EXPERIENCE, RESEARCH, SOCIAL CHANGE

EXPERIENCE, RESEARCH, SOCIAL CHANGE

Critical Methods

by Colleen Reid, Lorraine Greaves, and
Sandra Kirby

Third Edition

UNIVERSITY OF TORONTO PRESS

www.utppublishing.com

Library and Archives Canada Cataloguing in Publication

Kirby, Sandra L. (Sandra Louise), 1949–, author

　　　Experience, research, social change : critical methods / Colleen Reid, Lorraine Greaves,
Sandra Kirby. — Third edition.
Revision of: Kirby, Sandra L. (Sandra Louise), 1949-. Experience, research, social change.

Includes bibliographical references and index.
Issued in print and electronic formats.

ISBN 978-1-4426-3605-7 (hardback).—ISBN 978-1-4426-3604-0 (paperback)
ISBN 978-1-4426-3606-4 (html).—ISBN 978-1-4426-3607-1 (pdf)

　　　1. Social sciences—Research—Methodology—Textbooks.I. Greaves, Lorraine, author
II. Reid, Colleen, author　III. Title.

Q180.55.M4K5 2016　　　　　300.72　　　　C2016-905440-3
　　　　　　　　　　　　　　　　　　　　　　　　　　C2016-905441-1

We welcome comments and suggestions regarding any aspect of our publications—please feel free
to contact us at news@utphighereducation.com or visit our Internet site at www.utppublishing.com.

North America
5201 Dufferin Street
North York, Ontario, Canada, M3H 5T8

2250 Military Road
Tonawanda, New York, USA, 14150

ORDERS PHONE: 1-800-565-9523
ORDERS FAX: 1-800-221-9985
ORDERS E-MAIL: utpbooks@utpress.utoronto.ca

UK, Ireland, and continental Europe
NBN International
Estover Road, Plymouth, PL6 7PY, UK
ORDERS PHONE: 44 (0) 1752 202301
ORDERS FAX: 44 (0) 1752 202333
ORDERS E-MAIL: enquiries@nbninternational.com

This book is printed on paper containing 100% post-consumer fibre.

The University of Toronto Press acknowledges the financial support for its publishing activities of
the Government of Canada through the Canada Book Fund.

Printed in Canada.

EXERCISES, FIGURES, AND TABLES

TABLES

INTRODUCTION

Research can be exciting and is often important. In this third edition of *Experience, Research, Social Change* we provide an entry point for aspiring researchers interested in contributing to research and assisting in the creation of knowledge with the goal of social change. We have written this book from a critical standpoint and hope to encourage undergraduate students, graduate students, community-based researchers, practitioners, clinicians, service providers, and policymakers in undertaking meaningful research. Research can also feel daunting, and it may be that you do not consider yourself a "researcher." In this book we guide you, step by step, through the research process using clear and accessible language, exercises, and many examples. We distill complex concepts into meaningful terms. We believe that research can make a difference in the world and contribute to positive social change, and we want to share this journey with you.

How to Read This Book

In this book, we, the authors, chose to use second (you) and third (we, us, our) person throughout the text. We made a conscious choice to do this as a way of actualizing our belief that we, the authors, and you, the reader, are all in this research process together. Unless it is stated otherwise in the text, as it sometimes will be, "we," "us," and "our" refer to the authors, the readers, and the collective voice of people contributing to the research process. To make things clearer, examples and narratives are found in text boxes throughout the text, and selected exercises will be found in text boxes off set from the main text. At the end of each chapter are some further questions for discussion and reflection and additional readings for those of you who want to delve into a topic in more detail.

A Perspective of Research

Knowledge is power. We live in a world in which knowledge is produced and used to make change, stand as evidence, inform others, support a perspective, or justify an action. Hence, the question of who produces knowledge and how knowledge is used, and by whom, is central to understanding how power is created, taken, or maintained. Being able to produce knowledge, then, is a route to power, empowerment, and influence. This book is about how to do critical social research with an emphasis on understanding how research can make social change and improve people's lives. Social research that makes change often reflects points of view not generally seen in the mainstream, but that may be more commonly seen in the margins. We support and explain a critical view of methodology and research design, focusing on enhancing relevance and the change-making power of critical social research.

Learning how to do research is empowering in itself. It is also a route to a wider understanding of social life and a tool for interpreting the vast amounts of information and knowledge that surround us. It is a route to acquiring power, influence, and a voice as a result of documenting and producing knowledge. Indeed, bringing research processes to a wide array of groups is a route to diffusing the "power elite" and strengthening the impact of experiences that are not usually studied. It is our hope that the processes and content we describe in this book will contribute to these efforts.

Most of us have not had the opportunity to do research or create knowledge that is rooted in and representative of our own experiences. Historically, many groups have been excluded from participating in, describing, and analyzing their own reality. In many ways, understanding and doing research can be seen as a form of literacy. Without understanding the research process and being able to engage in that process, research remains distant, enabling the maintenance of the status quo rather than changing it. We believe that research that does not reflect on and analyze the social context from which it springs serves only its creators and does not enable us to engage with the nature of the knowledge and its relationship and relevance to others in society.

In recent years, some have argued that research has not represented their experiences. Indeed, research and knowledge are typically produced in a manner that represents the political and social interests of a particular (usually dominant) group. Further, research has often been a tool used to help perpetuate and maintain power relations and inequality or a limited and narrow view of what we "know." These critiques can apply to all types of research on any topic from bench research to social research. This influence extends throughout the research process. For example, the research questions or issues that are pursued are often reflective of dominant interests. Analyses of data can be circumscribed, or erroneous assumptions can be made about results, reflecting the limitations of the questions or methodological approaches.

It is important to all of us that the processes of investigating the world not remain a specialized or elite activity. Everyday life skills of data collection, reflection, analysis, and interpretation can be enhanced with basic research training. Indeed, by claiming access to the research enterprise, you can produce or interpret evidence in ways that reflect your reality and contribute to a more comprehensive view of life.

What to Expect from This Book

Reflecting of this book's title, we have divided it into three sections: Experience, Research, and Social Change. Part A, "Experience," includes three chapters. In Chapter 1 we demystify research language and the research process and explain research terminology that is used throughout the book. An overview of some theoretical and methodological perspectives that inform how we think about and conduct critical social research is covered in Chapter 2. In Chapter 3 we discuss the role of the researcher in terms of her or his reflexivity, positionality, voice, and representation, as well as research ethics.

Part B, "Research," is composed of seven chapters that move you step by step through the research process. We begin with formulating the research question (Chapter 4), and then cover literature reviews (Chapter 5), research methods (Chapter 6), sampling and recruitment (Chapter 7), data collection (Chapter 8), data analysis (Chapter 9), and writing the final research report (Chapter 10). In Part B we provide many hands-on exercises as well as examples from a diverse range of research projects. This section of the book is meant to be read consecutively—one chapter leads to the next.

Part C, "Social Change," is the final section. It has one chapter that discusses the myriad things we can do once the research is complete. Drawing on knowledge translation and advocacy concepts and examples, we provide many suggestions on how to be innovative and creative with your research products.

How Can This Book Be Used?

Questions about research spring up everywhere. This book will help answer some of them. As the three of us work in our respective domains, we encounter women and men who want to better understand and interpret research, and sometimes participate in the research process. We teach research methods to undergraduate students, supervise graduate students, and work with community groups who want to participate in research. We encounter many who need evidence on which to base decisions about changes in programs, policies, or legislation. All of these people have needs that are key to doing research differently, and they make up audiences for research and users of research. This book will speak to all who not only want to understand and follow the sequence of research steps, but also want to think more deeply about the issues involved in the production and use of knowledge.

This book will also explain the context of research. Research is done by particular people in specific social and historical contexts and is often funded by specific bodies, which means that it is both temporal and evolving and can reflect vested interests. Increasingly, social research reflects the experience and concerns of people who have traditionally been marginalized by the research process. This affects the manufacturing of knowledge and, ultimately, the placement of ideas on the public agenda.

This book will contribute to action and change. We believe that involving more and different people and groups in the research process is a necessary part of action for change. We also believe that access to and understanding of research is necessary to begin to share our various truths and expose the wider experiences of a democratic society. For example, survivors of incest or sexual abuse can engage in and use research to understand their experiences and make change by taking action. People developing systems or policies on urban transport or health care can contribute to the research process with practical perspectives from their sector, appropriate methodologies, and opportunities and methods for transferring knowledge. Nonprofit service providers working directly with people in the community can develop research questions and engage in research based on the real-life questions that arise in their practices.

This book humanizes research. When we engage in research we involve ourselves in a process in which we are constructing meaning and, ultimately, knowledge. Since the social world is multifaceted (i.e., the same situation or experience is able to give us many different kinds of knowledge), when we "do research" we involve ourselves in a process of revealing different kinds of knowledge. The knowledge we are able to observe, construct, and reveal is directly related to our vantage point and where we stand in the world. Every researcher's interaction with the social world is affected by such factors as gender, ethnicity, class, sexual orientation, age, ability, and geographic and social location. This does not mean that facts about the social world do not exist, but that what we see and how we go about constructing meaning is often a matter of context and interpretation.

Who Are We?

Colleen Reid

In 1991, when I was working on my Master's degree, I met a woman on a train who was reading the first edition of *Experience, Research, Social Change: Methods from the Margins* (Kirby & McKenna, 1989). We had a conversation about the book; I was instantly intrigued and bought the book the following week. As I read it, I felt that it had been written *for me*—in clear and accessible language it named my values, passions, and commitments as a researcher. It fundamentally changed what I thought was possible with research and inspired me to pursue participatory and feminist research in my graduate degrees. Ten years later, as a postdoctoral researcher at the British Columbia Centre of Excellence for Women's Health, I met Sandi Kirby who was a visiting scholar there at that time. After sharing many stimulating conversations about research she invited me to co-write the book's second edition with Lorraine Greaves. It was a tremendous gift to work with experienced researchers on a project that held such personal and professional meaning for me.

As we publish the third edition, where I have taken on the role of first author, it is gratifying to see how this book has evolved and the circle it has travelled. Today I am an educator and community-based researcher in the Faculty of Child, Family, and Community Studies at Douglas College in Vancouver. I am also an adjunct professor at the University of British Columbia (Rehabilitation Sciences, Faculty of Medicine) and Simon Fraser University (Public Policy, Faculty of Arts). The central themes in my work are to examine health in the contexts of oppression, suffering, and stigma for marginalized groups; and to use community-based research approaches to study and promote health for marginalized groups. To that end I draw on the theories and practices of engagement, transformative learning, social change, and feminism to teach and research in the areas of health promotion and public health, gender and women's health, inclusion and mental health, community development, and therapeutic recreation.

Lorraine Greaves

I have been interested in social change and action research for many years, first as an activist in the women's movement and later in academic, advocacy, and policy circles. Spanning these worlds has anchored my career and illustrated to me how important it is to understand research processes and to engage others in contributing to the development of evidence. As Senior Investigator and former Executive Director of the British Columbia Centre of Excellence for Women's Health in Vancouver, I had the rare opportunity to create a research centre that translates and carries out "women-centred" research and that values the change-making potential of research for improving women's health. Previously, I led the Centre for Research and Education on Violence Against Women and Children in London, Ontario, where anti-violence goals underpinned an action research agenda and influenced the choice of research questions, the research partners, and the process of approaching the research. I learned a tremendous amount from all of the partners and collaborators at both of these centres. I was also involved in thinking about the development of the Institute of Gender and Health at the Canadian Institutes for Health Research launched in 2000 and promoted the inclusion of specific attention to women and gender.

What questions we ask in research, who gets to be involved in the research process, as well as what we do with knowledge when we discover it are all critically important to understanding the impact of research, the development of knowledge, and human life. What questions we ask and how we frame those questions affects the knowledge-creation process. All of these issues continue to matter and concern me in my daily life and work and have been amply demonstrated to have an impact on our collective well-being. I continue to write books and articles, speak, do research, and consult on how to integrate equity and gender into programs, policies, and research initiatives in several countries around the world. Research usually underpins all of these efforts.

Sandra Kirby

I am a Professor Emerita at the University of Winnipeg and have been an educator, activist, coach, athlete, and researcher for virtually all of my adult life. My own understanding of doing practical research began when, as a Master's student at McGill University, I did a quantitative study on preferred leadership styles among athletes at the novice and high-performance levels. I tried to distance myself and be objective and removed from the research as it developed so that I could present the consequences of the study as if it all mattered equally. But, as an Olympic athlete, my own experiences were intertwined with the research project. I cared about how it would turn out and what it might change. However, the research methods of the day had no room for my experience in my research. Fortunately we are now in a much different research methodology place.

My research path includes many social change areas: athlete retirement, gender equality, sex and gender issues in sport, sexual abuse, homophobia and disability, home care and palliative care, and racialized communities and police services. The main thread of my work has almost always been connected to equity, safety, health, and sport. From a small core of researchers addressing harassment in sport (most notably Celia Brackenridge in the UK), Lorraine Greaves and I completed the world's first national quantitative study on sexual harassment and abuse of athletes in 1996 and, from that, published the world's first book on the subject, *Dome of Silence: Sexual Harassment and Abuse in Sport* (Kirby, Greaves, & Hankivsky, 2000). Sport has not been the same since, so we know our research joined with that of others to bring about positive social change. Now I am one of the founding members of an organization called Safe Sport International (http://safesportintl.org.uk) and the world of sport is much more aware and responsive to child protection issues.

My attention continues to be on action research, feminist approaches, and making change. This was the essence of the first edition of *Experience, Research, Social Change: Research Methods from the Margins*, co-authored with Kate McKenna in 1989, and for me it remains true for this third edition, which reflects advances in thinking about perspectives, methodologies, ethics, technology, and knowledge translation in critical social research.

How We Wrote This Book

Developing this book has been a collaborative effort. Some of the examples that we use throughout the book come from research projects that we have been involved in over the years in research centres, communities, colleges, and universities across Canada. They often involved many other researchers. The insights they provide have contributed to our understanding of and our commitment to the expansion of both the process and content of social research with a view to making social change.

Contributors

We are indebted to our colleagues, students, and friends who willingly offered examples and insights from their research. We are pleased to include contributions from the following people:

Maya Alonso
Samantha Bertolone
Maggie Bosse
Ellexis Boyle
Devin Carlson
Melanie Carlyle
Shayna Dolan
Olivier Ferlatte
Alison Greaves

J. Hofley
Louise Joycey
Deirdre Kelly
Katryna Koenig
Ania Landy
Danielle Lawless
Robin LeDrew
Paloma Leon
Jennifer Mullett

Colleen Pawlychka   Sheri Steffen
Nancy Poole   Allison Tom
Shelagh Smith   Chera Yellen

PART A

Experience

CHAPTER 1

DEMYSTIFYING RESEARCH

In this chapter we explore key concepts and issues that shape the research process. We discuss the evolution and focus of this book and the broader issues surrounding the production of knowledge. Then we address the following questions: What is research? What is a research paradigm? How does a world-view influence a person as a researcher? What are the stages and processes of research? Who does research? Who are you as a researcher? During and after your engagement in research, we hope that your own reflexivity and ongoing questioning will not only improve your research literacy but also generate a lasting interest in pursuing research and analyzing the context of research and its uses.

Experience, Research, Social Change: An Evolution and a Call to Action

Each edition of *Experience, Research, Social Change* has been a call to action that reflects and responds to current societal issues and concerns. *Methods from the Margins*, the first edition, published in 1989, was a clarion call to question and participate in the domain of knowledge production. The dominance of research by some to the exclusion—and at times harm—of others was its central theme. Authors Kirby and McKenna suggested that diverse individuals were beginning to question "the monopoly that certain powerful groups hold over information" (1989, p. 15). The first edition was at the forefront of the movement to democratize and demystify the research process. The "margins," understood as individuals and groups who were rarely considered or included in research, were brought to the centre of the inquiry process with the onus on the researcher to integrate her or his reflexivity and subjectivity.

Methods beyond the Mainstream was the second edition (Kirby, Greaves, & Reid, 2006). After 17 years our context had changed. While we remained concerned about the margins, we recognized that some progress had been made in addressing issues of academic power and control. The second edition emphasized the growing attention being placed on collaborative and participatory research approaches as promising strategies for engaging in research with those on the margins. It was a more substantial text that included a greater number of methods for the researcher's and research team's "toolbox." As well, the second edition placed a heavier emphasis on researcher responsibilities and research ethics.

This third edition integrates the strengths of the first and second editions. It includes an updated and in-depth description of research ethics and methods to provide the researcher with a range of tools in the toolbox. We have conceptualized the third edition as a re-centring by pointedly asking two questions: *Why is this book necessary?* and *Who is this book for?* Re-centring, which means to move something to the centre again, can also mean to understand anew. Re-centring the margins requires a constant examination of how we understand the margins and who continues to occupy that space. In 1989, Kirby and McKenna wrote that they "believe research must begin to reflect the experience and concerns of people who have traditionally been marginalized by the research process and by what gets counted as knowledge" (p. 22) because historically many groups are marginalized from the production of knowledge (e.g., women, Indigenous peoples, racial and ethnic groups, recent immigrants and refugees, individuals with disabilities, people who identify as LGBTQIA [lesbian, gay, bisexual, transgender, queer, questioning, intersex, and asexual]).

Some progress has been made since 1989 in terms of who has been seen as worthy of study and how research has been conducted with marginalized groups. For example, documents such as the Canadian Institutes of Health Research "Guidelines for Health Research Involving Aboriginal People" (CIHR, 2013) and "Sex, Gender and Health Research Guide: A Tool for CIHR Applicants" (CIHR, 2015b) signalled an increasing awareness of the ways that research had historically excluded or made invisible some groups. Some groups from the margins are now participating in research, sometimes in highly democratic and authentic ways. For instance, Indigenous beliefs, customs, and approaches to community life must now be reflected in the processes of investigation, knowledge building, and ownership of information. Indeed, with the emergence of feminist, Indigenous, and anti-oppressive methodologies; community engagement mandates at academic institutions; and participatory and community-based research approaches (see Chapters 2 and 3), traditional conceptions of who does research and controls knowledge production have expanded significantly.

As our context continues to shift and strides toward greater equality and inclusion in research are made, we must concomitantly remain vigilant in our interrogation of who or what remains in the margins. There are many examples to draw on to illustrate this point. Recently the Canadian Broadcasting Corporation blocked all comments on Indigenous-related articles because it had observed "a disproportionate amount of racist and ignorant hate speech targeted at First Nations people" (Luger, 2015). There is a persistent gender wage gap; today women make 74 cents for every dollar earned by a man, and statisticians estimate that as much as 10% to 15% of the gender wage gap is due to discrimination (Pay Equity Commission, 2016). In Canada access to mental health care relies on the ability to pay, resulting in many under- and unserved individuals (Picard, 2013). Anti-immigrant and anti-Muslim sentiments can be read daily in newspapers around the world, and many US states have banned Syrian refugees outright (Fantz & Brumfield, 2015). What these examples reveal is that the work of exposing and investigating the margins continues. Despite advances, discrimination, misunderstandings, unintentional biases, and fear perpetuate a margin that requires our attention. Even in the context of progress we need to continue to examine oppressions that exist while countering assumptions that social justice has been achieved.

The Truth and Reconciliation Commission of Canada (TRCC) articulated the role of research in reconciliation. In its final report, it stated:

> Research is vital to reconciliation. It provides insights and practical examples of why and how educating Canadians about the diverse concepts, principles, and practices of reconciliation contributes to healing and transformative social change. The benefits of research extend beyond addressing the legacy of residential schools. Research on the reconciliation process can inform how Canadian society can mitigate intercultural conflicts, strengthen civic trust, and build social capacity and practical skills for long-term reconciliation. First Nations, Inuit, and Métis peoples have an especially strong contribution to make to this work. Research partnerships between universities and communities or organizations are fruitful collaborations and can provide the necessary structure to document, analyze, and report research findings on reconciliation to a broader audience. (Truth and Reconciliation Commission of Canada, 2015, p. 126)

As articulated by the TRCC, research for social change requires collective organizing among people who have been historically unacknowledged, misrepresented, abused, or used. They must be integrally involved in reforming societal systems and structures and the research process itself. In this edition of *Experience, Research, Social Change* we encourage you to see beyond power relations and commonly held understandings to create new ways of making research choices based on your reflexivity and positionality, ethical principles and practices, and desire for social action (see Chapter 3). The methods appropriate for critical social research are grounded in a political awareness of a need for change. Hence, choosing a research approach and method becomes a political choice. Critical social research focuses principally on describing reality from the perspective of those who have traditionally been excluded as producers and consumers of research. At times, critical partnerships form between those with the experience at the centre of the research, those who are primarily researchers, and those who are responsible for program or policy creation. Ideally, partners learn from each other and knowledge transfer and social action are positive outcomes.

We believe research activities should empower people to not only be participants in the research experience but also to develop and take a lead in research that is personally or collectively important to them. By asking "Who is this book for?" we reach the nascent neophyte researcher. This may include anyone engaging in critical social research for the first time: the undergraduate student completing an Honours thesis project, the graduate student working on a thesis or dissertation, the service provider in a nonprofit organization, the front-line practitioner in an agency, the community-based researcher, or the government policymaker or policy creator. What these researchers likely have in common is their uncertainty or hesitation in conducting research. They may not consider themselves "researchers," and some may have perceptions about who can do research and what kinds of research are most valued. Yet, as described in the first and second editions, all of these prospective researchers have important contributions to make to knowledge production. These researchers may share a passion for their work or their communities, a desire to make evidence-based decisions, or a commitment to social change. They may possibly want to contribute to the critique of research that only serves to perpetuate the ivory tower. We believe that bringing the neophyte researcher from the margins to the centre will produce more democratic, complete, and authentic knowledge. To enable the student, practitioner, service provider, or policymaker to become a researcher necessitates an engaged conversation to inspire passion, insight, and learning. In this third edition we integrate relevant examples and hands-on exercises throughout to build the research skills of any emerging researcher.

Fundamentally, the path and product are important: The path or route you choose for research is as important as the meanings or substance you might discover. Either way, the research path requires a continual reflexive interrogation of the margins for both the researcher and the researched. As you focus on your substantive area of interest, keep your research processes and choices transparent and visible to others. In this way, others can make the research journey with you and you can contribute to the democratization of research. This encourages a greater diversity of knowledge to be recorded as part of human experience.

What Is Research?

The everyday research we do is driven by curiosity and intellectual discovery. For instance, we might do some research before buying a car or deciding to have elective surgery. But unlike the day-to-day research that most of us do to make decisions, critical social research demands a more rigorous approach. As the researcher you are accountable for asking questions you may not have thought of as you move beyond meeting your own needs or satisfying your own curiosities. For example, there is a big difference between reading a handful of online reviews to find a restaurant to eat at (to satisfy your hunger and to have a place to dine with friends) versus administering a survey of all restaurants in a suburb of Toronto based on a range of criteria to determine which restaurant is cheapest, uses the greatest number of organic ingredients, has the most vegetarian options, and so on. In formal research, you move from meeting an individual or personal curiosity to imposing a structure for systematically and reliably gathering information.

We define research as the process of discovering or uncovering new knowledge using techniques, theories, and methods. The defining characteristics of research are that it is a *systematic, purposeful, and disciplined process* of discovering reality structured from human experience. Research is a matter of process as well as outcomes; it is distinct from our everyday musings and problem solving because it involves a systematic inquiry into a phenomenon of interest. Research aims to contribute to what is known about a phenomenon and to contribute to action and social change to solve a practical problem or issue. It involves identifying what you are interested in finding out, reading up on the area, and focusing on a research question(s). It requires a sound design, which includes choosing the right participants and the appropriate methods and mode of analysis. These steps can be complex and involve many different decisions.

Principles of Critical Social Research

Critical social research aims to be simultaneously scientific, critical, and action oriented. It is scientific in that it is research that is conducted transparently and systematically. The research route taken is accounted for and documented with a well-practised and disciplined recording of observations or other research methods. Critical social research is "critical" in two different ways. It can reveal how the broader social, structural, or cultural factors shape people's experiences and understandings. As well, it explicitly interrogates the role and influence of the researcher him or herself. Reflexivity, discussed in depth in Chapter 3, allows the researcher to account for how and why the research is being done, who is being researched, and how the researcher behaves as an instrument of research. It exposes and articulates these taken-for-granted positions. For example, why is it that a researcher chooses one research foci but not another, specific participants in a particular social context but not outside that context, or a particular data gathering method rather than another? Finally, critical social research is practical, action oriented, and adopts a political stance. It seeks to educate its audience to take action that transforms its situation (Adams, Hollenberg, Lui, & Broom, 2009; Kincheloe & McLaren, 2005; Lincoln & Guba, 2005; Njelesani, Gibson, Nixon, Cameron, & Polatajko, 2013).

As critical social researchers, we take the position that the researcher should not shy away from the experience being studied. If you care about a research topic, that caring will sustain your energies through to the end of the project. Your caring may also mean that you have a position in relation to the topic that needs to be clearly stated as you begin your work. It is a bias—a bias that needs to be accounted for and made visible. It is normally the covert biases that are harmful to research, not the overt and accounted-for ones. In this way, the researcher is visible and the context of the new information is incorporated into the research. The consumer of the research, the reader, is thus provided with research that is contextualized from the perspective of the researcher.

The First Step in Becoming a Researcher: Reflecting and Recording

The way we have written this book is consistent with our belief that the production of knowledge should be available to everyone. This book is a conversation between us, as authors with diverse research experiences and backgrounds, and you, the reader. In order to have this conversation we pose questions and exercises throughout the book so that you can actively engage in the ideas presented rather than passively reading information. In addition, engaging you with questions and exercises in which you document your thinking, decision making, and rationalizations will establish your documentation processes—a hallmark of rigorous and reliable research.

From this point forward we're asking that you engage in the material covered in this book as actively, inquisitively, and openly as possible. There will be different ways to engage with the material, most of which require some kind of writing or documentation. This process can be personal to you and may also involve drawing or other artistic means that help you explore ideas and make research decisions. Here we briefly discuss reasons and strategies for "research writing." We'll return to this topic over the course of this book and in a lot more detail in Chapter 4. Research writing has three purposes:

1. *Writing for learning and clarification* will help you get clear on what you want to research and the decisions you need to make. It is also done to keep track of decision making and milestones in your research project. The purpose of learning and clarification is to deepen your understanding of research and clarify what is meaningful for you to pursue in your own research project.

2. *Writing for reflexivity and positionality* will document how you as a researcher relate to and are engaging with the questions arising from your research interests. This allows you to document and clarify your biases, assumptions, and worldview and how these things shape yourself as a researcher and your research interests.

3. *Writing as a source of data* is how a researcher documents her or his observations in the field. The researcher's observations are documented in fieldnotes and become a source of data. As such, the researcher is a research instrument.

For now, we ask that you create a space to begin documenting your insights regarding "learning and clarification" and "reflexivity and positionality." We call this space your *research journal*. Again, the research journal is discussed in depth in Chapter 4, though we ask that you begin it now as you engage with the following exercises.

Exercise 1.1: What does research mean to me?

Reflect on and write about the following questions. They are intended to help clarify what research means to you and what types of research and research topics have meaning for you:

- What does the word "research" mean to me? What images does the word "research" conjure up for me?
- What kinds of research am I familiar with?
- How do I envision myself as a researcher?
- What kinds of questions might inspire me to engage in research?
- What kinds of values do I feel are important for guiding research?
- How do I envision benefiting from research (generally) and the research I'm interested in (more specifically)?
- What historical and institutional factors shape the way I view research? (Adapted from Reid, Brief, & LeDrew, 2009)

The word "research" can bring up an array of images or understandings. It is typical to think of research that involves filling out a survey or being tested in a lab. These common or mainstream understandings of research are shaped by historical, cultural, and institutional factors. However, as we explore throughout this book, there are more diverse approaches to research that can be used to ask and address a wide range of social issues.

Research Paradigms

Why certain approaches to research are chosen often goes unquestioned, even unmentioned. But all research is driven by tacit theories even if the values underlying research are not made explicit. We suggest that you bring the values and principles that permeate your research to the fore in an attempt to understand its broad implications and to identify the kinds of evidence that are particularly relevant. In critical social research there is a systematic approach to "bringing to the fore" the values and principles that underpin our work. The point is to be clear and consistent in naming your position and identifying your research paradigm. An overall question that may guide you is "How does my worldview influence me as an investigator—ontologically, epistemologically, and methodologically?" But before addressing this question it is first necessary to understand the meanings of epistemology, ontology, paradigm, theory, methodology, and research methods.

Epistemology is a theory of knowledge, including assumptions about how we come to know what we know (Carter & Little, 2007). It answers questions about who can be a "knower" and what tests beliefs must pass to be legitimated as knowledge. Ultimately, one's epistemological stance addresses the kinds of things that can be known. For instance, can subjective truths count as knowledge (Harding, 1987)? Does knowledge only include those things that can be measured?

Ontology is a theory of existence and includes assumptions about what is real and what is knowable (Scotland, 2012). It can also be understood as a way of seeing and constructing the world.

A *paradigm* is a worldview or a belief system about the nature of knowledge and existence. It can also be understood as a broad, overarching intellectual framework or architecture of assumptions (Ostrom, 1999; cited in Carpiano & Daley, 2006, p. 568). It is a constellation of theories, questions, methods and procedures that share central values and themes (Mesel, 2013).

Theory is a formal explanation of a phenomenon or set of related phenomena (Poland, 1998). A theory is an analytical structure designed to explain a set of empirical observations. Theory does two things: (a) It identifies a set of distinct observations as a class of phenomena, and (b) it makes assertions about the underlying reality that brings about or affects this phenomenon.

A *methodology* is how we gain knowledge about the world or an "analysis of the assumptions, principles, and procedures in a particular approach to inquiry" (Schwandt, 2001, cited in Carter & Little, 2007, p. 1317). A methodology is "the study—the description, the explanation, and the justification—of methods, and not the methods themselves" (Carter & Little, 2007, p. 1317)

Research methods, or "tools in the toolbox," are specific data collection and analysis procedures and techniques. A research method can also be understood as a technique for, or way of proceeding in, gathering evidence.

The research paradigm in which the researcher is located ultimately determines or directs all other decisions made within a particular research endeavour. Yet identifying your worldview and making systematic research choices presents many challenges to new researchers. Sometimes it is difficult to distinguish clearly between labels that denote an epistemological stance and those that refer to method (Mesel, 2013). As well, there are as many ways of delineating different research paradigms as there are disciplines and researchers. Each inquiry and inquirer brings a unique perspective or understanding—the possibilities for variation and exploration are limited only by the number of those engaged in inquiry and the realms of social and intrapersonal life that become interesting to researchers. What additionally confuses matters is that currently there exists a confluence and convergence of paradigms whereby "various paradigms are beginning to 'interbreed' such that two theorists previously thought to be in irreconcilable conflict may now appear, under a different theoretical rubric, to be informing one another's arguments" (Lincoln & Guba, 2005, p. 191). Categories are fluid, and what should be a category keeps changing and the boundaries between paradigms are shifting (Lincoln & Guba, 2005; Szyjka, 2012).

Despite the shifting terrain in defining and distinguishing research paradigms, it is necessary to outline some fundamental differences in worldviews that can help anyone new to research navigate the research literature and her or himself in the research process.

The *positivist* paradigm is characterized by traditional, scientific, quantitative, and experimental knowledge (Tubey, Rotich, & Bengat, 2015). Researchers operating within this paradigm are concerned with controlling physical and social environments and the replicability of their research studies (Scotland, 2012). This paradigm is based on the arguments that the world is objectively given, that through the application of objective methods truth can be acquired, and that there is one true set of events or facts that are discoverable (Arghode, 2012).

The *interactive* paradigm, also known as constructivist, naturalistic, ethnographic, and qualitative knowledge, is derived from lived experience (Scotland, 2012). Knowledge is obtained by participating subjectively in a world of meanings created by individuals. What exists is what people perceive to exist. It is based in meanings and interpretations and has a theoretical base in phenomenology, symbolic interactionism, and grounded theory. Theory captures an understanding of people in their environments. It is an attempt to give a direct description of our experience as it is in itself without taking into account its psychological origin or its causal explanation (Tuli, 2010).

The *critical* paradigm examines societal structures and power relations and how they play a role in promoting inequalities and disenabling people while promoting reflection and action on what is right and just (Reimer-Kirkham et al., 2009). Theory is used to attempt to explain underlying structures that influence phenomena. What really exists cannot be ascertained simply through empirical research, and the world of appearances (what we experience) does not necessarily reveal the world of mechanisms (what causes the world of appearances; Lincoln & Guba, 2005). The critical paradigm is founded on reflective knowledge and comprises critical, materialist, structural, feminist, postcolonialist, Indigenous, and queer theories (Reimer-Kirkham et al., 2009). Power issues are central for all research originating from a critical paradigm.

As we discuss in more depth in Chapter 2, critical social research that is explicitly focused on social change resides in the critical paradigm. We believe that the critical paradigm can include research that is interpretive and positivist because it brings together many different stances on the state of knowledge and what counts as knowledge, but with a strong focus on reflection and taking action in the world.

Current debates about research paradigms require researchers to probe where and how paradigms exhibit confluence and where and how they exhibit differences, controversies, and contradictions (Lincoln & Guba, 2005). One strategy for identifying a research paradigm involves probing the basic values that guide one's research. *Values* that feed into the inquiry process can be understood as preferences for courses of action and outcomes. Values guide the choice of problem, paradigm to guide the investigation of the problem, context, theoretical framework, data gathering and data analysis methods, and formats for presenting findings. The questions we ask are at the core of understanding paradigms, for they are powerful shapers of the world we see (Carter & Little, 2007). At the end of this chapter we point to a number of additional readings on research paradigms and encourage you to further explore current thinking in this area.

Another way to think through one's research paradigm is to consider how you as a researcher view and choose to deal with notions of objectivity and subjectivity. The positivist paradigm is centred on the notion of objectivity. *Objectivity* can be understood as splitting reality into subjective and objective realms. From this perspective, knowledge is limited to the objects and the relationships between them that exist in the realm of time and space. On the other hand *subjectivity* recognizes the centrality of values in driving the research process and that more objective accounts can create a "false dichotomy" of knower and known, observer and observed. With the increasing acceptance of subjective forms of inquiry, there has been a concomitant visibility for research designs that are interactive, contextualized, and humanly compelling because they invite joint participation in exploration of research issues (Bettez, 2015). These forms of inquiry have critiqued the traditionally dominant positivist paradigm for creating a vision that leads us to believe that the world is simpler than it is, for reinscribing enduring forms of historical oppression (Lincoln & Guba, 2005), and for neglecting crucial aspects of life that cannot be easily measured (McCoy, 2012). These debates indicate important issues that are worth considering as you prepare to do your own research or read someone else's research.

Research Methodologies

The research paradigm shapes everything else that occurs in a research study, including the methodology. A research methodology is a set of rules and procedures about how research should be conducted. Although there are many methodologies articulated in the literature and a vast and growing body of literature, most research methodologies fall into one of two categories: qualitative or quantitative. *Qualitative methodologies* are most consistent with the constructivist or interpretivist paradigms, while *quantitative methodologies* fit most closely with the positivist paradigm. With the increasing acknowledgement that blending qualitative and quantitative methodologies can be the most effective way to answer some research questions, there is growing interest in mixed methodologies. Similarly, researchers within the critical paradigm can use both qualitative and quantitative methodologies to answer their questions. In Table 1.1 we distinguish qualitative and quantitative methodologies.

Qualitative research occurs in natural settings, often requires multiple methods, is grounded in the lived experiences of people, and is naturalistic, emergent, and evolving (Marshall & Rossman, 2016). Qualitative methodologies embrace the complexity of social interactions as expressed in daily life and with the meanings the participants themselves attribute to these interactions. On the other hand, observations of some social experiences can be quantified or categorized in numerical ways. Such quantification may make the observations more clear and could open up the possibility for statistical

TABLE 1.1 Qualitative and Quantitative Methodologies

	QUALITATIVE	QUANTITATIVE
Assumptions	Assumes multiple and dynamic realities, contextual	Assumes single, stable reality that is divisible or fragmentable
Theory	Captures an understanding of people in their environments	Scientific laws that are formal and predictive
Orientation	Discovery: Theories and hypotheses are evolved from the data collected	Verification: Predetermined hypotheses are tested
Research setting	Natural setting, uncontrolled observation	Controlled observation, experimentation
Sampling	Nonprobability sampling	Probability or random sampling
Results	Valid: The focus is on design and procedures to gain "authentic," "rich" accounts	Reliable and valid: The focus is on design and procedures to ensure accuracy and replicability
Goals of research	Interpretation	Prediction and confirmation

analysis and applications. Some research concepts are relatively easy to quantify. For example, research requiring the nature and scope of a particular phenomenon could lend itself to a quantitative approach, while research concepts such as the measurement of happiness or fear would be more difficult, though not impossible, to approach from a quantitative perspective. Often, researchers use labels to derive assumptions about others' work to either endorse or discount their research. We should be careful not to fall into these traps, as false dichotomies between research approaches are often artificial and serve to limit thinking. As critical social researchers we embrace both qualitative and quantitative approaches and encourage the use of a combination of methods to reveal useful data.

Example: Diet Study

A researcher is interested in learning more about individuals' eating habits. If she uses a qualitative approach, she could speak with participants about a number of things, including the meanings they attribute to eating, why they buy and eat certain foods, how eating certain foods makes them feel, how they deal with food cravings, and so on. If the researcher decides to use a quantitative approach, she may ask participants to do the same amount of exercise and eat the same number of calories and then measure changes to body weight and muscle. She could also have two groups of participants who eat different kinds of foods (high fat and low fat) and compare body fat measurements after a month. Another option might be to measure the weight of the participants before and after the experiment and analyze the participants' blood for choles-terol. As you can see, a research topic like "eating habits" can proceed in many different directions. As we will restate in subsequent chapters, the research question must guide the methodology that is used.

Exercise 1.2: What can you know?

You can do this exercise on your own or with a partner. For each topic listed below brainstorm two research ideas: one that uses a qualitative methodology and a second that uses a quantitative methodology. Do not worry about any of the study specifics or feasibility. Consider this an opportunity to play with different ideas.

- Native languages among Indigenous Canadians
- Childhood obesity
- Effectiveness of dietary counselling for weight loss
- Depression in older adults
- Effective marketing strategies on children under five
- Students' attitudes about recycling
- Sense of community in northern rural towns
- Women's roles as paid caregivers
- Cultural competency among social workers

While you have arrived at one qualitative and one quantitative question, there remain many more questions that could be asked.

The Research Process

Critical social research is a continuous and iterative process that begins with a concern that is often rooted in experience. This concern can spring from your personal life, your professional life, or your community life. It can be rooted in an observation, a fact, or a feeling. It may be linked to someone else's research, which spurs you into thinking about an additional research question.

From our perspective, critical social research involves the continuous revision of one's plans and expectations and engaging in a process of self-reflection as a participant in the process of creating knowledge. As in any journey, there are choices of routes, modes of travel, and various forks in the road. You can design your own trip, or you can replicate a trip that someone

TABLE 1.2 Demystifying Research Language

WHAT DO I WANT TO KNOW? WHAT IS MY AREA OF INTEREST?	IDENTIFYING THE RESEARCH TOPIC, PURPOSE, AND QUESTION
What do others know about my research interest?	Reviewing the literature
What's involved in answering the research question?	Operationalizing the research question by answering the 5Ws and an H
What kinds of responsibilities do I have as the researcher?	Addressing research ethics
What information will answer my research question?	Collecting data
How will I make sense of the information I gather?	Analyzing data
What do I do with what I learn from the information?	Dissemination, knowledge translation, and taking action

else has already defined. You will be faced with choices and new ideas along the way. Regardless of your particular journey, it is crucial to apply a systematic approach to ensure your conclusions are valid and to make them useful to others who are interested in the same issues. There are some basic principles of design, data collection, and analysis that enable the systematic creation of knowledge. In Table 1.2 we demystify some common research language.

For example, your research question must be precise and phrased in a way that allows for new knowledge to be discovered and that invites all findings. It may become necessary to revise your research question as you go along, making it more specific and reflective of your emerging understanding. Your methodology must fit the question, the people, or the issues you are interested in knowing more about. Will the methodology lead to an answer to your question? Will it avoid harm, minimize risk, and create benefits for society? Is it feasible? Will there be cooperation and collaboration where you need it? The research methods you choose will both limit and enable your research project. Will your methods generate information that will be illuminating and meaningful? Finally, the analysis matters to you, the users of your research, and your research participants. What approach will you take? How will you describe your analysis and link it to existing knowledge? Who will be involved in analyzing the research? How can you assure the reader or user of your knowledge that your analytical approach is valid? Critical social research rarely unfolds according to plan. Modifying the research question, reassessing the methodology and methods, and ensuring a responsive and iterative analysis are distinct possibilities. The context and emerging issues may shift the question and the environmental factors shaping the project. In addition, as the researcher you have an effect on how the research evolves.

As critical social researchers we embrace the notion of subjectivity surrounding the research process, sometimes invisibly. We must be aware of our subjectivity and be capable of identifying its impact while continuously interrogating it. Research methodologies and methods have always been developed by people who see the world in particular ways, so every time a research tool is used the researcher must be aware that it contains the perspectives of those who created it. Being constantly aware of and responsive to potential assumptions or tacit theories in ourselves and others is the essence of reflexivity. Reflexivity requires that we embrace our subjectivity and actively identify its impact on the research process. In other words, how can you, the researcher, continuously reflect upon your own worldview, the impact of the question you ask, the issues you explore, and the methods of investigation and analysis that you employ? Further, how can you use the knowledge that results from your research responsibly and ethically to make a positive difference?

Summary

This book is about conducting critical social research. This involves asking the following questions: How do you make clear observations, record the data accurately, analyze it fully and appropriately, and distribute the findings to others? Good research results provide enough information to adequately describe, explain, and generate further questions about the issue. Poor research results, like poorly constructed maps, do not describe the terrain clearly enough to be of use to anyone or to invite further exploration.

A researcher needs the basic skills of an explorer: curiosity, good observational skills, flexibility, a goal, and a vision of the utility of exploring the issue at hand. In addition, the researcher needs a method for recording her or his observations and a facility for analysis and knowledge building. Creators of new knowledge must outline why a question is important, why a particular method has been chosen to study the research question, and how the data collected shed new light on the issue.

Considering the issues raised in this chapter encourages us to reflect on the ultimate purpose of research. Is it to uncover new facts and describe them, or to document trends to give advice to the ruling elite? Is it to solve human and social problems, or to make changes? Is it for social transformation? Is it to increase representation and visibility of all citizens, or to control behaviours of citizens? Is it directed at empowering those without power, or assisting those with power? Or is it to build social relationships and citizenship? Perhaps all of these goals exist. However Maiter, Joseph, Shan, and Saeid (2013) reflects on Paulo Freire's belief that the goal of research is to develop a critical conscious-ness that enables all to speak the truth, particularly when oppressed, and to contribute to praxis and reflection in everyday life. "He implies that a negotiated critical consciousness will provide the researcher with the capacity to enable the participants to transform from their position of vulnerability or oppression and find their own voice bringing their cultural and sociopolitical construction of self and experience to the foreground" (Aluwihare-Samaranayake, 2012, p. 67).

Questions for Discussion

---

1. How can "the margins" be defined?
2. What is "research"? What is critical social research?
3. What is a research paradigm? What is a research methodology? How are the two related?
4. What does "iterative" mean and how might this affect you as a researcher?

Our Recommended Readings

Arghode, V. (2012). Qualitative and quantitative research: Paradigmatic differences. *Global Education Journal, 2012*(4), 155–163.

Lincoln, Y. S., & Guba, E. G. (2005). Paradigmatic controversies, contradictions, and emerging confluences. In N. K. Denzin & Y. S. Lincoln (Eds.), *Handbook of qualitative research* (3rd ed., pp. 191–215). Thousand Oaks, CA: Sage.

Mesel, T. (2013). The necessary distinction between methodology and philosophical assumptions in healthcare research. *Scandinavian Journal of Caring Sciences, 27*(3), 750–756. http://dx.doi.org/10.1111/j.1471-6712.2012.01070.x Medline:22935081

Tubey, R., Rotich, J. K., & Bengat, J. K. (2015). Research paradigms: Theory and practice. *Research on Humanities and Social Sciences, 5*(5), 224–228.

CHAPTER 2

CRITICAL AND CONTEMPORARY APPROACHES TO SOCIAL RESEARCH

In this chapter we introduce some current approaches that are components of a critical approach to social research. These approaches and their inherent perspectives reflect the ever-changing nature of research, and social research in particular. Within these descriptions we point to other resources and references for additional reading, fuller explanations, or tools. We also weave in examples or exercises to have you begin to consider your research questions and how your interests may relate to these approaches or benefit from employing them.

As we discussed in Chapter 1, research is not a static endeavour. Times change, research questions emerge or get answered, and ideas about how to approach research shift. This chapter first examines selected critical, contemporary perspectives in social research and discusses how they might work and how they could make a difference to research processes, methods, results, and impact. We discuss these separately, even though they are not mutually exclusive nor collectively exhaustive of each other or other approaches. Then, we discuss approaches to engagement, a key element in social research. The level and process of engagement can differ from project to project, but some connection with and understanding of the people affected by your research question is needed. Whether or not you are using a formal participatory methodology, there are ample opportunities for consultation and involvement, from developing preliminary research ideas all the way to using the results of the research in practice. Further, engaging with individuals and groups is respectful of the group's interests and points of view and offers a platform for them to contribute to the research question, its methodology, and the analysis. Most important, though, is that if engagement is started early and is respectful and rewarding, knowledge translation processes go much more smoothly and productively. It stands to reason that those who have a stake in the research from the outset are also going to be invested in sharing the results of the research when it is completed.

Finally, we give examples of some specific methodological approaches that formally involve the people who are the focus of the research. Specific research methods that require participation and action on the part of the people who are most affected by the research include participatory action research and community-based research. We define and discuss these two options and illustrate how they can make a difference to the outcomes of social research.

The Critical Paradigm

In this book, we take a deliberately critical stance in relation to social research. As discussed in Chapter 1, a *critical paradigm* examines societal structures and power relations and how they play a role in promoting inequalities and disenabling people while promoting reflection and action on what is right and just (Reimer-Kirkham et al., 2009). A theory is used to attempt to explain underlying structures that influence phenomena. Indeed, what really exists cannot be ascertained simply through empirical research, and the world of appearances does not necessarily reveal the world of mechanisms (Lincoln & Guba, 2005). The critical paradigm is founded on reflective knowledge and comprises critical, materialist, structural, feminist, ethnic, and queer theories (Reimer-Kirkham et al., 2009). Power issues are central for all research originating from a critical paradigm.

We choose this stance because critical social research that is explicitly focused on social change resides in this paradigm. Similar to many other researchers, we believe that the critical paradigm can include research that is both fundamentally interpretive and positivist. Indeed, the critical paradigm brings together different stances on the state of knowledge and what counts as knowledge with a focus on reflection and taking action in the world. Choices such as this often rest on values; hence, they require some self-probing. Values that feed into the inquiry process can be understood as preferences for courses of action and outcomes. Values guide the choice of the problem under investigation, the paradigm that guides the investigation, the context of the research, the theoretical framework used, the data gathering and data analysis methods used, and the formats for presenting findings. Considering what questions we ask is at the core of understanding paradigms, for the questions we ask are powerful shapers of the world we see (Carter & Little, 2007).

Some Critical Contemporary Approaches

Transdisciplinarity

Much of our education, professional lives, and understanding of expertise are identified or categorized by discipline. Chances are, most university students are enrolled in a "major" discipline and are required to take a minimum number of courses in that discipline. Likewise, professors are hired by "departments" that exist to advance and reflect a particular discipline. Some institutions have "interdisciplinary studies" where students are encouraged to explore and study in several disciplines to prepare for a degree.

Disciplines have a long history as an organizing framework of knowledge that is useful for the academy, and they often lead to specific professional roles or job categories in working life. The *Oxford English Dictionary* defines discipline as "a branch of learning or scholarly instruction." Disciplines have and teach specific approaches to knowledge, including methods, theories, and scope of subject area for study. Disciplines are not only sources of knowledge and scholarship, but also sources of socialization for their adherents. As a result, adherence to a discipline or education in a discipline is likely to lead to a clear identification with that discipline and its perspectives. This identification creates solidarity and allows for specialization to occur, thereby advancing disciplinary depth. It also serves as a basis for training students and new practitioners of that discipline.

At the same time, discipline-based training creates divisions between learners and scholars. By definition, boundaries around disciplines are drawn and serve to separate as well as to protect disciplines. Some observers identify the negative effects of discipline-based education on the pursuit of knowledge:

> While the disciplines may share a common ethos, specifically a respect for knowledge and intellectual inquiry, differences between them are vast, so much so in fact that discipline has been referred to as the major source of fragmentation in academe. Disciplines have been distinguished by styles of presentation, preferred approaches to investigation, and the degree to which they draw from other fields and respond to lay inquiries and concerns. Put simply, scholars in different disciplines "speak different languages" and in fact have been described as seeing things differently when they look at the same phenomena. (Del Favero, 2016)

Society comes to see knowledge as divided among or coming from certain "experts," divisions that are reinforced by the media, the professions, universities, and the public as meaningful, maybe even vital, but separate contributions to understanding life. Some disciplines are more known or understood than others, but all disciplines have some identity in the public eye. Disciplines also have reputations among themselves—that is, disciplinary adherents judge each other as well as themselves.

Having such divisions raises some questions for the critical social researcher: How do disciplines relate to the critical social research endeavour? Are social scientists (sociologists, psychologists, economists, anthropologists, geographers, etc.) best suited to pursuing critical social research? Are there other disciplines that are relevant to critical social research (such as public health, medicine, philosophy, engineering, literature, music)? To some extent, this depends on what your research question is. Does it involve a complex, multifaceted issue? Would its study ideally involve different perspectives? Or, perhaps more importantly, would its study be disadvantaged by taking a singular disciplinary perspective?

Some researchers have asked these questions, and several identifiable approaches have developed as a result. *Interdisciplinarity*, *multidisciplinarity*, and *transdiciplinarity* are all responses to the limitations that some researchers have seen in taking a unidisciplinary approach. Each of these is different. Interdisciplinarity occurs when a conscious attempt is made to involve different disciplines and have them contribute to each other in the quest for new knowledge. Multidisciplinarity occurs when several disciplines contribute to the study of a question or problem, often in parallel. These two approaches are well established in social research. Transdisciplinarity, however, attempts to reach a different, and lofty, goal. It aspires to bring together the contributions of multiple, relevant disciplines to bear on an issue or problem and to create a new approach. This might include a common language, a shared methodology and theory, or a common purpose established through drawing on the contributions of various disciplines. It requires a commitment from researchers and a willingness to learn from and listen to each other's perspectives. It requires the active adoption of some new language, or even the creation of a new language, among the team members. It requires openness and the willingness to dispense with rigid disciplinary approaches from our past so that we can address new questions with new, more complex approaches that transcend our own past limitations.

The benefits of transdisciplinarity can be immense. They include merging different kinds of science, methods, theories, and considerations, or raising and forming new questions and approaches. Transdisciplinarity offers a route to integrating both positivist and interpretative research, which can be critical to understanding many difficult issues that are resistant to or badly need social action and change. But most of all, transdisciplinarity promises new answers. Patricia Rosenfield (1992), an economist for the Tropical Disease Research program at the World Health Organization (WHO), is largely credited with introducing the concept of transdisciplinarity in health sciences. Based on shortcomings that she observed in scientific collaborations, she felt that transdisciplinarity was the answer to cracking some complex problems.

When Rosenfield joined the WHO in the late 1970s she found that the post-war ideals of her predecessors of integrating social and biological perspectives were not being fully honoured (Kessel & Rosenfield, 2008). Rosenfield observed that review processes were dominated by medical doctors with little representation of social scientists, leading to the marginalization of social perspectives in health issues. Despite the success of some interdisciplinary collaborations, Rosenfield observed that cross- disciplinary work remained a fad and the WHO lacked a deeper conceptual and institutional commitment to working with new theories and methods that could generate more complex and innovative ways of framing and understanding health problems. Kessel & Rosenfield (2008) reflect:

> What was called multidisciplinary or even interdisciplinary research involved primarily separate input of different disciplines, but *not* creative ways to blend those to yield deeper understanding of the problem or integrative solutions that would be both more acceptable to the population at risk and more cost-effective in the long run. (p. S226)

More recently, the idea has been applied to policymaking, suggesting that intersectoral action in government could be achieved through a transdisciplinary or "transectoral" policy approach, one that by definition was not rooted in a particular ministry or department (Greaves & Bialystok, 2011, p. 409). Intersectoral action is a relatively new frontier in policy and suggests that if various government interests worked together, then core priorities could be enhanced more easily. The health-oriented version of intersectoral action is "health in all policies" (HIAP). HIAP contends that transport, economic, environmental, and other policy all needs to be made with health in mind so that unintended and negative consequences do not emerge when one department works on its own. Transdisciplinarity is fundamentally a critical approach to research, as it delves into the (often arbitrary) boundaries between disciplines and tries to rise above them by melding the best contributions of each. It is particularly useful in addressing complex problems where historical unidisciplinary approaches have not yielded effective solutions.

ADDICTION: A COMPLEX PROBLEM

Addiction is an example of a complex and persistent social and health issue that has challenged individuals and their communities for centuries. Addiction has no easy definition, explanation, or solution. Many disciplines, however, have studied addiction and offered theories, methods, and solutions, usually from a particular perspective. For example, disease models of addiction see it has a neurobiological condition that needs therapeutic treatment (Jellinek, 1960). Social models of addiction see it as a function of connection, culture, history, and social context (Carlson, 2006; Peele, 1987). Legal models see addiction as a criminal, regulatory, or deviance issue in need of deterrence, punishment, and policy. Yet others see addiction as a moral issue, or one derived from spiritual vacuums (Alexander, 2008; Maté, 2010).

The book *Transforming Addiction: Gender, Trauma, Transdisciplinarity* (Greaves, Poole, & Boyle, 2015) argues that transdisciplinarity is crucial to reaching a better understanding of addiction in research and that such an approach will enhance treatment approaches as well. Based on a 12-year research training program in addictions and mental health research called "Intersections of Mental Health Perspectives in Addiction," this book brings together a range of disciplines and sectors, professionals and trainees, to discuss examples of how working in transdisciplinary ways has transformed their understanding of and approach to addiction. Chapters in the book demonstrate the value of an integrated approach to addiction that recognizes the issues that intersect and influence experiences of addiction such as trauma, violence, and mental health. *Transforming Addiction* calls for a paradigm shift in addictions research that embraces a three-pronged approach: transdisciplinary collaboration, inclusion of sex and gender at all stages of research and treatment, and the adoption of an integrated approach to addiction and its related issues.

The reason transdisciplinarity is suggested in the study of addiction is because of the many possible causes of addiction and its wide range of effects. No single discipline will provide all the answers to addiction issues, nor create research or treatment options that will provide all the solutions for individuals or society. There are many other social issues that could benefit from a transdisciplinary approach, given their complexity.

Feminist Methodologies

In keeping with our shared values, we are highlighting feminist approaches to research. There has been a long tradition of exclusion of women in research, either as scientists, subjects or participants, and beneficiaries. This reflects a long history of patriarchy, often solidified by restricting access to higher education, influential positions, decision making, universities, and governments. In some parts of the world, immense progress has been made in rectifying such exclusions, but much remains to be done both in Canada and globally. The net result of such exclusions is that knowledge construction is distorted and not reflective of all perspectives and experiences.

Historically, power has been unevenly distributed between men and women, and among women and among men, reflecting complex social processes and practices such as discrimination, sexism, racism, homophobia, and classism, among others. Feminist research approaches directly address the power imbalances in everyday life, political and economic institutions, and education and access to resources. They introduce subjectivity into research as a key element in understanding life and doing research by asking questions about who gets to know and create knowledge. The ultimate aim of feminist research is to achieve praxis—a bringing together of theory and practice.

Feminist approaches to research emphasize the inclusion of women's viewpoints and concerns; highlight the influence of gender and sex on research questions and outcomes; recognize factors that limit or extend power, such as race/ethnicity, income, class, location, ability, age, and so on; and delve into different research values and goals that can be characterized as "masculine" or "feminine." Indeed, such characteristics are reflected in attributes that have often been assigned to types of research (positivist = hard, interpretive = soft) or areas of study. These attributes, exclusions, and differences in power can have real impacts on our collective understanding of research and knowledge. As Lorraine Code points out, some areas of knowledge that are traditionally feminine have been suppressed or unrecognized as scientific. Code reminds us that knowledge construction is not value free and that "subjectivity" has become associated with females and devalued as a result, while "objectivity" has been associated with males. She tells us that there are many stark reminders of this, including the devaluation of women's accumulated wisdom in areas such as midwifery, horticulture, cookery, and home remedies (Code, 1991, p. 27).

Implicitly, an emphasis on gender in research in recent decades has facilitated the clear delineation of women's issues and viewpoints, men's issues and viewpoints, and increasingly gender questioning or transgender viewpoints. Highlighting and exploding the concepts and categories of gender has shone a light on the impact of both sex and gender on human life and has implicitly set the stage for understanding the complexities of human existence as affected by other social factors, such as race/ethnicity, indigeneity, socioeconomic status, or ability in conjunction with gender.

Sex and Gender Analysis. Many research questions may have different implications for women compared to men, or boys compared to girls, or transgendered persons compared to cisgendered persons. The way to investigate this is to consciously include and measure sex- and gender-related factors in the research. Indeed, because of feminist research and advocacy there are now increasing requirements to include sex and gender issues in research, practice, and policy as governments, funders, and the general public increasingly want to know if research and policy affects women and men or boys and girls similarly or differently (see Canadian Institutes of Health Research, www.ciw-irsc.gc.ca). Answering these questions requires designing research and measuring factors in ways that will reveal these potential differences.

Including sex and gender in research is a critically important contemporary approach. In North America and Europe, this approach has been gaining momentum over the past 15 years, with funding agencies and government bodies demanding more detail on these elements of research, treatment, and policy. The main idea behind including sex and gender in research is that assuming knowledge is equally applicable to all people is not warranted. Therefore, it is essential to consciously include sex- and gender-related concepts and variables that are often overlooked.

"Sex" generally refers to the biologically based elements of human and animal organisms, while "gender" generally refers to the cultural or socially constructed elements of human life. Sex and gender are both fluid, context-specific concepts. This means that while we can define them, they are interpreted differently in different time periods, cultures, or settings and hence get redefined continuously. This also means that they can change and they often exist on a continuum, not as two distinct, dichotomous variables. This fluidity is essential to understand since it sets the stage for understanding gender and sex as changeable factors, rooted in time, tradition, or culture and interacting with a range of other factors that affect human life. It also sets the stage for social action, a key element of feminist approaches to research.

Sex includes biological elements that are different in and among many women and men, such as hormones, muscle mass, body size, and anatomy. If they are not taken into account in research on disease trajectories or physical strength or responses to drugs then the results are unlikely to be sensitive to all. Similarly, workplace and occupational policies or labour market analyses need to account for such sex-based factors. But much research and policy in the past has been based on a male model, either in animal studies, cell lines, or in social policy research, with assumptions made about applicability and generalizability to all people or animals regardless of sex.

Gender includes categories such as male, female, or other and is shaped by the social or cultural factors that affect humans. For example, access to power, money, resources, political positions, or jobs are often gendered, with more power and resources being allocated to male individuals in almost every society. Gender is a fluid and context-driven factor that includes an individual's gender identity, gender roles and norms that affect relationships, and institutional gender rules and laws that influence resource distribution. Views on gender also affect practices such as voting rights, inheritance, rituals (such as female genital mutilation), access to public space, expectations of body image and dress, engagement in social life or political affairs, among many other human practices.

The Institute of Medicine released a key report in 2012 that outlined the importance of including sex differences in health and medical research, especially to women's health, where such inclusions may have traditionally been overlooked. For example, women are generally underrepresented in clinical trials, and where they are included the data are rarely segregated by sex. Inclusion criteria for clinical trials related to cardiovascular disease focus on early age of onset of myocardial infarction and chest pain as presenting symptoms, unconsciously favouring men since women more often present with different symptoms, such as unstable angina, stroke, or unrecognized myocardial infarction. This leads to the underestimation of cardiovascular disease in women. Inclusion criteria for animal models also reveal a substantial sex bias in research, where mostly male animals are used to create models of disease. This bias creates crucial limitations for identifying and understanding potentially important sex differences in the progression and treatment of disease. It also leads to an assumption that "maleness" is the norm in both human and animal research.

While the impact of biology and culture on human health is clear, sex and gender also affect other kinds of research. Economic policies may affect women and men differently (because women typically make less money than men), as do housing policies (because women often have children to house and make less money) and urban design (because women are more vulnerable to sexual assault than men). Sex and gender sometimes interact directly, such as women being more vulnerable to HIV/AIDs transmission because of the structure and biology of the vagina, as well as experiencing less power to control sexual relations (Johnson, Greaves, & Repta, 2007). Another example is the vulnerability of women to small-cell lung cancer from using light or filtered cigarettes and succumbing to the gendered advertising promoting such products to women.

SEATBELT TESTING AND PREGNANT CRASH TEST DUMMIES

A case study compiled by Gendered Innovations at Stanford University provides a prime example of how taking one body as a norm for others (i.e., male bodies as the norm) not only limits knowledge but can be harmful. Safety belts in motor vehicles were initially developed in the 1960s based on the body of the fiftieth-percentile man. Thus, conventional seatbelts do not accommodate bodies of different sizes and shapes, such as those of pregnant women. This has a fatal implication given that motor vehicle accidents are a leading cause of accidental fetal death due to maternal trauma. With an estimated 13 million pregnant women across the European Union and United States each year, the use of seatbelts during pregnancy is a key safety concern. (Schiebinger et al., 2011–2015)

In recent years, many helpful manuals and training sessions have been developed to convince researchers how much sex and gender matter and to suggest ways in which research can be adjusted or policy developed that will be more sensitive to women, men, boys, and girls. Examples include the following:

- Susceptibility to lung disease from smoking among men and women
- Contraction of HIV through heterosexual intercourse
- Symptoms of heart disease for men and women
- Use of X-rays for judging levels of disability and chronic pain as experienced by men and women
- Experiences of being overweight and obese among boys and girls
- Efficacy of international tobacco control policy for men and women (Clow, Pederson, Haworth-Brockman, & Bernier, 2009)

Other documents focus on training researchers on how to address sex and gender in research, either using simple techniques for reanalyzing data or by designing new research entirely. For example, *Better Science with Sex and Gender* (Johnson et al., 2007) offers the following suggestions for redesigning research to take into consideration sex and gender: revisit an original study; augment an existing research plan; or incorporate a sex- and gender-based analysis from the outset. Sex and gender categories are in the process of being exploded by increasing advocacy and visibility of transgendered individuals as well as feminists. For example, some individuals who question their assigned sex or gender (the one they were assigned at birth based on their physical characteristics) can deliberately change their identities by using hormone blockers, hormone therapy, or surgery. Gendered identities, relations, and roles can also be questioned, rejected, embraced, or adopted, either by individuals who question their own imposed limitations or by social movements that question gender categories and social limitations assigned to whole groups. These shifts and questions serve to illustrate how important, fluid, and contextual sex and gender categories are.

Despite these increasing complexities, the aim of including sex and gender in research is to make research more sensitive and relevant and to generate better evidence for tailoring policies, programs, treatments, drugs, products, or services to fit men and women, boys and girls, or other categories of people more specifically. These adjustments reflect better science and social and biological realities and could save lives, or at the very least improve life for all. It is heartening to see that in 2016 there are more funding agencies and governments requiring a sex and gender analysis be included in research, policy, and treatment, and more public and media interest in understanding and accepting a range of gender categories in addition to male and female.

Gender Transformative Concepts. Sex and gender analysis is a tool for change and an essential aspect of planning and carrying out research. It is a dynamic and critical area, constantly changing and challenging gender constructs and pointing out how gender interplays with almost all issues, problems, and social constructs affecting human life.

In recent years, the concept of gender has been used to guide and analyze social action and programming as well as policy, treatment, and research. In these areas, persistent problems such as violence against women, unequal caregiving or employment opportunities, maternal health risk, lack of political representation, or HIV/AIDs transmission quickly emerged as areas where gender played an important role. For example, violence against women is often predicated on imbalances of power between men and women. Unequal caregiving is predicated on assumptions about gender roles as well as sex-linked reproductive roles. HIV/AIDs transmission is also affected by sex-linked vulnerabilities and gender power imbalances. Progressive thinkers have suggested that instead of just noting these gender imbalances, it is important to try and change—or *transform*—negative gender relations and harmful gender stereotypes to diminish the inequalities and risks. Hence, gender transformative work has progressed in a range of areas, focusing on how to shift gender stereotypes, norms, and practices from negative to positive along with improving health, reducing risk, and increasing equity.

IMPROVING HEALTH *AND* GENDER EQUITY

Making It Better: Gender Transformative Health Promotion (Greaves, Pederson, & Poole, 2014) argues that the field of health promotion, for example, could benefit from the application of gender transformative concepts. Typical approaches to health promotion don't take gender into account, and if they do they don't necessarily aim to change gender stereotypes. Rather, they often focus on generating individual behaviour change to reach health goals. In designing health promotion, or indeed health interventions, research, or policies, gender can be ignored, perceived as neutral or irrelevant, or integrated in sensitive and specific ways. But sometimes gender is used in exploitative or accommodating ways by programs or in policies that still leave negative gender norms intact. The authors offer a framework, a tool, and a training course (www.promotinghealthinwomen.ca) for all who might like to understand and then change negative gender relations, roles, or practices—making gender transformative shifts to an issue or population.

For example, negative gender stereotypes about women and girls that underpin sexual harassment and abuse can be addressed and shifted by overtly engaging men in awareness-raising campaigns and encouraging bystander engagement in stopping these practices. Engaging men in positive fathering classes or in reframing masculinity to equate gentleness with strength are other examples of programs that try to shift gender relations as they apply to single mothering, caregiving and parenting, teen pregnancy, or violence against women. Other examples focus on shifting approaches about women who smoke tobacco or drink alcohol to using positive gender notions, as opposed to negative ones, to make change. For example, much programming aimed at getting women to quit smoking focuses on negative cosmetic concerns, such as wrinkles, premature aging, or diminishing heterosexual attractiveness. Gender transformative approaches would focus on quitting for health, independence, freedom, liberation, or power.

Intersectional Analysis.[1] Since the early 2000s, intersectionality has arisen as a major development in feminist theorizing and research. The term "intersectionality" was coined by Kimberlé Crenshaw (1989) in the late 1980s, but the underlying principles have a long and rich history in social sciences, particularly among black feminist scholars. There are multiple definitions

1 This section is adapted from work contributed by Olivier Ferlatte.

of intersectionality, but it can be described as a research framework that investigates and interprets how multiple interlocking social locations (such as sexuality, gender, race/ethnicity, class) that are shaped by intersecting sociocultural forms of power and privilege (such as heterosexism, sexism, racism, classism) affect peoples, individuals, and collective identities and experiences (Hankivsky, 2012; Shields, 2008).

In recent years researchers have increasingly applied intersectionality to the investigation of problems and inequities to acknowledge its potential to capture the breadth of individuals and populations' experiences (Bowleg, 2012; Hankivsky, 2012). Often, social science researchers have studied the effect of social locations by looking at one social location at a time (Bauer, 2014), such as investigating the effect of sex and/or gender or being a woman on HIV vulnerabilities. To embrace the complex experiences of those whose lives cut across a range of identities it is often necessary to consider the intersections of gender and other characteristics or processes. For example, the experiences of racism and colonization that shape Indigenous women's experiences with HIV are also integral to how they experience gender and inequity. Intersectionality researchers try to illuminate the intersections of different social locations, power relations, and experiences that shape health, economic status, or other experiences.

Intersectionality researchers argue that human lives cannot be reduced to a single characteristic; that human experiences cannot be accurately understood by prioritizing any one single factor or adding together a constellation of factors; that social categories are socially constructed, fluid, and flexible; and that social locations are inseparable and shaped by the interacting and mutually constituting social processes and structures that are influenced by both time and place (Hankivsky, 2012, p. 1713). Like other critical approaches, intersectionality is not a research method but rather a research framework that represents a set of underlying beliefs that inform the research process. Intersectionality does not offer or dictate a particular methodology to conduct research. However, Hankivsky and colleagues (2012) have proposed a set of principles that can guide intersectional health research and can be adapted to other forms of social science research:

- *Intersecting social locations:* Intersectionality research rejects the idea that health inequities are shaped by a single social location or that one social location is most important. Rather, intersectionality conceptualizes social locations as interacting and co-constituting.
- *Multilevel analysis:* Intersectionality research is concerned with and tries to elucidate the effects of social locations between and across different levels in society, including macro- (global and national level structures), meso- (provincial and regional structures), and micro-levels (community level or individual).

- *Power:* A critical consideration of intersectionality research is what is revealed about power (i.e., homophobia, racism, classism, sexism; Dhamoon, 2011). Intersectionality researchers bear the responsibility of interpreting their data within the context of power that is shaping the lives of those under investigation.
- *Reflexivity:* One way researchers also attend to power in intersectionality research is through reflexivity, which is a process where researchers explicitly examine how their own social positions, personal beliefs, and emotions enter the research process (Hsiung, 2008).
- *Time and space:* Intersectionality emphasizes the importance of time and space in analysis, meaning that geography and historical events shape the meaning of social locations.
- *Diversity of knowledges:* Intersectionality recognizes the existence of different forms of knowledge and seeks to include the knowledge of traditionally marginalized groups, such as the traditional knowledge of Indigenous populations, to disrupt power and build new evidence.
- *Social justice:* Intersectionality explicitly works toward social justice, meaning that the improvement of all populations and the fair treatment of those socially disadvantaged is improved (Gostin & Powers, 2006).
- *Equity:* Closely tied to social justice, intersectionality seeks equity, which is the advancement of policy and health interventions that promote equal outcomes between privileged and less-advantaged groups.

Many of these principles overlap with other feminist research approaches and with the goals of sex- and gender-based analysis. There is little disagreement that multiple factors affect human life and social interactions and that they need to be taken into account in research. Intersectional analyses draw attention to the necessity to consider concurrent variables and processes in examining human life in research and remove the challenges of developing methodologies that achieve this aim. Some argue that while certain factors may be more dominant than others in some situations, factors such as gender are integral and influential in *all* other factors, characteristics, and processes. The challenges in applying intersectionality frameworks in developing research methodologies are significant, but when applied they can yield interesting data.

SUICIDE RISK AMONG GAY AND BISEXUAL MEN

Written by Olivier Ferlatte

Suicide, like many other health inequities, is unevenly distributed among the population, with marginalized groups being the most affected. In Canada, suicide particularly affects gay and bisexual men, Indigenous peoples, and people living in rural and remote communities. While the populations affected by suicide are not mutually exclusive—for example, someone can be a bisexual Indigenous man living in a remote community—the suicide prevention literature tends to treat these groups as such. Very little attention is given to diversity within groups; for example, we know very little about which gay and bisexual men are most at risk of committing suicide (Ferlatte, Dulai, Hottes, Trussler, & Marchand, 2015).

We therefore used intersectionality as a framework to study recent suicide attempts among gay and bisexual men. We found that 1 in 58 men reported a suicide attempt in the last 12 months (1.7 per cent), but that not all gay and bisexual men were equally affected by suicide, with some groups being more vulnerable. First we found that gay and bisexual Indigenous men reported a higher number of suicide attempts; 1 in 23 Indigenous men said they attempted to end their life in the last 12 months (4.2 per cent). We also found that men that had both a lower education and a lower income were at significantly higher risk of suicide; these factors appear to work together so that men who find themselves at the intersections of these two social locations reported suicide attempts in a proportion of 1 in 23 (4.2 per cent). Meanwhile, men who had either a lower education or lower income (or neither) were not at increased risk of suicide attempts; less than 1.2 per cent of these men reported a suicide attempt in the last 12 months.

In addition, our analysis also revealed that partnership status affected the vulnerability of bisexual men while it had no effect on gay men. Bisexual men who were in a relationship with a man reported a suicide attempt in the last 12 months in a proportion of 1 in 27 (3.7 per cent). This is contrasted with bisexual men partnered with a woman, who reported suicide risk less frequently: 1 in 125 in the last year (0.08 per cent). This suggests that heterosexual partnerships may protect bisexual men from stressors such as homophobia and biphobia that are generally associated with suicide, while same-sex partnerships may have the opposite effect. While homophobia can be blamed for contributing to the excess of suicide among gay and bisexual men, our research revealed that for some gay men issues of classism and racism might increase their vulnerability. Therefore, it is critical that prevention strategies take into account the unique experiences of those most vulnerable to suicide, including Indigenous gay and bisexual men, those with a lower income, and same-sex partnered bisexual men.

Indigenous Methodologies

In recent years, Indigenous scholars and researchers across the globe have worked to promote and highlight Indigenous perspectives in research and community building. The production of knowledge through research is always culturally and socially bound and defined, so it is important to ask how science and research have come to reflect dominant "Western" values. It is equally important to ask how Indigenous perspectives have been hidden, obliterated, or ignored. There has been a long history of considering Indigenous peoples as "others" in research, especially in colonial times. As Denzin and Lincoln write:

> In this period, qualitative researchers wrote "objective" colonializing accounts of field experiences that were reflective of the positivist scientist paradigm. They were concerned with offering valid, reliable, and objective interpretations in their writings. The "other" who was studied was alien, foreign, and strange. (Denzin & Lincoln, 2000, p. 12)

Indigenous scholars and allies who are working collaboratively with Indigenous scholars have thought through this history and examined the assumptions underlying "Western" and Indigenous approaches to research and offered alternative methodologies. For example, Brown and Strega (2005) reflect on the paradigm of mainstream research that highlights positivism and objectivity, which can downplay ethics, location, and experience and thus often further marginalize certain groups. Their collection is intended to be radical and highlights Indigenous, critical, feminist, and anti-oppressive approaches to research: "In Canada, Indigenous peoples' commitment to reclaiming traditional ways of knowing has also led to questions and critiques of research practices" (Brown & Strega, 2005, p. 7).

Thus, Indigenous scholars resist hierarchical, objectivist research that privileges quantitative methods and empirical work and diminishes the role of subjectivity in research. Indigenous researchers and their allies are often invested in linking experiences, past and present, to research studies and overtly seeking social justice. Some Indigenous perspectives emerge from holistic, community-oriented social structures that often question or reject binaries of gender, private ownership, or non-Indigenous government, but offer a frame for family and kinship structures and, in recent decades, seek to collectively recover from colonization, discrimination, and trauma. One approach emerges from the Indigenous medicine wheel and reflects some of the perspectives for underpinning community life, health and recovery, and research. The medicine wheel offers a structure of equality and nonhierarchical thinking where various components of life work together in harmony and equality to create results.

Kenny and colleagues (2004) proposed another framework for policy research detailing the components of an Indigenous approach that took gender into account. They suggest the following three components: honouring the past, present, and future; honouring the interconnectedness of all things; and honouring the spiritual, physical, emotional, and mental aspects of human beings. The authors also note the negative history of research on Indigenous issues in Canada, detailing the following errors and historical obstacles:

- Lack of partnerships with communities
- Researchers in control of all aspects of the research procedures
- No meaningful participant involvement
- Lack of trust in researchers by the participants
- Conflicting worldviews of researcher and participants
- Lack of understanding by participants on purpose and impacts of research
- Failure to obtain informed consent
- Irrelevant research methods that are not compatible with Indigenous culture
- Community not involved in identifying solutions
- No follow-up or reporting back to the participants (p. 10)

A decade later, these ideas and approaches are now embedded in the Tri-Council Policy Statement with formalized guidelines that attempt to rectify these imbalanced research relationships and to replace them with new paradigms. Conducting ethical research with Indigenous individuals and communities is explored in more depth in Chapter 3.

Other researchers have proposed Two-Eyed Seeing, *Etuaptmumk* in Mi'kmaq, to indicate an effort to integrate ways of thinking. Two-Eyed Seeing is an approach to Indigenous knowledge, health, and well-being that originated with Mi'kmaq Elders Murdena and Albert Marshall (Bartlett, Marshall, & Marshall, 2012). Marshall describes this approach as "learning to see from one eye with the strengths of Indigenous Knowledges and ways of knowing, and from the other eye with the strengths of Western Knowledges and ways of knowing . . . and learning to use both these eyes together, for the benefit of all." This approach is inherently integrative and transdisciplinary in that it draws together multiple perspectives from within and across Western and Indigenous knowledges. It involves a careful weaving back and forth between Indigenous and Western knowledge systems, which are founded on different belief systems and valuations of evidentiary sources (Castellano, 2000; Fornssler et al., 2013).

Two-Eyed Seeing is also considered a "decolonizing methodology" because it aims to honour Indigenous ways of knowing and needs in the process of working with Western approaches so that culturally specific meanings are not lost or demoted in translation through Western methods. This approach also embeds a broader Indigenous Knowledge Framework (Hopkins & Fornssler 2014) that perceives well-being for Indigenous peoples as involving multiple aspects of life: physical, spiritual, mental, and emotional wellness.

THE HONOURING OUR STRENGTHS PROJECT

"Honouring Our Strengths: Indigenous Culture as Intervention in Addiction Treatment" (Hopkins & Fornssler, 2014) is an example of the application of Two-Eyed Seeing and Indigenous methodologies toward supporting the integrated wellness of Indigenous communities. Bringing together a multidisciplinary and intersectoral group of quantitative and qualitative researchers, therapeutic front-line workers, executive directors, and Indigenous knowledge keepers, the aim of this project was to develop a wellness instrument to measure the efficacy of culturally based addiction treatment services for Indigenous clients. The "Honouring Our Strengths" project offers a promising model and products such as the Indigenous Knowledge Framework that can benefit Indigenous populations and addictions more generally because it integrates mind, body, heart, and spirit within one framework.

There are many implications for both researchers and practitioners of adopting any of these decolonizing methodologies and theories. For example, Michael Yellow Bird (2013), an Indigenous social worker and researcher, suggests that emergent neurobiological theories and findings indicating the potential of the brain to reprogram itself can be melded with an Indigenous point of view to undo the effects of trauma and colonization. Yellow Bird adapts the notion of brain neuroplasticity and applies it in clinical practice to create "neurodecolonization" processes—undoing negative brain processes and replacing them with optimistic, positive brain processes in Indigenous peoples and societies. In short, Indigenous approaches to research offer insight and guidance to all researchers on rethinking evidence, building relationships, and approaching research more holistically.

Anti-Oppressive Research

A cluster of research approaches that hold reducing oppression (and increasing emancipation) at their centre have emerged in recent decades. Oppression can be levelled at any social group or individual, but some groups have overtly named oppression as deleterious to their well-being and progress. For example, disability researchers, Indigenous researchers, or those whose aim is to raise the profile of women, immigrants, people in poverty, or gay and queer people have all contributed to articulating this perspective. Oppression often assumes structures and dominant philosophies and stances that contribute to silencing or ignoring various less-powerful groups. These can be in the form of governments, capitalism, patriarchies, "white" or "Western" thinking, or simply purveyors of discriminatory practices such as homophobia, ableism, or racism.

Anti-oppressive research practices have emerged from anti-oppressive practice, which is often located in social work (see Brown & Strega, 2005). Academic social workers and other social scientists have focused on the dual goals of relieving oppression via their work and introducing elements of anti-oppressive thinking into research practices. A central element of anti-oppressive research is to name and then disrupt oppressive thinking by deliberately asking questions that illuminate these processes. Another central element is to question standard research assumptions such as "objectivity" or "hierarchies of evidence" of positivism. Taken together these disruptive questions open up space for research that overtly questions oppressive practices, with a view to reducing them in the name of emancipation. Brown and Strega (2005) put it this way when describing the contributions to their book:

> Questions about who knowledge is created for, how it is created and for what purposes are interwoven with concrete descriptions of how politically committed researchers can address these concerns in their work. (p. 4)

These questions have flowed in several directions. At their base, they highlight ethical approaches to engaging with both oppressed groups of people and their issues and in naming appropriate research questions, methods, and goals. But more critically, they aim to counter traditional, positivist research approaches and to unearth other "truths"—either new information from or about oppressed people or to uncover previously hidden "truths." Hence, anti-oppressive research is deliberately countering the very essence of positivist science by challenging assumptions about scientific method and "truth." Indeed, in keeping with a range of recent perspectives, such as feminist research or Indigenous research, there is an acknowledgement that "value-free" science is elusive at best, and imaginary at worst.

This approach acknowledges that various oppressions often work in concert to create disempowerment among populations. For example, a Toronto-based study to determine best practices in creating culturally competent, anti-oppressive housing was based on an understanding of intersectionality, social justice, and anti-oppression (Warner et al., 2008). It concluded that diversity is a key component in understanding and planning for supportive housing, and that the engagement of people requiring housing needs to be fundamental in design of services.

Anti-oppressive research builds on the rich legacy of Paulo Freire, who wrote the important book *Pedagogy of the Oppressed* (1970/2000) where he identified how traditional education focused on filling students up with information as if they were vessels. He argued for a critical pedagogy aimed at the "co-creation" of knowledge, a process that identified the political stance of the teacher and empowered the student based on a relationship between student, teacher, and society. Freire developed his theories based on teaching literacy to people in Brazil and suggested that, ultimately, freedom from oppression is the result when a balance between theory and practice is achieved—that is, a state of praxis. Building on these principles, people have created practice, research, and educational approaches to generate a more balanced power structure between groups in society, the essence of anti-oppressive work.

These critical approaches reflect value positions of many researchers who are interested in social change. All of these selected approaches have critical thinking in common, and they all address entrenched assumptions about knowledge creation and traditional research approaches with a questioning eye. Further, all offer more complex and representative approaches that recognize the diversity of experiences in human society. While some of them emphasize one element over another, they are all aimed at increasing equity and generating new knowledge that will aid in rectifying social problems and increasing social justice.

Engagement in Research

In addition to generating new approaches to research that critique existing paradigms and offer new ones, engagement with participants in and users of research is increasingly important in planning research projects. Engagement covers a range of approaches, but generally refers to how groups affected by the research question, or potential implementers of research results, get an opportunity to engage in research processes. This can include generating research questions, deciding on methods, or suggesting how to apply the results. While there may be little time or resources for engagement within many student research assignments, it is well worth understanding how important engagement is in the broader research world.

There are various goals in engaging those affected by research, such as respecting their voices and roles, using their wisdom and advice, and making sure that research is done with their collaboration and permission. Some of these goals reflect the need to redress past injustices in the name of research, such as using materials and stories with no benefit going to the community or objectifying groups as a result of little engagement with their goals, aspirations, and humanness. Sadly, lots of research in the past has been done in this fashion, prompting many groups to state "nothing about us without us" as a rallying cry for engagement. Of late, the disability rights movement and mental health community have popularized this slogan to indicate a deep desire to acquire power and independence and to alleviate the effects of paternalistic treatment. Its use has since spread to other groups making the same point about engagement.

Sometimes, of course, the participants, subjects, and users of research are one and the same, but often several groups in society are likely to be affected and ought to be engaged. There are similarly important goals in engaging antic-ipated users of research in research processes well in advance of finishing a research project. For example, canvassing the key questions or needs that prac-titioners or policymakers have can inform the research question and design. Involving practitioners and policymakers or community groups in the research team can be equally important, as this deepens the relevance of the research and makes it much more likely to be used and supported by key sectors. This type of engagement can also be critical to getting access to research commu-nities or participants while also building confidence in groups of people about the purpose, value, and utility of the research project.

Integrated Knowledge Translation. Integrated knowledge translation has been adopted by research funding agencies, in particular the Canadian Institutes of Health Research (CIHR). The knowledge-to-action process is conceptual-ized as an iterative process leading to more effective application of research findings. One way to maximize this is via collaboration, or engagement, in research. According to the CIHR,

> In integrated KT [knowledge translation], stakeholders or potential research knowledge users are engaged in the entire research process. By doing integrated KT, researchers and research users work together to shape the research process by collaborating to determine the research questions, deciding on the methodology, being involved in data collection and tools development, interpreting the findings, and helping disseminate the research results. This approach, also known by such terms as collaborative research, action-oriented research, and co-production of knowledge, should produce research findings that are more likely to be relevant to and used by the end users. (Canadian Institutes of Health Research, 2015a)

This type of engagement is heralded by funding agencies as indicative of genuine partnership and as likely to lead to more relevant and valuable research results. Accordingly, it is now often required as part of funding proposals.

FUSION: A COLLABORATIVE MODEL

In 2001, 80 women's health researchers from across Canada were brought together to develop a framework for doing collaborative health research that would meet both interdisciplinary and engagement principles. The result was *Fusion: A Model for Integrated Health Research* (Greaves & Ballem, 2001). The process involved not only identifying ideal processes of collaborative, engaged research, but also revealing the key power and structural issues that create barriers or opportunities for engagement. For example, contrasting goals were identified, such as those of academics to produce peer-reviewed publications and acquire university promotions versus those of community groups or policymakers to use research knowledge to make immediate changes or to support advocacy requests. In addition, issues of territoriality, power and control, establishing authentic partnerships, finding funding for engagement processes, and addressing stereotypes and differences of worldview were all seen as challenges for carrying out integrated research. In contrast, there is increasing interest and pressure for more voices, disciplines, and sectors to be involved in research and to marry academic thinking with community and practice "know-how" to carry out research and apply the results.

Community-Based Research. Community-based research (CBR) has a long history with roots in Kurt Lewin's participatory action research and Freire's work with oppressed communities in Brazil (Minkler, 2005).[2] CBR is "research rooted in community, serving community interests, encouraging citizen participation and geared towards affecting social change" (Flicker, Savan, McGrath, Kolenda, & Mildenberger, 2008, p. 241). Reid, Brief, and LeDrew (2009) describe CBR as an approach to research that is collaborative, inclusive, and action oriented. It can use either qualitative or quantitative research methodologies to generate knowledge. The community is at the centre of CBR because the research is conducted by, with, and for communities (Reid et al., 2009). By placing this importance on the "community," CBR is inclusive of different ways of seeing the world and incorporates multiple perspectives.

---

2 Related research traditions also include participatory research, action research, and feminist participatory action research.

It recognizes "local knowledge systems as valid on their own epistemological foundations and views them as contributing to a larger understanding of the world and the place of humans in it" (Fletcher, 2003, p. 32).

CBR aims to deconstruct power relations, democratize knowledge, create opportunities for community capacity building, and create spaces for political advocacy and action (Horowitz, Robinson, & Seifer, 2009). Ochocka, Moorlag, and Janzen (2010) view community engagement as a "research entry" process that goes beyond gaining entrance to the community and recruitment of the participants and involves "a long-term relationship with community members that is 'continually negotiated' with power imbalances to be constantly navigated" (p. 3). Increasingly, CBR is being seen as a catalyst for social innovation, for public policy improvements, for solving complex community issues, and for promoting democracy in which local knowledge is valued in building local solutions (Ochocka & Janzen, 2014).

A key value and principle of CBR is the democratization of knowledge through the democratization of the research process itself. In this context "democratization" means that anyone can know anything: A body of knowledge can be shaped and directed by the people and not necessarily by experts alone. As such, everyone involved in the research—participants, researchers, practitioners, supporters— engage in co-learning (or learning with and in communities). It "reminds us of our equality and provides a frame for developing mutual, non-appropriating learning from and with one another" (Curry & Cunningham, 2000, p. 81).

CBR emphasizes not only the democratization of knowledge production but also the importance of context in the development and interpretation of the knowledge itself: Money, politics, culture, and environment all influence our perceptions of the world around us (Fletcher, 2003). Ochocka and Janzen (2014) refer to democratization as "community relevance." Research must have practical significance to communities, and it is relevant when community members, especially those most affected by the issue under study, gain voice and choice through the research process (Smith, 2012). Ideas about the democratization of research and using research as a tool to inform both informal and formal actions have been central to not only CBR but also to feminist, Indigenous, and anti-oppressive approaches to research.

In CBR, community members and researchers equitably share control of the research agenda through active and reciprocal involvement in the design, implementation, and dissemination of the research (Ochocka & Janzen, 2014). Engaging people democratically and reciprocally in the research process results in stronger, more-empowered communities that develop the capacity to create social and individual change (Reid et al., 2009). The process and results of CBR should be useful to community members in making positive social change and in promoting social equity (Ochocka & Janzen, 2014).

IMAGINING INCLUSION

"Imagining Inclusion" was a community-based research collaboration between the Thrive program at Open Door Group and the Department of Therapeutic Recreation at Douglas College. The purpose of the study was to explore how people with lived experiences of mental illness experienced community inclusion, health, and well-being. The 32 research participants were women and men of diverse ages and ethnicities, most of whom had incomes of less than $11,000 per year. Their mental health issues included major depression, bipolar disorder, post-traumatic stress disorder, borderline personality disorder, psychosis, schizophrenia, and anxiety, and many of them had other and multiple health conditions. We used photovoice, a CBR method, to engage participants in exploring their lived experiences of mental illness. Photovoice allows for "the possibility of perceiving the world from the viewpoint of the people who lead lives that are different from those traditionally in control of the means for imaging the world" (Wang & Burris, 1997, p. 372). It is a participatory process where individuals use photography to answer specific questions and tell a story. For 10 weeks participants photographed their responses to different questions, such as, What are your communities? What does community inclusion look like? In your day-to-day life, what do your experiences of social isolation, exclusion, poverty, and stigma look like? What does recovery mean to you?

Discussions of the photos were audio-recorded, and participants wrote reflections to develop a narrative for each of their photographs. The data set included over 300 photographs and reflections, 34 meeting transcripts, 40 sets of fieldnotes, 14 one-on-one interviews, and demographic data from the 32 individuals.

Throughout "Imagining Inclusion" the research participants' lived experiences remained central in data collection, analysis, dissemination, and knowledge translation. Research participants were involved in analyzing data, planning photo exhibits, writing newsletters, and public speaking to increase awareness of mental illness. They became catalysts for change, and many found their prolonged involvement in the project was transformative. It engaged them intellectually, brought purpose to their day-to-day lives, and enabled them to network with professionals and others with lived experiences of mental illness.

CBR seeks to bring together action and reflection, theory and practice, in participation with others in the pursuit of practical solutions to issues of pressing concern to people and their communities. CBR has different purposes, is based on different relationships, and has different ways of conceiving knowledge from academic or more traditional research approaches. These are fundamental differences in the nature of inquiry, "not simply methodological niceties" (Reason & Bradbury, 2001, p. 3).

Summary

This chapter has brought together selected approaches to critical social research and discussed some fundamental issues and approaches to engagement in research. These critical approaches illustrate the links between values and research and how diverse research perspectives can advance those values. Further, these critical perspectives shine light on using research to do advocacy and effect social change. All of these critical approaches question power distribution and seek to improve equity. In order to achieve such goals, it is often deemed helpful or even necessary to engage with community participants, practitioners, or policymakers to develop and carry out research projects that matter and will make a positive difference. While there can be obstacles to effective engagement, the opportunities for engagement in research are now increasingly recognized and supported by research funders. Effective engagement requires time and resources, but it is often the key to successful research and knowledge translation.

Questions for Discussion

1. What are the differences between inter-, multi-, and transdisciplinarity? In what ways does transdisciplinarity address the shortcomings of inter- and multidisciplinarity?
2. Define "gender" and "sex." How are they fluid concepts? Can you think of examples of people or groups that illustrate this in real life?
3. How will exploding the gender binary (of male and female) to include "other" affect research project designs?
4. Describe the negative history of research with Indigenous peoples. What strategies and approaches have attempted to overcome this history?
5. What are the differences between a sex and gender analysis and intersectional theory? What are the principles of intersectionality, and how might they be applied to a research project?

6. What is community-based research? What are its main values, principles, and practices?
7. What are the similarities between feminist methodologies, Indigenous research, anti-oppressive approaches, and community-based research?

Our Recommended Readings

Brown, L., & Strega, S. (2005). *Research as resistance: Critical, Indigenous and anti-oppressive approaches.* Toronto: Canadian Scholars' Press.

Crenshaw, K. W. (1989). Demarginalizing the intersection of race and sex: A black feminist critique of antidiscrimination doctrine, feminist theory and antiracist politics. *University of Chicago Legal Forum, 1989,* 138–167.

Fletcher, C. (2003). Community-based participatory research relationships with Aboriginal communities in Canada: An overview of context and process. *Pimatisiwin: A Journal of Aboriginal and Indigenous Community Health, 1*(1), 27–62.

Flicker, S., Savan, B., McGrath, M., Kolenda, B., & Mildenberger, M. (2008). "If you could change one thing …" What community-based researchers wished they could have done differently. *Community Development Journal: An International Forum, 43*(2), 239–253. http://dx.doi.org/10.1093/cdj/bsm009

Hankivsky, O. (2012). Women's health, men's health, and gender and health: Implications of intersectionality. *Social Science & Medicine, 74*(11), 1712–1720. http://dx.doi.org/10.1016/j.socscimed.2011.11.029 Medline:22361090

Johnson, J., Greaves, L., & Repta, R. (2007). *Better science with sex and gender: A primer for health research.* Vancouver: Women's Health Research Network.

Ochocka, J., & Janzen, R. (2014). Breathing life into theory: Illustrations of community-based research—Hallmarks, functions and phases. *Gateways: International Journal of Community Research & Engagement, 7*(1), 18–33. http://dx.doi.org/10.5130/ijcre.v7i1.3486

Oliffe, J., & Greaves, L. (Eds). (2008). *Designing and conducting gender, sex and health research.* Thousand Oaks: Sage Publishing.

Websites

Academic Disciplines: http://education.stateuniversity.com/pages/1723/Academic-Disciplines.html

Canadian Institutes of Health Research: The Knowledge-to-Action Process: www.cihr-irsc.gc.ca/e/29418.html#ktap

Gendered Innovations: https://genderedinnovations.stanford.edu/case-studies/crash.html

Gender Equity through Health Promotion: www.promotinghealthinwomen.ca

Honouring Our Strengths: Culture as Intervention in Addictions Treatment: www.addictionresearchchair.ca/creating-knowledge/national/honouring-our-strengths-culture-as-intervention

Imaging Inclusion: www.imagininginclusion.ca

Institute for Integrative Science and Health: Two-Eyed Seeing: www.integrativescience.ca/Principles/TwoEyedSeeing

CHAPTER 3

BEING A RESEARCHER: LOCATING YOURSELF AND RESEARCH ETHICS

Critical social research places specific demands on the researcher. It requires self-awareness and deep consideration of approaches to engaging with others in the research process. A central demand is *intersubjectivity*: creating and maintaining an authentic dialogue between participants in the research process whereby all are respected as equally knowing subjects.

The purpose of this chapter is to discuss the importance of investigating your locations both within the research context and in broader social contexts. In order to investigate one's social location we outline some of the central ideas on researcher positionality (Holloway & Biley, 2011), reflexivity (Berger, 2015), voice, and representation. While we address research ethics throughout this book, in the latter part of this chapter we discuss the principles and practices of research ethics and how they relate to critical social research.

Locating Ourselves and Our Research

All of us express and represent elements of ourselves in every research endeavour. The questions we ask, the observations we make, the emotions we feel, the impressions we form, and the hunches we follow all reflect some part of who we are as person and researcher (Cole & Knowles, 2001). Critical social researchers view social phenomena holistically, use complex reasoning that is multifaceted and iterative, systematically reflect on who they are in the inquiry process, and are sensitive to their personal biography and how it shapes the study (Marshall & Rossman, 2016). One of the standards of rigorous critical social research is the visibility of the researcher in a research account. There is an impetus for researchers to be attentive to the influences that shape what we hear and how we interpret (Josselson, 2007)

It is important to remember that *all* research reflects a point of view, whether it is declared or not. Unlike more traditional or positivist research approaches that claim objectivity, in critical social research the researcher does not need to minimize his or her own interest or investment in the issue on the pretense of remaining objective. While stating research questions in ways that predict or prejudge answers must be avoided, a researcher's familiarity with the issue will increase her or his potential understanding of it. Researchers who are passionate about their area of interest can offer interesting and insightful knowledge and inspire others to investigate the issue further. While researchers who base their work on their passions have been accused of bias and politicization, many critical social researchers are now trained to declare such passions and subjective "locations."

Researcher Positionality

In the last three decades much has been written about the researcher's location within the research context. Understanding one's location as a researcher is central to most research endeavours and is vitally important for a critical social researcher who aims to engage in research that will result in meaningful social action. There has been considerable debate around the notion of "double consciousness," "dual perspectives," and "double knowledge."[1] People who occupy the margins, such as people of colour or Indigenous peoples, for instance, have more than one perception of reality. They are forced to not only view themselves from their own unique perspective, but also to view themselves as they might be perceived by the outside world. As a result, people on the margins can suffer from a damaged self-image shaped by the stereotypes perpetuated by mainstream culture (Kristin Does Theory, n.d.). Double consciousness can also be understood as a sense of always looking at one's self through the eyes of others and of being defined by dominant and subordinate cultures (Krause, 2013).

In this context *positionality* is understood as the way that one's position in the social hierarchy vis-à-vis other groups potentially "limits or broadens" one's understanding of others. Members of the dominant group have viewpoints that are "partial and perverse" in contrast to those from subordinated groups, who have greater potential to have fuller knowledge (Wolf, 1996, quoted in Roer-Strier & Sands, 2015). The vision of the dominant group is more partial and perverse than the vision of the subordinate group (or someone living on the margins) because the subordinate group needs to understand not only themselves but also the dominant group (Henwood, 2008).

Some have argued that we should be "as close as possible" to the oppressed group being studied. Yet just how close should we be to our research participants? Across the boundaries of gender, sexual orientation, race, ethnicity, disability, class, and age, can we score two out of six and still explore subjectivity?

....

1 Double consciousness is a concept that W. E. B. Du Bois first explored in the 1903 publication *The Souls of Black Folk*.

What are the boundaries and under what circumstances can they shift (Watts, 2006)? It is presumptuous to argue that a person could have knowledge of only the sorts of things she has experienced personally and that she would be unable to communicate any of the contents of her knowledge to someone who did not have the same sorts of experiences (Edwards & Ribbens, 1998). It is also presumptuous to suggest that the condition of being female, for instance, guarantees that one will necessarily see women or gender more perceptively (Watts, 2006). Women of colour have repeatedly pointed out that forcing people into a single identity—whether it is based on gender, race, class, or sexuality—advances colonization, isolation, and violence (Carbado, Crenshaw, Mays, & Tomlinson, 2013).

Who you are and where you are situated does make a difference to the knowledge you produce. In practical terms, when a researcher shares the same ethnicity as participants, rapport may be enhanced, which may increase the willingness of participants to respond. Yet when interviewers share similar experiences or backgrounds that include norms of conversation and interaction, interview strategies must also be explicit to avoid interferences and assumptions (Locke, 2015). As well, in some cases research participants may be more comfortable with a relative outsider as researcher. While there have been ongoing debates in the literature about the static separation of insider and outsider roles, a challenge to this division may lie in a reflexive problematization of identity, which involves thinking about how identity is an ongoing process that is co-constructed in the research experience. Typically when identity is discussed as a dilemma in conducting critical social research, it has been restricted to the problematizing of the baggage we bring to the field, with the underlying assumption that "the researcher's biography with regard to race, class, and gender is already formed prior to the research experience rather than being an emergent feature of the research process itself" (Best, 2003, p. 908, cited in Day, 2012). A reflexive understanding of identity tries to make explicit the ways in which identity is formed through the interactions of the research relationship. This is the difference between asking "what impact did the researcher's race/gender/class have on the research relationship?" and "how are race/gender/class made meaningful in this relationship?" in (Best, 2003, cited in Day, 2012).

Outsiderness and insiderness are not seen as fixed or static positions; rather, they are ever-shifting and permeable social locations that are differently experienced and expressed. As researchers we are never fully outside or inside the community. Even if we are conducting critical social research within our own community, we necessarily adopt some degree of outsiderness by virtue of becoming a researcher. In the practice and art of critical social research one is faced with the need to constantly negotiate between the positions of insider and outsider rather than being fixedly assigned to one or the other. More than simple assumptions about location and identity are the power differentials and class inequities that divide those insiders and the division between the researched and researcher that are created by the act of observation (Day, 2012). Rather than constructing a rigid distinction between "insiders" and "outsiders," we need high standards of reflexivity and openness about the choices made throughout any empirical study, considering the implications of practical choices for the knowledge being produced (Day, 2012). "Identity work" during the fieldwork process requires more than simple reflection. There is a need to make reflexive accounts explicit within research publications (Allen, 2004; McCabe & Holmes, 2009).

Reflexivity

Critical social researchers advocate high standards of reflexivity, openness, and transparency about the choices made throughout any empirical study (Ali, 2015; Josselson, 2007; McCabe & Holmes, 2009; Nicholls, 2009). Critical social research requires critical reflection or reflexivity. *Reflexivity* is a researcher's self-critical questioning about how knowledge of participants is generated and how relations of power operate in the research process (Sheppard, Newstead, Di Caccavo, & Ryan, 2000; Taylor & White, 2000). Reflexivity involves the researcher's capacity to locate her or his research in the same social world as the phenomena being studied (Nencel, 2014). Through being reflexive one recognizes and accounts for relations of power in the generation of knowledge (D'Cruz et al., 2007; Fook, 1999; Taylor & White, 2000).

Reflexivity, or engaging in a reflexive process, involves openly and honestly recognizing one's location and experiences and deeply considering the implications of one's power. As such, researchers are expected to be transparent and to appreciate methodological, epistemological, and political influences, contradictions, and complexities in all stages of research (Etherington, 2007). Through personal accounting, researchers should become more aware of how their own positions and interests are imposed at all stages of the research process— from the questions they ask to those they ignore; from who they study to whom they ignore; from problem formation to analysis, representation, and writing—to produce less distorted accounts of the social world (Mosselson, 2010). The goal of being reflexive is not to resolve "power plays"; rather, it is to deliberately increase the complexity of the research process by employing an analytical approach that doubles back on itself (McCabe & Holmes, 2009).

Voice and Representation

As discussions of positionality and reflexivity make clear, the researcher is inescapably at the centre of the research account. However equal the methods of access and data collection, researchers still hold the power when we take our participants' private worlds into publication or academia. As long as a researcher is seeking to be heard by a public audience, he or she cannot evade the necessity to interpret the worlds and understandings of others into a knowledge form that can be understood and accepted within the dominant frameworks of knowledge and culture (Day, 2012).

For critical social researchers this can pose a dilemma: One is in a position of power to translate and interpret (Ali, 2015), yet implicit in engaging in critical social research is establishing more equitable research relationships where the researcher checks her or his own power and privilege and makes systematic efforts to honestly and authentically portray the lived experiences of her or his research participants. The concepts of *voice* and *representation* are central to shifting power relations in the research process. Although reflexivity encompasses voice, voice focuses more on the process of representation and writing than the processes of problem formation and data gathering. The notion of voice has multiple dimensions: the voice of the author, the presentation of the voices of one's respondents, and the self as the subject of inquiry (Etherington, 2007).

When a researcher takes into consideration voice, he or she engages in dialogue between the presentation of his or her own self while simultaneously writing the respondent's accounts and representing them. Who has a voice and who does not is related directly to the power relations in the research context. Critical social research that seeks to hear other people's voices requires understanding the research relationship as one of speaking and listening and therefore requires us to understand who can speak to whom and be heard. As researchers we must be willing to hear what others are saying, even when it violates our prior expectations or threatens our interests (Day, 2012). It is important to consider whether, and how, people are able to speak, how we obtain access to "private" and "personal" voices, and the ways in which research tools and theoretical orientations can affect how researchers listen to the voices (Etherington, 2007).

Critical social researchers are active participants in the research process. As previously discussed an important first step is to understand one's location within power hierarchies and within the constellation of gender, race, class, and so on, as explored in intersectional theory (see Chapter 2). Critical social researchers must also find representational strategies for presenting and contextualizing participants' experiences. We must not simply gather data on others to fit into our own paradigms, but we must extend the conversation through checking back with our research participants to sensitively negotiate issues of interpretive authority (Cannella, 2014; Locke, 2015). These challenges and representational strategies are particularly relevant when we opt to engage in social struggles with those who have been exploited and subjugated. By reflexively examining and understanding the margins, researchers probe who we are in relation to the contexts we study and to our informants, understanding that we are all multiple in those relations (Fine, 1994). Interrogating at the margins requires "coming clean"—questioning how we write and represent, and how we coproduce the narratives we presumed to collect. As critical social researchers we have a responsibility to talk about our own identities, why we interrogate what we do, what we choose not to report, on whom we train our scholarly gaze, and who is protected and not protected as we do our work (Mosselson, 2010).

Strategies for Being Reflexive

As briefly discussed in Chapter 1, we are engaging you in many questions about the research process by asking you to record your reflections in a *research journal*. While "conceptual baggage" (Kirby & McKenna, 1989) and an "invisible backpack" (McIntosh, 1989) are related terms that can be found in the literature, we are asking you to document your "reflexivity" throughout the research process. A research journal is where you can begin considering yourself a critical social researcher by recording and tracking your evolving ideas about the research. In it you can record candid and overt reflections, account for existing biases, and document reflections on content and analyses. The research journal can help you record your comments on the research process, your responses to conversations and the circumstances surrounding them, your hopes and dreams for the project, and your preliminary analyses or early attempts to make sense of what is happening and what you are discovering in the research process. In essence, journalling can help tease out real-world observations, the complexity of relationships, unspoken theories, political commitments, affinity to certain methods, growing research interests, frustrations, and reasons to celebrate (Reid, Brief, & LeDrew, 2009).

Maintaining a research journal is an important skill and resource for you as a critical social researcher with a commitment to being reflexive. Reflections documented in a journal can capture different kinds of ideas and questions—ones focused on processes and relationships within the research itself, and ones focused on clarifying the overall purpose of the study. It is best to keep all your journal entries in one place—put handwritten reflections in a binder or electronic notes in a file on your computer—and date your entries so you can keep track of how your ideas have shifted or remained consistent throughout the research process.

Exercise 3.1: Starting your research journal

Although you were introduced to the research journal in Chapter 1, you are now prepared to reflexively engage in journal writing with an understanding of concepts including positionality, voice, and representation. The purpose of this exercise is to help get your journal started, help you become more comfortable with reflexive writing in general, as well as ground you in your own interests and desires for doing research. Review all of the questions listed below and then pick three to five that resonate with you and start writing the thoughts and responses that emerge from reflecting on the questions:

- What are my passions? What am I thinking about when I feel most alive?
- When have I had a conflict with someone about a social justice issue (e.g., poverty, homelessness, pay equity, universal health care)? What do I believe in strongly?
- What questions do I need to answer that would result in social change for the better? What would change look like? How does this relate to me personally (family, work, friends, neighbours, etc.)?
- What is my worldview? Can I identify and name it? How do my assumptions and understandings influence what I am interested in and the work I want to do?
- How would I like to describe the significance of my research?

Research Ethics

The moment the researcher thinks of a research focus, the fundamentals of ethical decision making need to be considered. To act ethically involves knowing what we are sensitive to and how we come to understand or interpret the experiences of others (Paul & Elder, 2005). Discussions of ethics need to be incorporated into the entire research process, and research participants and researchers alike need to be protected by those ethics.

By research ethics we mean two things. First, the behaviour, values, and attitudes of a researcher must conform to the standards of conduct for critical social research. This includes how a researcher does research. Does she or he design and conduct research in ways that are recognized as ethical? How does he or she conduct him or herself in relation to the research participants and other research team members? It also includes whether a researcher follows the general tenets of the profession or discipline. Most professions (e.g., medicine, social work, occupational therapy, therapeutic recreation, physiotherapy) have ethical conduct guidelines that must be adhered to in any research endeavour. Second, a duty of care must be upheld and exercised by all those involved in the research. That is, how are the principles of voluntary participation, safety, equity, inclusion, fairness, openness, transparency, and ownership integrated into the research process in meaningful ways? Ethical procedures are generally understood as protections for participants, but they are also protections for researchers and others involved in research.

ETHICAL MISCONDUCT IN RESEARCH

The nature and role of ethics in research has been a hotly contested terrain for decades. A number of experiments done on concentration camp inmates by the Nazis in the early 1940s were revealed at the Nuremberg trials in 1947, raising questions about the neutrality of science, the harm to (and sometimes death of) research participants, and captive groups and notions of consent for research. An early study about the trajectory of syphilis in black men from Birmingham, Alabama (approximately 1932–1965) was the subject of considerable public attention in the mid- to late 1960s when it was finally revealed that a number of men had died unnecessarily over the course of the study (Brandt, 1978; NOVA, 1993). Questions arose in the Tuskegee Syphilis Study about issues such as the nature of informed consent, racism, the misrepresentation of diagnostic tests for research as if they were *medical treatments*, and the withholding of effective medical treatments to ensure a clean research protocol. Professional researchers involved in the study are on record in the 1960s as saying that the demands of pure science meant that the study should have been allowed to proceed to its logical end. The end point was determined as the death of the 400 research participants, thereby completing the tracking of the progression of syphilis through the full life course of each participant. Penicillin had been actively withheld from these participants after its discovery as an effective treatment for syphilis and despite widespread use during World War II. Scientists in the Tuskegee Syphilis Study have said that ethical issues raised at the Nuremberg trials had not given them second thoughts about their own ongoing study because "They were Nazis" (NOVA, 1993). There are numerous examples of studies where scientists have crossed the line on what is now considered ethical practice (see, for example, Punch, 1994).

Research Ethics Boards

In Canada, current debates and challenges in research ethics include the changing notions of what constitutes research and therefore requires a formal ethics review from a research ethics board (REB). An REB, also known as an institutional review board or ethical review board, is a committee formally designated to approve, monitor, and review biomedical and behavioural research involving humans. The purpose of the REB is to ensure that all human subject research is conducted in accordance with all federal, institutional, and ethical guidelines (American Public University System, 2016; Office for Human Research Protections, 1993). As an undergraduate or graduate student or academic or researcher you must gain ethical approval for your research study from your institution's REB. Although REB approval is not required consistently in community-based research in the not-for-profit setting, funded research projects most often require REB approval before the money is dispersed. The need for REB approval has inspired more community–academic partnerships, with the academic partner taking the lead on the REB approval process. REBs in Canada are governed by the Tri-Council Policy Statement: Ethical Conduct for Research Involving Humans (TCPS). TCPS is a joint policy of Canada's three federal research agencies: the Canadian Institutes of Health Research, the Natural Sciences and Engineering Research Council of Canada, and the Social Sciences and Humanities Research Council of Canada. This policy expresses the agencies' continuing commitment to Canadians to promote the ethical conduct of research involving humans. An overview of the TCPS, as related to critical social research, is presented below.

Core Principles of Research Ethics

Respect for human dignity has been an underlying value of the TCPS since its inception. It requires that research involving humans be conducted in a manner that is sensitive to the inherent worth of all human beings and the respect and consideration that they are due. Respect for human dignity is expressed through three core principles: respect for persons, concern for welfare, and justice. These core principles transcend disciplinary boundaries and are complementary and interdependent. (The following information is adapted from Panel on Research Ethics, 2014.)

1. *Respect for persons:* This principle recognizes the intrinsic value of human beings and the respect and consideration they are due. It encompasses the treatment of people involved in research directly as participants and those who are participants because their data are used in research. Respect for persons incorporates the dual moral obligations to respect autonomy and to protect those with developing, impaired, or diminished autonomy. Autonomy includes the ability to deliberate about a decision and to act based on that deliberation.

    An important mechanism for respecting participants' autonomy in research is the requirement to seek their *free, informed, and ongoing consent.* This requirement reflects the commitment that participation in research should be a matter of choice and that, to be meaningful, the choice must be based on as complete an understanding as is reasonably possible of the purpose of the research, what it entails, and its foreseeable risks and potential benefits, both to the participant and to others. Specifically, consent should be voluntary; it can be withdrawn at any time, and if a participant withdraws consent the participant can also request the withdrawal of his or her data. Consent needs to be informed and full disclosure must be provided. Informed consent is an ongoing process, meaning that researchers have an ongoing duty to provide participants with all information relevant to their ongoing consent to participate in the research.

2. *Concern for welfare:* The welfare of a person consists of the impact on individuals of factors such as their physical, mental, and spiritual health, as well as their physical, economic, and social circumstances. A contributing factor to welfare is privacy and the control of information about the person.

   a. *Privacy* refers to an individual's right to be free from intrusion or interference by others. An important aspect of privacy is the right to control information about oneself. The concept of consent is related to the right to privacy. Privacy is respected if an individual has an opportunity to exercise control over personal information by consenting to or withholding consent for the collection, use, and/or disclosure of information.

   b. The ethical duty of *confidentiality* includes obligations to protect information from unauthorized access, use, disclosure, modification, loss, or theft. Fulfilling the ethical duty of confidentiality is essential to the trust relationship between researcher and participant and to the integrity of the research project. Depending on the purpose and procedures of the study, data may be identifying, de-identified, or anonymous. For a fuller description of confidentiality, see Chapters 7 and 8.

   c. *Security* refers to measures used to protect information. It includes physical, administrative, and technical safeguards. Physical safeguards include the use of locked filing cabinets and locating computers containing research data away from public areas. Administrative safeguards include the development and enforcement of organizational rules about who has access to personal information about participants. Technical safeguards include the use of computer passwords, firewalls, anti-virus software, encryption, and other measures that protect data from unauthorized access, loss, or modification.

   d. *Harm* includes any negative effects on welfare, broadly construed. Participants must be provided with enough information to be able to adequately assess the risks and potential benefits associated with their participation in the research. To do so, researchers and REBs must ensure that participants are not exposed to unnecessary risks, and they must attempt to minimize the risks associated with answering any given research question. They should attempt to achieve the most favourable *balance of risks and potential benefits* in a research proposal.

3. *Justice:* The principle of justice refers to the obligation to treat people fairly and equitably. Fairness entails treating all people with equal respect and concern. Equity requires distributing the benefits and burdens of research participation in such a way that no segment of the population is unduly burdened by the harms of research or denied the benefits of the knowledge generated from it. Treating people fairly and equitably does not always mean treating them the same. Differences in treatment or distribution are justified when failures to take differences into account may result in the creation or reinforcement of inequities.

   An important threat to justice is the imbalance of power that may exist in the relationship between researcher and participant. Participants will generally not understand the research in the same way and in the same depth as does the researcher. Historically, there have been instances in which this power imbalance has been abused, with resulting harm to participants.

   a. Researchers should be *inclusive* in selecting participants. Researchers shall not exclude individuals from the opportunity to participate in research on the basis of attributes such as culture, language, religion, race, disability, sexual orientation, ethnicity, linguistic proficiency, gender, or age unless there is a valid reason for the exclusion. Women, children, older adults, or any individual or group whose circumstances may make them vulnerable in the context of research should not be inappropriately included or automatically excluded from participation in research on the basis of their circumstances.

   b. *Vulnerability* is often caused by limited decision-making capacity or limited access to social goods, such as rights, opportunities, or power. Individuals or groups in vulnerable circumstances have historically included children, the elderly, women, prisoners, those with mental health issues, and those with diminished capacity for self-determination. Ethnocultural minorities and those who are institutionalized are other examples of groups who have, at times, been treated unfairly and inequitably in research or have been excluded from research opportunities. People or groups whose circumstances cause them to be vulnerable or marginalized may need to be afforded special attention to be treated justly in research.

c. The *recruitment process* is an important component of the fair and equitable conduct of research. Participation should be based on inclusion criteria that are justified by the research question. Inequity is created when particular groups fail to receive fair benefits of research or when groups, or their data or their biological materials, are excluded from research arbitrarily or for reasons unrelated to the research question.

Indigenous or Traditional Knowledge. The TCPS 2 (the second edition of the TCPS: Panel on Research Ethics, 2014) outlines a number of considerations for Indigenous research that may be relevant to questions and approaches adopted by critical social researchers. Indigenous or traditional knowledge "is usually described by Aboriginal Peoples as holistic, involving body, mind, feelings and spirit" (Panel on Research Ethics, 2014, Chapter 9, p. 108). Indigenous knowledge is rarely acquired through written documents, but rather is a worldview adopted through living, listening, and learning in the ancestral languages and within the contexts of living on the land. Engagement with elders and other knowledge holders is acknowledged as valuable and vital to knowledge transmission within the context of Indigenous peoples living in place. Both Indigenous knowledge content and processes of knowledge transmission are, thus, embedded in the performance of living, including storytelling, ceremonies, living on the land, the use of natural resources and medicine plants, arts and crafts, singing and dancing, as well as engagement with more than the human world. Indigenous values that need particular consideration in any research endeavour include reciprocity, community, and respect, relevance, and contributions:

- *Reciprocity* is an important value in Indigenous ways of knowing in that it emphasizes the mutuality of knowledge giving and receiving. In the context of research, the emphasis on a co-creation model should result in reciprocity in the form of partnerships and collaborative practices, which can include identification of research objectives and methods, conduct of the research, ethical research protocols, data analysis and presentation, and transmission of knowledge. It also recognizes that access and benefits are, thus, integrally connected.
- *Community*, in the context of Indigenous research, can refer to places or land-based communities as well as thematic communities and communities of practice. Furthermore, community-based, community-initiated, and community-driven research can involve varying degrees of community engagement; the research outputs will be negotiated, taking into account the interests of relevant Indigenous community members.

- *Respect, relevance, and contributions* refers to the fact that Indigenous research must respect relevant community research protocols and current goals as well as the contributions to and from the community that are likely to emerge or are in place. A respectful research relationship necessitates a deep level of collaboration and ethical engagement. This may include engaging with existing, distinctive research processes and protocols for conducting ethical research reviews in the community, learning within language or traditional knowledge systems, collaboratively rebuilding or revitalizing processes that have been displaced or replaced, or co-developing new processes based on the community's expressed interests. (Adapted from Social Sciences and Humanities Research Council, 2015; see also Panel on Research Ethics, 2014, Chapter 9, for information on respecting rights, shouldering responsibilities, and building relationships in Canadian research.)

Women as a Vulnerable Group. Vulnerable groups were identified earlier, under the discussion of the TCPS principle of justice. One vulnerable group that has historically been inappropriately excluded from participating in some research due to a range of concerns is women. This exclusion of women, where unwarranted, has delayed the advancement of knowledge, denied potential benefits to women, and exposed women to harm when research findings from male-only research projects were generalized inappropriately to women, as has often been the case in clinical drug trials. The inclusion of women in research advances the commitment to justice, improves generalizability of research findings to women where that is a goal of the research, and is essential to ensure that women and men benefit equally from research (Panel on Research Ethics, 2014).

Community-Based Research. As discussed in Chapter 2, research is increasingly conducted by a wide range of groups, such as not-for-profit organizations, governments, pollsters, independent consultants, think tanks, community organizations, community researchers, and many others. These researchers may not have access to institutional REBs. Nevertheless, they are still concerned with maintaining ethical research standards that help to ensure no harm comes to those who choose to participate in their research (Community Research Ethics Office, 2012).

In partial response to this need, the Community Research Ethics Office (CREO) in Waterloo, Ontario, was created to assist community-based researchers and their sponsors in understanding the principles and requirements outlined in TCPS 2. CREO aims to strengthen and support community research by responding to the needs of community researchers to easily access an ethical support and review process. It offers a supportive environment that encourages community researchers to participate and collaborate in a process of reflection to promote awareness of ethical issues and maximize ethical conduct of research. CREO's work aligns with the three core principles in the TCPS 2 and includes a fourth principle reflecting the impact research has on communities as well as individuals:

- Respect for persons: free and informed consent, autonomy and voluntariness, vulnerability
- Concern for welfare: balance of risk and benefits, participants' perspective, confidentiality
- Concern for justice: equitable treatment, appropriate inclusion, power
- Respect for community: understanding the community, respecting the community, community inclusion

In community-based research, informed consent is often understood as having both individual and community components. However, there remain challenges in determining who represents the community, who represents the subgroup being asked for participation, and how both levels of consent can interact and support each other. A central issue is whether it is legitimate for researchers to interview individuals in their own right as individuals, without regard to the interests of the group as a whole and without seeking permission from any group authority or spokesperson or, conversely, when the approval of the community as whole should be required (Panel on Research Ethics, 2014).

While we have covered the main components of research ethics as outlined by the TCPS 2, it is essential to review in detail the ethical guidelines articulated by the REB where you will seek ethical approval. As well, it is helpful to be familiar with the most current issues and debates in research ethics. Online tutorials are available for that purpose; for example, go to https://tcps2core.ca/welcome.

Ethical Considerations in Research

The field of research ethics is expanding to better reflect the considerable challenges critical social researchers (and others) face in conducting their research. Traditionally, research ethics were understood in terms of informed consent, avoidance of harm, and confidentiality. While these concepts are still crucial and relevant, they do not adequately capture the depth and breadth of research ethics. For this discussion we will outline the key considerations through phases of research: recruitment, fieldwork, and writing and dissemination.

Recruitment. Informed consent was traditionally understood as the "gateway" to initiating research relationships. Informed consent involves receiving consent by the research participants after having carefully and truthfully informed them about the research. According to the TCPS 2, consent shall be given voluntarily, can be removed at any time, and if a participant withdraws he or she may also withdraw his or her data. The voluntariness of consent is important because it respects human dignity and means that individuals have chosen to participate in research according to their own values, preferences, and wishes (Panel on Research Ethics, 2014).

As a critical social researcher it is your responsibility to describe all of the ways in which your research participants will be involved in the research. You need to take deliberate steps to describe the strategies that are in place to minimize or manage the risks for research participants and other potentially affected individuals. While there are few examples of critical social research involving physical harm, there are many instances where harm may be in the form of emotional risk. Examples include long-term involvement in a research project that is time consuming or being subjected to personal and difficult questions. It is important to note that in qualitative methods, and particularly in research that aims to establish and nurture relationships with multiple stakeholders, there is a certain degree of unpredictability. It is often difficult for a researcher to fully describe the extent or nature of everything the research will entail, often because the research does not know. Critical social researchers must remain mindful of this unpredictability and consistently discuss with their research participants the ways that the research is shifting. If considerable shifts have occurred, it may be necessary to receive informed consent a second or third time from your research participants.

Recruitment not only involves the more formalized process of informed consent but also involves building rapport with your research participants (this is discussed in more depth in Chapter 8). This includes building reciprocity into research relationships and taking into consideration cultural sensitivities that may not be caught by formal ethics review boards. Indeed, the notion of informed consent can be expanded to involve giving information, reciprocating, and collaborating. Informed consent also includes confirming with research participants their entitlement to withdraw from the research at any time. With the expanded understandings of informed consent, it is now necessary for researchers to allow for culturally appropriate ways for participants to withdraw.

Fieldwork. Traditionally, the main ethical consideration associated with fieldwork has been avoidance of harm. In any research endeavour the good or benefit should outweigh the harm or risk. Flinders (1992) expanded the notion of avoidance of harm to avoidance of wrong, imposition, and detachment. He asks crucial questions to guide all fieldwork: What principles should guide a researcher/participant relationship? When does research constitute an imposition? What does participation mean within a participant's primary culture? Who benefits from the research (Flinders, 1992; Stutchbury & Fox, 2009)? Let's look at an example:

> Louise wanted to speak with caregivers of adults with dementia to better understand the role of adult day programs in relieving caregiver burnout. While she had intimate knowledge of this population group because she worked at an adult day program, after encountering difficulties with recruitment she learned that caregivers' involvement in fieldwork—in her case one-on-one interviews—imposed a significant burden on many caregivers who had little time during the week without the loved one for whom they were caring. She questioned whether the demands of her fieldwork compounded caregivers' experience of burnout. As a result, she expanded her recruitment strategies and plans for fieldwork by including service providers as research participants.

What is central to ethical considerations in fieldwork is how the research participants benefit from their involvement in the research. The notion of reciprocity is important for critical social researchers. Issues and mechanisms for ensuring reciprocity can include payment for research participants (honoraria), the creation of new opportunities, developing skills, advocating for the community, or enabling the research participants to access and use the findings in some tangible way. It is also important to consider who within the community will benefit from the research.

Writing, Dissemination, and Knowledge Translation. Many formal ethics review processes miss the opportunity to fully examine how research findings are reported and disseminated. The main criterion for most ethics processes is that the research participants' confidentiality is maintained. Raw data may include a name or other identifiers, such as a code or membership in a group, that can be used to link the data to the subject's name. The research team has access to this information, but it should not be included in the final reports of the research, nor should anyone other than those specified in the consent form be given access to the data. If participants wish to have their comments attributed, this should be specified in the consent form (Office of Research Ethics, 2004).

Yet confidentiality extends far beyond withholding identifying information. It also includes a sense of fairness in that participants should not be upset at how they are portrayed, and the information should not be used for exploitative purposes or to embarrass the individual or the community. Responsive communication—acting responsibly in making public what we have learned about the lives of our participants—is a component of confidentiality (Kaiser, 2009). Researchers have two obligations that are frequently in conflict: the requirement to describe research participants in enough detail so that others can understand the general applicability of findings, and the ethical obligation to avoid unfairly stereotyping vulnerable segments of a population or unwittingly providing data that allow others to unfairly stereotype them. According to these stipulations, researchers are required to justify the need for collecting data on such demographic features as race and ethnicity, age, birthplace, gender, geographic location, domestic status, and sexual orientation and must prove that these data will not be analyzed in such a way that unfair stereotypes may be drawn and that reports will not allow others to use the data to create unfair stereotypes.

Fundamentally, confidentiality is about representation and reflexivity, deeply listening to the research findings, and asking "Did we get it right?" and "Were people overlooked or ignored?" Integrating member-checking, a validation interview, a follow-up focus group, or some other form of checking back with your informants can help with this process (see Chapter 9). As a critical social researcher the first ethical decision you make is whether to collect certain kinds of information at all. Once that decision is made, you are responsible for what is done with the information, and you must protect informants from becoming emotionally burdened (or worse) from talking to you (Josselson, 2007).

Summary

In this chapter we presented the various dimensions of the critical social researcher's roles and responsibilities through an in-depth exploration of the concepts of reflexivity, positionality, voice, and representation. Critical social researchers must investigate their own locations, assumptions, biases, and worldviews while engaging in research with others. The research journal, introduced in Chapter 1 and revisited in this chapter, is one way to bring the researcher's reflexivity into the research process. In this chapter we also introduced the guiding values and practices of research ethics as outlined in the Tri-Council Policy Statement. We encourage all readers to review the TCPS and become familiar with current research ethics principles, values, and practices (see the Readings section below).

Questions for Discussion

1. What does "intersubjectivity" mean and why is it so important to critical social research?
2. What does "reflexivity" mean?
3. What kinds of questions can a researcher pose to get a better understanding of how issues of voice, representation, and positionality play out in a research study?
4. Why are research ethics important and to whom?
5. What are the principal issues around power and ethics in research?
6. What are the three key principles in research ethics? What is the fourth principle in community-based research? Describe each one and how it relates to the research process.
7. What are the three values of Indigenous or traditional knowledge?

Our Recommended Readings

Community Research Ethics Office. (2012). Ethics and community research. Retrieved from http://www.communityresearchethics.com/background/

Day, S. (2012). A reflexive lens: Exploring dilemmas of qualitative methodology through the concept of reflexivity. *Qualitative Sociology Review, 7*(1), 60–85.

Josselson, R. (2007). The ethical attitude in narrative research: Principles and practicalities. In D. J. Clandinin (Ed.), *Handbook of narrative inquiry: Mapping a methodology* (pp. 537–566). Thousand Oaks: Sage. http://dx.doi.org/10.4135/9781452226552.n21

Panel on Research Ethics. (2014). Tri-council policy statement: Ethical conduct for research involving humans. Retrieved from http://www.pre.ethics.gc.ca/eng/policy-politique/initiatives/tcps2-eptc2/Default/

Reid, C., & Brief, E. (2009). Confronting condescending ethics: How community-based research challenges traditional approaches to consent, confidentiality, and capacity. *Journal of Academic Ethics, 7*(1–2), 75–85. http://dx.doi.org/10.1007/s10805-009-9085-0

A Step-by-Step Approach to Research: Doing a Project from Beginning to End

INTRODUCTION

This is the "how-to" section of the book and includes Chapters 4 to 10. This section is a practical outline that moves you through the research process. By using the following chapters as a guide, you can find a research focus and a research question, identify a research method or methods, gather data, analyze the data collected, and produce a report of your findings.

In previous editions of *Experience, Research, Social Change* we described "operationalizing" the research question. Operationalizing a research question involves planning the practical steps in the research project by answering the five Ws and an H: what, why, how, who, when, and where.

WHAT?   What do I want to know?
WHY?   Why do this research? Why those people? Why now?
HOW?   How will I answer the research question? How will I gather data?
WHO?   Who has the information I am seeking?
WHEN?   When can I best undertake data gathering?
WHERE?   Where is it most appropriate to collect data?

In this section we move through the how-to section by addressing these questions. In Chapter 4 we provide strategies for identifying a research interest, focus, and question (What do you want to know?) and ideas for managing research files and documenting the research process. Chapter 5 covers literature reviews to address the "why" of the project (Why do this research? Why now?). We cover a range of research methods that are relevant to the critical social researcher with full descriptions, examples, samples, and exercises in Chapter 6 (How will you answer the research question?). With examples we illustrate that even the most experienced researchers are faced with critical research decisions and challenges. Despite very sound methodological reasoning, researchers sometimes make mistakes and it is the correction of these mistakes that adds to our understandings of good practice. Since research methods and ethics are closely interwoven, we integrate ethical considerations into the presentation of methods. In Chapter 7, participant criteria and sampling strategies as well as other study logistics are described (Who will participate in this study? When and where will you collect data?). By the end of Chapter 7 you will have addressed the five Ws and an H in your research proposal and ethics application and will be prepared to begin data collection. In Chapter 8 we help you navigate the data collection process and describe strategies for managing your data set. Chapters 9 and 10 describe the analysis and writing processes, respectively.

This how-to guide is only as good as the research topic that is chosen. The more meaningful the research topic is to you, the more useful the how-to guide will be. Research is both challenging and complex. Being a researcher is a disciplined, thought-provoking, exciting, exasperating, and daunting activity. What follows are some of the essential skills needed to carry out research projects and numerous examples to show how the skills are used. This book is part of our research journey, and we hope that as you read this there are useful ideas, exercises, skills, and recommendations for you on your journey in search of knowledge. The search for knowledge can be one of the most important activities in life. Enjoy the journey as you go.

CHAPTER 4

WHAT? THE RESEARCH QUESTION AND ESTABLISHING WRITING AND ORGANIZATIONAL PROCESSES

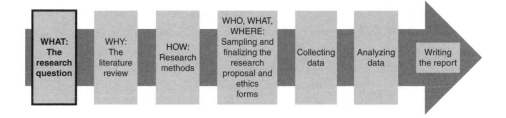

FIGURE 4.1: The Research Process

In this chapter, we review several key points from Part A on the creation of knowledge and research as discovery. The research process is then explored through the following stages: identifying a research focus, creating or finding a research question, and situating yourself in the research.

Getting ready for a research activity is akin to warming up for a physical activity: You have to get ready and then start slowly on the right path (Janesick, 2004). Overall, planning a research project means that first you have to move from general topics of interest to a research focus. Then you need to determine the best question to ask and plan for how you can gather data to answer the question. This narrowing—from a research interest to a more exact research focus to an even more precise research question— takes careful thought and time. Once you have the research question, you can progress toward answering the question. You can gather information, undertake data analysis, then report on the answers to the research question based on the evidence found. Importantly, getting these initial stages of the research process clear, concise, and correct makes the rest of your research project flow with more ease.

Most researchers start by focusing on the substantive area of interest but with no clear question in mind. Articulating the research question in straightforward language may take a lot more time than you anticipate, or it can emerge from a serendipitous conversation or a sudden insight and take no time at all. Unfortunately, there is no direct correlation between the time it takes to define the research question and the quality of the question. And the research question is only the beginning.

Research as Discovery

As simplistic as it sounds, research is like embarking on a voyage of discovery. As the voyage takes place, the researcher maps or charts the process of exploration. For example, if you explored Canada and created your own maps as you went, you would be doing research. Thinking about *what* is to be studied and *what routes* are to be used might indicate that Canada is a country bounded by a border to the south and by western, northern, and eastern shores. How can this territory best be explored? Has it been inhabited and explored before, and if so by whom and with which routes? Determining those answers would be the equivalent of doing a review of literature—that is, documenting what is already known about Canada and who knows this land well.

To begin your own exploration, you might choose to use only existing routes like public roads or well-travelled paths. You would then limit your exploration to those areas where roads or paths have been established. You would not have access to remote terrain or to fly-in communities or to land on less-travelled paths or where no paths yet exist. Think about how you might explore this country and with whom you would like to do the exploration. Canada is a big country, and choices must be made about what parts of the country will be explored and how you can record what you are observing on your explorations. The rules (such as strategies and criteria) you choose for these will both limit and enable your research process.

Another approach to doing research is to replicate someone else's research. This means that you would take maps already created by some other explorer, travel the exact routes, and make your own observations. In all likelihood, there would be considerable overlap in the observations because both you and the person before you would likely pay attention to or "attend" to similar features, particularly to strong or outstanding ones. However, because you are a different person from the original researcher, you will also make unique observations about what is most interesting or compelling. Thus, even replicated research is not identical to or a duplicate of existing research, though the overall outcomes are likely to be similar if paths chosen and criteria for observational recordings are similar.

The Research Interest, Focus, and Question

The research process requires fine-tuning the initial concern into a research question, making a plan for gathering information, figuring out who has the information we may need and planning for their participation in the research, gathering data, making sense of it, and reporting the information back to participants and others. Concurrently, researchers engage in a process of self-reflection by using a research journal so that biases, preliminary analyses, and ideas for action are all recorded along the way. We introduced the research journal in Chapter 1. In this chapter and the rest of the book we have included exercises for you to use to fine-tune your thinking and develop skills for data gathering and analysis. At the end of this chapter we discuss in detail how you can use these exercises and strategies for filing and organizing your research journal notes and fieldnotes as you conduct your own explorations.

The first three steps in research include identifying your research interest, your research focus, and your research question. Imagine a funnel shape. Moving from your research interest to your research focus and finally to your research question(s) is much like moving through the wide top of the funnel to its narrow bottom (see Figure 4.2).

Anyone embarking on research needs to be clear about the research question. The research question is the "fulcrum" or "root" of any research project: It helps guide every decision in the research process. The process of identifying a research question that is doable and meaningful to you can be difficult and take some time, but early clarity will pay off by enabling you to stay on the research path. For this reason, the exercises below move you carefully through three stages—identifying your research interest, focus, and then question—so that you gradually narrow down or specify your research question. Use your research journal to explore the questions posed in these exercises.

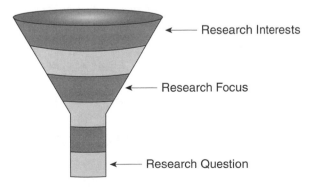

FIGURE 4.2: Conceptual Funnel

Step 1: Identifying Your Research Interest

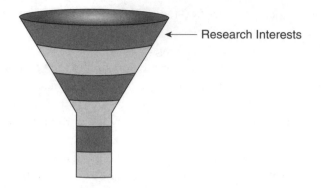

FIGURE 4.3: Conceptual Funnel: Research Interest

The first step is to identify the broad range of ideas or topics that may be of interest to you as a researcher. Lofland and Lofland (1995) refer to the beginning of a research process as "starting where you are." Your own research interests are your starting point, but remember that your research interests are broader and more vague than the research question. To figure out "where you are," engage in the reflective questioning of Exercise 4.1.

Exercise 4.1: What are your research interests?

To begin identifying what your research interests might be, you will need a blank page (paper or computer screen) with two columns. First, put a date on the page. Then, on the left, list words or phrases about things you are interested in knowing more about. These should not be in the form of questions; rather, it is just a "free form" list of, for example, topics, issues, things, people, or events that you are interested in. Try not to think too much about how you might find out more about the topics—just get the list going. Feel free to fill the entire left side of the page and go on to another if you really get going—this is part of the fun of starting research! No topic is too big, too small, too insignificant, or too grand at this stage. On the right side of the page, opposite each word or phrase, write why you are interested in it. This is a place for your thoughts, your reflections, or your relationship to the word or phrase. Exercise 4.1 has two functions. It gets possible research ideas flowing (substance) and it is the first step to recording what you are thinking and doing as you go (process).

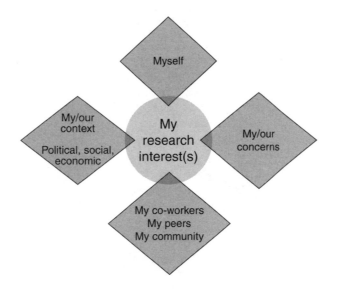

FIGURE 4.4: Where Do Your Research Interests Come From?

Exercise 4.1 illustrates the various ideas that can shape one's research interests. It poses broad questions that you can ask about yourself, your concerns, your peers and co-workers, your community, and your social, political, and economic context. The point here is to begin considering why you want to do research and what you hope to achieve from engaging in research (Reid, Brief, & LeDrew, 2009). The remainder of Exercise 4.1 is to identify where the research interests come from (see Figure 4.4), further probing them (Figure 4.5), and expanding on those that have potential (Figure 4.6).

As you consider "where" your research interests come from, you can pose a number of questions, including those in Figure 4.5. As you explore your research interest(s) you are focused on the outer boxes of the diagram. Consider the questions posed in those outer boxes and use your research journal to document your immediate responses. Some questions may be easier to answer than others. It is important to notice where you find the most "flow" in your exploration and where you feel stumped.

Once you have explored these questions in some depth, you can delve more deeply into the questions by employing an expand–focus strategy (see Figure 4.6).

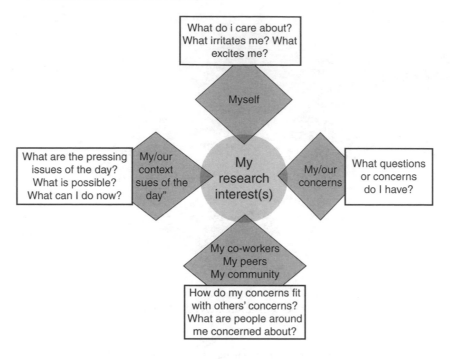

FIGURE 4.5: Probing Your Research Interests

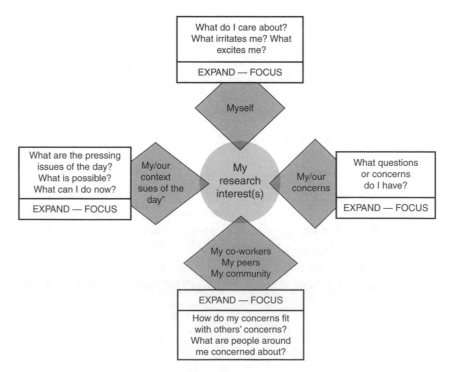

FIGURE 4.6: Expand — Focus

For each question you are asked to expand and focus your thinking. Again, start where the ideas come most easily. Some people tend to be expansive in their thinking, which can make it difficult to focus on one research question. Others tend to be too limited in their thinking and need to be encouraged to think more broadly or expansively. In your research journal, focus on the question(s) where you feel most energy, excitement, and flow. Probe these questions using an "expand–focus" approach:

What do I care about?

Expand:

- What is my fundamental worldview?
- How do I see the world?
- What issues are important to me?

Focus:

- What values and priorities are important in my life? What do I believe is important to how I live my life (honesty, integrity, trust, innovation, quality, equity, conduct, faith, etc.)?
- How do I envision my work (school, practice, day-to-day life) serving my values?
- How do I serve my values in other activities I do?

What questions and concerns do I have?

Expand:

- What do I wish I could change?
- What do I like and want to see more of?
- Where do I wish I had more skills and knowledge?
- What things keep (not) happening?
- Who/what do I wish I understood better?

Focus:

- Which concerns keep repeating in my thinking?
- What conversations do I keep having with colleagues or friends?
- Where am I beginning to see changes I want to pursue?
- What makes me frustrated?
- What skills can I build upon?
- Where can I make a difference?

How do my concerns fit with others' concerns?

Expand:

- Which of my colleagues or friends talk about this?
- How are their language and concerns similar to mine? How are they different?
- Who writes about concerns like mine?
- Who writes about concerns that are close but not the same?

Focus:

- Can I name any authors whose writing has affected how I think about these issues?
- Can I identify the parts of these writings that I identify with and want to build upon?
- What parts do I disagree with? What parts don't make sense to me?

What is possible?

Expand:

- What are all of the elements I can include?

Focus:

- Which piece of the research comes first?
- Which piece of the research makes me excited enough to put my heart into?
- What skills do I have? What am I best at?
- What feels manageable at this time?
- What can be saved or postponed for a future project?

Once you have spent some time exploring your initial research interests, write some rough notes about the context of these interests. These can be jottings about all kinds of things you are interested in. It is best if they are written in free form, like a brainstorming exercise where nothing is discarded in the initial stages. Don't get caught up in trying to find an "important" question. Allow the questions to flow and they can all be sorted out later. All points are considered equally valuable, even if some of them are humorous or nonsensical or not possible as research.

A few notes about your jottings: Although we do most of our writing and documentation on our computers, we often find that this kind of exploration is easiest with pen to paper or marker to whiteboard. It can allow for a more "free flowing" expression of ideas. You may prefer to draw diagrams, flowcharts or engage in mind or creative mapping. Use whatever strategy helps you most easily explore these questions. Also, no matter how rough or incomplete your documentation (jotted notes, writing in paragraphs, pictures, diagrams), keep them all! If you've done them on a whiteboard, take a picture. These should all be part of your research journal. Colleen's research journals are usually a binder with a collection of notes, jottings, diagrams, and musings. She begins each new research project with new materials—including a new book for journaling that she carries around with her at all times.

"Starting where you are" means that you can begin your research with some confidence by identifying your initial skills and interests in the research topic and using those as a bridge to get a clearer research focus and perhaps even a precise research question. Your position in relation to the topic of interest or concern is important—in fact, only you have that particular relationship or understanding of the topic. This means that you will need to spend time writing about your experience with the topic and how you understand it. You want to ensure that your research will answer the question it is asking. "Starting where you are" takes a bit of time to do well because you have to describe in some detail from where it is that you are starting and why.

We think of "starting where you are" as the beginning of the conceptualization of your ideas. While starting any research project is difficult, planning the research project is next to impossible until the central focus of the research is clear.

Step 2: Determining Your Research Focus

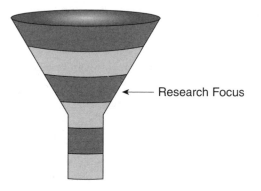

FIGURE 4.7: Conceptual Funnel: Research Focus

There are a variety of ways that you can come to a research focus and later (and more precisely) a research question. Consider the research interests you just identified in your research journal. Use your journal to mull these interests over and write about each one to unravel some of their potential. While you are alone, try sounding a topic or two out loud. In verbalizing a research focus, a research question sometimes bubbles to the surface. If you are quick enough to recognize and capture it in your journal, it can become a research question around which the research project develops. Which interests attract you more and which ones appear more doable because you can imagine gathering data on them? The interest you choose to pursue does not have to be the one you know most about. It might be the one you have the greatest curiosity about or the one that is the most risky to do. In the long run, it is helpful if you can find a research focus to which you feel some passion and attachment.

At this point a more specific research focus needs to be developed. Try formulating more specific questions. For example:

- What is the job market like for someone with XYZ skills and ABC experience?
- How do people a generation older than me view the challenges they will experience in their older age? How does that compare with my generation's views of these challenges?
- How can children with multiple disabilities form and keep friendships?
- Is there a relationship between moving (to a new town, province, or country) and personal health?

By asking questions you can narrow your interests into a research focus. Notice that none of the questions above provide any preconceived notion of what method of data gathering might be used. The possibility of working with one method or with diverse methods remains open until later in the process. Continue to explore reflexively. Record all of your thoughts, questions, insights, curiosities, and confusions in your journal.

A researcher's path to finding the research focus and the research question can be a straightforward linear path, a forked path, or even a path that looks like a river delta with myriad paths all diverging and converging without any apparent pattern. It is likely that your research interests will arise from your own experience or knowledge. To contextualize your work and situate your research focus you will need to think and position yourself around each possible research focus.

Let's look at an example. In Figure 4.8, Sandi put a research focus in the middle of the page: "palliative care work/workers." As you can see, this is general and broad. Around the research focus she brainstormed all of the questions and curiosities she had about that research interest. Some of them were not

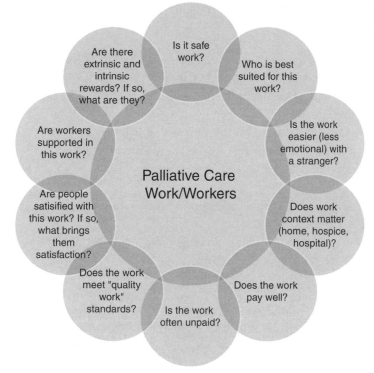

FIGURE 4.8: Palliative Care Work/Workers

related, and it was not necessary to logically move from one to the next. The point here is to document everything.

Exercise 4.2: Situating yourself

Put each prospective research focus at the centre of a blank page or computer screen. Similar to the example in Figure 4.8, write all around the topic—what you think about it, yourself in relation to it, what you have heard or read about it, and your questions or curiosities about it. Even if the page appears unwieldy and disorganized, this process will help you contextualize the topic and situate yourself in relation to it. Try to identify what you already know about the research interest in addition to what you think needs to be researched.

There are other useful, reflexive ways to situate your thinking about research interests. For example, you can talk to people who may inform your interests or ideas, you can "try on" different positions in relation to potential topics, or you can read articles to spark your thinking. Often, just speaking about a possible research topic brings some clarity, and this can be effective either alone or in conversation.

Once you have generated a list of research ideas and used Exercise 4.2 to situate yourself and achieve a greater focus, you can then try out different research questions. Drawing on the palliative care example, some possible research questions might be as follows:

1. To what degree are palliative care workers satisfied with their jobs?
2. What elements of palliative care work bring satisfaction to palliative care workers?
3. Does the context for palliative care work determine the effectiveness of the care?
4. How and why do palliative care workers get into, continue, and eventually leave palliative care work?

As you can see, there are a number of research questions that could be generated here. Two people could have similar research interests and research foci yet arrive at quite different research questions.

Another approach is to develop research from a body of literature. As you read, concepts you identify and links you make between ideas in the literature can help you expand or deepen your understandings of a particular research interest. This strategy for honing a research focus into a research question is explored in more depth in Chapter 5.

The research could take place in an environment that is already reasonably well researched and understood (e.g., a university or college, government organizations, not-for-profit organizations, public places). Or it could take place in an environment where very little is understood (e.g., drop-in programs for transgender youth) or in an environment linking unusual areas (e.g., web-based romances and global futures). As the research focus becomes clear to you, so should the nature of the research path you are on and the context in which your research focus resides: That is, you can begin to see how you might actually do the research.

After you have chosen a focus, it must be honed down to a real research question. This can be a challenging process, but you do not need to be in a hurry to get through this step. The research focus may come from observations from aspects of your life (work, family, community) and omissions you may have noticed. Louise's research question came from observations from her work:

As a recreation therapist who works with older adults I was interested in conducting research with caregivers I had observed in both my professional and personal life. I witnessed the daily struggles they encountered and the impact these struggles had on their health. I was struck by their dedication and commitment in supporting their family members with dignity while forsaking their own well-being. I work for an organization that provides adult day program services for older adults living with dementia. I knew that involvement in the program was making a difference in the participants' lives, but wondered if the programs made a difference for the people who cared for them— the caregivers. Caring for and supporting a person living with an irreversible progressive illness is challenging. I considered the fact that there was more focus being placed on the care recipient rather than the caregiver. I also discovered this tendency or bias when I began the literature review. I decided that I wanted to explore what benefits there may be *for the caregiver* when their loved one attended an adult day program. The intent was to understand and gain insight into their circumstance and learn from them what it meant to be a caregiver. In doing so I believed that I would enhance my own knowledge and gain tools to develop programs that could ease some of their challenges and improve their health. (Louise Joycey, BTR, Douglas College)

As discussed in Figures 4.4, 4.5, and 4.6, research questions can also arise from a general interest or concern about one's community. For example:

Sebastian was getting ready to vote in the municipal election and was discouraged by the voter apathy articles he was reading. The municipality offered small grants for a researcher to measure "voter interest" in the municipal campaign. He applied. Voter interest, he determined, was about intent to vote and interest in an expanding list of municipal issues. "I live in a really active community, and as I was getting interested in what our local candidates had to say about the issues in the upcoming election, I was also interested in what they were hearing as they went to the public forums asking for support. I thought it might be good to tag along to observe whether people said they were going to vote or not and what they talked with the candidates about. I could learn a lot about what my community said were issues that concern them.

The research focus can also be dictated externally. For example, a local food bank might need help determining the best way of keeping food varieties available each week. Or a local credit union is interested in better understanding access to banking for people who live below the poverty line. In these scenarios the food bank and credit union may seek the help of a student who is conducting research for an undergraduate honours project or a master's degree. These one- or two-semester projects can help local organizations better serve the community.

It might be that the research question comes from a more formal "call for research." In Chapter 1 we wrote about governments and not-for-profit organizations using research to make evidence-based decisions. Increasingly they rely on researchers and research communities to assist in the production of knowledge. To do this, they will advertise a "call for research" and identify the general topic area or policy focus they are interested in funding. The researcher or research team then matches their interests around the call for research. For example:

> The International Development Research Centre (IDRC) issued a call for proposals called "Cities and Climate Change," which aimed to support high-quality, demand-driven, policy-relevant action research that engaged local authorities, communities, and the private sector. Research projects were intended to help meet the adaptation deficit in small to medium-sized cities or well-defined subdivisions of large cities where demographic pressure and environmental stresses are particularly acute. (IDRC, 2015)

Such applications may be successful if they meet the criteria set out by the funders and if the researcher(s) show the skills, credentials, and community linkages or partnerships needed for the tasks ahead. Research proposals that do well in such competitions get to a clear research question quickly, explain in a step-by-step fashion what is proposed, and have reasonable budgets and timelines. Their starting point is always a good, clear research question. However, it is important to remember that even the most meritorious projects can remain unfunded because of the competitive nature of calls for proposals. As well, it is advisable to have some research experience before putting the time and effort into drafting a research proposal for external funding.

Live with your research focus for a while and then decide if it is what you want to do. Once you have lived with your general focus, or perhaps your favourite two foci, ask yourself these questions: (a) Does it feel comfortable and if so, why? (b) Can I talk to people about it with some ease? (c) Is it really what I want to do? and (d) What is the right way to ask this? If it doesn't feel quite right then it probably isn't and you may need to revise your thinking.

In this case it is important for you to re-examine the general focus. Ask yourself, "Is this really what I want to focus on?" "Is there a different approach to this that allows more room to explore the topic?" "Is this really the research that is needed?" Spend some time with these questions in your research journal. If you feel positive about the research focus and have a certain comfort with the way you have expressed it, you are ready to move to the next step of framing the research question.

Research Funding. Research is often funded by agencies or foundations. They provide research grants after assessing proposals using competitive processes. Such funding bodies often set priorities that determine the types of issues and approaches they will favour. Priority-setting dilemmas affect these funders, and a host of decisions affecting the funding process itself come into play. These choices often involve assumptions about the relative importance of research topics, the merit of certain data gathering methods, the qualifications of those wishing to conduct the research, and of course the pressing issues of the day.

In order for a research proposal to acquire funding, the following steps are often followed:

- Respond to an opportunity for funding or seek one (these can be for either general research or in answer to a specific call for proposals).
- Draft a proposal for the project.
- Submit the proposal for internal review among colleagues within a university, hospital, or institute (if applicable).
- Finalize the proposal, including the budget, partnership letters, and letters of support, and send it to the funder for review.
- At this point a peer-review process begins, typically involving external reviewers, a committee of reviewers, and a scientific officer from the funding organization.
- Funding decisions are made by ranking the proposals according to the call criteria.
- The top-ranking proposals are funded in accordance with the allocation of funds for the competition.

Academic research projects are often led by a "principal investigator" (PI) and, in the case of research teams, assisted by "co-investigators" (CIs). These roles indicate and imply the responsibilities that each investigator has in the project and sometimes reflects the level of experience with research and the topic being researched. These designations have been developed in the context of academia, and their use is encouraged by granting agencies. In academic settings, the institutions invest the responsibility for sound research design, ethical conduct, and financial accountability in their PIs. In turn, the PI is accountable to his or her department head or research officer. PIs in any context will take responsibility for the content of the proposal and, if successful, for the design and completion of the project. They will also be responsible for gaining ethical approval for the project, reporting to the funders, and solving problems or dealing with adverse events. The CIs usually take on an aspect of a proposal or a project and may offer different skills, experience, or talents to the project.

If research is being conducted using private funds from individuals, private foundations, or corporations, some different processes will apply. The interests of the funders will often be implicit in the types of proposals they initiate or the types of research they solicit or support. In some cases, vested economic interests drive a research agenda, such as internal research for pharmaceutical, tobacco, or automotive companies. In these settings, research takes place for many reasons and at many stages, such as product development, human trials, or marketing. It is for these reasons that academic journals require authors to identify their sources of funding, because the journal editors need to determine what is commercialized research and what is not. In Canada, both funders and universities are now increasingly interested in the commercialization of research (see, for example, the Canadian Institutes of Health Research Act), which blurs the lines between public and private knowledge even more. Other private funders support research that fits with their own interests, including noneconomic goals. Philanthropic organizations are often concerned with change for a particular group or on a specific issue and fund research to derive evidence to support these goals.

Step 3: Identifying Your Research Question

Decisions need to be made about which research question best captivates your research interests and foci. This is done by creating a descending list of questions in order of preference and assessing them against one or more of the following choices:

- A question with enough research scope but not so much that it cannot be answered
- A question that is straightforward and clear

- A question that you are able to gather information about and that is doable
- A question that is exciting or enticing and will sustain your interest and focus throughout the research process
- A question that is in line with anticipated results (though other results must have an opportunity to come to the fore)
- A question that resonates and is important to the community in which you will gather data

What kind of question will see us all the way through this research? Questions that are more quantitative usually ask about the nature and scope of an issue or experience. For example, one might ask how many people have a certain experience or what proportion of people think one way as opposed to another. Quantitative questions will result in data that answer "how many?" "what kind?" and "when and in what order?" For example: How many people put signs on their property during an election campaign? What proportion of the signs is for each candidate? How does this compare with the posted voting outcome for the area?

Questions that are more qualitative in approach may focus on the nature of an experience, innovation, program, or policy, or the meaning of something to selected individuals or groups of people. For example, qualitative research questions may focus on the following:

- The quality of a given experience, innovation, program, or policy
- The meaning or interpretation people may give to an experience or a component part of an experience
- Aspects of an experience or a perspective on an experience
- How an experience fits within a social context
- The institutional location of certain experiences and how individuals make sense of those in their lives
- The formal and informal ways in which an institution or organization functions
- How different or similar people make sense of their experience
- Overt and covert meanings people assign to a particular experience

Here are some examples: What kinds of people are located in the "food desert" in the centre of (our town)? Where do they shop for the food they need? How do they get their food home? What issues arise out of this?

To return to the conceptual funnel, the research question is at the narrowest end of the funnel. Here you are narrowing your focus to the point where one question emerges as most important, doable, and exciting.

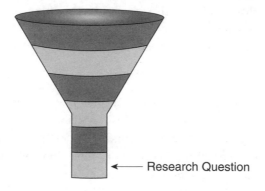

FIGURE 4.9: Conceptual Funnel: Research Question

The skill in formulating a research question is in finding something straightforward, clear, communicable, and important. Regardless of a researcher's experience, time must be spent identifying the right research question. When Shayna was introduced to research as an undergraduate student, she brought a lifetime of observations from her home community, a resource town in northern British Columbia, into her explorations of her research focus and question:

Embarking on the research process at the undergraduate level filled me with both excitement and apprehension. I have great respect and admiration for researchers and perceived them to be in a league far from my own. The idea of learning about and completing a research project within a semester-long timeframe seemed to be an impossible task. Initially I assumed that the research process began with the formulation of a question. I quickly realized that there is a lot of work to be done prior to deciding on a research question and that this work cannot be rushed or skipped, despite being on a tight timeline. Questions such as, "What do I care about? How do my concerns fit with others' concerns? What questions and concerns do I have? What is possible during this time?" helped me decide to conduct my research in my home community that was experiencing rapid social and ecological change. Having strong feminist values I knew I wanted to conduct my research with women in the community to explore how these changes were impacting their health and well-being. Being a member of the community I knew of many women who were experiencing negative health effects and had a desire to share their experience.

In wanting to explore the women's experiences living in the community I knew my research would be qualitative in nature. Although I was tempted to choose a narrow question hypothesizing what I would discover through my research, when I reflected back on my values, goals, and beliefs it became clear that I wanted to create an inclusive opportunity for women to share their experiences. After spending time talking to women in the community it became apparent that there was a particular experience that tied many of them together: their partners being repeatedly absent because of their employment in the oil and gas industry. This experience underscored many of the more specific issues I was interested in, such as mental health, substance use, community supports, and opportunities for empowerment. By formulating a broad exploratory question I had the potential to capture a range of experiences.

My research question then became, "What are the experiences of women whose significant others are repeatedly absent due to their employment in the oil and gas industry?" Once I committed to a question I used it as a "root" that would guide me through the rest of the project (Reid et al., 2009, p. 17). I had my question written in several places—on my notebooks, in my phone, and pasted above my desk. Whenever I became overwhelmed or felt lost I would look at my question and ground myself. This not only helped to answer the questions I was contemplating at the particular moment but strengthened the passion that I had for my project and participants.

Whether it's your first research project or your tenth, there is always the need to spend time reflecting on and honing your research questions:

Linda Tuhiwai Smith (1999), an established scholar, was interested in the "the power relations of domination, struggle and emancipation" (p. i). Her research question was "How does research become institutionalized and colonized, rather than respectful, ethical, sympathetic and useful?" (p. 9). She writes that she sought to understand "the significance of indigenous perspectives on research and attempts to account for how, and why, such perspectives have developed." (L. T. Smith, 1999, p. 3)

These examples show researchers beginning with a problem or concern. Their questions come from different places in their lives and identities. Yet they share a similar exploratory process with their willingness to reflect on what is important to them and to find the research focus and question that captures their curiosity. Once they achieved a clear focus, they both had a strong commitment to and conviction in their research question.

Your Research Proposal and the Ethics Application: Thinking Ahead

Although you are just beginning to get a clear sense of your research question and to view yourself as a researcher, it is important to have a sense of the requirements you'll face in having your research approved. You'll need to gain institutional and/or community approval to conduct your research, which involves completing ethics forms and other documentation. In addition, you will need to have a fully prepared research proposal, which includes the literature review, research question(s), descriptions of prospective research participants and recruitment strategies, plans for data gathering and data gathering instruments (e.g., the criteria for observation in a participant observation, the interview guide, the questionnaire questions, the category codes for content analysis), a plan for analysis, and the necessary unsigned consent or assent forms. In addition, if organizational consent is needed before data gathering (e.g., from a school, prison, care home, sports team), then a signed consent form or approval letter from them will have to be attached. Students engaging in research for the first time, as undergraduate or graduate students, often find research ethics board processes confusing and frustrating. It takes time to fully consider all of the details of your project and get everything in place.

A full description of research proposals and ethics requirements appears in Chapter 7. At this point, your task is to move through Chapters 4 through 7 and to use the exercises provided so you are making informed, logical, and ethical decisions in your research.

Being a Researcher: Writing, Reflexivity, and Organizing the Project

One of the defining characteristics of any kind of research is that it is a *disciplined* process. Bringing discipline to your role as a researcher requires the "orderly or prescribed conduct or pattern of behavior" ("Discipline," 2005). Here we describe the various writing files that you need to create and maintain over the course of your project. It is strongly advisable to do this now—set yourself up to document systematically and organize your thinking. Indeed, "*starting as you mean to go on*" will help you establish research habits (Chapter 3) and create efficiencies in your work down the road. And it is essential to conducting rigorous and reliable research.

In Chapter 1 we discussed the researcher's responsibility to keep written records throughout the research process. Written records are kept for three reasons:

1. To exercise and practise reflexivity, to check assumptions and biases, and to explore your positionality. In your *research journal* you document how you, as a researcher, relate to and are engaging with the questions arising from your research interests.

2. To learn and clarify your emerging ideas on what you want to research, your learning and insights regarding the research process, and your decision making and milestones in your research project. These records are documented in your *process fieldnotes* and *audit trail*.

3. To be a source of data from the field that documents your observations and reflections as you conduct research (observations, participant observations, interviews, focus groups, etc.) in the form of *content fieldnotes*.

Based on our own experiences we recommend creating two spaces for research writing: one for journaling and a second for recording fieldnotes. The research journal and fieldnotes can be recorded either electronically or on paper, but either way they must be kept securely. Entries must always be dated. Keep in mind that fieldnotes that are used as data will most likely need to be converted into an electronic file for analysis, so it may be most efficient to begin recording fieldnotes electronically.

Research Journal

The research journal is where you document your emerging reflexivity to the research topic and question. The research journal includes descriptions of your personal engagement with, or "invisible backpack" (McIntosh, 1989) on, the research question and process, or the posture (Morse, 1994) or stance you take in relation to the research question. This is where you record your struggles about representing the experiences of others and ensure that your voice does not dominate the research but takes its appropriate place. Patton (2014) provides a number of questions to stimulate reflexivity; see Figure 4.10.

Those studied (participants):

How do they know what they know? What shapes and has shaped their worldview? How do they perceive me? Why? How do I know? How do I perceive them?

Reflexive Screens:

Culture, age, education, family, political praxis, language, values gender

Those who receive the study (audience):

How do they make sense of what I give them? What do they bring to the findings I offer? How do they perceive me? How do I perceive them?

Myself (as a critical social researcher):

What do I know? How do I know what I know? What shapes and has shaped my perspective? With what voice do I share my perspective? What do I do with what I have found?

FIGURE 4.10: Reflexive Questions: Triangulated Inquiry

Research journals are where researcher privilege can be dealt with. McIntosh (1989) writes:

> I have come to see white privilege as an invisible package of unearned assets which I can count on cashing in each day, but about which I was meant to remain oblivious. White privilege is like an invisible weightless knapsack of special provisions, maps, passports, codebooks, visas, clothes, tools, and blank checks. (p. 1)

Awareness of privilege is an important part of reflexivity, and your journal becomes a safe place to explore and account for privileges you may have. It is also a place where you consider others' perspectives and experiences and how these might influence the research process. The research journal may be highly personal and private, in which case it is not used as data or shared with anyone. Bear in mind, however, that some demonstration of your disciplined and consistent engagement in a reflexive process is a research practice or "action" that contributes to the credibility of the final analysis (see Chapter 9 on trustworthiness).

Process Fieldnotes

Process fieldnotes document how you do your research: the path you take and your thinking about that path. Process fieldnotes are a record of learning and clarification, exercises or tasks (found in this book or assigned by an instructor), research interests and focus, questions, uncertainties, and so on. One of the best reasons for recording process fieldnotes is that it is simply a good practice. A well-kept set of process fieldnotes is a disciplined, richly detailed repository for the following:

- Descriptions of the routes and decision making involved in getting to the research question
- Descriptions of each research-related encounter that, when recorded, adds to the steady accumulation of ideas, facts, reminiscences, reminders, and growing understanding
- Records of what other researchers have to say about your research
- Records of what people on the street say about your research (you become a magnet for information, albeit serendipitous knowledge, once a research project is underway)
- Records of your increasing comfort or discomfort with the topic over the course of the research or your vulnerability as the holder of certain kinds of information
- Chronological records of your methods, decisions, and commitments; a way to keep your tasks clear
- Records of your observations and analysis, preliminary conclusions, interesting or unexpected links, and a way to keep the analytical process iterative and dynamic

For example, Table 4.1 contains process fieldnotes that were recorded from a telephone conversation that helped move the research project forward. Note that the right column documents the researcher's reflections, insights, and feelings.

Audit Trail. Part of the process fieldnotes is documenting an audit trail. While your process fieldnotes may contain musings, jottings, and other kinds of notes that represent your emerging understandings of the research process, an audit trail is a transparent description of the research steps taken from the start of a research project to the development and reporting of findings. Consider an audit trail a high-level representation of all decisions made. It is important to keep an audit trail because there are a range of approaches that can be used in qualitative research, and the decisions you make need to be visible and clear. In addition, for replicability purposes it is important to have clear descriptions of the research path you take. This should include decisions made and actions taken regarding research design, sampling, data collection, the role of different data sources, data management and analysis,

TABLE 4.1: An Example of a Section of Fieldnotes

December 18, 2015

Winnipeg

Just received a phone call from Joseph.

He is delighted to be a partner to the research on the condition that it is a real contribution that he and his organization, MRac, can make. I suggested that in addition to a training site, the advisory group is where a contribution makes sense.

He said that sounded good and I told him I would present that to the research team and get back to him. That was fine with him.

MRac will be a great place for the research assistants to get some hands-on training with telesurveys, too.

Also, by chance, it looks like Stats Can may be really interested in helping us with the base info b\c they have some historical data that fit right into the question about donor patterns and experience with ill health.

Renata called to say she had the reference to the early background doc and was getting it for us.

Joseph is a keen research advocate and has shown a real interest in health issues, particularly to do with kidney disease, and issues related to getting better information out to the public about where their donation dollars get spent on research. He is high energy and will be a great asset!

Things are falling together nicely.

and reporting. Malterud (2001) underscores the need to provide a detailed report of the analytical steps taken in a study:

> Declaring that qualitative analysis was done, or stating that categories emerged when the material had been read by one or more persons, is not sufficient to explain how and why patterns were noticed . . . the reader needs to know the principles and choices underlying pattern recognition and category foundation. (p. 486)

Your audit trail can be recorded in a logbook. We suggest a simple approach where all decisions and actions are recorded in one place. For example, the following table is an easy format for maintaining a logbook:

DATE	ACTION OR DECISION	RATIONALE AND NEXT STEPS	QUESTIONS/ REFLECTIONS

Content Fieldnotes

Content fieldnotes document what you are learning about the research topic (focus or question). They are a record of a research encounter or interaction (observation, participant observation, interview, focus group, etc.) and are included in the data set for analysis. In the literature there are a myriad of suggestions for recording content fieldnotes. We recommend using a "double-entry" approach that divides the process into two phases: (a) observational/descriptive fieldnotes and (b) expanded/analytical fieldnotes. Remember, everything must be dated.

Observational Fieldnotes. Observational fieldnotes are descriptive notes you take while you are in the field that are based on your close observations. When in the field:

- Write down as much as possible—you never know what might become important later.
- Always write down the date, time, and place of observation at the beginning of your notes.
- Include conditions of colour, weather, light, shape, time, season, atmosphere, and ambiance.
- Write down specifics: Note the time something happens, what a sign says, and so on.
- When you are listening to people speak, write down their words. Specific words, phrases, and language can be very important. (If you write "conversation about food," there are hundreds of things that could mean. Don't expect your memory to be perfect.) As much as possible, write down conversations word for word. Create a glossary of insider phrases and words.
- Pay attention to nonverbal cues. How do people use body language? How do people understand/interpret body language?
- Describe what you see. What are people wearing? How do they adorn their bodies? How is the area you are in decorated?
- Write down your sensory impressions. What can you hear? What do you smell? Tastes, textures, smells, and sounds can be just as important as what you see.
- Map the space you're observing. Having a map that shows you the layout of the area and tracks people's movements can be extremely helpful to refresh your memory and to help others understand your site.

Expanded Fieldnotes. Expanded fieldnotes are analytical and reflective notes you take after you return from the field. Expanded fieldnotes require your ongoing engagement with what you have observed. Once you have left the field do the following or answer some of these questions:

- Respond to the notes you took.
- What questions do you have as a result of your observations?
- Are there things going on in the community that you'd like to know more about (the history of a story, where a specific expression comes from, etc.)?
- Ask yourself questions about what you've seen. What surprised you? What intrigued you? What disturbed you?
- Analyze your position in this community. What assumptions and expectations do you bring to your observations? Ask yourself questions like "Why do I focus on this aspect of the community instead of that other one? Why do I focus on the people I do? Where in my fieldnotes do I find evidence for this description? What have I rejected, and why?"
- Re-read your fieldnotes shortly after you've taken them. Take the time to fill in details that you didn't fully write down, to make sure that everything is legible and understandable for later, and to mark places that you're interested in researching further.
- Reflect on what you've written down. What data relate to your position as a researcher?
- What information confirms your initial hunches? What artifacts speak about your site and your informants? Which of your informants' words explain larger ideas about the subculture you're studying?[1]

Writing fieldnotes is an ongoing part of the research process. Use the expanded fieldnotes to go back to your earlier notes and rethink certain ideas or record new perspectives on earlier information. This is called *layering* and it can be done several times over the same material by adding comments, concepts, and links. As you cycle back through your fieldnotes, layering allows you to continually account for yourself in the process, including things like decisions you made and the reasons you made them, any thoughts you might have about doing research, and what other people tell you about the research when you talk to them about it.

External parameters sometimes organize and influence researchers' work and the knowledge created by that work. Because of this, you might also want to record the historical and political contexts in which your research occurs. You can do this by asking if any pre-established goals, assumptions, or

....

1 Descriptions of observational and expanded fieldnotes are adapted from Heidi Estrem's "Fieldnote Requirements" in *Guide to First-Year Writing at Eastern Michigan University.* Retrieved from www.emich.edu/english/fycomp/curriculum/pdfs/handouts.pdf

responsibilities influence or organize your work. These insights can also be documented as you work on the expanded fieldnotes.

There are various ways that "double-entry" fieldnotes can be recorded. Some prefer a table structure with observations recorded in the left column and expanded fieldnotes in the right. A second approach is to add the expanded fieldnotes after the observations in a narrative format. In the following example, the expanded fieldnotes are couched within the observations but separated with asterisks (★★★).

What: Analysis PTG Meeting
When: 10 February 2015
Where: [Organization's name], Activity Room 2
Whom: Maria, Joanne, Steve, Melanie, and Rebecca
Recorded by Melanie

I arrived at [organization] around 10:00. Maria and Joanne were already there, seated around the table in the activity room. I sat across from them. We greeted each other and talked about our weekends. ***It is nice that the group is getting to know each other.*** Shortly after this Steve arrived and sat beside me. ***This is the second week in a row that Steve and I have worked together. A while ago, Steve talked about how he prefers to do coding on his own. I wonder how he feels about working with me. Also, this is the second or third week Cathy has not come to the PTG meeting. I know she has not been feeling well and I wonder if Adia has called her to check in.***

Maria mentioned that we would be getting a visitor around 11:00—Rebecca. Joanne smiled and moved her hands in excitement. Maria introduced two tasks for the day—continue coding transcripts or work on the Excel spreadsheet documenting the relationships. Joanne said she would prefer to code transcripts first while her mind is sharp. Steve agreed with this, and so did I. We divided up the transcripts—Joanne and Adia started working on "suffering." Steve and I started working on "insecurity."

Around 11:15 Rebecca entered the room saying "Hello!" We all looked up and stopped what we were doing. Joanne jumped up to give Rebecca a hug. Maria gave Rebecca a hug next. Rebecca said hello to Steve and I, but we did not get up. ***The group, especially Joanne, is very excited and happy to see Rebecca. She was a big part of the Analysis Group in the fall and it seems that they really miss her.*** Maria asks Rebecca how her internship is going. Rebecca talks for about 20 minutes about her experiences at [hospital] and all the things she is learning. She talks about having to learn medical information about injuries and conditions. Joanne says "that's the part I would be interested in." ***Joanne has mentioned before that she always wanted to work in the helping field. She seems to be living vicariously through Rebecca in this moment.***

Maria asks Rebecca if she would like to help us code. She says yes. We decided to do it as a group. Joanne and Maria began—they read out a quote, and we talked about how to code it. Rebecca did not say anything, but nodded. ***Rebecca is learning the new process for coding. This must be somewhat strange for her, being so involved one minute and not involved the next.*** Steve and I went next, going through the same process. Afterwards, Rebecca said she had to leave to be at her internship site. We all said goodbye, and Rebecca promised to come back and visit again another time. ***Rebecca is excellent at maintaining rapport with people. She is truly connected to the participants and research team.***

A few important notes: These are fieldnotes from a meeting where the student (the person recording the fieldnotes) was a participant observer. Her expanded fieldnotes, which are demarcated by asterisks (★★★), contain not only her reflections and analysis but also her inferences—how she is making meaning of a particular exchange or moment. The student recording the fieldnotes is diligent about moving back and forth between her observations and her expanded notes. Note that the pertinent information regarding the meeting is recorded at the beginning of the document (what, where, when, who). It is extremely important to be systematic about how fieldnotes are named and the relevant information that they contain.

At the start of your research, recording your fieldnotes will help you formulate the question or raise concerns you might have about being a researcher. For example, "Catherine" (Kirby & McKenna, 1989, p. 175) had chosen incest as her research topic. She went back to her private journals to find references related to incest. It soon became apparent to her that everything was related. Rather than look at published works to find out about incest, she concentrated on the examination of her own experience. Some of this was reflexive (what she had thought and felt) and some were experiential observations (details) recorded when she was a little girl. Now, as an adult, she was able to formulate a research focus that incorporated the original information and her adult responses to it. Thus, the fieldnotes included intellectual thinking and observations, and the journal contained her emotional and reflexive comments. Together they wove together her personal experiences with her research interests.

Critical social research is a dynamic and continuous process. During the research itself questions, concepts, strategies, theories, and ways to gather and engage with the data require a constant reflexive approach and questioning by the researcher. Such flexibility, reflexivity, and responsiveness contribute to the overall strength and rigour of data collection and analysis (Panel on Research Ethics, 2014, Chapter 10).

Exercise 4.3: The touring exercise

We recommend that even the most seasoned researcher use the touring exercise to prepare for research. The touring exercise is a tool that can be used to develop and hone one's reflective abilities.

This exercise involves one hour of recording content and reflections at a location or site of your choice. It is a chance for you to play with information as it comes to you and as you attend to it. Here we describe the skills important to the exercise in Steps 1 and 2 and then describe the exercise in Step 3. The touring exercise provides you with an opportunity to practise gathering information and reflecting on it. It also reinforces your skills at recording field-notes. Let your curiosity lead you through an exploration. There is no outcome except the documentation of where you have been, what you have seen, and what you thought about it.

Given that disciplined recording is part of the skill of being a researcher, and because there is no such thing as being an impartial or unimpassioned researcher, the touring exercise allows you to not only follow your interests and instincts for searching, but it also allows you to record, in a disciplined way, your reflections about *why* you are thinking and searching in those ways. Your search will be unlike anyone else's because when you follow your interests you will be certain to arrive at a different conclusion. Rather than considering your interests to be limitations, consider them as enhancements of your vision, built on the diversity of your experience. As we explore ideas, a single piece of research often produces more than one equally plausible conclusion. Instead of debating which is more correct, we believe more than one outcome is likely. Even contradictory outcomes can emerge, but are really only illustrative of the fact that we do not yet know enough about a topic to confirm one single outcome. In qualitative research, with such a diversity of researchers as the creators of new knowledge, diversity of outcomes is part of the diversity of the human condition. Added together, these new pieces of knowledge can provide considerable understanding about the meaning of social experience. Let's go over how the touring exercise works.

Step 1: Freeing Your Thinking

How can you learn to be attentive and listen to the voices of those around you? In traditional research, you might begin by going to a library and completing a review of all the available literature on your topic . Typically you would look for answers to what information (content) might exist and what techniques you might need to find it.

Freeing your thinking in the touring exercise allows you to locate yourself in a stimulating environment where you can surround yourself with books and ideas and colours and voices. It allows you to pay specific attention to how it is that you—uniquely you—are an instrument of the research. Why do you hear and make sense of certain voices more readily than others? In the tour, why are you attracted to information presented in bright shiny formats rather than information presented in dull and heavy tomes? Why do you turn right, not left, when you come to intersections in the library, and why do you have more interest in things presented at eye level than at knee level? This is what the touring exercise is about. *It is an experience in thinking freely and reflecting on how you think.*

Being free to think means "getting rid of the *shoulds*," the things that tell you how you *should* think, what you *should* gather, and where you *should* go for information. It also means understanding that you think differently than anyone else and that this enables you to do unique research. At the end of the touring experience, you will feel like a more finely tuned researcher and more attentive and skilled in the practice of research observation and reflection.

Step 2: Getting Ready for Fieldnotes

The goal of this step of the touring exercise is to help you figure out how you think, how your interest moves from place to place, how you make links between observations, and if and how you move from observations to theories. Everything needs to be recorded in your fieldnotes, including:

- All content (the information gathered through observation)—these are your *observational fieldnotes*
- All reflections (thoughts about content and about the process of observing and about oneself as the observer)—these are your *expanded fieldnotes*

The touring exercise is a task to get you used to combining your search for ideas with an understanding of how you think and feel. Although there's a more detailed discussion earlier in the chapter on fieldnotes, the example provided in Table 4.1 illustrates a small section of fieldnotes. Entries are dated, and the observations and reflections are linked.

In the touring task, you have only to gather what information you attend to through seeing, hearing, and so on. There is no particular product expected nor is there a particular plan. All sorts of information are at your disposal, but with no uniform strategy for gathering the information, your own way of thinking becomes the guide to what you attend to and how you record it.

Step 3: The Tour Task

Choose a locus of attention. This could be a library, department store, grocery store, stadium full of people, product fair, court house, picnic, a tour of a three to four block area of a community, or a public exhibition—anywhere where it would not be too unusual for someone to walk about with a clipboard making notes. Places that are unsuitable are bars, restaurants, funerals, places of worship, classrooms, or any place someone with a clipboard would draw attention to themselves.

Choose a time. You have only one hour from the time you start the task until its conclusion. Make note of the time you start and finish.

Prepare a clipboard or notebook with a number of bifurcated pages in readiness for your observations. Or you may choose to use your laptop or phone, if appropriate. Either way you should be prepared to document your observations. Identify your location, date, and time on the first page.

Get started. Start at a pre-identified place at your site. Look around you. Remember that detail counts. Begin with a single word or idea and record it under "Observations" as your starting point. Now follow it wherever your interest takes you. Make note of each item that catches your interest, and continue your search through your site using each new reference point as a stepping-stone or guide to the next. You might even want to take along a camera or a sketchbook and use them to record items that catch your interest. During this time keep a record of what you are thinking. Take notes to fill in the context of your photo or sketch. As in the example provided in Step 2, record both content (what you stop to look at) and reflections (what you are thinking as you stop, select, record, and move along). These reflections are an ongoing record of how your mind works while you are engaged in research. Both content and reflections are integral features of the process of researching from the margins.

Immediately after your one-hour time limit, stop where you are and make preliminary observations about your overall sense of what the site looks like and your collected impressions of what the experience was like for you. You might, for example, have comments on the process and whether the tour captured your attention or was a boring and unsatisfying experience. Or you might want to comment on what it feels like to be an active and unique creator of knowledge. Anyone else could go to that same site, start at the same spot, and yet be unable to reproduce your account. The two would be entirely different accounts of the tour. Both are correct, though different.

Conclude the fieldwork with an evaluation statement of your experiences as an active creator of this new web of information, with its own texture, density, and colour. Answer the question, "What picture can I draw to describe how my mind works?" For example, from one tour the concluding statement was the following:

> I am so orderly. I have to go in straight lines, down one corridor and up another. I was afraid to wander randomly. I kept thinking about exactly what task I was supposed to be doing. My mind works in an orderly, logical, and linear way; it does not jump around. So I guess I miss the oblique thinking, the happenstance of something because I keep going in a set pattern. I get lots of detail down though—I really see what I focus on and am able to describe it well. I use lots of references to size and colour of things, so I think I am attracted to the big and the bright, sort of like a crow attracted to shiny things. A whole bunch of topics interested me and I have a lot of notes saying "come back to this for more information . . ." I hope I do.

Step 4: Layering and Refocusing

From your preliminary fieldnotes, you now have new ideas and experiences. You can begin to link them together in ways that make sense to you. Eventually, there are threads of thought that you can later weave into a fabric of ideas. The texture, density, colours, and patterns you use are all symbolic of the ideas you have linked through your personal understanding. Each researcher weaves differently and will therefore weave a different set of patterns depending entirely on the observations and reflections on those observations. Researchers develop a trademark or pattern that makes their work recognizable to others.

Since linking data together takes a lot of thought and some time, it is best to let the detailed observations and reflections you have made rest for a day or two. Then go back and fill in an additional layer to your thinking. Layering is your chance to reflect on your reflections. If you use different coloured ink or pencils each time you layer on to these reflections, it will help to illustrate the way your analysis develops over time. Researchers frequently make fieldnotes and then record them (with some on-the-spot editing) into a computer. Others wait until they are at their computers before they write their fieldnotes in any detail, working off brief written or tape-recorded notes taken on site. Some computer programs allow recording of dated layering. The purpose of this touring exercise is to show how the researcher is the key instrument of the research and to provide an opportunity for researchers to develop their skills in recording fieldnotes.

Organizing Your Project: The Keep, File, Protect (KFP) System

As you begin to plan your project and get a clearer sense of your research interests and focus, it is necessary to create a system for organizing your documents. You will have different kinds of documents to keep organized—literature (PDFs, notes on articles), process fieldnotes, content fieldnotes, research journal, research proposal, ethics forms, bibliography—and having a well-organized system for identifying and retrieving documents can be a huge time saver. On the other hand, we have worked with students and colleagues who have not organized their files from the outset, which has resulted in time wasted and a lot of frustration.

We recommend that you create or adopt some kind of organizing system that makes sense to you and enables you to find and identify what you need. Some people find the use of project management, data analysis, or bibliography programs helpful in keeping them organized, whereas others prefer a simpler approach of file management on their computer. We discuss the use of software and online programs for project management below. Regardless of your preference, it is important to imagine the breadth of your project and how it will make most sense to you in terms of organization, file management, and document retrieval. In principle, we use the KFP system (keep, file, protect):

- Keep and name all records.
- File everything: Be consistent, thorough, and diligent in documenting and filing.
- Protect your records and back up everything.

As you set up your organizing system, the first rule is to *keep and name all records.* Date all records and find a location in your filing system for them that makes sense to you. Do not discard anything. The more you keep or document at this point the less difficulty you will have later when you defend your decisions or report on your research process.

For instance, you may decide to record your fieldnotes and research journal as separate "kinds" of documents on your computer. In this case, you will want to consider how the files are named so that you can easily identify what they are. Here are some examples:

- PFN 20160908 → Process fieldnotes from 8 September 2016
- CFN INT 20160915 → Content fieldnotes from the interview conducted on 15 September 2016
- RJ 20161016 → Research journal entry from 16 October 2016

It is also extremely helpful to create a system for managing the literature you retrieve. When downloading an article from the Internet or a library database, the document's name rarely makes any sense. We find that renaming articles by author(s) last name and date is helpful for identifying a document, such as Reid, Landy, & Leon (2013). Use consistent information and formatting when labelling articles and resources that have been retrieved.

Digital files need to be clearly labelled to distinguish between data files, fieldnotes, journal entries, retrieved documents for the literature review, and so on. The point here is to be able to look at a file name and know exactly what it is. The practice of putting a date and some indication of the "kind" of file in the title of the document is one way to do this. Dating documents also helps distinguish between recent and older versions of the same file.

The second rule of record keeping is to *file everything*. Be consistent and organized. Find a logical place for items: Similar items go together, dissimilar items are located apart. Similar to keeping track of your house keys by always returning them to the same place, keeping track of bits of information means being disciplined about putting (documenting or recording) them in the expected places every time. Whatever you choose, be consistent in your filing and labelling.

The third rule is that you need to *protect your records*. All raw data must be protected, inaccessible to others, and located separately from the names of the people who provided it. If there are paper documents, these must be kept separately from the electronic files where we do most of our work.

There are many different ways of backing up or saving information. Some researchers save files onto an external hard drive or use web storage to keep their files (some examples include Google Drive, IDrive, Dropbox, Apple iCloud, Microsoft OneDrive, CertainSafe, CrashPlan, or SugarSync). It is important to fully understand the web storage you choose, including security options and where the data are kept. Some institutional ethics guidelines do not support the use of specific web platforms for saving sensitive and confidential data. If you work within a research team, the protection of files must include those who need and have legitimate access to the materials and exclude those who do not. Adding password protection or freezing access to certain files may be useful here. All files are dated in their titles, and most only need to be kept for as long as the information may be required to support or back up the research. Some files, such as those with identity information, records, results, or transcripts, might be kept longer, and the length of time that you must retain data will be dictated by the research ethics board. In general, we use a five-year rule and archive whatever we have promised to keep or are legally required to keep.

There are a growing number of Computer Assisted Qualitative Data AnalysiS (CAQDAS) software programs that support a variety of analytical styles in qualitative work, for example QSR-NVivo, ATLAS.ti, Citavi, and Xsight (we discuss the use of online survey management programs in Chapter 9). They have word-processing capabilities so that fieldnote records can be placed directly in document files for you to "write as you go." If you choose to use a CAQDAS program it makes sense to keep your fieldnotes as an electronically managed file. This enables easy data checks and frequency counts and can assist with interpretation, conceptualization, examination of relationships, and documentation of the process. CAQDAS programs can help you not only with the initial task of managing fieldnotes, but also with keeping good records. They also allow for transcribing digitally recorded files (interviews, fieldnotes) directly into the program and uploading audio and visual files for analysis.

The proliferation of bibliography and analysis software programs (see Chapter 5) has come with a side benefit that many offer free trials to attract potential users. The free trials are often limited in time or capability, and as such will most likely not meet the needs of a multi-year research project. Before committing to any program, consider your own needs and style of work, and reasonably estimate the time it will take to learn the functions of a new program. For highly complex research projects with multiple data sources and a group of co-researchers, analysis and bibliography programs are generally worth the time and financial investment.

Being a Researcher: Establishing Research Habits

As a researcher you now have taken on a "research schedule." This is something that you need to factor into your schedule on a weekly basis. Researchers cannot cram a night or two before the research report is due. First, it is simply not possible to complete research in this way, and second, it is highly unethical to rush or cram any kind of research activity that involves interactions with others as research participants. Therefore, embrace your role as a researcher, the responsibilities this carries, and create a plan for moving forward that will allow you to progress in your research with as little stress as possible.

By now we hope that it is clear that being organized is a research habit that will save you many headaches down the road. For some this comes easily, while for others it can be a challenge. If you struggle with being orga-nized, identify the hurdles you've encountered in the past and how you will work to overcome them. Some important strategies include the following:

1. *Plan your time.* Set aside at least one chunk of time each week to devote to your research, and don't let other demands interfere with this time. These chunks of research time should be at least three hours so that you can focus and immerse yourself in your study. Trying to do research in little bits of time is far more difficult and will, in fact, create more work for you in the long run.

2. *Create a timeline for your project.* Identify key dates in the timeline (such as when the proposal and ethics forms are due and, if you are relying on feedback from others, turnaround time to get that feedback), then back up from these deadlines. If you do not have any externally imposed deadlines, create some. From the deadlines, you can create weekly or biweekly to-do lists. This may change as you progress with your project, but a timeline and to-do list will help you move forward consistently. It is also important to try to stick to your timeline as much as possible.

3. *Be strategic about your research time.* Think about the best use of your time. Difficult tasks requiring intense thought often can't be done in short bursts, so plan these tasks when you have adequate time to devote to them. Other tasks are easier or less time intensive (such as reviewing fieldnotes, correcting proofs, or reading and taking notes) and can be fit into smaller periods of time.

4. *Keep going.* Always use your research time. If you get stuck on one piece of work, transition to another. There are always administrative tasks to do (formatting your reference list, designing a questionnaire, etc.).

5. *Turn off your internal editor.* When writing, regardless of what you are writing, keep writing. Get your ideas down. You can organize and edit your writing later.

6. *Create systems and processes that will serve you well.* Start thinking about how you like to work (entirely on your computer, with hard copies, or some combination?) and what's possible for you.

7. *Tap into and harness your inspiration for your topic.* Not all research tasks are equally engaging, but overall the research process should be exciting and should tap into your curiosity. When you do not feel excited or inspired, find ways to access this beyond your project. Attend a conference or workshop, search online for others engaged in similar topics, listen to podcasts, read the newspaper or online blogs, or have a conversation with an "interested outsider" who knows nothing about your topic.

Recognize moments where you are feeling stale and find ways to reinvigorate your passion for your work.

8. *Connect with other researchers.* Publicize your research and make connections with other researchers who are working in the same field or on the same topic. And remember that you are not bound by location—the Internet makes connecting with researchers on the other side of the world possible. Join relevant research networks or start your own. You can also strengthen your online presence to create further connections (your institution's webpage, Facebook, Twitter, Pinterest, Scoop.it, etc.).

9. *Get help when needed.* Don't allow yourself to stay stuck, uncertain, or confused. Reach out to the network you have established and ask for help from more experienced researchers.

10. *Give yourself breaks from research.* Take regular breaks, perhaps by going for a walk or a bike ride. Stepping away from your research can often give you the mental space you need to think through problems or develop an argument. Physical activity is surprisingly effective for unencumbering your thoughts. (Lupton, 2012)

Summary

This chapter is a practical starting point for you as you begin to do research. As you make choices about how you do research and who you study, your personal thoughts and feelings are important. This chapter helps you focus on an area of interest, examine whether it feels right, and begin the difficult process of finding a question. The chapter also explains the importance of creating systems for research writing—recording a research journal and fieldnotes—and organizing your project with various systems. It cannot be stressed enough to "start as you mean to go on." Thinking through how you like to work, what kinds of organizational systems make sense to you, and protecting time every week to work on your project will be a huge asset to you over the course of your research.

In this chapter we introduced a touring exercise to help you get used to recording fieldnotes and to learn to separate content from observations and reflections. One important theme of this chapter is to show the importance of stating your assumptions and contextualizing yourself in the research. By doing this, you change the traditional power dynamics or the hierarchy that tends to exist between the researcher and those who are being researched.

The researcher becomes another subject in the research process and another dimension is added to the data.

Questions for Discussion

1. What does it mean to "start where you are"?
2. How should you begin the research process, and in which order?
   a. Identify your research interest
   b. Focus
   c. Frame a question
   d. Keep a journal and record fieldnotes
3. What are the different kinds of research writing (research records, accounts) that you need to establish? Why are they important?
4. What is layering, and why is it important to being an attentive observer?

Our Recommended Readings

Janesick, V. J. (2004). *"Stretching" exercises for qualitative researchers* (2nd ed.). Thousand Oaks: Sage.

Lincoln, Y. S. (2005). Institutional review boards and methodological conservatism: The challenge to and from phenomenological paradigms. In N. K. Denzin & Y. S. Lincoln (Eds.), *The SAGE handbook of qualitative research* (3rd ed., pp. 165–181). Thousand Oaks: Sage.

Malterud, K. (2001). Qualitative research: Standards, challenges, and guidelines. *Lancet, 358*(9280), 483–488. http://dx.doi.org/10.1016/S0140-6736(01)05627-6 Medline:11513933

Marshall, C., & Rossman, G. B. (2016). *Designing qualitative research* (6th ed.). Los Angeles: Sage.

Reid, C., Brief, E., & LeDrew, R. (2009). *Our common ground: Cultivating women's health through community based research.* Vancouver: Women's Health Research Network.

Wolfinger, N. H. (2002). On writing fieldnotes: Collection strategies and background expectancies. *Qualitative Research, 2*(1), 85–93. http://dx.doi.org/10.1177/1468794102002001640

CHAPTER 5

WHY? THE LITERATURE REVIEW

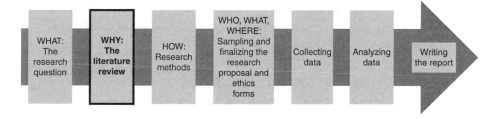

FIGURE 5.1: The Research Process

In this chapter we discuss the purpose and process of literature reviews. We focus on how to do an efficient and thorough review of the literature that culminates in a clearer articulation of the research focus and research question. The chapter concludes with an opportunity for you to clarify your research question and articulate a purpose statement as a result of the literature review.

Why do the review of literature now? In most research approaches, the literature review is usually recommended after the research focus and before the research question, or occasionally immediately following the research question. It is then used to set up the research design and determine the data gathering techniques based in the context of what other researchers have reported. In more emergent or exploratory research, a literature review is likely to expose gaps in the literature that reveal just how little is known about something. In that situation, the review of the literature may serve to point out what directions have not yet been explored or what problems may lie ahead in the unexplored terrain. Some researchers prefer to conduct an ongoing review of literature that runs parallel to data gathering and supports the analytical stages where literature is analyzed concurrently with new data.

A literature review is an objective, critical summary of published research literature relevant to a topic under consideration. Its purpose is to create familiarity with current thinking and research on a particular topic and justify future research into a previously overlooked or understudied area (Fry, n.d.). Literature searches may be done early in the research, particularly for topics where much is known already, or concurrently throughout the research process, such as in the case of truly emergent research. We position the literature review prior to conducting research because we believe it is important to have some understanding of what others have written about a chosen topic. Reviewing the literature before doing research can help with decisions that need to be made about the research question, research methods, and analytical approaches. Research proposals submitted for funding review usually have beginning sections on "general objectives," "background," and "theoretical framework" where the researcher frames the proposed research based on what has already been discovered and gaps that exist about the topic.

Organizing Your Literature Search: KFP System

The KFP (keep, file, protect) system was described in detail in Chapter 4. As you begin to search for information on your topic, you will find two things: First, information comes to you in many forms, and second, you need a disciplined and systematic process for recording the information and references you find. The three principles of the KFP system, as discussed in Chapter 4, also apply to literature searches.

You may have chosen to use a program such as ATLAS.ti or NVivo to organize and manage your entire project, including your literature and data. If this is the case, the program's manual will provide guidance for filing and tracking literature that is gathered on your topic. Alternatively, many researchers choose to use a program specific to literature searching to manage their references. There are many reference manager software programs available, such as BibBase, Bookends, Citavi, EndNote, Mendeley, Paperpile, refbase, Reference Manager, RefWorks, and Zotero. This is not an exhaustive list; it may be worth asking your peers, colleagues, and supervisor(s) which bibliography programs they use. If you are affiliated with a college or university, your institution's library may offer a free subscription to a reference manager program that is compatible with its library databases. But bear in mind that if you graduate or are no longer affiliated with that institution you will either lose your references or have to pay the program's subscription costs.

If you decide to use a reference manager program, try the free online trial version that many of these programs offer. These programs have a range of functions, compatibilities, and costs. Most of them store your references online and have functions that allow you to identify keywords and output reference lists in different styles (i.e., APA, Chicago). It is also possible to use these programs to create an annotated bibliography and to document other relevant information about the references you have retrieved. For example, you can create subfolders that house articles specific to one aspect of your project or that are, in your estimation, A+ or highly relevant/important articles. The appearance or interface of each program also varies, and some may be more visually intuitive to you than others. What is important here is that you spend some time exploring your options and what might work best for you.

Despite the proliferation of reference manager software programs, some researchers choose to use the organizing system within their computers (folders and subfolders) to manage their references. References are downloaded as PDF documents and saved in the folder system. It is strongly recommended that you rename all downloaded documents with the author(s) and date of publication so you can recognize the document without having to open it (see Chapter 8 for a description of naming documents). The limitation of this approach is that websites, blogposts, and other online references may not be downloadable nor saved easily within this system. Digital bookmarking sites such as Scoop.it, Pinterest, Delicious, or Bundlr can be used to save interesting material you have found on the web (Lupton, 2012).

The main decision here is to find a balance between how you need your reference organizing system to function and the time and cost of adopting a reference manager program. If you anticipate a fairly straightforward literature search for a one-term research project, using the filing system on your computer may suffice. However, if you are working on a master's or Ph.D. research project with diverse literatures and are also including materials from coursework, you may be well served in using a reference manager system. Finally, if you are an undergraduate or graduate student and decide to use a reference manager program, we recommend that you use it for all coursework and research activities. Reference manager programs are most effective when all library and online resources are stored within the program so that it becomes a "one-stop" location for your reference materials.

Whatever system you use, find a location in your filing system that makes sense to you. Do not discard anything. The more you keep and document at this point, the less difficulty you will have later when you defend your decisions or report on your research process. Most reference manager software programs store files virtually, which can be very convenient if you are working on different computers or with a research team. However, it is essential that the files also be kept securely on one computer or hard drive so that there is a backup of the literature that is gathered. Start a KFP system that works for you. The proof of a good KFP system will be the ability to file all bits of information, to relocate any information needed with ease, and to have timely access to the information you need.

Conducting a Literature Review

In a formal research proposal, the research purpose is stated followed by the research goals and the literature review. For our purposes, once the research focus is clearly stated the literature review can be used to examine what is known about that focus, what methods have previously been used to obtain data, and what might serve as an excellent research question. A literature review is a comprehensive account of what has been written or is known about your topic in the last 10–15 years. Consider the following purposes of literature reviews:

- To review what has been written on your topic. How much and what sort of information already exists, who is writing about it, and from what perspectives? As you review what has been written on your topic, you must map, record, and file all relevant sources. This involves being thorough and tracking everything. As you do this you will determine the variety of materials available on your topic, including those that are refereed and not refereed.
- To identify central arguments, concepts, patterns, and relationships between them.
- To locate useful definitions that will make conceptualizing your project easier. It may help you fine-tune your research question or inform the development of your interview or survey questions.
- To identify the gaps and research that have been overlooked in the literature, such as overt conclusions or a dominance of one methodology or research paradigm.
- To identify key experts and foundational articles/writings as related to your research interest. For example, is one person cited repeatedly by other authors? Is one article or book referenced as foundational?
- To construct an up-to-date reference list of authors whose work is important to the research. This will help you avoid possible plagiarism and make final reporting easier. (If you are using a reference manager software program's in-text citation feature, then this step is not relevant to you.)

With these purposes in mind, the search can become more focused and efficient. Each of the six purposes can serve as initial files in your burgeoning KFP system. Literature searches that used to be done manually have been replaced by online searches of published and unpublished literature of all varieties. Despite the enormous online library, many research topics may still require examination of the grey literature (i.e., not published in journals), discussions with other researchers or people working on the issue in the community, and other forms of searching. Books are very useful, but online versions that are spliced and fragmented can be hard to understand and are not as useful as the book itself.

Technology has increased the proliferation of information so that it takes a much more discerning eye to select references containing useful and trustworthy data. Broadly, there are two kinds of literature: refereed (peer-reviewed) literature and non-refereed. A *peer review* is the evaluation of work by one or more people of similar competence to the producers of the work. It constitutes a form of self-regulation by qualified members of a field or profession. Peer review methods are employed to maintain standards of quality, improve performance, and provide credibility. In academia, peer review is often used to determine an academic paper's suitability for publication. Peer review means that an article has been reviewed by other academics in the same field who verify that the research both makes a contribution to the field of study and has been conducted properly. Typically, peer-reviewed literature in academic journals and books or book chapters are considered to be the most legitimate or reliable sources because they have been evaluated externally for trustworthiness, meaning that there are presumably no false claims or overt biases.

Alongside such peer-reviewed literature there is now a field of information called grey literature. *Grey literature* refers to a type of information produced by organizations or governments outside of commercial or academic publishing and distribution channels. There is a vast quantity of literature that is published but not always peer reviewed, for example research and project reports, government reports, newspaper articles, blog posts, and self-published materials. Such literature crosses disciplines and the public/private divide and is often current and topical. Some kinds of grey literature are not published but are still useful, such as in-house documents and annual reports.

When considering the vast array of information that can be gathered, it is important to ask if all information is equal. Therefore there are now numerouse examples of bogus academic journals and predatory publishers that are not legitimate. Therefore some information is less solid and demands more skepticism from the reader. In many ways grey literature is the most topical and interesting but may be less disciplined. Nevertheless, it reflects the work of organizations and governments outside of academia and therefore is very valuable in informing many research questions.

Regardless of your research interest and research question, when you do a literature review you will want to do an efficient and thorough search for the following:

- Key information or knowledge that already exists and where it is located, including search engines, disciplinary journals, books and book chapters, newspapers or popular media, and so on
- Key concepts, theories, and definitions that inform your research topic
- Key "thinkers" or experts and their collaborators, as well as their key writings
- Possible data collection strategies that have been used and recommendations for other methods

A good literature review will thoroughly and systematically represent what is known about a topic and provide a critical appraisal of the information. It is a piece of discursive prose, not a list describing or summarizing one piece of literature after another. Organize the literature review into sections that present themes or identify trends, including relevant theory. You are not trying to list all the material published, but rather your task is to synthesize and evaluate it according to your research question. A literature review must (a) be organized and related to the research question, (b) synthesize findings into a summary of what is known and not known, (c) identify areas of controversy in the literature, and (d) formulate questions that need further research (Taylor, n.d.).

SAMPLE QUESTIONS TO STIMULATE CRITICAL THINKING ABOUT BOOKS AND ARTICLES

Ask yourself these questions about your process for compiling the literature:

1. What is the specific *thesis, problem, or research question* that my literature review helps to define?
2. What is the *scope* of my literature review? What *types of publications* am I using (e.g., journals, books, government documents, popular media or other grey literature)? What discipline am I working in (e.g., nursing, leisure and recreation, psychology, sociology, medicine)? What does the scope of my literature review tell me about the kind of information that is available?
3. How *good* is my information seeking? Has my search been *wide enough* to ensure that I have found all relevant material? Has

it been narrow enough to exclude irrelevant material? Is the number of sources I have used appropriate for the length of my paper?

4. Have I *critically analyzed* the literature that I have gathered? Do I follow through a set of concepts and questions, comparing items to each other in the ways they deal with them?

5. Are there any places where I have simply listed or summarized items rather than *integrating* them, *assessing their strengths and weaknesses*, and *how they relate to other components* of the literature review?

6. Have I cited and discussed studies that are *contrary to my perspective*? Have I allowed my own opinions, values, or beliefs to be challenged by the literature?

7. Will the reader find my literature review *relevant, appropriate, and useful*?

Ask yourself these questions about each book or article you review:

8. Has the author formulated a problem or issue? Is it clearly defined? Is its significance clearly established (scope, severity, relevance)? Can I articulate this? Can I write this?

9. Could the problem be more effectively approached from another perspective?

10. What is the author's research orientation (positivist, interpretive, or . . .)?

11. What is the author's theoretical framework (psychological, developmental, feminist, or . . .)?

12. Has the author evaluated the literature relevant to the problem/ issue? Does the author include literature that takes positions that she or he does not agree with?

13. In a research study, how good are the basic components of the study design (e.g., population, sampling, methods, outcome)? How accurate and valid are the measures? Is the analysis of the data accurate and relevant to the research methods? Are the conclusions validly based on the data and analysis?

14. In material written for a popular readership, does the author use emotional appeals, one-sided examples, judgmental language, or rhetorically charged language and tone? Is there an objective basis to the reasoning, or is the author merely supporting what she or he already believes?

15. How does the author structure the argument? Can you "deconstruct" the flow of the argument to see whether and where it breaks down logically?
16. In what ways does the book or article contribute to our understanding of the problem under study, and in what ways is it useful for practice? What are the strengths and limitations?
17. How does this book or article relate to the specific thesis or question I am developing? How would I rate its significance?

Source: Taylor, D. (n.d.). The literature review: A few tips on conducting it. University of Toronto Health Sciences Writing Centre. Retrieved from http://www.writing.utoronto.ca/advice/specific-types-of-writing/literature-review

Literature reviews can feel overwhelming for first-time researchers because of the amount of information available and the apparent authority of researchers who are publishing in their disciplines. You can always seek the assistance of library personnel to help you navigate the library and information world. They can show you a number of labour-saving approaches by, for example, directing you to known search engines, specific sites, annotated bibliographies, and collections of abstracts. But a literature review is an ongoing and iterative process; it is always incomplete and frequently uneven. While your task is ultimately to weigh all the evidence, the best you can do is assess the quality of the evidence, research design, and methods used in the literature that you have gathered.

A primary purpose of conducting a literature review is to know and be able to represent what has been written about your research topic. The information gathered from a literature review will help you hone your research question and research methods. In critical social research some research questions may require a literature review and an environmental scan. Consider the following research questions:

1. Which health care services in a municipality are available to women who are homeless and Indigenous?
2. Of the available health care services in that municipality, which ones are regularly accessed by women who are homeless and Indigenous?

See the difference between these two questions? It may be that there are a number of health care services available to women who are homeless and Indigenous, but that for a range of reasons, such as stigma and discrimination, location, timing, and so on, only a small percentage of those "available" services are accessed by women who are homeless and Indigenous. It paints a very different picture if all available health care services are accessed versus only a small percentage of them. To have a full appreciation for the findings from the second research question it is necessary to answer the first research question. With respect to these research questions, a literature review is necessary but not sufficient. An environmental scan will help to adequately answer the first research question, but it will take a more in-depth search to find the answer to the second, and perhaps more important, question.

Environmental scans, often called SWOT analyses (Strengths, Weaknesses, Opportunities, Threats), can be done to determine where your research question is in relation to the current environment or context. Table 5.1 shows a SWOT analysis about whether to start up a local welfare organization to help children at risk in Winnipeg. It clarifies the arguments and context for any immediate action and indicates that potential risks and challenges are capable of being resolved by some proposed key strategies.

Strategies for Conducting a Literature Review

Though many researchers rely almost completely on the Internet and a range of search engines, we offer three important cautions. First, searching the Internet is, by itself, insufficient for literature reviews. Although many journals and other published information from recognized sources are now available online, the

TABLE 5.1 SWOT Analysis

	HELPFUL	HARMFUL
Internal	**Strengths** • Expertise and skills of start-up group • High-level network of contacts and previous partnerships working on the issue • Documented research expertise and evidence-based understanding • Excellent base of start-up members	**Weaknesses** • Funding not yet available • Not a legal entity • No office/staff • Dependent on voluntary contributions, which is not sustainable
External	**Opportunities** • Well-established trend for similar organizations on comparable welfare issues • National organization has similar recommendations • Existence of multiple agencies bringing welfare to the centre of their organizations' concerns • It is right to support better welfare systems	**Threats** • Perception of difficulty stemming from lack of capacity leading to rejection • Lack of awareness in some constituencies • Lack of national consensus on definitions of welfare—where would we fit? • Differing individual agencies in the environment

Internet does not have *all* available information. Using the Internet can be the base of a literature search, but it needs to be balanced with material in other more obscure documents, with new information in journals and newspapers and periodicals that do not link to the Internet, and with publications that may not be caught in scans by search engines. Likely to be underrepresented are local community materials, materials from marginalized groups, materials from groups that typically have limited computer access, and less formal materials such as letters, diaries, and memos. Material in nonmajority languages is also likely to be underrepresented.

Second, the information available can be uneven. Some of it is peer reviewed and has met accepted academic standards; other information has never been reviewed. New researchers must learn how to discern information that is strong and reliable enough to be useful. Though university libraries can be commonly accessed through the Internet, it is not always evident that the information is presented accurately.

Third, Internet searching can lend itself to a narrow focus on information rather than a broad, more systematic outward search. The tendency online is to move sequentially from one page to the next as ideas or links appear. A systematic and thorough literature search requires cycling back to the search terminology and strategies to ensure adequate coverage of the topic. If you are using the Internet to initiate or carry out a literature search, we recommend documenting the strategy you intend to take so that you can cycle back to the terminology, as well as documenting the route you took to the literature that you found. In short, a number of ways exist for conducting thorough and efficient literature reviews. Our recommendation is that you use the Internet for your literature searches but that you augment that search with information secured from documents from a variety of offline sources.

Step 1: Identify Key Concepts and Terminology. At this point you may have a rough or finely tuned research question in mind. Regardless, you can identify the concepts and terminology that are central to your question. The point here is to imagine the search terms that may elicit the literature needed to inform your literature review. Any research question can be broken down into its individual parts and expanded to create a list of search terms.

Consider the following research question: *What factors influence retired women's involvement in daily physical activity?* The key terms in the research question can be expanded in the following ways:

- "Retired women"—older adults / senior / nonworking / age / gender / female
- "Daily physical activity"—exercise / recreation / leisure / sport / activity

This will allow you to both find a range of literature that will contribute to your literature review and to better define the terms used in the research question.

Step 2: Imagine the Argument and Outline of Your Literature Review. Constructing a literature review, like most aspects of critical social research, is an iterative process, meaning that it does not happen in a linear fashion but often requires "cycling back" to revise, hone, or tighten. Before launching fully into the literature review, imagine the argument that supports your research question. Often the argument comes from the list of problems that led to the research question, as discussed in Chapter 4.

Using the research question, "*What factors influence retired women's involvement in daily physical activity?*" a rough argument could unfold like this:

- There is a well-documented problem with osteoporosis in women who are older—this remains true today despite awareness programs and other strategies (nutrition, supplements, exercise) to remedy this.
- Girls' physical activity levels begin to drop off in adolescence; girls are less active than boys, diet more, and use cigarette smoking and controlled eating to manage their weight.
- Women generally take on the burden of care work (taking care of husbands, children, etc.), which means they often have less discretionary leisure time.
- On average women live longer than men (by 6–7 years), so it is important to address their health and quality-of-life issues as they age.
- Quality-of-life issues are important, both to women who want to improve or maintain their daily physical activity and to the entire health care system, which can benefit from reduced health care costs for those engaged in daily physical activity.

Sketching out the arguments or outline of your literature review will help you focus on the areas you need to cover. When reviewing the literature, always ask yourself, "How does this relate to my question, and why is it important to include?"

Step 3: Build Key Definitions and Context. As the literature review progresses, keep an ongoing list of definitions of terms with references as well as any new terms and their subsequent definitions. This will become a useful mapping tool showing how the research focus is being discussed and how it is shifting and growing. Where there are overlapping definitions, the interconnections between them can be used for understanding relationships and competing discourses and for developing indicators for measurement. As the researcher, you choose the operational definitions for the research project. You might choose broader definitions for projects that are more exploratory or less defined in the earlier stages of research. Conversely, you might choose more narrow definitions if the field of study is complex, has a lot of competing concepts under study, or if your research is focused on a narrow target. We recommend making the choice of definitions only after the array of choices is evident. The definitions chosen then become part of both the limitations (how the research is now limited or circumscribed) and the delimitations (how the research is now enabled or reaching further).

One might also search for frameworks or patterns in what has been written about a topic: How has this phenomenon been understood before, and in what context does that understanding rest? Is it a historical context; a social, political, or economic context; or a biographical context? Gaps evident in definitions or contexts are excellent places for beginning new research.

Step 4: Pursue Jump Offs. As you gather information, each text can serve as a jumping off text for other readings. When reading a document related to your research, look at the reference list. Are new and related references listed? The following example shows how this works:

> In the recently published *Critical Strategies for Social Research* (Carroll, 2004), the concluding chapter on convergences, complementarities, and tensions was thought provoking. The notes and the reference list held several keys for where to search next for information. I made special note of the following:
>
>> Campbell, M., & Gregor, F. (2002). *Mapping social relations.* Toronto: Garamond.
>> Fraser, N. (1997). *Justice interruptus.* New York: Routledge.
>> Reid, C. (2000). Seduction and enlightenment in feminist action research. *Resources for Feminist Research, 28*, 169–188.
>
> Since I was interested in homophobia in sport, I found the concept of cultural positivity (Fraser, 1997) essential to getting away from the binary and into more transformative politics around such discriminations. For participatory action research (PAR), I found Campbell and Gregor (2002) useful for their reconceptualization of institutional contexts. They did this by using power relations to rethink social settings so that the resulting analysis is "in the interest of those

about whom the knowledge is being constructed" (Carroll, 2004, p. 386).
For feminist action research (FAR), I found the notion of
democratizing the interpersonal relations among research participants
and voice appropriation in Reid (2000) to be a useful overall
constructs for my work. (Kirby, 2005)

Step 5: Track and Map Authors. Make a list of authors who appear in the literature and conduct an "author search" on each. Use the following questions to
probe the authors you are seeing:

- What else have they written and is it useful for this topic?
- Do the various authors on the list reference each other? Is it a closed
  network of authors communicating with each other, or is it a loose
  link of a wide variety of authors who write only tangentially about this
  research topic?
- Do some of the authors make themselves visible in the texts they write
  by providing biographic information?
- Who are the principal or central authors referred to in virtually all the
  references?
- What are their main points of agreement and where do they disagree?
  What gaps are evident in their debates?

If there are some authors who have written extensively on your topic,
you may consider searching for their professional website that contains a list
of publications.

Step 6: Establish a Personal Search Pattern. Marlene Boersch, an agricultural
economist, gave the following description of how she conducts literature
searches using search engines. Her work is largely oriented to recently published
materials and to grey literature. First, she recommends that searchers think from
big to small. The best search engines are more concrete and can save lots of
time. Locate search engines tied to the topic: for example, some are focused
on agricultural topics, sport topics, health topics, and so on. Narrow it down.
Record the sites you really like (into "Favourites" on the drop-down menu,
for instance). Some people maintain a long list of favourites, particularly if they
change topics frequently. Others group their favourites into *subfiles* for easy,
regular access. Boersch describes the following approach:

I write an outline of what I want to find. I copy the web addresses by
topic into the outline. Since I search frequently, I search by topic and
I make note of where and what is useful in each address. Then I start

> back through and look at the material in detail . . . I keep what I want
> by copying into my base file at that point. I keep a reference list going
> as I look for material on the second look through. I take the references
> down and drop them into an EndNote program; I also put an asterisk
> or other highlighting feature to mark a particular file as very useful
> for cross-projects. I keep key web addresses to link into networks
> of information I use frequently. Also, I keep the web file address
> right in the document for interactive material that I might use, such
> as a video clip or an interview transcript record. (Boersch, personal
> communication, 17 January 2005)

Boersch recommends that you create a single file. Everything then can be copied into the one file and a backup can be regularly maintained. Whatever the format, it is essential to date files as changes are made, such as adding material or reorganizing material. If more than one person needs access to the file (in the case of a research team or for editing purposes), the files can be clearly labelled.

Step 7: Use Academic Databases to Ensure a Thorough Search. There are hundreds of academic databases—some require subscriptions and others are free. Typically college and university libraries have a wide range of search engines available to their students and faculty. Academic libraries have a wide range of indexes and databases that can guide literature searching. For example, the University of British Columbia's library has its indexes and catalogues organized by subject, and within each subject there are 1 to 14 databases listed and described.

Step 8: Link Qualitative and Quantitative Searches. Dedicated sites can be used to search repositories of information. Statistics Canada databases (e.g., Census Program, www12.statcan.gc.ca/census-recensement/index-eng.cfm), the General Social Survey in the United States (http://gss.norc.org), and World Bank international data (http://data.worldbank.org) are examples of different databases maintained that are accessible to the general public. Universities, organizations, businesses, and governments may maintain versions of dedicated sites for use by authorized individuals and more general sites for public use. There are also websites created specifically to serve as repositories for particular information, for example on AIDS research, tobacco use, poverty, employment figures, and so on.

Step 9: Ensure a Thorough Search. When conducting a review of the literature, we recommend that you combine Internet searches with more traditional reviews of material (documents, books, articles, newspapers, magazines, peri-odicals, laws, etc.), usual and atypical sources and sites, and primary with sec-ondary sources. Information located in such searches may be uneven, and you will learn to recognize which is which and how to attribute weight to differ-ent forms of information. While peer-reviewed materials carry the academic "stamp of approval," the grey literature can also be reviewed by peers and exists outside the academy for many reasons—accessibility, freedom, speed of publication, different knowledge translation goals, and different audiences—and is valuable in its own right.

You will need a variety of literatures from a variety of publishing contexts that may be uneven in theoretical and methodological strength. But the review of the literature includes the raw material for analysis of the theoretical and methodological positions taken to date on the research question. As such, the review provides the background information for the arguments a researcher makes for the need for and direction of a study. Secure copies of and complete references for material (whether it came from an interlibrary loan, was an elec-tronic copy, etc.) are important, and whenever possible information should be tracked back to its original source and read first hand, rather than in a pre-interpreted or second-hand form. For example, if something interesting from LaRiviere (2004) is quoted in Jamieson (2005), search for the original LaRiviere document and use it in the review. It is important to ensure that it is *your* reading and interpretation of the material.

Step 10: Create a Literature Map. One strategy for gaining a "high-level" understanding of the literature you are covering, and for ensuring that you have conducted a comprehensive literature search, is to create a *literature map*. Creswell (2014) describes literature maps as a useful approach to conceptualize and organize a literature review. It may also be more effective for people who think and work in more visual ways. The map provides a high-level summary or overview of the literature that will be covered. It can be organized hierarchically, circularly, or as a flowchart. The central idea is that you begin to build a visual picture of existing research about your topic and question. Follow Exercise 5.1 to create your own literature map.

Exercise 5.1: Creating a literature map

- Write your topic or research question at the top or side of the page. If you choose the top of the page, the organization will be more hierarchical. If it's at one side of the page, the map will be a flowchart. And if the topic is in the middle of the page, it will demonstrate more circular relationships.

- Review the materials you have gathered for your literature search. Organize them into broad topics. Topics can be identified by unpacking the "arguments" that will justify your research question. Or a topic may be a concept or theory that is central to your study.
- Examine closely the articles, books, and other materials you have gathered. Determine subtopics within the topics. Ask yourself, "How and in what ways does this study help me understand my research question?" You are moving toward greater specificity.
- Consider levels in the literature map. Not all subtopics or ideas within them are equal. Major topics lead to subtopics, which then lead to sub-subtopics.
- Some branches of the map will be more developed than others. This will depend on how much literature is available and how deeply you examine the literature.
- After drafting the literature map, consider which areas of the map, or which branches, provide a springboard for your own study.

Adapted from Creswell, 2014.

Step 11: Avoid Plagiarism. Plagiarism is presenting "another person's words or ideas as if they were your own. A kind of theft" (Payton, 2005, p. 23). Avoiding plagiarism can be done by keeping meticulous records of ideas and from where they have come. Paraphrasing, copying ideas, and summarizing a list of ideas need referencing, albeit in slightly different formats (Babbie & Benaquisto, 2010). Referencing and quoting from sources are hallmarks of both the skill of the researcher and the thoroughness of his or her literature review. What counts as plagiarism can be confusing for many new researchers. We recommend using a tool such as Turnitin (www.turnitin.com) to help learn about and identify where you are at risk of plagiarism. We cover additional issues regarding plagiarism when we discuss the final report in Chapter 10.

Literature reviews typically result in large volumes of material that need to be brought into some form of rationale or argument useful for proposing the research project. Keep the literature search straightforward. Locate and use information that is directly rather than tangentially connected to the research question. Keep it organized and keep an up-to-date listing of all sources. Establish a framework for the arguments to be used as soon as feasible, and fill in the framework with information as it becomes available. If the search has been diligent, what is missing at the end can be considered a gap in the research. At this point, the review of the literature should be a stand-alone document, though in the case of emergent research the process of reviewing and analyzing the literature may not be complete until the project itself is drawing to a close.

The format for a review of the literature varies depending on the topic, the amount of information available, and the rules of a funding application, thesis, or published article. A helpful hint is to look at a table of contents for a book, thesis, or dissertation (see the box below), or look at the titles and subtitles used throughout a text. It is relatively easy to find the overall structure for various reviews of literature in this way.

SAMPLE OUTLINE OF A LITERATURE REVIEW

Title: Sexual Exploitation: Swimming Coaches Perceptions and the Development of Role Conflict and Role Ambiguity

Chapter 2: Contextual Background
    2.1 Introduction
    2.2 Historical and Cultural Context
    2.3 Legal Context
    2.4 Swimming Context
    2.5 Backlash and Critique
    2.6 Summary
Chapter 3: Sexual Harassment and Abuse in Sport: Concepts and Research
    3.1 Introduction
    3.2 Concepts
    3.3 Prevalence of Sexual Exploitation in Sport
        3.3.1 Introduction to Prevalence Studies
        3.3.2 Prevalence of Sexual Harassment in Sport
        3.3.3 Prevalence of Sexual Abuse in Sport
        3.3.4 Critique of the Prevalence Studies (and Methodologies Used)
        3.3.5 Qualitative Research on Survivors Experiences
    3.4 Summary
Chapter 4: Epistemology, Theoretical Perspective, and Methodology
    4.1 Introduction
    4.2 Epistemology
    4.3 The Fallacy of the Qualitative/Quantitative Divide
    4.4 Grounded Theory Methodology
    4.5 Evaluating Research
    4.6 Quality in Qualitative Research
    4.7 Computer-Assisted Qualitative Data Analysis

Bringer, J. (2002). *Sexual exploitation: Swimming coaches' perceptions and the development of role conflict and role ambiguity.* Unpublished doctoral dissertation, University of Gloucestershire, UK, p. vii.

Note the expanded section of Chapter 3, where the detail of the subsection shows just how prevalence was introduced, described, and critiqued. This is an excellent example of the literature presentation pattern that includes the essentials of describing and critiquing information on the content and substance of the literature and of the methods used.

After the review of the literature, the research question can be revisited and possibly reconceptualized. For explanatory or descriptive research, this might mean reaching for more precision, more clarity, more simplicity, or more definition. For exploratory work, this might mean ensuring that the direction the research question points the researcher in is appropriate and comprehensive enough for the task at hand. The questions "have to be answerable, at some level, with reference to the empirical world (the world of the senses)" (Esterberg, 2002, p. 28). In contractual research, the research question that is provided to you needs to be pulled into its component parts, definitions attached to each of the keywords or concepts, and then put back together again. Then you must check with the contractor to ensure that there is a clear understanding of the research task at hand.

Table 5.2 shows additional examples of how questions have been clarified after the review of the literature is well underway. The first draft of the research question is followed by a more precise and hence more answerable second question.

How do you know when you have the right question? The research question is correct when (a) you live with it for a while and it remains the same; (b) you communicate it verbally or in writing to a few others and it holds its shape and order; (c) it makes sense in the real world and is answerable; (d) it does not create subquestions (such as "Which people?" "What

TABLE 5.2 Example of Research Question Drafts

Is abortion a good or bad thing? (Esterberg, 2002, p. 30)	What is the experience of abortion like for urban women over the age of 30?
What is the nature and scope of violence against gay men?	What is the nature and scope of physical violence against gay youth in rural and remote areas of Canada?
What is the role of creative arts activities for people living with concurrent disorder and their recovery?	In what ways do creative arts activities influence the recovery of people living with concurrent disorders?

do you mean by the terms X, Y, and Z?" or "Are there not three or four different questions in here? Which are you after?"); (e) it does not lead to a close-ended "yes" or "no" answer; and (f) the meaning and definitions assigned to the question can be supported with the literature. A good research question will suddenly feel right. It will feel simple and to the point. The possibilities for how to find data to answer the question begin to percolate, and the focus of the researcher shifts rapidly into brainstorming for ways to answer such a question. In sum, it is right when you are comfortable enough with the question and feel it will sustain you through the rest of the research process.

Refining the Research Question and the Research Purpose

The literature review will help you think more carefully and critically about your research question. Are you asking a question that is answerable? Is your question important to answer, and if so, why? Who will want to hear about your research? Has anyone attempted to address this question in the past? Which disciplines are engaging in discussions related to your research question?

In Chapter 4 we moved through the conceptual funnel (Marshall & Rossman, 2016) to help you narrow down your research question: You moved from interest to focus to question. Now, with some understanding of the literature that relates to your question, you can confirm that your question is exciting, important, and doable. You may also find that some refocusing is needed.

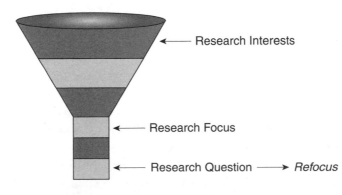

FIGURE 5.2: The Conceptual Funnel Revisited

To confirm the research question, "say it out loud." Does the question you have selected make sense, is it clear, and will it be something to which you can commit? Does it describe the research interest? Is there a way to reword it for greater clarity? Every word in the question must count and be precisely chosen. If one part of the question doesn't work, continue to refocus it. A useful strategy for refining your research question is to consider the research topic, problem, and purpose.

Exercise 5.2: Clarifying the research question

Approaching your research question from different perspectives can be helpful. Clearly and concisely answering the following questions should enable you to refocus and refine your research question:

- *What is the topic?* This is a statement of your general research interest(s).
- *What are the problems*? This can relate to what is known in the literature; what you have experienced in your life, your community, at work, or at school; or a societal issue that is concerning to you.
- *What is the purpose?* This is a statement of what you want to accomplish with your research. Why is this research important to you?
- *What is the research question?*

Once you have answered the questions in Exercise 5.2, consider the following example:

Topic: Career trajectories in therapeutic recreation.
Problems: Therapeutic recreation practitioners report low job satisfaction, job instability, and high turnover.
Purpose: To better understand the factors that lead to job satisfaction in the field of therapeutic recreation.
Research Question: What factors are most important in career satisfaction for recreation therapists?

This example is drawn from a student's one-semester research project. It was a doable and realistic project and reflected her own interests in her chosen profession. It was also an important question to pursue since the field of therapeutic recreation is relatively new and struggling for greater professionalism.

Thoughtfully engaging in this reflexive process by exploring these questions will reveal whether the nature of your research is primarily exploratory, descriptive, explanatory, change oriented, or some combination of these. Each is defined in Table 5.3, with examples.

TABLE 5.3 Kinds of Research Questions

Exploratory research - To investigate little-understood phenomena - To identify or discover important categories of meaning - To generate hypotheses for further research	Example: What is happening in this program? What kind of impact does it have?
Descriptive research - To document and describe the phenomenon of interest	Example: What are the most important aspects (actions, events, beliefs, attitudes, social structures, processes) of the program?
Explanatory research - To explain the patterns related to the phenomenon in question - To identify plausible relationships shaping the phenomenon	Example: Which participants are most likely to report a positive experience with the program and why?
Emancipatory/social change research - To create opportunities and the will to engage in social action	Example: What factors enable participants to take action to improve the program?

Ask yourself whether you are exploring a new and relatively unknown phenomenon, or whether you are describing something—an experience, sensation, or observation—or trying to explain a relationship between two things or between a type of person and some kind of experience. Drawing on the literature can help you determine the purpose of your research. You may learn that the phenomenon is not well understood or investigated in the literature and therefore your purpose is exploratory. Or you may uncover a range and depth of literature, in which case you may consider a more explanatory purpose to contribute to what is already known. Many social change researchers explicitly name social change as the intention of their research. The project aims to identify changes needed, generate a list of recommendations, and so on. Sometimes it is not entirely clear if the project is exploratory, descriptive, explanatory, or social change oriented, and indeed some projects are blended in purpose. Regardless, it will be necessary for you to be able to clearly and concisely articulate the topic, problem, purpose, and question of your research project.

Particularly in exploratory and descriptive research, research questions can change direction midstream. This is not a sign of weakness or poor thinking; rather, it indicates that as one engages in the research the question becomes clearer because more becomes known about the phenomenon of interest. Here's an example:

In partnership with the Coalition for Women's Economic Advancement, Colleen conducted a three-year community-based research project in four British Columbia communities to answer the question "What is the relationship between women's work and their safety, health, and well-being?" The project emerged from observations made by service providers who reported that important community and provincial supports were no longer available, government policies were increasingly "unfriendly" to women, women were more likely to be involved in precarious and dangerous work, and women's health and safety were at risk. As the project progressed, the research team revised the research question to be more precise: "What factors shape diverse women's employability across British Columbia?" and "What is the impact of being seen as employable on women's subjective health and well-being?" (Reid & LeDrew, 2013)

It is essential to work with a well-defined research question. A concise and clear question will mean that the data you gather are more likely to be directly related to your question rather than related only in a tangential way. Patience is key, since even the most experienced researchers often find framing the right question difficult. Persevere; use your friends, colleagues, co-researchers, or people in your community to better define the question; live with the question for a while to see if it makes sense to you and others; then commit to it. This will help to maintain your focus throughout the research process.

AN EXAMPLE OF A SECTION OF A LITERATURE REVIEW

The research questions guiding this study were (a) What factors shape diverse women's employability across British Columbia? (b) What is the impact of being seen as employable on women's subjective health and well-being?

Employability-Based Approaches

Initially, the concept of employability described a disabled person's capacity for employment. As liberal labour market policies strove to "wean the hardest-to-employ people off long-term state programs" the concept shifted to include delinquents, ex-convicts and eventually women (White, 2001, p. 6). These same market policies also maintained that the state had neither the responsibility nor the capacity to create jobs. The causes of unemployment were conceived in individualistic and behavioural terms: the old problems of demand deficiency and job shortage were dismissed, and policies needed to focus on the motivations and expectations of the "work-less class" (Peck & Theodore, 2000, p. 729). Not taking into consideration the supply and demand of labour perpetuated the idea that credentials, knowledge and social status alone guaranteed a good position in the labour market (Brown & Hesketh, 2004).

Although women in both developing and developed countries saw significant improvements to their socioeconomic status after World War I, "economic adjustments undertaken globally since the 1980s halted and even reversed this progress" (McDaniel, 2002, p. 127). Employability-based approaches to labour market policy are typical examples of these economic adjustments. Over the last 30 years, many industrialized countries have shifted the responsibility for the social safety net from the state to women's own shoulders by classifying them as employable (Baker, 1996; Baker & Tippin, 2002; Day with Brodsky, 2007; Morris, 2000; Stratigaki, 2004; Porter, 2003). However women face challenges to their employability for societal as well as individual reasons. The unavailability of quality childcare, the lack of public affordable transportation and the inflexibility of employment opportunities can hardly be viewed in individualistic terms (Berry, 2008). According to Peck and Theodore (2000), "employability-based approaches are not sufficient to the task of tackling unemployment, social exclusion, and economic inequality" (p. 731). Certainly, they address neither women's chronic poverty nor the nuances and implications of women's unpaid care giving work.

Source: Excerpt from Reid, C., & LeDrew, R. (2013). The burden of being "employable": Under- and unpaid work and women's health. *AFFILIA: Journal of Women and Social Work*, 28(1):79–93. doi: 10.1177/ 0886109913476944

Research should fill a knowledge gap, make it possible to facilitate change to make someone's experience better, or create a policy that can direct future changes. Research might give people a new perspective on their experience. It might provide new understandings of experiences so that more people have access to and engage in debates about it. Research might add to the way we currently understand the world—giving something a new spin, a new direction, or a new shift. What we find out might make a difference to someone in this world. With research people can change how they think about something, hear things for the first time or in a new way, or act because they understand the world differently than before.

Summary

The review of literature section is an important part of the ongoing process of building knowledge and choosing research routes that are feasible for you. We consider literature like voices: Some get heard more often or more easily than others. In the case of peer-reviewed publications, others have approved them as contributions to knowledge. Much other knowledge may come to you by other means. We encourage you to search wherever you can and to carefully balance the knowledge gathered.

In this chapter we described and provided support for conducting a disciplined and focused literature review that can be used to refocus and refine your research question. We present numerous tips for conducting a literature review in a context where information is rapidly available through a wide variety of sources. We hope you develop a discerning eye to determine what information is reliable, useful, and appropriate to your research needs. It is important to be as clear and concise as you can on the research question before you progress much further. By this point in your research process the overall conception of your research project should be clear. Next, choices must be made about the appropriate techniques for data gathering and analysis and the presentation of the data.

Questions for Discussion

1. Why conduct a literature review? What is the purpose?
2. What are the differences between peer-reviewed and grey literature? Published and unpublished literature?
3. What are the most effective strategies for conducting a literature review?
4. How can you be sure that you have done an adequate job with your literature review?
5. How does the literature review help you refine your research question?
6. Why is your study important? What is the problem you are seeking to address?

Our Recommended Readings

Cooper, H. (1998). *Applied social research methods series: Vol. 2. Synthesizing research: A guide for literature reviews* (3rd ed.). Thousand Oaks: Sage.

Fink, A. (2014). *Conducting research literature reviews: From the internet to the paper* (4th ed.). Los Angeles: Sage.

Ridley, D. (2012). *The literature review: A step-by-step guide for students* (2nd ed.). Los Angeles: Sage.

CHAPTER 6

HOW? RESEARCH METHODS

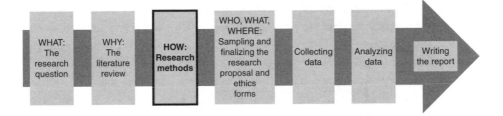

FIGURE 6.1: The Research Process

In this chapter you will learn about investigating the research question and making informed choices about which methods to use. The approaches to critical social research that are included in this chapter are observations, interviews and focus groups, questionnaires, and content analysis. Examples of case studies, photovoice, digital storytelling, and life histories illustrate the use of single and multiple methods. For each method described, exercises are provided so you can develop your data gathering skills. While a range of other methods are covered elsewhere (see Creswell, 2014; Marshall & Rossman, 2016), we focus on these methods as they are most commonly used in social change-oriented research. By the end of this chapter you will be able to choose the method(s) that will best answer your research question.

Investigating the Research Question

Quantitative approaches are capable of clearly laying out the rules for defining and establishing changes in variables (Del Basto & Lewis, 1997) because quantitative data are numerical—that is, they represent relationships between numbers. The notion of "measurement" in qualitative research is used differently because many social experiences cannot be precisely measured with variables and qualitative data can include text, images, music, colour, texture, and so on. Qualitative data provide meanings people attach to things, the ways that experiences are interpreted, and so on. Although qualitative research takes place in the natural world, and as such focuses on context and is "emergent and fundamentally interpretive" (Marshall & Rossman, 2016, p. 3; for a discussion of qualitative research, refer to Chapter 1), research tools can assist with the quantification of certain types of qualitative information. For example, research participants' demographic information, such as age, sex, education, income, occupation, and country of origin, can provide indices for more precise measurement. The collection and use of demographic information is covered in more depth in Chapters 7 and 9.

Whether you are using qualitative, quantitative, or mixed methods, it is necessary to develop operational definitions for terms critical to the research question. For example, if you were interested in measuring the distance travelled between school and home, you would specify that distance is defined as the number of kilometres travelled door to door, one way, on a school day. If you were interested in feelings of fatigue experienced on the trip between school and home, you might ask for a description of how one travelled from home to school and how one felt on this trip on different days of the week. Qualitatively you might determine that descriptions of the experience of fatigue are different depending on which day of the week the person is travelling. Quantitatively you might determine that female participants with lower incomes reported highest rates of fatigue. To complete the operationalization of terms, you must set the criteria for data gathering. In this way, you can describe or measure what is needed to answer the research question.

Operationalizing the research question involves completing four steps, which will move you all the way from defining your key terms or factors to selecting methods for data gathering. The four steps are as follows:

Concept → Indicators → Measurements → Methods

Operationalizing Your Research Question

A good way to illustrate how to move through the four steps of operationalization is to follow a specific example. If we take the example of sexual harassment and abuse in sport through the operationalization steps, it might appear as follows:

Research question: What are female athletes' experiences of sexual harassment and abuse in sport?

Concepts: sexual harassment and abuse in sport

- Social context for the terms harassment and abuse and overlap between the terms
- Absence of definitional consensus among researchers
- Consent as an issue for children and adults
- Unwanted attention of a sexual nature
- Need to protect children
- Pedophiles and abusers
- Sexual exploitation within the family
- Sexual exploitation within the "sport" family
- Sport as a social climate/culture where discrimination is tolerated
- Intention of the harasser or abuser

Unpacking the concepts related to the research question appears as a list of things to consider. Choices need to be made about precisely what counts as sexual harassment for the study. The literature review can help identify and shape the precise concepts and terms that will be used for the study. If key concepts or terms are not included for consideration in the study, then it is important to be able to articulate why you chose not to use them.

In this example, the following terms were repeated in the literature and held the research question together and thus became part of the definition: Harm to athletes in a sport environment is defined as nonaccidental violence or maltreatment through harassment and abuse (Mountjoy et al., 2016). Within that, sexual harassment and abuse is defined as unwanted attention of a sexual nature and/or sexual exploitation (Brackenridge, 1999; Bringer, 2002; Kirby, Greaves, & Hankivsky, 2000).

Indicators: multiple

- Rates of detection of abuse in the sport context
- Reports of risk
- Rates of trauma
- Number of perpetrators
- Experiences of unwanted sexual attention
- Vulnerability to sexual attention
- Number of suggestive comments
- Number of obscene phone calls
- Experiences seeing or hearing about sexual abuse

- Sexual orientation
- Transgender and transsexual issues
- Relationships with persons central or peripheral to the athlete's sport experiences

What was needed was a selection of available indicators, each of which could be measured and which together covered the nature and scope of the harassment issue. Indicators chosen included descriptions and accounting of athletes' most traumatic experiences in the sport environment of (1) suggestive comments, (2) sexist jokes, (3) forms of discrimination in the sport environment, (4) pornography, (5) sexual touching, and (6) sexual assault, including intercourse with a person on whom the athlete is dependent.

Measurement: qualitative and participant demographics

The need to capture athletes' perspective suggests that an interactive method be used to measure the quality (meaning) of the athletes' experiences and to capture their stories about those experiences. We settled on a four-part approach: (a) what the athletes know about sexual harassment, (b) what they have seen or heard about it among athletes, (c) what they have personally experienced, and (d) what actions they took, if any.

Measurements chosen included a sampling of athletes who have had any one or more of the above experiences and develop questions to allow them to indicate which of the experiences (1 to 6) they have had and to prepare a narrative for each. Probes included descriptions of the sport context, the age and level of sport performance of the athlete, the perpetrator, and the event (how it developed, action that was unwanted, short- and long-term outcome for the athlete and the perpetrator, whether the sexual harassment or sexual exploitation was reported).

Methods: one-on-one interviews and face sheets

From one-on-one interviews, we identified the accounts athletes provide about each of the indicators (1 to 6). We also identified other indicators that arose from the narratives. Component parts of each account were coded (a coding strategy in an iterative, reflexive manner was developed). Other indicators that arose during the analysis of the narratives were fully incorporated into the research.

In research proposals, operationalization contributes to the precision of the research and has multiple design implications for the researcher. The farther you move along the operationalization path, the more specific and precise the research becomes.

Exercise 6.1: Operationalizing a research question

The research question is "In what ways does the use of social networking sites influence postsecondary students' social relationships?" In your journal document the following:

Concept → Indicators → Measurements → Methods

Ensure that you move logically from one step to the next. Use a peer or colleague to debrief your responses.

Large and small projects alike follow the same path of operationalizing the concepts, indicators, measurements, and methods. Importantly, the choice of methods comes after the development of the research question. It is surprisingly common for researchers to choose the method before identifying the research question; however, we believe that it is important to choose what you will research before you choose how to research it.

Use operational definitions to solidify the intended meaning of a concept (e.g., length = kilometre; sexual harassment = unwanted sexual attention) and the agreed-upon meaning assigned to the term(s) (Babbie & Benaquisto, 2010). Failure to operationalize carefully can be disastrous later in terms of low validity or reliability. It can mean collecting and analyzing data but never answering the question. As much as possible, be precise with your definitions so that they are relevant and measurable. When possible, identify more than one dimension of the concept and use multiple indicators. It is important to be consistent when moving from concept to indicator. Concepts and indicators must be closely aligned since the indicator is how you will investigate the concept. You can rely on the literature for key concepts, indicators, and definitions; in fact, looking to the literature can help you generate new ways of thinking about or looking for data to answer the research question. Finally, you may find it useful to get help with operationalization from classmates, instructors, co-workers, friends, key informants, or whoever is available.

Designing a Research Plan

How can you get the information needed to answer the research question? We recommend that you move from paradigm to research design to data collection. In Chapter 1 we wrote that research needs to be guided by ideas about how things work (the paradigm) and that, as researchers, we adopt a position about how we can know ourselves in the world. For the research plan, we recommend that you start with a rough map:

- Identify which paradigm (positivist, constructivist, critical; see Chapter 1) you are using.
- Determine which design you are using and why—state the rationale for your choices.
- Sketch out possible research designs and some strategies for data gathering.

Paradigm → Research Design → Data Collection

At this point you need to go back to the big picture. How you do research is inextricably linked to how you see the world. Methodology, theory, and ideology are intertwined. Methods, which are derived from methodology, are the means by which information is gathered. Methods are your tools in the toolbox, and a unique mix of tools may be needed to answer your research question. Researchers choose particular methods to unearth information because some methods permit them to gather types of information they think are important. Again, we position the research question *before* the choice of methods and encourage multiple methods. Whether or not to use a particular method "is not a methodological choice but a choice of what is to be studied. It is defined by an interest in an individual case, not by the methods of inquiry used" (Stake, 2005, p. 443).

CHECKING ASSUMPTIONS

Written by Deirdre Kelly and Allison Tom

Research that focuses on learning how people actually conduct their lives is exciting and demanding. Done right, it can confirm or challenge our assumptions and can also bring previously unnoticed assumptions and patterns of behaviour to our attention.

During the "second wave" of feminist activism and research in North America, attention focused not only on gender inequalities in the public spheres of politics, law, and employment, but also on gender inequalities within the domestic sphere. Specifically, these feminists argued that the work of maintaining a home and raising a family continued to be distributed unevenly between men and women even when women were employed as many hours as their male partners were. This gut feeling that irked many individual women was explored and substantiated by interviews with and observations of employed married couples by Arlie Hochschild and her associates in the project that generated the classic book *The Second Shift* (Hochschild & Machung, 1989). Hochschild was able to demonstrate that women in such couples spent significantly more time caring for children, preparing and cleaning up after meals, and doing housework than their husbands, while men spent more time watching television and sleeping.

Research can also challenge our initial assumptions. Anthropologist Mark Moritz (2013), in the context of teaching ethnographic methods to graduate students through conducting a collaborative research project, shared his initial assumption that students' use of social media, smartphones, and other mobile technologies during class impeded their learning. In a collaborative inquiry into this question, Moritz and his students actually found no evidence for this; indeed, the biggest factor affecting students' in-class engagement (used as a proxy for learning) was the (often ineffective) way instructors used PowerPoint!

Finally, research can bring previously unnoticed patterns of behaviour to the fore. When Allison Tom teaches research methods courses, she asks students to observe how individuals manage personal space on public transit. Students have often begun their assignment with the belief that residents of Vancouver, British Columbia, live comfortably and easily within the city's diversity of ethnicity, immigration status, language, and class. As they notice and record how people boarding the bus choose where to sit, they are often surprised to discover that individuals not only follow the familiar North American pattern of first choosing to sit in unoccupied seats or rows but then, as the bus fills and seats must be shared, choosing seat mates in clearly distinguishable patterns. When choice is available, they notice, women tend to sit next to other women, men and women both tend to sit next to others who appear to belong to their ethnic group, and both men and women tend to sit first beside people of their own age. Students have discussed and analyzed how these seating patterns challenge their assumptions that Vancouver residents mix with each other without "noticing" or reacting to observable differences between them.

In Chapter 1 we made the case that the selection of methods is a critical and political aspect of research and is usually based on worldviews as well as the kind of information sought, from whom, and under what circumstances. It is important to recognize that methods appropriate for gathering abstract, theoretical information will not be appropriate for gathering subjective experiences. Also, different kinds of knowledge require different data gathering methods. The research plan is designed to cover, in a step-by-step manner, how the data are to be gathered, from whom, when, and where. It also includes the data gathering instruments (e.g., questions on questionnaires, criteria for observations, interview questions), a plan for managing the data, and an analytical framework to make sense of the data and to answer the research question.

The data that you will gather come in the form of numbers, words, or images. *Data* are a collection of information or facts usually gathered as the result of experience, observation, or experiment. The four data gathering methods explored in this chapter are (a) observations (including participant observations); (b) interviews (including one-on-one and focus groups/group interviews); (c) questionnaires (including in person, online, and telephone); and (d) content analysis (including print, visual, and auditory). These methods were chosen because they are used most often in critical social research and because developing your familiarity and skill with them is foundational for tackling more complex methods.

For the methods described in detail in this chapter we have included specific practice exercises and additional readings. The exercises give you an opportunity to improve your research design and data gathering skills and are also intended as fun and instructional experiences. We recommend that you "try on" some data gathering methods, as identified in the practice tasks, to see which ones work best for you and are appropriate for your research focus. In addition, we ask that you refer back to Chapter 3 to the section on research ethics. You can be as creative in the practice exercises as you like as long as you are always aware that, as a researcher, you must be respectful of others. Since you are using the exercises to develop your skills, choose general topics that will allow you to practise but will not compromise or harm the people who are helping you learn the skills in any way. As a researcher, you have ethical responsibilities. Your overall goal is to gather a small amount of data with each practice task in a helpful and safe manner.

Method 1: Observations

Observation is an everyday skill, and the information we gather allows us to make our way through each day in a relatively orderly and reasonable way. Observation is the cornerstone of the inquiry process since it begins an investigation and continues throughout it. It involves a researcher's disciplined, repeated, and focused observation "in the field" of people's behaviours, evidence of those behaviours, and the meanings people attach to them. Observation involves the researcher observing social life in its natural habitat. Richly detailed qualitative data allow researchers to closely describe and explain people's behaviours and the patterns that emerge, and also to propose theories that help to explain those patterns. Fieldnotes are the observations written by a researcher at a research site, during an interview, and throughout the data collection process; see Chapter 4 for a complete description of fieldnotes.

Generally, there are three types of observation: researcher as participant, participant observation, and unobtrusive observation. A number of research methodologies are associated with social observation, including ethnography, ethnomethodology, phenomenology, social constructionism, grounded theory, trace or forensic analysis, and case studies. In critical social research, observation most often involves direct contact with individuals or groups of people in their natural environment. As a researcher you might, for example, sit on a park bench and record the activity in a nearby area, talk with a person who sits on the bench for a short time, offer a bandage to the boy who fell off the swing, and teach one of the girls to do a forward roll when she asks. Information gathering involves various degrees of participation. For our purposes the two forms of observation that are most commonly used in critical social research—researcher as participant and participant observation—are discussed here.[1]

Before determining what kind of observation you'll conduct or how you will record your observations, it is necessary to consider *why* you may choose observations. Here we draw on several examples. In the first, Allison and her colleagues used observations to better understand a research site. Allison explains:

> I often use mapping as an early activity when I am beginning research at a new site. It provides an excellent way to be introduced to people who work, live, or study in the area.
>
> When I began my research project into the ways adult literacy programs were and were not living up to their mandates, my first activity was to map the classrooms, office spaces, lunchroom, and open study space of this large program. An experienced teacher and I walked through the entire site, and he described to me the different activities that took place in the various rooms. Students were introduced to me in a causal way, and we invited

....

1 Unobtrusive measures are "any method of observation that directly removes the observer from the set of interactions or events being studied" (Denzin, 1988, p. 260). If you observe a group from a position distinctly outside the group, this would be unobtrusive. We feel that it is ethically indefensible to gather information about people's interactions without having permission to do so unless such information is on public record or unless extremely unusual circumstances make such permission unobtainable.

them to help us estimate the sizes of the rooms, identify spaces' important features, and collect examples of the uses to which the spaces were put.

This mapping allowed me to collect fresh pictures of how the program appeared to me when I was still an outsider, it engaged both students and teachers in neutral activities that showed my interest in learning about what happened at their school, and it gave me an excellent overview of both formal and informal aspects of the programs that research participants might not have remembered otherwise. For example, it brought to light the fact that there were no spaces that were off limits to students in the program. This detail supported and illustrated how the teachers and administrators in the program really did create an environment of maximum equality and respect between themselves and the adult students learning with them. (Tom et al., 1994)

Regular, systematic observation and participation allow researchers to capture moments that illuminate important social dynamics. During Deirdre's ethnographic research about teen sexuality and parenting in high schools in British Columbia, she was struck by the contrast between students' relatively high rate of sexual activity and adults' silences around sexuality issues of all kinds:

I observed a similar "don't ask, don't tell" policy at work in an elective class, Human Behavior 11. The teacher had invited a public health nurse to speak on contraception, and she relied on an up-to-date and comprehensive fact sheet prepared by Planned Parenthood. But the teacher announced that it was too difficult to get school and parental permission to distribute the brochure, and the samples being passed around would have to be collected at the end of class. Only one fact sheet made it back to the teacher, however; the rest were quietly slipped into student backpacks. The facts that contraception was available through a local health clinic without parental consent for those 14 years and older and was free to low-income youths and for a minimal cost to others were neither publicized nor widely known. (Kelly, 2000, p. 154)

This observation revealed that students valued information about sexual health and gathered it when they could.

A particularly useful type of observation is shadowing participants through their daily activities. Deirdre has used this strategy in all of her school-based qualitative studies. Shadowing allowed her to learn the in situ vocabulary used in a particular setting before ever conducting a formal interview. It provided (a) background information that allowed for asking better questions, (b) a check on what people were saying in formal interviews, and (c) a powerful reminder of what secondary schools typically demand of students and teachers, both emotionally and physically. Deirdre comments:

> After a day spent shadowing a young mother nursing her baby at the school's onsite daycare, through various academic courses, then to the bus stop, my fieldnotes were filled with comments about what a long, exhausting day it had been. In another school ethnography, one of my research assistants commented, "Strange phenomenon to structure and live one's life according to 60 minute periods—this is how the world gets constructed, 5 days a week, 5 periods a day for teacher and student alike." Besides capturing the mundane schedule, shadowing also revealed the occasional break in the routine. For example, while shadowing one student to the "smoke pit" during lunch, I bumped into an administrator taking a smoke break of his own. At another school, one of my research assistants made a trip to the vice-principal's office when the student he was shadowing ran afoul of a teacher during lunchtime.

Researcher as Participant

Critical social research allows for the possibility that the researcher is a participant, one who already occupies a legitimate group position. A nonparticipant stance is unlikely for this person, hence a participant or member role with a researcher's skill applied to the research task may be the best combination. Such a participant continues to be a participant after the research is completed.[2] Since the participant observer is known in the group, the degree of involvement is negotiated between the researcher, the participants, and the setting or context of the observations. Sometimes researchers take the unusual position of seeking total involvement as a way into the role being studied—for example, becoming a lifeguard, going through military boot camp training, learning to row boats, working the night shift at the hospital, and so on. They may even become invisible. With total involvement, the researcher is immersed, if only temporarily, in the experience that is being observed and attempts to understand it as completely as possible as a full participant. For example:

> I would learn a lot more about the sidewalk [street vending and pan handling in New York City] if I worked as a vendor myself, than I would by merely observing or doing interviews . . . So I proposed that I work at his

....

2 When a researcher participates fully in an experience that is being researched, the early methods books described it as the researcher "going native." "Going native" implies a politic of colonization, of researchers observing natives, a "we versus them" statement filled with hidden intentionality. In this enlightened age of postracism, postsexism, and postclassism, such a term would never be used. This observational style has all but been replaced by the more interactive, egalitarian methods of action research.

[Hakim's] table for three months and give him the money I made. "What will the fellas think when I have a white guy working for me all summer?" he asked. We decided he should just tell them the truth—I was there to do research on a book about the block. When I told Hakim he had reservations. Would I be safe on the streets? Could Marvin look after me? Would the toughest and most violent men on Sixth Avenue accept what I was doing as worthy of respect? Meanwhile, Marvin called from a pay phone in New York to accept my offer. I would begin in June. My summer internship, so to speak, had been arranged. (Duneier, 1999, p. 334)

Seeking a vantage point close to the experience is a way for a researcher to learn and create new meaning. Even though a complete understanding is impossible, a measure of assurance about understanding can be gained from being immersed in the research setting.

A note of caution: Think through the potential consequences of being a participant in the research process. Being a participant provides an opportunity to develop greater "felt meaning" for the experience being researched but may come at the cost of not being able to establish enough distance to do a fair job of observing. This was learned by some of the early researchers who had to problematize how involved to get with communities. In *Hookers, Rounders and Desk Clerks*, authors Prus and Irini (1982) describe how they participated as fully as possible without actually getting involved in the sex trade, while Krieger (1983), author of *The Mirror Dance,* participated fully in a women's community but had great difficulty reporting on her research until after she had fully withdrawn from the community.

It is essential that as a participant who is also a data gatherer you recognize the obligation to inform those in the setting about the research (i.e., what sort of research it is, for what purposes, and who is involved). Research from a covert or manipulative perspective is not generally acceptable. The values underpinning critical social research are that it is conducted honourably with overt relationships and direct communication. These values have been criticized for jeopardizing results. That is, people who know they are being observed behave as they think they should.[3] However, we think it is important that people are as fully informed as possible about the research. Since critical social researchers most often work directly with people in the field and possibly among participants as well, a concentrated effort has to be made to maintain an "honest relationship between researcher and research participants" (Klein, 1983, p. 95).

....

3 The Hawthorne effect is a well-documented phenomenon that affects many research experiments in social sciences. It is the process where human subjects of an experiment change their behaviour simply because they are being studied. This is one of the hardest inbuilt biases to eliminate or factor into the design (Shuttleworth, n.d.).

Researcher as Participant Observer

A combination of participation and observation is most common. Participant observation is considered the fundamental and most essential qualitative research method. We are always observing regardless of the kind of methodology and methods. Good science is systematic observation and good observation leads to good science (Johnson & Sackett, 1998). Adler and Adler (1994) call this the active-member researcher, where the researcher negotiates various levels of involvement depending on her or his status as a participant, research skills and experience, and level of energy and time to invest. Participant observations are of verbal and nonverbal behaviour so that the actual behaviour is recorded as well as people's accounts of their behaviours.

Learning and sharing how others experience the social world is a difficult and often daunting task. Difficulties may include finding a position from which to participate and make observations, recording accurately so that little information is lost, finding ways to describe the masses of data, being ethical in the research process, and documenting accurate descriptions in the research report. As a researcher becomes familiar with the people involved in the experience being observed, inquiries can be made to those being observed about the relationship between what is observed (behaviours) and what the participants think about their behaviours (expressed attitudes and apparent meanings attached to them). Researchers are seekers, analyzers, and interpreters as well as data gatherers. Any events described and thoughts recorded by the researcher become observations and reflections, respectively. All is part of the research data. Just as the researcher affects the data, the data will be affected by the researcher. As you engage as a participant observer with the data you are collecting, your consciousness about the research question will be raised and ideas for action and social change will bubble to the surface. With participant observation, the research process can shift or be "emergent" over time.

With participant observation it is important that the researcher's involvement be both noninvasive and noncolonial. *Noncolonial* means that while the researcher is likely to have a different way of doing things and of making sense of the experience, the researcher's way of doing or understanding is no more or less correct than the ways of those being observed. A participant observer diligently avoids projecting her or his own meanings onto the experiences of those being observed. Being noncolonial also means that the researcher does not intend to conform those observed to her or his ways; any commitment to action would be mutually agreed upon. Importantly, researchers are in a temporary and privileged position who briefly share the lives of participants as a respectful and nonjudgmental visitor.

There are many benefits of participant observation, including the generation of an enormous amount of data to advance understandings of different
groups of people and their behaviours. New data are collected and particular to the contexts and biographies of the participants. The drawbacks to
participant observation include issues of bias and overidentification, as well
as challenges with replication and confirmation that result from the lack
of structure around the observations. However, the main drawback to this
method is usually the sheer volume of data collected that must be analyzed.
In any case, the method has demonstrated usefulness for certain research
questions where observation of limited samples of people over a set amount
of time is required.

Exercise 6.2: Onsite observation

Observations are recorded as fieldnotes. These notes are then used as data for
analysis. Recording double-entry fieldnotes is described in Chapter 4. As an
introduction to field research, become an observer or participant observer by
following these steps:

1. Locate a data site. This is a site that you think would be appropriate for
   observations. It should be relatively public, describable, and safe for all
   concerned. Get permission if required or if you think it might be ethically
   necessary.

   For example, Heather went to a laundromat every Sunday and decided
   to practise recording the happenings at the laundromat for two consecutive
   Sunday mornings. She was not looking for anything in particular, just a general
   understanding of who came in and what they did.

2. Plan your trips to the data site and prepare your fieldnotes (see Chapter 4). Make two trips to the data site for a set period of time (one
   hour each). Think carefully about when you go to the data site and
   how the visits are spaced. Remember, who you are (or appear as) will
   have some impact on how those at the data site interact with you. You
   must also consider how you will document fieldnotes. For example, is
   it appropriate to use a laptop at the data site, or is a pen and pad of
   paper more appropriate?

   Heather made the two trips, once with her daughter and once alone. She
   recorded in an unobtrusive fashion who came in and what they did. Since she
   was a "regular" and often did schoolwork while waiting for her laundry, no one
   paid her much attention.

3. Record what you are observing using the double-entry approach. Prepare a running description, including accounts of previous visits that come to mind if you have been there before. Capture verbal and nonverbal interactions. Record what you sense of the emotional levels, background noise, and even multiple roles you see being played out. Further, record any interactions you experience and any onsite reflections about yourself as a researcher.

Heather's long descriptive passages included what people wore to the laundromat, what time they arrived and with whom, some of the bits of conversation overheard, people's patterns in doing laundry, and any comments they made.

4. Record your expanded fieldnotes after your site visit. These include your analysis and reflections on what you are observing with the goal of building understanding. Why are things as they appear? What ideas or inferences can you make about the observations?

Heather documented the unusual clothing people wore when they did laundry. She speculated that some simply wore whatever clothing they had left by Sunday and others seemed to wear "doing laundry clothes." The patterns of behaviour, such as who regularly used what machines, how full they made them, what they did while the clothes were being cleaned, and so on, formed the basis for describing people's patterns in the laundromat. Their conversations varied from plans for the trip to England next week to arranging the children's lunch.

5. After the two data collection forays, describe what you have observed. You may then discuss the meaning of what you have observed, your voice during the observations, and how you might, upon reflection, alter the participant observation process.

Heather suggested that the same people arrived at approximately the same time and followed similar patterns during the observational periods. She also suggested that those who came in alone seemed to want little interaction and kept themselves occupied in a variety of ways. Heather thought that her routine was well integrated—that is, she fit in with the behaviour patterns of others. Further, she recognized that as a participant she simply went about doing her laundry, but as an observer she remained onsite after her laundry was finished, although she had no real reason for remaining. She also had to send her daughter off to do something else because of the distraction to the ongoing recording. Heather reflected on her own voice as a Sunday morning regular and about being a focused observer at a familiar site.

6. Determine if it is important to provide feedback to the research participants.

Heather was able to talk to a few people in the laundromat while she was making observations. Afterwards, when asked what she had been doing, she simply replied by describing her overall task and providing a sample of what she had been recording.

Participant observation takes practice. One observer will record much differently and may become much more engaged in the activity than another. In situations where the participant observer becomes a full participant, extensive records of experiences and reflections will form a large portion of the data. In some situations it is helpful to determine, before you are at the data collection site, the kinds of things you will pay attention to as you conduct your observation. The box below contains an example of a guide to recording fieldnotes that Colleen used for her doctoral research.

> SAMPLE FIELDNOTE GUIDELINES FOR OBSERVATIONS OF PROJECT TEAM MEETINGS AND SUBGROUP MEETINGS
> 1. Logistical information (e.g., date, time, location, attendance at meetings, agenda items)
> 2. Meanings and understandings of health (e.g., meanings of good health, meanings of poor health, decision making about health, health concerns, responsibility for health)
> 3. Experiences and understandings of the stereotype of low-income women, low-income single mothers, and low-income elderly women (e.g., specific anecdotes of incidences and stories, confrontations and challenges with the stereotype, critiques of this stereotype, experiences with authority figures)
> 4. Implications for stereotyping on the women's health
> 5. Action plans for addressing stereotyping and health for this group of low-income single women

Method 2: Interviews

Interviews are an interaction between people to elicit information by asking questions. An interview is a process in which a researcher and participant engage in a conversation focused on questions related to a research study. These questions usually ask participants for their thoughts, opinions, perspectives, or descriptions of specific experiences (deMarrais, 2004). Maccoby and Maccoby (1954) defined the interview as "a face to face verbal interchange in which one person, the interviewer, attempts to elicit information or expressions of opinions or belief from another person or persons" (p. 499; cited in deMarrais, 2004). It is a way of gathering information about things that we cannot directly observe, including people's feelings, thoughts, and intentions, and things that happened previously or outside the range of observation. Generally, though not always, the researcher develops the questions and the participants have the experience and information of interest. Formats for interviews are usually described on a continuum of control from structured to semi-structured to unstructured (see Table 6.1).

TABLE 6.1 Structured to Unstructured Interviews

STRUCTURED INTERVIEWS AND QUESTIONNAIRES	SEMI-STRUCTURED INTERVIEWS; QUESTIONNAIRES WITH CLOSE-ENDED AND OPEN-ENDED QUESTIONS	UNSTRUCTURED INTERVIEWS
Close-ended questions with no room for expansion; responses can be quantified; questions types: yes/no, multiple choice, Likert scale	Interview protocol (set questions for everyone to answer) established with ability to prompt and gain further insight	Open-ended questions; "go with the flow" style of interviewing with only broad topics to cover
No variability in questioning	Some variability in questioning, mostly in terms of the order of the questions and probes used	High variability in questioning

One-on-One Interviews

The *structured interview* consists of a one-on-one interaction where the interviewer asks a set of questions in a precise order. This highly controlled format is usually good for large-scale studies where a number of research assistants are trained to deliver identical research conditions at each data gathering opportunity. The idea is that if the data gathering conditions are the same, differences in outcomes must be due to differences in experience or characteristics. Examples include structured interviews to measure demographics, purchasing patterns, attitudes toward current public issues, or even knowledge of particular topics. The researcher's role is always neutral, inflexible, and predetermined. There is no unsolicited interaction between the researcher and interviewee since it would add variation to the data gathering protocol.

The *semi-structured interview* is a one-on-one interaction in which the interviewer asks a set of questions but allows for some variation in the order and format of questions. There is some "give and take" between the researcher and the interviewee as adjustments can be made. This format is particularly useful when a skilled researcher who is very familiar with the topic and the questions to be asked is comfortable with a less ritualized experience and also when the research requires repeated interviews with the same participants over a period of time. Most often there are fewer questions in a semi-structured interview than in a more structured interview, and probes are used to deepen or expand participants' responses.

EXAMPLE: IN-DEPTH ONE-ON-ONE INTERVIEWS

Lorraine used semi-structured interviews with women who smoke cigarettes. She wanted to find out how they attributed "meaning" to smoking and what role smoking played in their lives and, most importantly, in their identity. Because there are competing theories as to why women smoke that are based on different interpretations of the meaning of smoking cigarettes (freedom or burden? seeking equality or reacting to life's burdens?), Lorraine interviewed two distinct groups of women in two countries. She spoke to women who smoked who were self-described feminists and women who were residing in abused women's shelters, having experienced violence. She used 10 probing questions and interacted with the women in interviews to get them to elaborate on their answers. The interviews lasted from 1 to 3.5 hours. The resulting book, *Smoke Screen: Women's Smoking and Social Control,* described the results, provided an analysis of the interviews, and offered a theory of women's smoking (Greaves, 1996).

Most often, interviews can be enhanced with observations. Close description through observation can support good interviewing. For one year Shauna Pomerantz (2008) conducted an ethnography of girls' cultural practices by exploring the contextual significance of girls' style as a mode of self-expression, identification, and agency. Her questions included, How do girls use style to engage with intersecting identity categories such as gender, race, ethnicity, class, and sexuality? How do girls use style to insert themselves into a social world—as individuals and as members of groups? How do girls use style to signal belonging, friendship, politics, resistance, ambivalence, anger, lifestyle affiliations, individuality, image, and personal taste (pp. 2–3)? Observations were essential to building her interview questions. She observed the clothing styles of young women and incorporated questions about what their dress meant in her interviews. Through observation she was able to ask more specific questions, thus eliciting more in-depth descriptions of different social groups.

An *unstructured interview* is closer to a guided conversation where the researcher's goal is to elicit from the interviewee rich, detailed materials that

EXAMPLE: A CASE STUDY USING ONE-ON-ONE INTERVIEWS

A case study is an intensive analysis of an individual unit (as a person or community) stressing developmental factors in relation to the environment. The decisive factor in defining a case study is the choice of the individual unit of study and the setting of its boundaries. If you choose to do a case study, you are making a choice of what is to be studied (Flyvbjerg, 2011).

Shelagh Smith (2014), a master of rehabilitation science student, used an embedded multiple case study approach in her study "Seeking Wellness: Living with Depression and Chronic Pain." Multiple embedded case studies use data from multiple sources to describe the real-life issues and dilemmas of a phenomenon, or case, bound within a specific context (Baxter & Jack, 2008; Crowe et al., 2011; DePoy & Gitlin, 2011; Salminen, Harra, & Lautamo, 2006; Yin, 2009). The purpose of Shelagh's study was to use a multiple embedded case study approach to better understand the experience of living with co-morbid depression and chronic pain and expectations for personal recovery. Shelagh's study involved three groups each composed of three people: a person with co-morbid chronic pain and depression, a family member, and a clinician. Data collected from semi-structured interviews were thematically analyzed within and among cases and among participants. The research design allowed for the thematic analysis of perspectives within and among the groups and between participants, although data collected from each participant and group can be considered a complete case study unto itself (DePoy & Gitlin, 2011). The emerging themes highlighted the experience and expectations for recovery, including the importance of connections, the struggle to move from a pain-centred to a function-centred life, empowerment, and seeking wellness.

can be used in qualitative analysis (Lofland & Lofland, 1995). In unstructured interviews, the general questions and direction for data gathering are understood ahead of time, but the format and wording of questions and probes are developed as the interview progresses. Unstructured formats are particularly good for emergent and longitudinal research such as life histories and case studies and allows for unanticipated information to arise.

One-on-one interviews can be conducted over the phone or online with different programs (such as Skype, Montage, etc.). Conducting an interview from a distance can enable the researcher to reach a wider range of participants or to expand her or his research question to include participants from different geographic locations. Phone or online interviews can sometimes be easier to arrange for people with busy schedules. However, there are major considerations when conducting telephone interviews. There must be a way for recording the conversation, and it needs to be possible to save the recording in a file version that is usable for transcribing and analysis. For instance, if you are using NVivo for transcribing and data analysis, you will want to ensure that the digital file of the interview can be easily uploaded into the NVivo program. In addition, the introduction to the study and discussion of informed consent will have to occur over the phone, and a signed consent form will need to be sent to the researcher prior to the interview (e.g., by scanning and emailing the document). Yet the most significant limitation to phone interviews is that, as the researcher, you are not able to see the interviewee's body language or facial expressions, which means that you may be miss some major cues that can help shape and direct the conversation, particularly if the interview is semi- or unstructured. This is less of a factor for structured interviews.

Some researchers prefer to record their interviews using video (Skype, Montage) rather than simply audio. Bear in mind that video recordings have different ethical considerations, and prospective research participants may be more cautious or uncertain about agreeing to a video recording. However, video recordings can be effectively used for dissemination and knowledge translation purposes. The British project *Health Talk* (www.healthtalk.org) is an excellent example of the effective use of video interviews for raising awareness about a wide range of health issues.

EXAMPLE: LIFE HISTORY USING PHOTOGRAPHS, INTERVIEWS, AND LETTERS

A life history is a "presentation of the experiences and definitions held by one person, one group, or one organization as this person, group or organization interprets those experiences" (Denzin, 1970, p. 220). In 2012, Alison Greaves interviewed her 93-year-old grandfather, Alec Greaves, as part of a two-part project committing his recollections and wartime letters to media memory. Alison was interested in documenting the memories and feelings of being a young man in England during World War II. Alison's reasons for doing this project are encapsulated in the following statement:

Through time we tend to forget; however, a photograph can provide us with a trigger for reflection on a previous moment in time. (Re)collection examines the experience of recalling the past through photographs that return him to a particular moment in time, recalling memories as well as noting absences.

The first part of the project yielded the multimedia presentation entitled *(Re)Collection.* Her technique was to use old photographs to prod recollections in Alec, reinforced by Alison's questions to further prod Alec's memories and stories. The results were committed to two videos (one of Alec's hands and one of Alison's hands) and an audio track, which were displayed for public viewing. Alison was interested in interviewing to access stories and recollections but needed a device for doing that. The photos were the device, but her input into the process was also important in generating memories and recollections. This element of the project was based on the work of Annette Kuhn and Kirsten McAllister who, in *Locating Memory: Photographic Acts* (2006), spoke of the importance of dialogue in generating memory and understanding. Alec had a relationship to the images, the ability to speak in greater detail, and to reference surrounding events of where, when, and why a particular image was taken.

Alison was the person in dialogue with her grandfather. She recognized that for many people memory cannot be determined or measured easily as it is always "recording." The audio reflected this process, illustrating the never-ending collection of thoughts and recollections. The audio also portrays the successes and failures of memory and the speed of the recalling process. The videos were separated to reflect the relationship of the two parties. A relationship and conversation was created with two perspectives on the same collection of images. The relationship between these two films reflects the originator and the response and the paths of information cued by the photographs.

This process reflects the iterative process of interviewing, using questions and building on answers, and using photographs as props or cues, as in photovoice. The videos and audio record this process in an accessible way, using media other than the written word to document the interview materials. Alison went on to do document analysis on 2000 wartime letters between Alec and his wife, Rene. She committed the themes of this analysis to video in a second project entitled *Sent and Received.*

Group Interviews

Focus groups, expert groups, and group interviews follow all of the guidelines of one-on-one interviewing. The focus group process has long been used in starting up a research project where little is known, in market research, and in testing research instruments prior to using them in actual data gathering. The expert group, using a similar though more flexible process, has been used more recently for assisting with analysis of complex data, designing policy recommendations for completed research, and identifying directions for further research.

In general, the participants in any kind of group interview are actively recruited and invited to a session where the researcher presents the research topic, the questions, and the parameters for the discussion. Once the ethics agreements and interaction format are settled, the researcher may choose to heavily facilitate the process (vertical process) or, particularly in the case of the expert group, sit back, be nondirective, and let the interactions freely occur (horizontal process) while recording fieldnotes. While some authors recommend much more, we find that generally five to eight questions for four to six people for approximately two hours of interaction works best in most situations. It is also helpful if the participants are not known to each other but have a particular contribution to make to the topic. Refreshments are always welcome at these sessions.

Focus groups can be used effectively to gain clarity on findings from another data source. In Sheri Keller's master's research she used a focus group with practitioners to enhance understandings of the journaling data she had collected from them:

JOURNALLING AND A FOCUS GROUP

The research question for my master's project was "What factors influence recreation therapists' clinical decision making in mental health?" This question was investigated with a two-phase approach to data collection, including both journaling and a focus group. A journaling format was used to learn about therapists' behaviours, strategies for practice, decisions, and day-to-day experiences in a clinical setting. This approach allowed the therapists to record their clinical decision-making information at the time it occurred, which increased the reliability of the information, limited recall bias, and captured patterns throughout the four-week process. Participants were asked to choose a two- to four-hour period of the day to focus on their journaling. The second phase of data collection was a focus group. The purpose of the focus group was to explore the participants' journaling experience, clarify and expand on experiences and reasons for making their clinical decisions, and present a preliminary analysis of the journaling data. Data from the focus group supported and reinforced the themes and codes generated from the journaling data. The journaling data provided information on what decisions were made, and the focus group allowed for further investigation and an in-depth understanding to why those decisions were made and provided more context and understanding. The focus group also revealed that the journaling process in and of itself was a reflective process where participants gained insight into their own day-to-day practice. (Keller, 2015)

The advantages of group interviews are that a large quantity of data can be collected in a relatively short period of time, and they can be used to engage in analysis or a member-checking process (refer to Chapter 9 for a fuller discussion of member-checking). The excitement generated as individuals key in on ideas and stimulate each other is considerable. The disadvantages relate to the facilitation skills required and the challenge of transcribing multiple voices.

EXAMPLE: GROUP INTERVIEWS AS THE PRIMARY DATA SOURCE

In the "Imagining Inclusion" photovoice project (led by Colleen Reid and Maya Alonso), the group interviews, which were the primary data source, were elicited with the use of photography. The purpose of "Imagining Inclusion" was to explore how people with lived experience of mental illness experienced community inclusion, health, and well-being. For 10 weeks the 32 research participants photographed their responses to different research questions. Some of the questions posed in the weekly photovoice sessions included, What are your communities? What does community inclusion look like? In your day-to-day life, what do your experiences of social isolation, exclusion, poverty, and stigma look like? What does recovery mean to you? Group discussions of the photos were audio recorded, and participants wrote reflections to develop a narrative for each of their photographs. The data set included over 300 photographs and reflections, 34 meeting transcripts, 40 sets of fieldnotes, 14 one-on-one interviews, and demographic data from 32 individuals.

Many participants found that their involvement in a photovoice process was transformative. It engaged them intellectually, allowed them to learn about photography, and created a platform from which to discuss their shared and unique experiences. The photographs and narratives were used in a community photo exhibit, which was set up and hosted by several of the participants. Photovoice is an example of a research method that uses a creative process (photography) to elicit rich and meaningful group discussions of lived experiences. It allowed for "the possibility of perceiving the world from the viewpoint of the people who lead lives that are different from those traditionally in control of the means for imaging the word" (Wang & Burris, 1997).

Group interviews require that the researcher have good interviewing and facilitation skills. By nature it is harder to maintain control in group interviews, and interpersonal dynamics and diverse communication styles can be difficult to manage. The researcher must troubleshoot to get the questions answered and to keep the group interactions from becoming one sided or going off track. There also may be a need to encourage quieter participants to speak up or to discourage more verbal participants from taking over the process. From time to time, a focus group will develop into "group think" (McCauley, 1989), and individual differences will be in danger of being lost. If possible, it is beneficial to have two researchers in the room—yourself as the lead researcher who is posing questions and facilitating the discussion and a second "research friend" who can record fieldnotes and document interpersonal dynamics. Ideally, the two researchers should sit at opposite sides of the room to allow for different perspectives on the group interaction.

A note of caution: The promise of confidentiality you offer to participants is not within your power to ensure. You may have the group verbally agree to maintain confidentiality, but you cannot guarantee that each participant will have their confidentiality guarantees respected by other participants. It is important to state this upfront and to encourage participants to remember the limits of confidentiality as they share with the group.

Guidelines for Developing and Administering Interviews

(a) Follow a Clear Interview Format and Flow. The set of questions normally begins with questions that are basic and open, for example, "Can you tell me about X?" Order the questions easy to more difficult, direct to indirect, simple to complex, and public to more private and introspective. It is good practice to say each question out loud then reduce it to the clearest and, for you, the most comfortable way of asking it. If you can't articulate the

question when you are alone, it is unlikely that you will be able to do so with a participant in front of you. Whether structured or unstructured, interviews should follow a general format or flow:

- *Introduction*: Discuss the purpose and length of the interview and how the data will be used, review the consent form, and ask permission to tape record and take notes.
- *Warm-up*: Begin with easy, inviting questions that help the participant relax and settle in. Often the warm-up can be used to gather demographic data (see the section on face sheets in Chapter 7).
- *Main body*: This section of the interview contains questions that relate most directly to your research purpose. They are the most "meaty" questions of the interview.
- *Cool-down*: Include one or several questions to wind down, if needed. This can include "Did I miss anything?" or "Do you have anything else to add?"
- *Closure*: Thank your participant for spending his or her time with you, clarify any questions he or she might have (especially regarding ethics and access to data), determine if there is any possibility for follow-up to clarify responses, and establish a process for member-checking.

(b) Develop a Variety of Interview Questions that Will Answer Your Research Question. The basis of all interviews is the question (Denzin, 1988). The research question must be operationalized into specific questions with the help of your fieldnotes and literature review, and perhaps a self-interview (see p. 158). Staying close to the research question will help participants respond to questions about their own experience in insightful and thoughtful ways.

Where do the interview questions come from? First, they come from your jottings. As you became interested in doing the research, you had questions to which you sought answers. Identify these as questions you need to ask. Second, questions come from what other people ask you or tell you. Again, carefully decoded reflections about the research process will yield these gems. Third, questions will come from some understanding of the research literature. What have other researchers asked? What do other researchers say about the inquiry process? As you have been reading about the research question, other questions will emerge. What questions emerge for the stories you read? In all cases be prepared to jot questions down and date them for recording in your fieldnotes.

There is an integral relationship between your research interest, focus, and question and the interview questions you choose. Always ask yourself if the questions you ask are answering the research question and what other kinds of questions might help you move from the research question to the answers. You will know if you are answering the research question if, for example, a number of participants respond with clarity and focus to your questions and provide insights that expand your knowledge about the research question. Alternatively, you will know your questions are not working if the participants offer widely divergent information in response to your questions; interpret your questions in various, possibly unrelated, ways; or if the information, however coherent, does not address the research question but something else entirely. It is time to regroup, refocus, and restart if these things happen to you.

It is useful to consider developing interview questions from different stances or perspectives. As you look at the interview question ideas you have jotted down, consider if any of them can be asked differently based on the following:

- *Demographic/background*: Regarding age, education, gender, and so on; these questions are used to situate the participant in relation to other participants or other people.
- *Experience/behaviour*: Find out about experiences, behaviours, actions, and activities that the researcher could have observed if present (e.g., How long have you been attending the program? How often?).
- *Opinion/value*: What people think about something (e.g., How has the program affected your day-to-day life?).
- *Feeling*: Aimed at understanding people's emotional responses through experiences and thoughts (e.g., How do you feel when you go to the program?).
- *Knowledge*: Find out about factual information related to the research topic (e.g., How many people come to this program? What services does it offer?).
- *Sensory*: Describe what participants see or hear (e.g., What do you see when you walk into the program?)

Different interviews follow different patterns. The pattern chosen should be related to the kind of questions asked and the nature of the information sought. For example, in the unstructured interview the interviewer has a general understanding of the research topic and asks highly detailed, individualized, exploratory questions that will vary somewhat with each research participant. In the structured interview the goal is to ask participants to make choices from among the options given. Another goal might be to obtain, in a preordered form, specific information from each participant. In this case a "shopping list of information required" is kept, and the interviewer solicits information and fills in the gaps as best as possible during the interview. Regardless of the type of interview chosen, you must pay attention to the components of good interviewing to maximize the encounter for yourself and your participants.

(c) Check and Double-Check the Wording of the Interview Questions. It is important that the wording of the interview questions be precise, clear, and straightforward. Interview questions should be examined, edited, read aloud, and piloted with a friend or colleague. In order to avoid questions that will confuse participants or lead to confusing or unclear findings, check for the following:

- Questions that are close-ended (that result in a yes or no response)
- Questions that are not yet ready to be asked because you are unclear about the main concept or they have an unclear relation to the research question
- Questions that are long and meandering
- Questions that ask more than one thing
- Questions with jargon or unfamiliar words
- Leading questions or questions with bias or evident intent
- Questions about a third-party opinion

(d) Develop and Practise Strategies for Probing. In the case of semi-structured and unstructured interviews, your comfort and ability at probing your participants' responses will expand and deepen what participants share with you. There are a variety of ways to probe to get at meanings and experiences:

- *Clarifying:* These questions ask participants to say more about something that is a bit unclear. Example: "You mentioned that your discussion with your child's teacher was not very nice; can you say more about what was 'not nice' about it?"
- *Summarizing:* These questions illustrate that you are actively listening and help to refocus a conversation or topic. Example: "So basically you are saying that while working at that job you could not afford daycare, a bus fare, and rent. Did I get that right?"
- *Elaborating:* These questions are designed to get more information about something the participant has said. Examples: "Can you tell me more about that?" "What else happened?" "What other ways of coping have you tried?"

- *Validation and feedback*: These are statements designed to let participants know that they are being helpful and to encourage them to continue sharing information. Examples: "That's really helpful," "That is a very important point you raised," "I appreciate your willingness to share that," "You've said something really important here; can we talk more about that?"

(e) Experience the Interview as Both an Interviewer and a Research Participant. Good interviewing is a skill that takes thought and practice. When you feel you have a final version of the interview questions, conduct a practice interview with a friend or colleague. This practice interview should parallel the circumstances (i.e., setting and format) you wish to establish with research participants. Begin with the introduction and description of the consent form and any ethical issues. Use the interview questions and the probes and clarifications you have prepared in advance. This will illuminate where the order of the questions needs to change or where the language needs to be adjusted. In addition, the practice interview will give you a sense of approximately how long the interview will take and whether there is enough variety to give the interview a natural flow. The timeframe is an important consideration for people consenting to participate.

Another way to develop interview skills is to do a self-interview. As a friend or colleague asks your interview questions to you, you experience the interview from a participant's position. Some questions will be answerable and others will need reformulating in light of your experience. Record the interview in the proposed fashion and record in your notes any comments about the interview content and process between you and your colleague. By experiencing an interview, you, the researcher, learn first-hand about the process of being interviewed with the proposed research questions.

(f) Account for Yourself in the Research Process. Similar to any method used in critical social research, it is essential that you account for yourself in the research. For example, you might choose to do a self-introduction, including why you are interested in the topic, why you think the topic is relevant, and perhaps something about your own related experience. Potential research participants may accept or reject an invitation to participate in the research process based on this. Ethically, participants must be informed about *what* the research is about, the *destination* of the information at the conclusion of the research project, and to some degree who you, *the researcher*, are. You also account for yourself in the research when you keep thorough records of your changing attitudes in relation to the research topic, including how you change throughout the process. The fieldnotes are essential for accounting for this.

(g) Recognize the Investment Made by Research Participants. In a research setting, interviews are voluntary and either party may leave at will. Either the participant or the researcher can break off, withdraw, retreat for a time, ask questions, respond to questions, or choose to share or not share particular experiences. In the case of interviews conducted with more than one participant, the nature of the data gathered varies because of the more public nature of the settings. The group dynamic affects the experience, and everyone in the group has an effect on it.

The research participant is not a passive participant who is simply there to talk about her or his experience. The participant may know better or clearer questions to ask and may recognize gaps in the interview plan or in the selection of potential participants. If the interaction between researcher and participant allows for an optimal degree of sharing, both may reach new personal and political insights in relation to the research focus. Interviews seek to discover information about the experiences of the interviewee in the language and gesture of that person. Our suggestion is that you remain flexible enough in the data gathering process to use the research participants' experiences, as they share them, as a guide for conducting the interview.

Participants and researchers are both involved in the data gathering. Even if participants accept an honorarium, they are usually volunteers who agree to participate because they are asked, their experience is important, or they are curious about the interview experience. They may also be passionately committed to research outcomes. Your participants are contributing their time and effort, and in return it is important to respect their time commitment, make it as easy as possible for them to participate, thank them for their time, and ensure at a minimum that they receive feedback on their participation. Typically, the individual interviewed is a willing and cooperative participant who seeks to describe and explain, as best possible, her or his experiences and the meaning of those experiences as they relate to the research question. Good rapport between the interviewer and participant is fundamental to good interviewing.

(h) Understand and Be Prepared to Deal with the Ethics of Conducting Interviews. The investment made by all participants is not equal, just as interest and personal goals for the research are not identical. However, it is essential to recognize that each participant is an autonomous human being with thoughts, feelings, and experiences. To presume that you can "take the data and run" is inappropriate. So too is leaving a participant to deal with the aftermath of sensitive interviews without being able to call upon the researcher in a capacity other than researcher. Remember that a researcher and a counsellor are different roles. For example, Ponic and Jategaonkar (2011) describe and reflect on the ethics and safety protocol for conducting photovoice research

with women who have experienced intimate partner violence. They were balancing the tensions between maintaining the confidentiality and safety of participants, using the data for action, and working to destabilize traditional power relations between researchers and participants. They developed a protocol framed by the primary guideline that all decisions be made through the lens of safety and autonomy, which shaped the ways that informed consent, confidentiality, and safety were managed during the research project. Regardless of your research question and participants, your efforts must always be directed toward minimizing any harm that might occur and, in your role as researcher, to protect and support your research participants.

Exercise 6.3: 15-minute interview

This task consists of preparing and conducting an interview, transcribing the recording, and summarizing how you facilitated the data gathering process. This exercise will familiarize you with the complexities of interviewing.

1. Choose a sample research focus; here are some examples:
   • Fears, as a woman (as a man), about growing older
   • Decision making about having a child
   • Being the only (volunteer/woman/hearing-impaired person) in group of (workers/men/those who can hear)
   • Physician-assisted suicide as a way of dying
   • Body image, diets, and politics
2. Describe your research goals:
   • Describe the research focus (X) and ethical considerations
3. Record fieldnotes on your research focus:
   • What do I already know about X?
   • What do I want to find out about X?
   • Are there any theoretical issues that guide this research focus?
4. Plan the interview:
   • Develop questions from fieldnotes and other immediate sources
   • Order questions for logical interviewing sequence
   • Prepare the introduction and role of interviewer
   • Write one goal for the research
5. Determine selection of participants:
   • Consider inclusion criteria for participants
   • Arrange the time and place (use personal contact, prepare the setting for no interruptions, distractions, or overlapping activities)
   • Ask permission to record
   • Assure confidentiality and the right to withdraw
   • Inform participants about the approximate length of the interview

6. Prepare the interview:
    *   Ensure that you understand how the recording device works
    *   Pre-record on tape your and the participant's identity, date, time, place, and topic
    *   Check the volume and get ready for recording; then press pause
    *   Have a paper and pen for jottings, a copy of the interview guide, and extra batteries with you
7. Conduct the interview:
    *   Introduce yourself and the topic
    *   Seek permission to record the interview
    *   Release the pause button, record the participant's name and his or her agreement to confidentiality
    *   Explain how the participant can go "off the record" any time by turning off the recording
    *   Agree on the approximate length of the interview
    *   Introduce the interview
    *   Start with a warm-up (easy, inviting questions that help the participant relax and settle in), such as "Could you begin by telling me . . ."
    *   During the main body of the interview, conduct the interview by asking, one by one, the questions on your list. Add more questions if they seem appropriate.
    *   Practise more in-depth questioning (have a probe or two ready for this, avoid leading questions and third-person questions)
    *   Try asking questions out of order or forming them differently than you planned
    *   Practise probing: clarifying, summarizing, elaborating, and validating prompts
    *   Begin the ending with the cool-down (questions to wind down if needed)
    *   Closure (thank-you, invitation to participant for further contact and feedback)
8. Be attentive:
    *   Conversation after the tape is turned off is usually very rewarding and helpful to the research focus (though it is impossible to reference it with this particular interview or participant in any way)
    *   Immediately write notes about your reflections of the content and the process of the interview
    *   Transcribe the interview if you have recorded it and write more notes on the participant's responses to your questions as soon as you can after the interview

9. Provide feedback to the research participant:
    *   Answer the research question, as best you can, for them
    *   Ask if they have any further comments on the content and whether they have any recommendations for you to improve the process

Occasionally, a researcher can lose sight of the research question or become lost themselves in the project. After doing the interview you will find yourself much more attentive to your voice as the researcher's voice, to the usefulness of the questions, to your active listening skills, and to engaging in focused data gathering with optimal rapport.

The basis of all interviews is the question (Denzin, 1970, p. 128). You must transform your research question into many specific questions that will help you, the interviewer, stay close to the research question and help the participant respond to questions about her or his own experience in an insightful and thoughtful way. The way in which you word the questions, the order in which you ask them, and what the participant thinks you might be seeking are components of the interview process.

Method 3: Questionnaires

Much has been written about research designs where questionnaires can be used, so in this section we focus on the major considerations surrounding questionnaires in critical social research. A questionnaire is a set of printed or written questions with a choice of answers that is devised for research purposes. Since questionnaires are noninteractive, they can typically collect information from a wider sample than interviews or other interactive forms of data collection. Generally, questionnaires are understood to be a quantitative method, which means that they are standardized and their findings are reliable, valid, and generalizable to the larger population. Typically, quantitative questionnaires are gathered through random sampling so that the results are representative of the population from which they are drawn.

Although qualitative and quantitative questionnaires can have the same appearance in terms of the kinds of questions and flow, they have fundamentally different approaches to sampling and trustworthiness. For example, a qualitative questionnaire may be used to gather structured data (i.e., by using mostly close-ended questions) from a purposively sampled group of third-year students in a particular academic program (Chapter 7 covers sampling approaches). Or a qualitative questionnaire may be used to evaluate the effectiveness of a particular program for those who were enrolled. In these kinds of research projects, statistical analyses with programs such as SPSS are not used; rather, the researcher compiles a spreadsheet and provides frequencies, percentages, means, medians, modes, and standard deviations. All of these "numeric" data can be easily computed by the researcher to describe a phenomenon. The main distinction between quantitative and qualitative questionnaires is that random sampling is used to gather quantitative data, which are then analyzed statistically in an effort to generalize to a larger population, whereas qualitative questionnaires employ purposeful sampling with a discrete group of individuals to describe a phenomenon that is particular to the participants sampled. The findings from a qualitative questionnaire, similar to other qualitative methods, will be transferable should other contextual factors be the same (trustworthiness criteria are covered in Chapter 9).

The qualitative questionnaire is a popular method for conducting research with a large sample. It is generally a cost-efficient, relatively quick way to gather information from a lot of people. Since the questionnaire is a more formalized and less interactive process for data gathering than interviews, it is useful for gathering information that does not require any social interaction. Often, questionnaires can be completed at a time and place of the participant's choosing. And since questionnaires produce data in a cogent and organized format, data entry and analysis can be straightforward with results available soon after data collection. Though the information gathered in questionnaires is not in-depth, it can still be very useful. For example, where certain clearly defined facts or opinions have been identified by more interactive qualitative methods such as interviews or focus groups, a questionnaire can explore how generally these apply. Alternatively, a questionnaire might be used first and be followed by a more interactive method on a sample of participants to fill out certain features of the questionnaire replies. Interaction among techniques in this way is typical of qualitative research and is encouraged for triangulation purposes (see the discussion of triangulation in Chapter 9).

In terms of creating a questionnaire, we suggest the following steps. First, unless a perfect questionnaire for answering the research question already exists (i.e., there is another questionnaire that you can replicate), take the research question, break it down into a set of possible questions that "cover the territory," and seek outside input. This involves breaking down the major concepts into indicators and determining how the questions need to be constructed to measure each indicator. Second, with the input of other people who have a stake in the research topic, build additional possible questions. Then the questionnaire is further developed with consideration to the order, format, and variety of questions and the overall look and feel of the questionnaire. Consideration should be given to accessibility and formatting (e.g., print size, overall length, white space between questions, space to answer open-ended questions, two-sided or one-sided presentation, sections, page numbers).

It is increasingly common to use an online tool to create and administer a questionnaire. Some common tools are SurveyMonkey, FluidSurveys, Zoomerang, SurveyGizmo, and Polldaddy. For most of these tools you can use a limited version for free, such as creating and administering a questionnaire with 10 questions or fewer. Generally speaking, however, you will only gain the benefits of using an online tool if you buy a subscription that allows for greater functionality. There are some advantages to using an online tool. First, online tools deal with all of the formatting needs of your questionnaires; these tools create visually appealing and easy-to-read questionnaires and can "brand" questionnaires with specific colours, fonts, and logos. Second, they facilitate the administration of your questionnaire in that a link to the questionnaire can be embedded in a recruitment email or on a social networking site, which means that you are not required to print completed questionnaires or be left with a stack of questionnaires that have been completed by hand. All completed questionnaires are kept securely online and can be accessed easily from a computer. Third, online tools allow you to design more complex questionnaires that include "skip logic" (skipping a question), "piping" (pulling answers from one part of the questionnaire into another part), and "question randomization" (randomly ordering questions). Finally, online tools can facilitate basic data analysis of numeric data. Frequencies, percentages, tables, charts, and basic reports can be created with ease using one of these tools. The data can also be exported to an Excel document if you prefer to do your analysis with a spreadsheet.

When the questionnaire needs to be administered face to face, such as in a convenient sample of program attendees, students in a classroom, or participants just completing a focus group, an online questionnaire will not suffice. And when you, as the researcher, are not present for data collection (such as when a participant is completing a questionnaire online), other issues may arise, such as incomplete questionnaires and losing control over who completes the questionnaire. Finally, there is a burgeoning conversation about the ethical issue of where these online tools store data and who has access to them. However, since there are advantages to using online questionnaire tools in terms of questionnaire design and management and analysis of data, in some instances we have used an online tool to create the questionnaire then administered it face to face in paper format; participants' responses are then inputted into the online tool. Though this adds the cumbersome step of data input, it can ultimately be more efficient than the traditional pen-and-paper approach.

Questionnaire Format

Questionnaires are usually "book-ended." A consent form, cover sheet, or information letter introduces the researcher, the topic, the questionnaire, and the ethical issues. Often, those who receive questionnaires do not sign consent forms but give tacit consent by reading a cover sheet or information letter and then completing the questionnaire.[4] All instructions and questions need to be self-explanatory, and the questionnaire should look attractive and be easy to follow. A back sheet contains the thank-you for participating, the promise for feedback (if appropriate and possible), the manner in which the participant can contact the researcher, and possibly an invitation to indicate whether she or he would consider being included in subsequent data gathering (if applicable). There may also be a space for the participant's comments. The questions can take a variety of forms. They may be constructed so that they are closed-ended (with a limited number of choices) or open-ended (a question followed by room for comment and expansion by the participant). Table 6.2 (p. 166) provides examples of the types of questions that can be used in qualitative questionnaires.

Strategies for Constructing a Questionnaire

- Begin with relevant demographic information, including questions about age, sex, race/ethnicity, education, employment, occupation, income, religion, and housing accommodation.
- When possible, use tick boxes or drop-down menus rather than open-ended questions, especially for demographic information.
- Create sections. Describe the purpose of each section so that the person responding understands the flow of the questionnaire. It is often necessary to provide explanations or definitions.
- Ask for similar information in different ways (cross-checking your findings).
- Ensure that all of your questions are posed clearly. There will be no opportunity for explanation.
- Avoid leading words (could, should) and leading questions ("The government should force you to pay higher taxes").
- Review your questionnaire and identify ways respondents could get stuck with either too many or no correct answers. For example, "What is your age?" Answer options: 0–10; 10–20; 20–30; 30–40; 40+. In this case there is overlap between the age categories.
- Limit the number of open-ended questions. Do not rely on respondents filling them in since they are time consuming and may result in low overall return rates.

....

4 We encourage you to consult the ethical guidelines of the institution where you are doing your research or where you will seek ethical approval to do your research. Different institutions have different practices and expectations regarding gaining consent for administering questionnaires. Additionally, ethical guidelines will now stipulate requirements for administering online questionnaires.

TABLE 6.2 Types of Questionnaire Questions

TYPE OF QUESTION	EXAMPLE
Tick box (one response only):	What is your highest level of educational attainment? □ Some high school □ High school □ Some college or university □ College certificate or diploma □ University degree □ Some postgraduate □ Postgraduate degree
Tick box (check all that apply):	Which community-based programs do you access? □ Library □ Recreation centre □ Pool □ School/educational program □ Religious group/synagogue/church/mosque/temple □ Visual, performing, or music arts □ Work or paid employment □ Volunteering □ Neighbourhood/housing □ Other: _____
Fill in the blank:	What is your ethnicity? _____
Answer all that apply, with hanging questions:	Which degree(s) have you obtained? Bachelor's? □ Yes □ No Master's? □ Yes □ No If No, go to question 17. If Yes, which university? _____Year_____ Discipline_____
Rank ordering:	Please indicate which factors influenced your decision (rank as many as you feel are relevant, beginning with 1 as the most important:) The subject area was interesting _____ Positive influence of others _____ Demands of family _____ I was needed _____ Have you ever felt discriminated against when trying to access work? What are your goals for attending this program? Other (please specify)_____
Likert scale:	1 2 3 4 5 On many occasions Often Once or twice Hardly ever Never _____ _____
Please provide additional feedback:	_____ _____

- Likert scales range from 1 to 7, 1 to 9, 0 to 4, and 1 to 5. Odd-numbered scales have a middle value that is often labelled "neutral" or "undecided." Even-numbered scales have no middle neutral or undecided choice, which means that the respondent is forced to decide whether they lean more toward the "agree" or "disagree" end of the scale. Always indicate what each value on the scale means so that it is not open for interpretation. Group scale questions together to simplify the questionnaire visually. Tables work well.
- Order the questions from easy to more difficult, from direct to indirect, from simple to complex, and from public to more private and introspective.

Questionnaire Pretesting

Once you have reviewed your questionnaire using the tips listed above, it should then be pretested (also called a trial or pilot) for such things as wording, style, response options, and flow. When pretesting the questionnaire, do the following:

- Sample participants who are close in characteristics to your actual population.
- Have participants complete the survey and ask them to answer additional questions about the content and the format.
- Check the clarity and order of questions; engage in sober second thought on the format and content.
- Identify gaps and create new questions.

The feedback from participants who pretest the questionnaire is used to revise it. The questionnaire can then be prepared for distribution to prospective participants (sampling techniques are presented in Chapter 7). Data gathered in pilots or pretests are not usually used in final questionnaire counts because the questionnaire may have been altered for data collection with the feedback from the pilot.

Administering Questionnaires

There are a number of ways to administer questionnaires, including in person, through email, online, via telephone, or by mail. In-person questionnaires are usually those done in offices, schools, or at specific programs or organizations. With questionnaires administered over email or online, researchers have little control over who receives and completes the questionnaire. Some questionnaires are delivered verbally, as in phone questionnaires or questionnaires done with people for whom auditory delivery is the only communication strategy appropriate. Although questionnaires are not usually interactive, they are occasionally administered by the researcher. Common examples include a quick survey of people on the street or a physician's diagnostic exercise; both are conducted in person. Though it used to be common practice, questionnaires are rarely distributed by mail. In the rare occurrence that questionnaires are mailed, they should include a stamped envelope for the return post.

Paper surveys may be delivered and then picked up when they are completed. In cases where the timeframe is restricted or the participants are in a local area, it is sometimes possible to administer the questionnaire in a slightly more personal manner. The following is an example of such a research plan:

> The task was to do a "women's issues report card" on candidates running in the 2015 federal election. Candidates received a brief survey with questions about their support for a number of issues. As planned, all candidates were informed of the report card process, received a hand-delivered survey, and arrangements were made to pick up their completed surveys within the following three days. Most chose to respond. All responses were used to assist with the preparation of "town hall" all-candidates meetings in several of the ridings.

Another delivery mechanism is to place questionnaires where prospective participants will see them, pick them up, read them, answer them on the spot, and return the completed survey to a lock box nearby. This is a method frequently used for such things as feedback on customer service, participant comments on a workshop or speech, or workers' comments on a possible policy change. Though these do not require much labour, distribution quality control is poor. For example, there is no way for the researcher to guarantee that one person does not answer more than one questionnaire.

For smaller, locally done questionnaires, information is usually collected at one specific point in time and analyzed soon afterward. However, for large-scale questionnaires many individuals may provide information at different points in time and in different contexts. These questionnaires are usually designed so that such differences do not affect the data gathered. The returned questionnaires need to be monitored (number returned per day, from where, etc.) and the information needs to be checked for completeness, identification information, and requests for further involvement. Normally, researchers use the monitoring to predict when reminders might be sent out and to whom. Also, monitoring helps get everything ready for the data management and analysis steps required next. Regardless of how the paper questionnaire is delivered, some thought must be given to how respondents will return the questionnaires. A stack of completed questionnaires cannot be left unattended on a desk, for example. The way that respondents return completed questionnaires has ethical implications, and accepted processes for returning completed questionnaires are articulated by most institutional research ethics boards.

Questionnaire Return Rates

Not all selected individuals respond to questionnaires sent to them. The return rate or response rate is based on the original population size and calculated using the percentage of the sample size (those who receive the questionnaire) who complete the survey. The return rate will be lower if the questionnaire is lengthy, poorly thought out, unattractive, difficult to complete in one sitting, and so on. The return rate can be improved with reminder notices, if possible, or with a hand delivery and subsequent pickup process.

We are often asked about what counts as a "good" response rate. The numbers vary depending on the size and randomness of the sample. When random sampling is used, return rates for moderate-length questionnaires on important topics might be considered "good" at 50 to 70 per cent (Babbie & Benaquisto, 2010; Sedlack & Stanley, 1992). For a specialized population study (e.g., university professors, individuals living with multiple sclerosis) where no random sample is drawn, the questionnaire is complex and lengthy, and no reminder steps are taken, a return rate of 20 per cent might be considered good. Questionnaires conducted internally, such as with a group of employees, usually approaches the 90 per cent response mark (FluidSurveys Team, 2014). While any response rate will enable a researcher to draw conclusions, the confidence with which the results are stated as true is severely weakened by proportionately small sample sizes and lower response rates.

The return rate will likely be higher if the sample is interested in the topic, the instrument is accessible and orderly, and if one or two follow-up reminders can be sent. However, there are exceptions where no matter what is done the return rates might remain low. Some groups or communities can become "fatigued" after being over-researched, such as a particular constituency of people (e.g., young offenders, Rhodes scholars) or segment of society (e.g., Indigenous peoples, circumpolar people). Other examples include lack of interest in the topic (e.g., "Could you take 30 minutes to complete the attached survey on toothbrush preferences?") or repeated surveying on the same question (e.g., "Do you feel the government is doing enough to take action on climate change?").

Exercise 6.4: Pretesting a questionnaire

The type of questionnaire you develop depends on what you want to ask, how you want to ask it, and where your participants are located. Questionnaires that have a variety of detailed questions allow you to evaluate participants' accounts of their experiences. Here are the steps to complete a pilot test of a questionnaire:

1. Research question
   - Choose a topic of interest: What is it that you want to know?
2. Fieldnotes
   - What do you think about the research focus and question? Jot enough notes about what you think, already know, or have experienced. Comb through these notes for possible questions to ask.
3. Create a questionnaire made up of five to seven questions
   - Order the questions you have and determine if there are other questions that you might want to ask.
   - Check to see that the questions you have identified get at what you want to know.
   - Make the final question a feedback question so participants can write what they think about the questionnaire questions and format.
4. Who can I ask?
   - Organize a list of 10 potential participants whom you already know and who have the experience you are interested in.
   - Contact participants to ask if they are willing to participate and give them a brief account of the research question and research task.
5. Conduct the pretest
   - Pretest the completed questionnaire with five people you know by arranging for it to be delivered by hand and returned the following day.
   - If you are doing an online questionnaire, send the invitation to your participants by email with the link to the questionnaire.
6. Analyze the data
   - Scan the returned questionnaires and answer the following: How many participants answered your questions? How did the participants respond to each question? What questions did they want to add? What comments did they make about the format? Are there other questions you would have liked to have asked? What have you found out about the research question?
7. Feedback and thank-you to participants
   - Write a short summary and thank-you to participants.

Some researchers conduct a small sample questionnaire to determine what questions need to be asked and in what ways they can be asked most effectively. You may want to think of this exercise as a small but important part of a larger research project. The feedback to participants is essential. Participants have shared their experiences with you and expanded your understanding. Providing a summary for participants is an inclusive and ethical way of communicating results.

Method 4: Content Analysis

Content analysis is a technique used for the systematic and focused measurement of content. The content in question can be virtually any form of recorded communication, including the following:

- Archival records in the public library about who owned arcades in Edmonton prior to 1950
- Newspaper clippings about the athletic career of Olympic and World Champion cyclist and speed skater Clara Hughes
- Early diary entries about Grandmother Rowe's trip from Saskatchewan to Nova Scotia in 1923
- The performance of a skill that is captured on DVD, film, or audiotape (e.g., the Aborigines way of cooking a kangaroo in the Australian outback)
- Layers of drawings and paintings under Leonardo da Vinci's paintings
- Film and the hand of the director visible in the production of the film

In content analyses some content is designated as primary—that is, it is content that someone with experience is presenting to you first-hand. Diaries or first-person accounts of events fall into this category. Secondary content is a retelling of the event by someone who was not at the event. For instance, the newspaper clippings of Clara Hughes's athletic career are secondary, but her writings or recorded interviews when she talks about her races and training are primary content. The primary and secondary designation is important because the more layers or filters the materials go through in the telling, the less accurate they become. Note that content analysis is most often done on material that was prepared for another purpose. While insights can be obtained from those materials, it is sometimes a tedious process of searching through a mass of less-than-relevant information for the things that are relevant to your research.

Content analysis is based on the notion of objectivity, "a systematic approach, quantitative enumeration and a focus on manifest (rather than latent) content" (Sedlack & Stanley, 1992, p. 263). Sedlack and Stanley (1992) add that "objectivity" is not value-free work, but rather work with clear, well-defined criteria for observation established and then used consistently on all the content being analyzed. The systematic approach to materials means that materials for analysis are selected according to some pre-established criteria that are applied consistently to all eligible material. Quantitative enumeration includes frequency of occurrence, length of text, size of titles, location of an article or advertisement on a printed page, number of colours used, volume of the voice, and so on. Manifest content refers to explicit information that appears and can be counted or described or analyzed, while latent content refers to material revealing underlying layers of meaning. While latent content can be interesting and revealing, it can be difficult to analyze with consistency and might risk producing an analysis that is not replicable by others.

In its simplest form, all that is needed for a content analysis is a piece or segment of content that is stable—that is, that you can review over and over again according to the pre-established analytical criteria called "code categories." Examples include most forms of communication, a written text, a piece of video that can be replayed, a recorded voice speaking or singing, a painting, or a photograph. In more complex, large-scale analyses, some selection or sampling of content may occur. If a random sampling technique is used for selection, then it is possible that the resulting analysis will be somewhat generalizable to the larger body of material.

Particular research questions will lead to a content analysis. You might choose to structure your inquiry as a content analysis because of the form in which data are available to you. What data on your topic exist, and how will you select data to answer the research question? If you are interested in sexism in advertising, how will you narrow down the sheer volume of data? For example, you might focus on television commercials and magazine advertisements in the 1990s. Once you have the content selected, you then have to consider what you want to know and the kind of analysis (and the codes or categories) that will enable you to answer your research question. The categories are determined by the broad focus of the research and might determine how many or what percentage of content is focused on each of your key themes, the tracking of who says what to whom, what trajectories or shifts in meaning exist in the data, supporting evidence for each predetermined code category, and whether additional categories are warranted.

Given the central importance accorded to broad influences upon health—especially "social determinants"—in federal and provincial health policy documents in Canada, Hayes and colleagues sought to determine the distribution of health news stories in Canadian newspapers. They developed a taxonomic framework to categorize the relative frequency of health topic coverage based on the document *Toward a Healthy Future* (Federal, Provincial, and Territorial Advisory Committee on Population Health, 1999). This document was organized into six chapters corresponding to the major identified influences shaping the health status of populations: (a) the socioeconomic environment, (b) healthy child development, (c) the physical environment, (d) personal health practices, (e) health services, and (f) biology and genetic endowment. Newspapers were purposively chosen from across Canada. Each had to be a major daily, be available electronically, reflect a mix of ownership, and include papers published in both official languages (English and French). One day of the week was randomly chosen for each calendar quarter of the five study years (yielding 20 constructed weeks), and all news items meeting the inclusion criteria for the study were selected from each of the newspapers for every day of each constructed week (Hayes, Ross, Gasher, Gutstein, Dunn, & Hackett, 2007).

Denzin and Lincoln (2003) write that the discipline of content analysis depends on several criteria. First, are the data adequate? Is there enough data and are they central and useful for the study or are they marginal or tangential? Second, is there an audit trail (see Chapter 4)? This involves the careful documentation of the entire research process. This would allow other researchers to follow the same path—to analyze the same data according to the same code categories and, presumably, to arrive at the same conclusions. Third, are there mechanisms to ensure that the analysis stays on track? These might be feedback loops to reanalyze some of the data or the use of secondary informants to view the analysis as it progresses. Fourth, using multiple analyzers improves the veracity of the outcomes. If all four of these criteria are in place, then content analysis can be an appropriate method.

Content analysis is a useful method because the data, or content, are stable and the researchers can work independently or work with others to do an analysis on their own time. Obscure materials can be brought to light, materials that are not alike can be studied together, writings from different centuries can be put in the same sampling frame, and primary and secondary materials about the same subject can be studied together.

Exercise 6.5: Content analysis

Select any three-minute clip of a videotape for analysis. The topic is to determine, by the evidence available, how the producer of the material put the segment together and for what purpose. You will need a video or DVD player and several bifurcated sheets of paper on which to record your analysis. Category codes are assigned as follows: (a) visual representations (the various physical settings and characteristics of each as they change; the people on the screen and their location as central, to the sides, or in the foreground or background; the actions that take place) and (b) auditory (who says what, background noises, use of music).

Step 1:

Watch the three-minute clip several times with the volume at zero. Record all information you can about each of the subsections of (a) above. Detail counts!

Step 2:

Listen to the three-minute clip several times with no visual screen. Record all information you can about each of the subsections of (b) above. Again, detail counts!

Step 3:

Watch the three-minute clip in its entirety (visual and auditory combined) and make any additional notes about (a) and (b) above.

Step 4:

Using the evidence made visible through Steps 1 to 3, what can you conclude about the "hand of the producer" and, in particular, how the producer put the segment together and for what purpose?

Summary

This chapter addressed data gathering options. The methods used most often—observations, interviews, questionnaires, and content analyses—were described in considerable detail. We intentionally selected these research methods based on the "kinds" of data they produce. Observations, interviews and focus groups, questionnaires, and content analyses produce different kinds of qualitative data and have different considerations and implications for analysis. What these methods have in common is that they allow the researcher to engage in the research as a visible and curious person. We provided sample tasks to assist with acquiring the data gathering skills. In all methods that are interactive, we have included information about the relational aspects of being a researcher and repeatedly addressed the importance of recording fieldnotes.

Often, the methods described in this chapter can be used together within the scope of a methodology, such as life history, case study, photovoice, and so on. If you are considering using two or several research methods, ask yourself the following questions: How will the various data be managed to be ready for analysis? Are you clear on which methods different participants will be asked to use? Have you accounted for the time the various methods will take for data gathering? These questions are explored further in Chapters 7, 8, and 9, but it is worth considering some of the implications of using multiple methods early on in the research process.

Research is about people and how they live their lives. As a researcher it is up to you to make those lives visible and to leave the legacy of a well-described and analyzed social world for the next generation. Critical social research is part of a continuous process of learning how to create knowledge as the process is experienced. It is a dynamic and emergent process. In this chapter you have moved through the operationalization of the research question to a presentation of choices a researcher can make about the methods or tools for data gathering.

Questions for Discussion

1. What are the four steps to operationalization and why is the time spent on doing these well so important to the research outcome?
2. What type of data gathering method is best for the kind of information you seek? What assumptions underlie this method?
3. Does the method "fit" you and fit your research question? Is it doable given the resources you have or can marshal?
4. Could you combine two or three of the methods to gather information about your research question (triangulation)?
5. Can you account for choosing one method or a combination of methods over others in a rational way?

Our Recommended Readings

deMarrais, K. (2004). Qualitative interview studies: Learning through experience. In K. deMarrais & S. D. Lapan (Eds.), *Foundations for research:*

Methods of inquiry in education and the social sciences (pp. 51–68). Mahwah: Lawrence Erlbaum Associates.

Flyvbjerg, B. (2011). Case study. In N. K. Denzin & Y. S. Lincoln (Eds.), *The SAGE handbook of qualitative research* (4th ed., pp. 301–329). Los Angeles: Sage.

Greaves, L. (1996). *Smoke screen: Women's smoking and social control.* Halifax: Fernwood.

Johnson, J. M., & Rowlands, T. (2012). The interpersonal dynamics of in-depth interviewing. In J. Gubrium, J. A. Holstein, A. B. Marvasti, & K. D. McKinney (Eds.), *The SAGE handbook of interview research: The complexity of the craft* (2nd ed., pp. 99–114). Los Angeles: Sage. http://dx.doi.org/10.4135/9781452218403.n7

Kamberelis, G., & Dimitriadis, G. (2011). Focus groups: Contingent articulations of pedagogy, politics, and inquiry. In N. K. Denzin & Y. S. Lincoln (Eds.), *The SAGE handbook of qualitative research* (4th ed., pp. 545–561). Los Angeles: Sage.

Marshall, C., & Rossman, G. B. (2016). *Designing qualitative research* (6th ed.). Los Angeles: Sage.

Miller, W. L., & Crabtree, B. F. (2004). Depth interviewing. In S. N. Hesse-Biber & P. Leavy (Eds.), *Approaches to qualitative research: A reader on theory and practice* (pp. 185–202). New York: Oxford University Press.

Patton, M. Q. (2015). *Qualitative research & evaluation methods* (4th ed., pp. 243–518). Los Angeles: Sage.

Sanjek, R. (Ed.). (1990). *Fieldnotes: The makings of anthropology.* Ithaca: Cornell University Press.

CHAPTER 7

WHO, WHERE, AND WHEN? SAMPLING AND FINALIZING THE RESEARCH PROPOSAL AND ETHICS FORMS

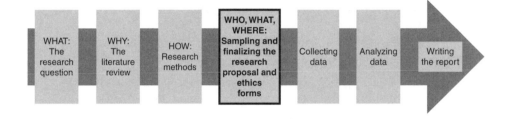

FIGURE 7.1: The Research Process

In Chapter 6 we provided a detailed description of a variety of data gathering methods and some exercises for you to develop practical skills before you begin your own research project. Now that you have learned a number of research designs and data gathering techniques, we encourage you to commit to the final version of your research question and to identify the practical steps you will take in your research. In this chapter you will choose a method or combination of methods for your research. You will learn about participant selection, which includes strategies for identifying an appropriate participant pool, preparation of selection criteria, the sampling process, and strategies for engaging with your participants from first contact to the conclusion of the research.

Choosing Your Method(s)

Now that we have examined various research methods, you must commit to your research question, research method(s), and data gathering plan. There are many things to consider as you commit to a specific method of inquiry. Among them are the kinds of data gathering you want to do, how prospective participants can be selected, where you are willing to go for information, how much time you have to do the research, how you will go about recording the information, and who can help you with various tasks. There are three steps remaining to determine the data gathering approach best suited to your purposes: reaffirm the research question; ask yourself about expectations, risks, and benefits; and select your methods.

Reaffirm the Research Question

Write out your research question yet again. Occasionally, at this point, the research question is suddenly too big and you must hive off a section to make it more practical. In the following example the initial focus of racial profiling would have been difficult to do, and the researcher would have been lucky to find even a few participants. With another look at the question, the real problem came clear and the research question, in its new form, became a much more doable piece of research:

> I wanted to research the media, and I was interested in racism. It seemed natural that I would do interviews with press reporters about their racial profiling tendencies and I thought they would simply tell me what they thought. It never occurred to me that if they knew racial profiling was wrong, they'd already be doing something to eliminate it. It was then that the research question became a question of "intentionality"—does racism with or without intent exist in crime reporting in print media? (Kirby, 2009)

Make any last changes to the research question at this point. Once the question has been set, you are ready for the next step.

Ask Yourself about Expectations, Risks, and Benefits

- *What do I expect to find?* Is it specific information? More questions? Certain answers? It is important that you understand and record early expectations of the research process in your fieldnotes.
- *What benefits do I expect to gain?* Do I hope to make the world a better place? To get an answer to a nagging question? To learn about the research process? It is less important to come up with a specific response than it is to consider the question itself.
- *What benefits and risks will this have for participants, and how might this affect their lives after the data gathering is over?* As a researcher, in what ways can you maximize the benefits for participants and minimize any risks? Are there ways that you can construct the research so that the knowledge gained from this is a real resource for participants as well as for you?

- *What responsibilities do I have to others, and how might they shape the research?* Things you might consider are the institutional context of the research (Who pays the bill for this research? Is there a link between the funder and the researcher? If so, how does this affect or shape the research enterprise?); the location of the researcher (undergraduate or graduate student; academic, community, or both; senior or junior position; secure or insecure position; established or new in the research field); the roles of community (as leaders, advisors, participants, consumers, analysts, or some combination thereof); and the scope of the research question (How much research is truly needed to answer this question well? Can justice be done to the research question through the research efforts that are going to be made?). The research may be shaped differently depending on your obligations to academic institutions, other organizations, grassroots groups, or political parties.

As the researcher, you will become a more informed person and this means you will carry the additional responsibility of having that knowledge. New research participants will also become more informed and will share that responsibility or burden of new knowledge. Be aware that new knowledge is not always easy to carry and can sometimes lead to major changes in the lives of both researchers and participants.

Select the Research Method(s)

Which research method(s) will help you answer your research question? To choose the method(s), consider the following in as much detail as possible:

- What kind of data are needed to answer the research question?
- What are all the choices in methods?
- What methods are most suited? Why?
- What methods will not work? Why?
- What mix of methods might work well? Why?
- What methods are best suited to the prospective participants with the experience I need? Why?
- What methods best suit you? Why?

List all the possible ways to get the information that could answer your research question. Map the possible methods and narrow the list to the single method or combination of methods. From mapping the possibilities, discuss with your supervisor, research team, colleagues, or knowledgeable others the merits of the chosen methods. Work through the choices and imagine how each method might be practically carried out. Be creative: combine, alter, and adjust. As in the touring exercise in Chapter 4, follow your instincts and remember to record your thinking and reasoning. This includes your reflections on the different methods and your plans for making the research "doable."

Narrow your choices to what fits you and your research question best. Make an informed choice about the best method or combination of methods that can be used to answer the research question. In a multiple-methods approach, the combination of methods means that after you gather your data from various methods you must have some way of combining the data to provide a cumulative view. Triangulation occurs when two (or more) methods are used in a study to check the results. Overlaps are seen as confirmatory—you can be more confident with a result if different methods lead to the same result. In choosing the methods, you will need to develop a plan to bring different data together in preparation for the analytical steps that follow. (We cover triangulation in more depth in Chapter 9.)

Remember That You Have Responsibilities as a Creator of Knowledge

As a researcher, your quest to answer your research question may occasionally get clouded and confused. Creating knowledge requires that you be attentive to what you experience and to what others experience around you. Critical social research must, at a minimum, describe and explain what happens in the social world. Not all research is good research. As you are now aware, whenever something is written about your experience but does not seem to represent what *you* know to be true, both the knowledge and the research methodology are questioned. Some groups of people frequently have this type of experience with researchers and soon rebuff attempts by researchers to learn more about them or their experiences. As a researcher, if participants in your research cannot see themselves in your reporting, then your research process and conclusions need to be re-evaluated.

Choosing Your Research Participants

The population of participants are all those who have the experience you are interested in. You then use a sampling method to select prospective participants for your study. The first step in choosing participants is to think about who has the information you are looking for. Given that different people have different knowledge and that knowledges exist in different forms, consider who has the information and experience you are seeking to understand. Think about who will be potentially affected by the research that is being proposed. Considerations for identifying who might be appropriate are listed below.

Demographics and Experience

Do your potential participants have the experience or criteria you are interested in investigating? How do you know? It might be that you have a clear understanding of who your research participants will be and that the "inclusion criteria" for their involvement are simple and straightforward. For instance, if you are interested in understanding the health practices of undergraduate students, your inclusion criteria may be as follows:

- Enrolled at X, Y, or Z institution in full-time study
- Between the ages of 18 and 25
- Female or male

Consider the range of participants you may get and how you may be able to use some of their demographic information (e.g., sex) as a point of comparison. In another example, Danielle wanted to retrospectively explore the experiences of siblings of children with cancer. She was able to identify some inclusion criteria—19 years of age or older, lived with a sibling with cancer during childhood—but then determined that she needed to be more specific about her inclusion criteria, such as gender of the participant and the sibling, family income, and geographic location at the time of cancer treatment.

Typically, a quantitative researcher who plans to investigate the relationship between two factors will need to consider the possibility of confounding variables. A *confounding variable* is "an extraneous variable whose presence affects the variables being studied so that the results you get do not reflect the actual relationship between the variables under investigation" (AlleyDog.com, n.d.).

In quantitative research there are statistical strategies to help control for confounding variables. Whether you are administering a quantitative questionnaire or qualitative interviews, the concept of confounding variables must be considered. In the example above, Danielle interviewed eight participants about their experiences growing up with a sibling with cancer. Her research question was "What supports do siblings of children with a history of cancer need?" Danielle needed to closely consider the confounding variables in her study. She collected a range of demographic data (gender, ethnicity, family income, family composition, and domestic status) as well as specific information about the family situation and the sibling's experience of cancer. To gain a clearer answer to the research question Danielle needed to know the sibling's cancer diagnosis, the outcome of the sibling's cancer (cancer-free or deceased), and the age of the participant when the sibling had cancer. Although these experiences are not "controlled" for in qualitative interviews as they might be in a quantitative research design, they are nonetheless essential considerations in comprehensively answering the research question.

When considering the experience you want to examine, think closely about how similar or diverse a sample you need. Do your participants need to have similar demographics, experiences, communities, and locations? And if so, which ones are most important? The *inclusion criteria* (or demographic commonalities) that are pertinent to some studies may not be to others. Participants with a greater number of similarities may allow for stronger findings and a greater chance of data saturation and rich accounts (see Chapter 9 for trustworthiness criteria), although the narrower the inclusion criteria, the more difficult it may be to recruit willing participants. It is always advisable to be clear about the demographic information and lived experiences you are interested in and to find ways to gather consistent data from your participants about these factors. Face sheets with open- and close-ended questions can be used in qualitative and quantitative research (see Figures 7.2 and 7.3). Often they are a good way to begin a questionnaire or do a "warm-up" of an interview.

Participant Face Sheet

Name: _____

Age: _____

Domestic status:

☐ Single

☐ Divorced

☐ Separated

☐ Widowed

☐ Common-law partner

☐ Other?

How would you describe your ethnicity/race?

_____

Do you have children?

☐ Yes

☐ No

If yes, how many children do you have and what are their ages?

_____

Where do your children live?

_____

What is your education level?

☐ Elementary school

☐ Some high school

☐ Completed Grade 12

☐ Some college

☐ Completed college diploma

☐ Some university

☐ Completed university degree

☐ Other: _____

FIGURE 7.2: Sample Face Sheet #1

INTAKE INTERVIEW

Pseudonym:	Consent form signed? Yes ☐ No ☐	Participant Number:	Cluster Group Number:
Photo identifiers:			

First name:		Last name:	
Phone:	Email:		Best way to contact you:

Socio-demographic Information

Age:	Gender:	First language spoken:
Highest level of educational attainment: ☐ Some high school ☐ High school ☐ Some college or university ☐ College certificate or diploma ☐ University degree ☐ Some postgraduate ☐ Postgraduate	Current employment status (check all that apply): ☐ none ☐ part-time ☐ full-time ☐ disability benefits PWD ☐ PPMB ☐ social assistance ☐ volunteering ☐ pension plan CPP ☐ TVP ☐ other: _____	Current living situation: ☐ with family ☐ with roommate ☐ alone ☐ with partner ☐ with partner and child(ren) ☐ supported housing ☐ group home ☐ other: _____ ☐ pets: _____
Domestic status: ☐ Single ☐ Partnered / common-law ☐ Married ☐ Separated ☐ Divorced ☐ Widow/widower ☐ Other: _____	Average annual income: ☐ less than $10 000 ☐ $11 000 - $15 000 ☐ $16 000 - $20 000 ☐ $21 000 - $25 000 ☐ $26 000 or higher	Ethnicity : Religion or spirituality:

Mental Health History

Diagnosis:	Since when?	Length of time involved in mental health system:
Currently, who is your primary contact for your mental health care: ☐ Mental Health Team ☐ EPI ☐ Private psychiatrict ☐ No one ☐ Family doctor		
Are you currently accessing any other support services within the mental health system? ☐ YES ☐ NO		
If "yes", which ones? ☐ Community Link ☐ Housing ☐ Art Studios ☐ CMHA ☐ Other: _____ ☐ Coast		
Do you have any other health issues? (e.g. addiction?) Please list them:		

FIGURE 7.3: Sample Face Sheet #2

As you can see, these face sheets are very different, asking different kinds of questions and eliciting different amounts of information and detail. When in doubt, gather the face sheet data you believe will be relevant to your study.

Accessibility

Are the potential participants willing to share their experiences? Can you locate them or can others identify them for you? Do they live in a geographic location that you can access? In some instances individuals or groups of individuals with the experience you are interested in are clearly identifiable. You may know who you want to research, but they may be hard to find. Perhaps they have been dispersed, changed names, or sought anonymity on purpose. For example, women who were pregnant and unmarried prior to the 1970s were often forced or pressured to give up their babies for adoption. In later decades, when many jurisdictions opened their adoption records and adoptees began to search for their biological mothers, only some of the mothers wanted to be found. While some women have banded together and been vocal about getting assistance in dealing with their experiences, others have wanted no part of being found by their children or discussing the issues surrounding relinquishing them.

Identity

Do your potential participants identify themselves as having the experience? Will they identify themselves to you as the researcher? It can be difficult to identify those who have the experience you are focusing on. In work on the health and social services needs of older gay and lesbian individuals (Kirby & SQS, 2000), the identification of what types of people was quite straightforward: older (+55 years), gay or lesbian, within the boundaries of the City of Winnipeg, and willing to complete a questionnaire. The difficulty was finding the people or letting them know how to find us, the researchers. This was a community "deep in the closet" who had lived through the 1950s to 1970s in Canada when homosexuality was considered by many to be a psychiatric illness, a disease, a sin, or a crime. A number of public information meetings were held around topics of interest such as financial planning, mobility assistance, gardening, and travel destinations. With each meeting the list of contacts remained short, but the number of questionnaires handed out to as yet unidentified people in the community grew quickly. Few were interested in sharing their stories in a public way, but the strict confidentiality measures we had in place enabled even the most timid to complete a questionnaire and return it to us without having to "come out of the closet" or in any way feel unsafe. The meetings and snowballing technique soon created a substantial number of completed questionnaires.

Communication

Does the language of communication of your potential participants match your linguistic capacities and the instruments for gathering data? There are circumstances where *basic communication* is difficult. For example, does a prospective participant's language of communication match yours (the linguistic capacities of the research team and the language used for the instruments for gathering data)? You may be faced with a telephone interview or you may need to communicate with a participant who has a hearing impairment or who speaks a different language than you. In order to reach the best level of communication possible, full translation or mediated communication might be necessary. Every attempt within reason and available resources must be made to ensure that open communication is established between you and the participants. Consider the ethics and translation issues that arise when the communication between research participants and researchers is mediated. Since communication is mediated, the translator or mediator must sign the ethics agreements of confidentiality. Also, they must be asked to provide direct, unaltered translation. The same holds true when participants are those who can only communicate through an attendant. Often being fully inclusive is resource intensive: It can take considerably more of the researcher's time and it can be expensive. Efforts to be inclusive have to be sustained, well thought through, and sometimes require compromise.

Another issue in basic communication is the use of our own language or our first language for communication. For example, the Truth and Reconciliation Commission (2015) revealed that many survivors and their families are focusing on healing themselves, their communities, and their nations in ways that revitalize Indigenous cultures, languages, spirituality, laws, and governance systems. Indigenous languages are connected to identity and culture. Consider this narrative challenge from Young's (2005) work:

> In her ethnographic study of the residential school experiences in British Columbia, Haig-Brown (1998) added that "Not only were the students not allowed to speak (their language) in school, they were also convinced that their use of the language was an indication of inferiority" (p. 120) . . .
>
> Both my [Young's] parents offered me another way of looking at education as a whole, my experiences and the world for that matter. Wherever I go, wherever I am, I will always remember I am *Anishinabe*. I will speak it even if no one understands: it is a way of centering myself (p. 11) . . .
>
> They reminded me that I came from another place and I was carrying a different kind of knowledge. Teachings and educations I received from my parents, I had forgotten to attend to this embodied knowledge (p. 135) . . .
>
> I hope you recognize the importance of speaking our Aboriginal languages and how they are so important to our identity and to who we are as a people. I wonder how you see yourself helping us to achieve our wishes . . . *Kwa yuk ka kwe pimosata.* Let's walk in a good way. (pp. 153–154)

What this suggests is that if we want to research in areas where other languages are used, then the research must occur in those languages. Young asserts that much of her identity is lost when she does not use her

Indigenous language. This stance is now taken in most research with Indigenous communities and is supported by the First Peoples' Cultural Council among other groups and organizations. Researchers need to value and have research conducted in the participants' language rather than have the participants come to the language of the researchers.

Rapport

Do you have the insight and diplomacy to work with this group or these groups (St. Denis, 2004)? Is establishing a comfortable rapport to share information likely to occur? Rapport is a key component of communication and the need for rapport is evident in virtually all data gathering methods requiring social interaction. It is needed early in the research and must be sustained sometimes well past the end of the research. This means that whether you are gathering data or reporting on the research, communication skills are important.

Good rapport can be fostered by complete and straightforward introductions of the research focus and of you as researcher. Any information that will ease participants' concerns is appreciated; this could include such details as confirmation of meeting dates and times, arrangements made for participation and feedback after initial encounters, and information about where the data will be used. As discussed in Chapter 3, we believe that critical social research requires intersubjectivity: an authentic dialogue between everyone in the research process where each person is respected as an equally knowing subject. This does not imply that you and your participants are the same. Even though you may initiate the research interaction, the participants have the experience you want to know more about and their sharing will help shape the research. The communication between you should reflect the respect you hold for each other as individuals. Rapport is something to be fostered for the duration of the research and possibly beyond. Rapport is *not* to be developed as a tool of manipulation to solicit more information from a participant. It is, however, important to be as open, honest, and straightforward as possible throughout each of the participant's involvement in the research.

A word of caution: Rapport is essential to many research designs and is the hallmark of critical social research. However, there is ongoing debate in the literature about blurring researcher and friend roles or moving into a counselling relationship and the risk this may pose for the participant and the researcher (Bringer, 2002; Oakley, 1981). Also, remain mindful of the possibility of response effects—when participants want to please researchers by answering in ways they believe will be helpful to the researcher, or when participants purposefully divert the researcher. A classic example of this is Margaret Mead's landmark study *Coming of Age in Samoa: A Psychological Study of Primitive Youth for Western Civilisation* (1930/2001).

Sampling Approaches

There is an array of sampling techniques described in the literature. Probability or random sampling is used in quantitative research. Participants are selected or sampled in a way that is representative of the population in order to generalize the results to the original population.[1] In qualitative research, nonprobability sampling is typically used. Researchers select cases with a particular purpose or goal in mind. Nonprobability sampling techniques used in qualitative research include the following:

- *Cluster sampling:* The researcher chooses participants who are ready and able to participate, for example, surveying all students in a particular classroom.

- *Extreme case sampling:* The researcher seeks participants who are known to "exemplify the characteristics of interest" (Morse, 1994, p. 229) so that the questions become clear quickly.

- *Intense sampling:* The researcher chooses participants who have a variety of experiences over a length of time all of which are useful to the study (Morse, 1994).

- *Maximum variety sampling:* The researcher looks for common experiences and also for uncommon experiences to round out the description of the characteristics being studied.

- *Critical case sampling:* The researcher selects participants who typify critical incidents in what is being studied.

- *Snowball sampling:* The researcher asks each person interviewed or surveyed to identify another person who could be contacted. Its limitation is that it may reach a narrow part of an experiential community and may be problematic in terms of confidentiality.

- *Convenience sampling:* The researcher chooses participants who are close at hand and easily accessible.

- *Purposive sampling:* The researcher uses special knowledge of group or experience to select those "most" representative.

- *Quota sampling:* The researcher selects participants based on a percentage of the population who experiences a particular phenomenon: If 10 per cent of the population is "obese," we need 10 per cent of a sample that is "obese."

....

1 Probability sampling techniques include (a) random sampling: every participant has an equal chance of being selected every time. For example, random selection from a population means that, after each selection, the sample selected is then replaced into the pool; (b) systematic random sampling: the researcher wants 20 from 100 participants and then takes the fifth, tenth, and so on; and (c) stratified random: in order to select representatives from subgroups, the population is divided into strata and random selection is applied to the strata.

In all cases, we recommend that interested participants be asked to contact the researchers, not the other way around. Prospective participants can learn about the study from posters, flyers, listservs, social networking sites, or via a third party.[2] This prevents researchers from identifying and targeting prospective participants who may not know they have been identified as potential participants. It also means that, should they want to, a prospective participant could find out about the research project prior to volunteering to participate.

Ania used maximum variation sampling (a purposive sampling for gathering a heterogeneous sample) to recruit research participants for her master's thesis project. Here she describes her sampling approach:

> To gain multiple perspectives on ways in which gender, education, income, and mental health diagnosis interact to shape engagement within community-based research, this study will use the maximum variation sampling strategy (Creswell, 1998) to identify and recruit participants for in-depth interviews. Fourteen participants (14) will be selected based on their roles and the length of time of their involvement in the Imagining Inclusion project. The research entry process will be divided into 4 distinct stages: 1. *pre-engagement*, 2. *engagement*, 3. *assessment, reflection* and *feedback*, and 4. *ongoing maintenance* (Ochocka, 2010). I propose adding a fifth stage—*employment*, to represent paid engagement of peer researchers. (Landy, 2015)

Number of Participants

Sample size in quantitative research depends on the degree of confidence a researcher wants in the results. In this case a small sample usually means large room for error. In part, determining sample sizes in qualitative research is a matter of judgment and experience. It is necessary to evaluate the quality of the information collected against the particular research method and sampling strategy employed (Sandelowski, 1995). In qualitative research, sufficient sample size is usually determined by the volume and consistency of the data gathered. Data saturation occurs when the researcher is no longer hearing or seeing new information and when a depth of information has been achieved. Essentially, saturation is reached when no new cases add new information to

---

2 An example of using a third party for recruitment occurs when conducting research at one's worksite. The researcher, who is also a practitioner or clinician onsite, is in conflict of interest when recruiting research participants from the clients who access the service or program. In this case an administrator or nonclinician/nonpractitioner can step in to contact prospective participants and, in some cases, to be the first point of contact for participants who may want to participate in the study.

the existing body of information. For example, 5 to 10 participants may be all that is needed in an emergent piece of work on smoking among preteens, while 30 to 40 may be needed for research on smoking cessation programs for nurses working in critical care units. A participant observation can involve one participant intensely observed over a long period of time, or hundreds of people observed all at once for a short period of time. Data saturation is discussed in more detail in Chapter 9.

The Complexities of Sampling

Diverse Knowledges

There is knowledge in common sense, not-so-common sense, tradition, and authority, and in research and writing. *Common sense* is how each of us interprets or makes sense of the world around us on a daily basis: everybody knows, for example, that drinking and driving are not a good combination of behaviours because innocent people can get hurt. *Not-so-common sense* is unreliable but nonetheless accepted knowledge. For example, many North American hotels are built without a thirteenth floor; witness the elevator counter as it records 11, 12, 14, and 15 as it ascends. How is it that people know this superstition? *Traditional knowledge* is based on culture and heritage. People learn as they grow up in a particular culture what serves as true knowledge. For example, on the Chinese New Year preparing a fish with both its head and tail means that you value the beginning and end of things, and eating long noodles at the end of the meal means long life. Another form of knowledge is based on *authority*. This is knowledge we accept because someone in authority tells us it is right. It is authored, published, and appears to have currency in people's understanding of how the world works. But it also appears, for example, when we learn that vegetables are good for us because a parent tells us so. Knowledge can also be found in *research and writing*. Research provides the information and conclusions based on that information to support a particular research question. Research provides a "measure of proof" that particular knowledge exists and eventually it becomes part of public knowledge.

Critical social research involves four tasks that can unpack diverse knowledges:

- *Unmasking* refers to questioning existing knowledge to understand who created that knowledge and why, what concepts and rules were used, and whose meanings or experiences are being presented. Applying a social exclusion lens (see Chapters 1 and 3) to knowledge is a helpful tool here. Who does this knowledge represent and who does it benefit?

Who is not represented in this knowledge and what needs to be done to have a more inclusive knowledge base?

- *Creating* means building knowledge out of a basic understanding that social reality is constructed by members of society and that those on the edges or margins and those within the status quo experience different social worlds.
- *Affirming* refers to developing an understanding of the complex and subtle ways in which people beyond the mainstream are kept invisible and silenced, affirming the knowledge of those currently excluded, and participating in naming that social reality in a way that remains faithful to their experience and does not further exploit it.
- *Sharing and reconstructing* means acting as responsible knowers, working with others to use research skills to create knowledge for social change, and combining knowledge with action.

The Challenge of Inclusion

Sampling is not always a neutral event (J. Hofley, personal communication, 9 February 2005). Occasionally, sampling sets up a new "hierarchy of importance" in a community where some people are chosen and others are not. Consider the following example:

> [He] was a member of a research team exploring strategies to improve the performance of Indigenous students in high schools in Manitoba. As part of the research design, it was suggested that one group of students be divided into a control group and a treatment group. The treatment group would have harder tasks to complete and would receive various types of support and mentoring along the way. There are obvious benefits for those in the treatment group. The control group would have far fewer tasks to complete and no extra supports to assist them. The problem here is simple: One group gets benefits and the other does not. And benefits accrue to members of one group while equally talented but perhaps unlucky members of the control group receive fewer. As Hofley explained, the research design itself set up a fundamental inequality in an attempt to address an even larger inequality. This inequality was not acceptable to some and, as a solution, was partially ameliorated by a recommendation to change the research design to a matched pairs protocol to be selected from groups in different school years.
> (J. Hofley, personal communication, 9 February 2005)

Researchers have always selected research participants according to well-established selection criteria. However, in recent attempts to find more egalitarian research relationships sampling presents new dilemmas. For example, some who are excluded by "neutral sampling procedures" want to be included, while others want to be excluded from the research. Another example is that of sampling repeatedly from the same population. Despite the best intentions of researchers, some populations have been extensively over-researched, while others have received little or no research attention.

To reach a more inclusive goal, you may need to rethink the notion of selecting participants—Who are they? Why them and not others? Do all have a fair and equal chance of participating? Are they willing? Who gets to select them and why? and so on. In the above example, teachers, researchers, and Elders together could choose participants. Also, a researcher can visit a number of communities where participants are identified and consult with community members about research plans. At the same time, the researcher can seek their guidance and offer support.

Another way to think about inclusive research is to make accommodations to enable all people with the experience in question to have an equal chance of participating. Accommodations might include data gathering instruments that are in large print or presented orally and in a language familiar to prospective participants (e.g., Braille, American Sign Language, Italian), a data gathering site that is accessible to someone with mobility issues, a longer time limit for someone with a cognitive disability, or an alternative recording mechanism so that those with visual impairments can receive timely feedback similar to other participants.

Our recommendation in sampling is two-fold. First, you must be aware of the social context in which the participants live and take account of it in the selection of research participants. No researcher wants to exacerbate social exclusions that might already exist. Second, seek the advice and support of the community in which you hope to conduct your research. By virtue of having selection criteria, some people will not be included in your research. Sometimes the best you can do is to make your criteria transparent and clearly communicate why the criteria are important to the integrity of the research.

Researchers rarely conduct research with everyone identified as a possible participant. Some people will be unwilling to participate; others will resist the development of any rapport and will therefore not be suitable; others may simply be unable to participate in any organized data collection session; still others may retract their participation without explanation. If there is a great deal of difficulty in finding willing participants, the problem may be with the research focus, the access or consent processes, or the researcher. A good researcher will recognize this and make adjustments. If the research is inherently flawed, the researcher can always go back to the drawing board. Every part of the research process teaches us a bit more about ourselves and the world. It is not a matter of getting to the end at all costs. Rather, the way you get there and the process itself is part of the research.

Exercise 7.1: Thinking critically about sampling

Use the following questions to identify the characteristics of targeted research participants and to become fully aware of who may be missing from the study:

- Are there characteristics that are central to the study that are common among all participants?
- Which characteristics are less central and do not require uniformity (they are not the basis for inclusion or exclusion in the study)?
- Who is and is not participating in the project? Is it possible to be clear about why certain groups or individuals have not been included?
- Is attention being given to barriers to participation (i.e., transportation, language, childcare)?
- Is attention being paid to the methods chosen to advertise the research? Could the advertising method itself exclude certain populations? (adapted from Reid, Brief, & LeDrew, 2009)

The Appropriateness of the Data Gathering Site

You must go to where the information is located or bring those with the information to you. Lofland and Lofland (1995) recommend that potential data sites need to be evaluated for appropriateness, access, and ethics. Determining appropriateness means taking into account that *where* you gather data will influence *what* data you gather, what methods you can use, and even what questions you might ask. Lofland and Lofland offer three principles of appropriateness:

- If you choose participant observation, do your observations at a site where what or who you are interested in will be present.
- If you are interested in gathering information about some experience that doesn't occur in any specific site, more direct interaction through interviews or surveys is likely to be more useful.
- There are many varieties of the standard research methods and you may find that you have to adapt a particular method to suit your research needs. This may mean reconsidering data sites in light of the permissions you receive or your novel approach to data gathering.

Although these points are based on common sense and may seem obvious, they are important to remember when you are trying to decide where you will go for information. Many research projects have gone off track because of the inappropriateness of the data site. As a researcher, you bring your own characteristics to the study and need to account for these fully. Such characteristics and viewpoints need to be identified and accounted for as part of making choices in any research project. The process should be as open as possible to participants; an overt and mutually interactive experience between the participant and the researcher is possible. Participants need to know enough about the research focus to want to participate, to be able to share in the information gathering process, and ultimately to see themselves in the final report of the study.

Research Proposals

The research proposal lays out plans as part of an approval process where a researcher will have the research plans vetted for ethics. For the undergraduate, honours undergraduate, or graduate student researcher, the research proposal is often a class assignment or a requirement for partial fulfillment of the degree. In essence the proposal is exactly what it says: a *proposal* for the research that the researcher intends to undertake. A researcher prepares a proposal that details what she or he proposes to do and how he or she plans to do it. Essentially, the proposal requires a full explanation of the five Ws and an H: what, why, how, who, where, and when. Based on all the information gathered (literature review, methods texts, consultations with stakeholders or others), it contains the "best guesses" and rationale of how the research will unfold. Writing the proposal is a step-by-step approach to document what you anticipate doing in the research. The purpose of the proposal or research protocol is to write your argument (Morse, 1994, p. 226) and to communicate it to others (e.g., department, organization, potential participants, collaborators, ethics board, potential funders, graduate committees). Your proposal should persuade others that the research you want to do is interesting, important, and worthy of support and attention. And it should be convincing. Your proposal is your case—that is, a clearly presented and complete plan for what it is you want to research and how you plan to undertake the research. Consult Table 7.1 for a detailed outline of what is included in a research proposal.

All sections up to and including the methodology will contain details of what you have accomplished to date. The methods section details the type and location of data sources available and your criteria for selecting research participants. Things to be appended include the research data gathering instruments, biographical notes on research team members (if applicable) and the specific tasks they may undertake in the research, ethics forms (consent forms, assent forms, information letters, email recruitments, etc.), and any other documents significant to the research.

TABLE 7.1 Detailed Outline of a Research Proposal and Final Report

	RESEARCH PROPOSAL	FINAL REPORT
Title page (page 1)	• Project title and institution or organization • Name of principal investigator (P.I.) or student researcher • Names of members of the research team, supervisory committee, or course instructor • Date	
Abstract (page 2)	Summary of your basic message (i.e., what you PLAN to do in this research project and WHY the project is important)	Summary of your basic message (i.e., what you DID, what you FOUND, and SO WHAT?) In the final report write in past tense because it is now a completed study
Introduction	Specifications for abstracts, in terms of word count and format, vary by institution, publisher, etc. • Introduction and purpose of the research • Research goals and researcher's orientation to the research • Where did the research idea come from? • What research goals are to be accomplished and why? • What is the general research focus? • Rationale for the research (why this research, why now, why you?) • What can be/was accomplished with this research? • What expectations or fears do/did you have about doing this research?	

Literature Review	• Theoretical and contextual background
	  • What is already known about the research focus?
	  • What kind of research, using what methodologies, has been undertaken in the past?
	
	• Rationale for the research (why this research, why now, why us?)
	• Gaps, oversights, biases, or limitations of literature
	• What you have learned from and how you position yourself in relation to current discussions of your topic. Do you have a personal relationship to the topic?
	
	Your literature review may need to be revised for the final report. Some literature covered in the proposal may no longer be relevant. It is also possible that your research findings will require you to cover additional literature.	

Methodology	• Proposed participants and inclusion/exclusion criteria, recruitment strategies, target number • Data collection procedures, including rationale, number, format • When and where data collection will occur • Plans for data management and analysis • Your role as the researcher (positionality, reflexivity)	• *Rationale* for method(s) used • *Data collection process*: How was the data gathering organized (who, where, when)? What was the plan from initial to final contact with participants? Who participated and how many (include demographic information)? How did data gathering progress? Did it work? Was the data gathering plan appropriate? What was your "data set"? What reflections are recorded about the data gathering process?

- *Data organization and management processes*: How have the data been managed (transcripts, recordings, files)? How was security of files, participants, and research assistants managed? How has the accuracy of the data been confirmed with participants?
- *Data analysis processes*: How were data described (coding, emergent themes, categories)? How were data analyzed (links between codes, themes, etc.)? Are there any leftover data? If so, how can it be accounted for?
- *Trustworthiness criteria/credibility of the analysis*: Have various people participated in the analysis? In what ways can you confirm that the analysis is credible and trustworthy?

In the proposal you are "proposing" what you will do, which means that you are making "best guesses" at what will be possible. Typically, research will not unfold exactly as expected. In the final report document what you did, and do not worry about what you proposed in the proposal. In the final report write in the *past* tense because it is now a completed study.

Ethical Considerations	Ethical considerations and anticipated ethical procedures	What were the ethical considerations and how did you manage them? Did anything unexpected occur?
Research Findings	n/a	*Overview of findings*, usually organized by theme: Are the data presented comprehensively and sensitively? Can participants see themselves reflected in analysis? Is the reporting accurate, reliable, and valid? Are there linkages with concepts in the review of the literature? Are there new theoretical developments? Are you satisfied with the report?
Discussion	n/a	*High-level discussion of research findings and literature*: In what ways do the findings support what is in the literature? In what ways do the findings add to the literature, or conflict with what has been written? Author's reflections on the research
Study Limitations	n/a	Short overview of limitations encountered or limitations with the research design
Conclusion	General statement about why this research should be pursued and the rationale for the study	High-level overview of the importance of the research question(s), the rationale, and some or several statements to address "so what?" What do we know that we didn't know before? How does this research make the world a better place to live? Tell the readers why it counts and why it is important

(continued)

TABLE 7.1 Detailed Outline of a Research Proposal and Final Report (Continued)

	RESEARCH PROPOSAL	FINAL REPORT
Dissemination and Knowledge Transfer	Reporting and communication plans (dissemination and knowledge transfer)	*Plans for using the research* (applying the findings, communicating results, etc.): What actions and policies do you think are likely to bring about positive social change? What have the participants indicated about ways to bring about social change? What have other interested parties indicated about action and policy change? Have you indicated what your investment in any action or policy development might be? What are the directions for further research? Updated from the proposal
References	You will be well-served to know the formatting style that is required before you begin your proposal and to consistently follow this style through all stages of writing.[3]	
Appendices	• Timeline • Budget (if applicable) • Data gathering instruments (interview questions, questionnaire, observation guidelines) • Ethics documents (approval forms from institution, institutional ethics forms and supporting documentation, including consent forms, assent forms, information letters, recruitment emails, etc.)	• Data gathering instruments (interview questions, questionnaire, observation checklist, etc.) • Ethics forms • Signed ethics approval certificate from your institution • Data displays, including codebooks, data spreadsheet, analytical maps, and so on (if needed); do not include raw data

....

3 There are many formatting styles, including (but not limited to) APA style, Chicago Manual of Style, Bluebook, Business Style Handbook, Elements of Style, IEEE style, MLA Handbook, New York Times Manual, Oxford Guide to Style, Scientific Style and Format, The Sense of Style, Turabian.

The Ethics Application

In Chapter 3 we introduced some of the principles of conducting ethical critical social research. Once you have committed to your data gathering process and to the prospective participants in your research, it is time to complete the research proposal, as described above. In addition, you need to specify the ethics provisions you are making and submit the ethics forms to the appropriate organization for approval. Members of the research ethics committee, typically academic peers and sometimes representatives from the nonacademic community, review the submission and either approve, disapprove, or make recommendations for improvements of both the methods and ethical steps proposed. Where student research is being proposed, different institutions have different practices regarding ethics approvals. In some cases, such as a one-semester undergraduate research methods class, the course instructor gains "course approval" for all student projects and oversees and is responsible for the ethical dimensions of the projects that unfold in the class. Course approval is granted in the case when the students are engaging in research primarily for pedagogical purposes rather than research purposes. In the case of an honours undergraduate or graduate course, most often the student is required to gain ethical approval for his or her project and typically applies as a "student researcher" with the academic supervisor as the principal investigator. Once again, institutions have different practices and it is important to know how you will gain ethical approval for your project before you begin the process.

In the case of the first-time or student researcher, we recommend engaging in "minimal harm" research, which means that the research imposes little risk to the participants or organizations involved. Minimal risk projects can often undergo an expedited review. Expedited reviews are reserved for those proposals with little interpersonal interaction and no discernible harm. On the other hand, moderate risk reviews are for those proposals that have a lot of interpersonal interaction and may have a potential for elevated risk to the participants or others as a result of the study. High-risk reviews involve a much more intensive and exacting level of scrutiny, are reserved for those proposals that are seen to have a potentially high balance of harm to benefit.

All ethical guidelines seek to balance the regulations about research protocols and systems of approval with the rights of participants, researchers, and partners. Not only are research ethics boards tasked with ensuring that research follows ethical guidelines, they also assess the internal consistency in your documents (i.e., proposal, ethics forms, consent form, information letter, interview questions, etc.). If inconsistencies are found you will need to revise and resubmit all of your documentation. Your ability to be clear and consistent about what you are doing is a sign of systematic, transparent, and ultimately ethical research.

The Role of Ethics in Selecting Research Participants

There are two key ethical questions to address when considering sampling and access to data sites (Lofland & Lofland, 1995):

1. Should this particular group, setting, or question be studied by *anyone*? We are concerned with gathering information that will help us explore and transform current relations of inequality. We are less interested in pursuing research just for the sake of research. Examples of research that maintain or extend relations of exploitation and domination include eugenic engineering, mind control research, covert research on grassroots organizations, some forms of military weapons research, some forms of research with Indigenous peoples, and research that supports or legitimates racist, sexist, homophobic, ethnocentric, or classist actions or attitudes.
2. Should this group, setting, or question be studied by *me*? If the group does not want to be studied, or does not want to be studied by you, you need to back away and re-examine your motives and intentions, research design, and skills and attitudes. It may be possible to make some changes to gain access. Then again, there may be nothing to do but accept the wishes of the group.

Safe communication is essential to good research. As a researcher you may gain access to information that could be potentiality damaging to specific individuals, to groups, or to political movements. In some instances you will be asked if you can guarantee safety to your research participants. The researcher's job is not to guarantee that which cannot be guaranteed, as in the case of, for example, child sexual abuse disclosures that must, by law, be reported. If researchers intend to alter the course of events as a result of the research, these intentions need to be communicated clearly to the research participants, particularly about the guarantee of confidentiality and distribution of information at the completion of the study. You must adhere to what you have told the participants; any changes require renegotiation with the participants.

> **INFORMED CONSENT**
>
> Harriett was approached to participate in a video on women on the margins at a national conference held in Ottawa. The person who approached her said that the video was being made for use by faculty of a particular department of a university. Harriett agreed and participated in a three-minute taped interview on being a visible lesbian in a national organization. She was surprised to find out immediately after

the recording that the video was also going to be marketed nationally on educational channels. Weeks later, when the request for a signature of approval was received in the mail, Harriett did not sign it and wrote to the producer complaining of unethical treatment.

At the end of the data gathering experience, Harriett felt neither safe nor fairly treated and as a result she withdrew her contribution from the process. The insights she might have contributed were lost. The terms for Harriet's participation in the video—as discussed when reviewing the informed consent form—were breached. Researchers must guarantee, to the best of their ability, that they will adhere to the research plan and, if there is any deviation, particularly regarding the use of the information or actions undertaken, that the participants be informed and have the option to withdraw their participation. Researchers are responsible for establishing a safe communication pattern so that participants are comfortable sharing their experiences and know how their experiences or "data" will be used. If they feel "at risk," you might negotiate a different way of gathering the information, or simply accept the stance they are taking and respect their choices.

When you ask "who has this experience?" you are beginning to focus on information, not on people. That is, you are sampling the information available to you and should not be overly concerned about whether you have gathered the correct number of participants or a random sample or a complete population. Instead, if you think in terms of how much information is enough, you will soon recognize when data gathering is sufficient in certain areas of your research but lacking in others.

Consent forms are used to ask prospective research participants whether or not they agree to participate in the study and what their participation would involve. Once signed it becomes the contract between you, the researcher, and them, the participant. As such, they must be in a position to sign the form. First, this means that they must be capable of giving their consent. Although the most recent Tri-Council Policy Statement on ethical conduct does not overtly state an age of consent, generally speaking the age of consent is 16 in all provinces except Quebec, where it is 18. If the child is not of the age of consent, a parent or guardian must sign on their behalf and must not be in a position of dependency with regard to the researcher or the supporting institutions or with other organizations responsible for their care.

Researchers and research ethics boards should be aware that institutions, organizations, or other groups under study may have requirements for allowing access to their sites and participants, and some of these have established mechanisms (e.g., school boards, Indigenous communities, correctional services, and community groups; Panel on Research Ethics, 2014, p. 34). For example, an adult in a care home may fully understand the research and may wish to participate, but since the care home is legally responsible for him or her the care home would also have to consent to his or her participation before the research could be undertaken. Second, the research participants must be aware of what they are signing. The consent form must have enough information to communicate what is being asked of participants and what the researcher is promising to do. Third, they must know for how long they are giving permission to the researcher to gather data. The timeframe must be clear. Participants consent to certain data gathering and feedback activities over a certain period of time and not beyond. Fourth, consent must be freely given. The prospective participant cannot be coerced into signing or promised special treatment outside the purview of the research. Since the consent form is a legal contract, both the researcher and the participant should be protected by it. Both should know what they are agreeing to and should be bound by it.

When the participant is under the age of majority, regular consent forms are prepared for parents or guardians and an additional "assent form" (Gratton & Jones, 2004) is prepared for the child/dependent person. According to the Researcher Information Services (n.d.) at the University of British Columbia, "assent is to *concur with the decision of another* whereas consent is *to provide permission.*" Children old enough to understand the concepts described in a consent form should be provided with an assent form to sign. The consent form is essential. The assent form is a reminder to you that even though others may legally sign for a participant, you need to have the active agreement from the participant. In addition, if the ethics board agrees, there are rare cases involving "emancipated minors" where such persons can consent for themselves. The purpose of an assent form is to inform participants who are unable to legally sign for themselves about the study in a manner in which they can understand, and to serve as a vehicle whereby they may (or may not) indicate that they agree to participate.

Final Checklists

Use these final checklists to ensure that all is in order as you complete your proposal and ethics forms. As well, many institutional research ethics boards include checklists in their documentation so that researchers who are applying for approval can ensure that all is in order. Of course, you must have ethics approval before data gathering. It is also helpful to have a rough plan for data management and analysis and a general timeline for your research.

Research Participants

1. Demographics and experience
   - Which participant characteristics or criteria are central to your study and need to be common among all participants?
   - Which characteristics or criteria are less central and do not require uniformity?
   - Which characteristics might be confounding?
   - Which other experiences are central to your research and why?
2. Accessibility
   - Is the information you are interested in accessible?
   - Are the participants you've identified willing to share their experiences?
   - Can you locate them or can others identify them for you?
   - Do they live in a geographic location that you can access?
3. Identity
   - Do your prospective research participants identify themselves as having the experience?
   - Will they identify themselves to you as the researcher?
4. Communication
   - Are you able to communicate in the participants' first language? If not, is anything compromised by your inability to communicate in the participants' first language?
   - Do you have the resources (time and money) for translation? What are the implications of translation and what interpretations or nuances might be lost?
   - Do you have the insight and diplomacy to work with this group or these groups? (St. Denis, 2004)
5. Rapport
   - What is involved in reaching out and creating relationships with your prospective research participants?
   - Do you have the insight and diplomacy to work with this group of people?
6. Sampling technique
   - Which sampling approach will you take, and why?
   - How many participants will be recruited, and why?

Research Setting and Timing

- Where are the richest possible data sites? What are the characteristics of the setting? What data are available?
- Have you met with encouragement in the setting or resistance? What is the balance of benefit and risk?

- Have you achieved familiarity with and awareness of the dynamics of the setting?
- Do you have a reasonable plan for:
  - Getting into the field (existing access, informants, cold calls, overt/covert)?
  - Staying in the field (relational aspects of research, community, ethics)?
  - Getting out of the field (leaving an undamaged field); meeting responsibilities to participants, to the data (conceptualized and intact), to an improved social world?
  - Returning to the field (communicating results, being involved in social actions)?
- Can you communicate well in the setting, that is, engage in interactions with people in the setting?
- What are the community assets (e.g., knowledge, commitment, leaders, interest in the research question or change)?
- Is the setting appropriate? Can you gather data through the method(s) chosen in this setting? Is there a cultural competence in our research team?

Fieldnotes, Timelines, and Resources

A remaining point is to ensure that the discipline required to write fieldnotes is well established. You have already created a filing system for your fieldnotes. You now need a place to keep all the bits of information about why you are choosing a particular method, what you expect to learn from the research enterprise, and other information you will begin to collect. Refer back to Chapter 4 for a full description of the keep, file, protect system for organizing your project. When the time comes to account for why you constructed the research process as you did, the helpful information will be waiting in chronological order in your process fieldnotes and logbook.

We recommend that you prepare a visual timeline or schematic of the territory to be covered by the research. This could take the form of a chart or a rough sketch of information that could contain things such as who might have information that you are seeking and where they are located, how much time you might need for gathering information and making sense out of it, and, finally, when you anticipate finishing the research. This schematic functions as a set of signposts—a checklist to ensure that you stay on track. It can also help you see the entire picture when you have been working intensely on one small aspect of the work. Later on in the research process, if you feel overwhelmed by the sheer volume of information you have collected and you begin to think that you will never do justice to the voices you have heard, look back to the grid to see how far you have come in the process and think about how much more you understand now than you did at the start.

Finally, if you prepare a list of the skills and resources available to you during the course of the research, it will reinforce the point that you are an instrument of the research. For example, what research tools do you prefer? What personal attributes do you bring (e.g., tenacity, logic, order, critical thinking, creativity, inspiration, education, experience, thoughtfulness, reflection, discipline, insight, flexibility, dedication)? These are important because they determine, to a large degree, how you will approach the data gathering and analysis.

You are now at the stage in the research where you have all the plans in place, you have the skills to conduct the research, and you have the participants selected. After you have had your proposal vetted and the ethics approved, you can then begin to gather data.

Summary

Social interaction is at the root of all social knowledge. Thus, it makes sense that information is gathered about social interactions. Given that knowledge changes over time, the process used to discover knowledge needs to be both dynamic and adaptable to change. In critical social research we recognize—and indeed stress—these points. In this chapter you were invited to make choices about methods for data gathering and selection of participants. To assist you, there were a number of checklists to guide your decision making. We also presented some helpful ways for you to think about being a creator of knowledge and what that means when you are in the thick of a research project. We concluded by reminding you that once you have received ethics approval, you will be ready to actually begin the data gathering.

Questions for Discussion

The data gathering approach you choose must enable you to research peoples' lives, their experiences, and the meaning these experiences hold for them.

1. Have you reflected on the data gathering process? Have you prepared for ongoing reflections as you begin to gather data?
2. What is(are) the best way(s) for you to record new data?
3. Have you accounted for yourself in planning the research?
4. What criteria need to be shared among all of your research participants? Do the potential participants have the experience you want to know more about?
5. What is your approach to sampling?

6. How will you build rapport during the research process? What kinds of things will you need to be aware of in terms of rapport and reciprocity?
7. Is the research site optimal? Why or why not?
8. Is your timeline realistic and have you accounted for other activities that might take you off track?

Our Recommended Readings

Beitin, B. K. (2012). Interview and sampling: How many and whom? in J. Gubrium, J. A. Holstein, A. B. Marvasti & K. D. McKinney (Eds.) *The SAGE handbook of interview research: The complexity of the craft.* (2nd ed.; pp. 243–254). Los Angeles: Sage. http://dx.doi.org/10.4135/9781452218403.n17

Creswell, J. W. (2014). *Research design: Qualitative, quantitative, and mixed methods approaches* (4th ed.). Los Angeles: Sage.

Marshall, C., & Rossman, G. B. (2016). *Designing qualitative research* (6th ed.). Los Angeles: Sage.

CHAPTER 8

COLLECTING, ORGANIZING, AND MANAGING DATA

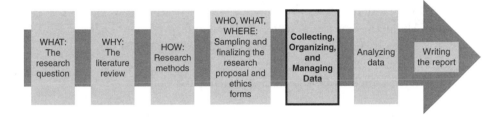

FIGURE 8.1: The Research Process

In this chapter we discuss a variety of ways of gathering data. To facilitate the data analysis, the data need to be methodically organized and maintained. We also describe how data can be handled, approaches to data management, and preliminary steps to organize data for analysis. Finally, we illustrate how data may appear at this point in the research process and how it is prepared for analysis.

Stages of Data Gathering

We covered a number of data gathering techniques in Chapter 6. Once you have committed to a particular data gathering process, you will need a system for keeping all data gathering efforts organized and on track. For example, in more structured research, this phase of the research process consists of marshalling all the data needed into one place for analysis. For more inter-active research, this means contacting prospective participants, arranging for the data gathering (questionnaire, observation, etc.), and conducting the data gathering. There are three steps here: preparing the checklist, making contacts, and arranging for and conducting the data gathering. The collected information is analyzed within its research context and then synthesized within a general social context to provide new insights and meanings.

Stage 1: Preparing the Checklist

For research such as content analysis, the data gathering phase includes applying the predetermined criteria to an existing data set, gathering the appropriate data, and preparing those data for analysis. The researcher needs to be certain about the following questions:

- What is to be measured and described?
- How is the measurement and description to be done?
- Who will determine the criteria and their measurement?
- Has permission been granted from research participants and the necessary ethics review boards to use these documents?

Sample checklist before data gathering for content analysis:

- Are the criteria being used to guide or structure the analysis pretested for clarity, utility (ease of use, practicality), and comprehensiveness?
- Are the analytical results the same when different researchers use the grid on identical nonstudy data?
- What are the parameters I need to use to frame the data set, and what selection criteria do I have in place to ensure I get an appropriate sample of data?
- Do I have permission to gain access to the field or the data I need if it is not publicly accessible?
- How do the data I want to gather relate to my research question? Have I created the category codes?
- Have I taken sufficient steps to ensure that I will understand the data correctly and that my analyses will be valid?
- Are there political or legal issues I need to be attentive to in this research?
- Are there any other issues?

For interactive data gathering, the "readiness" checklists are more comprehensive. Before contacting prospective participants, you must know precisely how to describe the research project, what is being asked of participants, and what will be provided to them. If possible, you can also inform participants about how and when the feedback will occur and any future role they may have in the research. To prepare, ask yourself the following questions:

- How am I going to introduce my research project?
- What am I measuring and describing?
- How am I measuring and describing?
- What are my recording methods? Am I prepared if my technology doesn't work?
- Do I need someone else to assist me in making contacts (gaining access)?
- Who is involved and in what capacity (collaborators, participants, peers, co-workers, colleagues, etc.)?
- Do I have clear plans for analysis and the destination of the research data?
- What assurances can I provide to the participants about the use of the information they provide and their role in any reporting or subsequent action related to the research outcomes?
- Do I have permission from the necessary ethics review boards?

Sample checklist before data gathering for observations:

- Is my role clear to me (degree of participation/observation)? Have I practised data gathering enough to know what I should focus on?
- Is the research focus clear?
- Am I fully prepared to gather information (prepared to go into the field, recording procedures clear, possible questions formulated)?
- Have I considered the timeframe (how long do I plan to stay in the field?) and the selection of the setting (physical environment, sociohistorical background, people and their relationships)?
- Do I have contingency plans so that I can gather information when and where it appears?
- Do I need to ease into the setting? Do I need an introduction, or can I just appear and start data gathering?
- Can I record my observations accurately? Is my grasp of the language and my understandings of the meanings clear enough to gather information accurately?
- Do I need assistance in the field (collaborators, co-workers, colleagues) to assist me in the gathering and interpretation of data? If so, who are they and are they willing to help me?
- Do I have permission from the necessary ethics review boards and from the community to do this observation for these purposes? How do I handle

individual rights in relation to participant observation of the whole social field?

▪ Other issues?

Sample checklist before data gathering for interviews and focus groups:

▪ Are the questions clear in my mind? Have I practised enough to be fluid in my delivery? Have I done a self-interview?

▪ Is the interview guide ready (detailed, comprehensive, orderly, clear)? Are my probes ready?

▪ What is my plan for contacting participants: by email, telephone, mail, listserv, in person, social networking site, other?

▪ How long will each interview take? Do I have a contingency plan if the time is insufficient to complete the interview? Is my exit strategy clear?

▪ Is the interview setting safe for me and my participants? Do I have a backup plan to ensure this?

▪ What degree of interview setting is most appropriate?

▪ Exactly what do I want to say in that first contact with a prospective participant?

▪ What kind of confidentiality can I guarantee?

▪ How will I handle introducing the recording device? What will I do if a participant does not want to be recorded?

▪ In scheduling, what amount of time do I need for each interview and for reflections afterwards?

▪ Do I want participants to prepare in some way—to think about the topic beforehand or to bring some documentation?

▪ What if they decline to participate?

▪ (For focus groups): Are the questions ready for people similar in experience, for people different in experience (Morgan, 1988)?

▪ Do I have permission from the necessary ethics review boards?

Sample checklist before data gathering for questionnaires:

▪ Is the questionnaire designed, piloted, edited, and ready to distribute?

▪ How can I explain the research so that the process is clear and understandable to participants?

▪ If sending the invitations via email, is the email drafted and clear?

▪ If conducting an online questionnaire, does the link work and do all questions function as intended?

- If the questionnaire is to be mailed, do I have the complete, most recent addresses of prospective participants? Is there a stamped return-address envelope included? Do potential participants have enough information to complete the questionnaire?
- For any kind of questionnaire, is there a follow-up plan in place to ensure that people are reminded to reply to or return questionnaires as soon as possible?
- Do I have a plan for managing the completed questionnaires?
- Is there a follow-up procedure in place so that people can be informed about the research results?
- Do I have permission from the necessary ethics review boards?
- Other issues?

Sample checklist before data gathering for life histories or case studies:

- Do I have permission from the person to be researched, his or her immediate caregivers or supervisors, or his or her estate? Do I have permission to examine this particular case?
- Have I successfully avoided the "top-down" approach and created a research design that allows for truly emergent work? Is this study examining the case/person in a natural setting or in a social context?
- In relation to my research question, how much information do I need? What kind of information do I not want?
- What kind of information will I give priority to? Are my questions flexible enough? Am I fully ready to examine the case in all its detail?
- Am I open to serendipitous data and findings, to new questions that might emerge?
- Am I ready for the long haul, since the research might not naturally conclude for a time?
- Who can be helped or hindered by this information or by the resultant analysis? Do I need to have supports organized in case the participants need aid or assistance at the conclusion of the data gathering?
- Who might need to review my report before it becomes a public document?
- Is there someone I might partner with or need to include in the process?[1]
- Do I have permission from the necessary ethics review boards?

....

1 For example, the Truth and Reconciliation Commission of Canada gathered thousands of stories from Indigenous peoples about their experiences in residential schools. Translators and supporters were often needed as the painful and difficult stories were told.

Sample checklist before gathering data from multiple methods:

- Initial questions include the combinations of prompts from the above checklists plus some consideration of who will gather which data and when.
- How will the various data be managed to be ready for analysis?
- Have I mixed the methods appropriately and found adequate support for my decisions? For example, have I embedded the interview process into the questionnaire process, added the fieldwork to case studies, or linked a qualitative observation with public records? Rank, 2004
- Am I clear on which methods different participants will be asked to use?
- Have I accounted for the different time the various methods will take for data gathering?
- Have I readied a plan for how I am bringing the data into analysis and when?
- Do I have permission from the necessary ethics review boards?
- Other issues?

Once you are fully prepared, you are ready to get access to the documents you need (non-interactive) or contact potential participants (interactive).

Stage 2: Access to Settings and Potential Participants

In Chapter 6 you identified the method(s) you will use to gather data for your research. Now your intention to do research is ready to be translated into action. Depending on your chosen method(s) there are various types of contacts to be made. You must contact potential participants or organizations, gain access to relevant documents, and/or negotiate access to particular settings.

Making contact is not always as easy as it may seem (Silverman, 2005). It is one thing to decide for yourself about interest, appropriateness, accessibility, and ethics, but it is quite another to get all interested parties to go along with your plan (Lofland & Lofland, 1995). Your contact may be directly with those who have the experience you are researching, as in the case of interviews, questionnaires, and participant observation. Or your contact may be indirect, where either you need a partner or "gatekeeper" (Guilianotti, 1995) to help you bridge the distance between yourself and potential participants. Gatekeepers are usually people who are known and trusted by the group of interest who agree to introduce you to the prospective research participants. Gatekeepers may also be the holders of documents that will be used for analysis. How you first contact participants will determine whether they trust you in return, and will also in some sense predetermine which parts of the group you see initially or subsequently. There is no best practice for entry into a setting or group. In all cases, you must consider the group, the social context, and the research you would like to do (Gratton & Jones, 2004).

Potential participants can be contacted in a number of ways. The usual approaches are through personal contact, telephone contact, email, listserv, social networking site, mail, or advertising (posters and flyers). Occasionally contact can be made through a third person (a colleague or collaborator) who might introduce the research to the potential participant and then, if it is agreed, introduce the researcher to the participant.

In recent years social networking sites (SNSs) like Facebook have gained popularity as a means to recruit participants. In studies of young adult smokers (Ramo & Prochaska, 2012), women in their first 20 weeks of pregnancy (Arcia, 2014), and low-income women (Lohse, 2013), Facebook advertisements were found to be a viable recruitment option for a reasonable cost. However, there are considerable ethical concerns that have been debated online. Facebook captures lots of information about its users that it accumulates based on the advertisements they view and the external URLs they click to (so if the ad for your study mentions drug use, for example, Facebook might infer something about the user who clicks on it). In addition, users' comments, likes, and so on are typically visible on their timeline and profile page, so sensitive data related to your study might be made very public (Zimmer, 2012). Caution should be exercised in using SNSs like Facebook.

As this is a relatively new practice and ethical concerns are only beginning to be articulated, Zimmer (2012) recommends safeguarding prospective participants and researchers by keeping the text in your ads or external URL links as generic as possible and avoiding any sensitive or controversial text. For example, instead of using the words "illegal drug use," perhaps "recreational activities" or something similar could be used. Also keep in mind that participants may avoid "liking" something related to your page because of privacy concerns, so other communication methods may need to be implemented.

Interviews. Regardless of your chosen recruitment method, a first contact will contain an invitation to participate and the following information:

- Introduction of researcher and research question
- Time and place of interview
- Description of interview setting
- Description of proposed recording methods
- Approximate length of time needed for the interview
- Particular mention of any sensitive material that might be covered
- Description of any preparation needed from the participant
- Arrangements for confirmation or alteration in these contact plans

Hello, is this _____? My name is Jasmine Willard. Harriet Springer has already talked to you about the research and has, with your permission, passed on your name and phone number to me. I am calling to ask you if would be interested in doing a recorded interview with me on your experience of being one of the breast cancer survivors who paddles with the Chemosabi group. I am a breast cancer survivor too and a researcher with the University of X. I am looking at the health and hopes of women living with breast cancer and how they got involved in the breast cancer teams. I would very much like to interview you about how you first found out about Chemosabi, your initial involvement with them, and your involvement with them now and what it means to you. My overall interest is in women's health.

If you are interested, the interview will take about 45 minutes of your time, and we could do it at a place convenient to you. And it would be great if you wanted to bring a picture or two of you paddling. [Organize details of the arranged interview time and place, and indicate that you will call the night before at 7:00p.m. to confirm arrangements.]

FIGURE 8.2: Prepared Text for Personal Contact

Figure 8.2, above, provides a sample of how one researcher conducted her first contact with a potential interview participant (note that this is a phone contact after a third person established initial contact and approval).

The participants are contacted well before the day of the interview. Some research ethics board guidelines require that researchers allow a minimum of 24 hours between contacting participants and data collection. This allows participants time to order their thoughts around the topic and prepare for the interview. They are likely to be just as nervous as you are, so providing lead time is one way to show respect for them. In cases where more than one person is to be interviewed at the same time (e.g., a married couple), it is important to get informed consent from each participant before arranging the interview time and place.

Questionnaires. For questionnaires, the first contact with a potential recipient consists of the same elements of information as the contact with the interview participants. However, in this case information is presented in the form of a cover letter or information letter. Regardless of the method for administering the questionnaire (in person, email, SNS), the cover letter and the questionnaire are usually delivered simultaneously, although an introductory letter could be sent out ahead of time in cases where participant preparation time or anticipation about receiving a questionnaire can be beneficial.

Cover letters include the identity of the sender, the purpose of the research, the reason for the recipient's selection, a guarantee of confidentiality, the length of time required to complete the questionnaire, the deadline for completion, instructions about the completed questionnaire, a request for an indication of willingness to be further involved, and a notice of where the results will be discussed, published, or posted.

Figure 8.3 shows a sample draft of an email recruitment used to generate interest in completing an online questionnaire.

Dear BCTRA member,

The TR Research Network arose from a gathering of therapeutic recreation practitioners in Metro Vancouver in June 2010. Along with Dr. Colleen Reid, they have been working toward identifying a research project in therapeutic recreation that will help advance the field. After six months of exploration and discussion, the TR Research Network identified the following research question: ***"What is the common language and shared identity of diverse therapeutic recreation practitioners (TRPs) in British Columbia?"***
The goals of this study are as follows:

1. Initiate a culture of inquiry in therapeutic recreation
2. Establish a common language and shared identity among TRPs in British Columbia
3. Identify areas where common language and identity are shared and lacking
4. Build research skills among a group of TRPs who are involved as co-researchers
5. Provide opportunities for TR students to further hone their research skills

This project involves both an online survey and face-to-face interviews. **We are requesting your participation in the online survey.** This survey will take 20–30 minutes to complete. As the field of TR is emerging, establishing a common language and shared identity will benefit any person who associates with or becomes a therapeutic recreation practitioner. As a result, your participation in this study will benefit you in your work and the field more broadly.

If you are interested in participating in the online survey, please click here {insert link} to read the consent form and access the survey.

Thank you!

FIGURE 8.3: Prepared Text for Online Contact

Note that the recruitment email in the example above was approved by the college's research ethics board before being sent out. Letters of introduction or permission may also be needed to gain access to certain documents, diaries, and letters. Such introductory letters should contain similar information.

Maintaining Confidentiality. It is important to be clear about the degree of confidentiality that can be promised in any study. Depending on the method(s) used, data can be identifiable, de-identified, or anonymized:

- *Identifying/identifiable data:* This is information that can directly or indirectly identify an individual and includes information (a) that contains an individual's personally identifying information (e.g., name, initials, address, telephone number, date of birth, personal health numbers, full face photographic images) or (b) for which there is a reasonable basis to believe the information could be used to identify an individual.
- *De-identified data:* Information where an individual's identifying information has been removed and where there is no reasonable basis to believe that the information could be used to identify an individual. De-identified data may nevertheless be coded (e.g., via a confidential master list created by the researcher) so that the information can be linked to the individual and to his or her clinical or other records when required. For security, the identification and the de-identified data must be kept in separate files.
- *Anonymous/anonymized data:* This refers to information that cannot be linked back to an individual either directly or indirectly (i.e., the information contains no identifying information, no master list or coding remains anywhere linking a participant to the information, and there is no reasonable basis to believe that the information could be used to identify a participant; UBC Office of Research Ethics, n.d.).

Anonymity can be promised if there is no possible way that a person's identity can be linked to the data. For instance, if you are administering an online survey and send the link to a professional listserv, receive 150 responses, and participants do not write their name or provide any information that would identify them, then the data are anonymous or anonymized. Depending on the method of recruitment, questionnaire data that are gathered noninteractively (where there is no face-to-face encounter) can maintain anonymity. In any interactive or face-to-face recruitment or data collection method it is more appropriate to promise confidentiality. Guaranteeing confidentiality means ensuring that no link can be made between a particular participant and a body of information he or she has provided. However, the researcher and some members of the research team (if applicable) will know the participants' identities and must keep that knowledge confidential. If you are conducting qualitative interviews, guaranteeing confidentiality might involve using pseudonyms or participant numbers and stripping all data of identifying information.

In rare occurrences participants' identities remain identifiable, in that they can be directly or indirectly identified in the research findings. Typically research ethics boards do not approve such research unless a strong case can be made for data remaining identifiable and that using identifiable data poses no risks to the participants. For example, a participant may want to be known, that is, to use your research as a way to achieve his or her public goals. If you are a first-time or relatively new researcher, we recommend that you de-identify your data by using various strategies for maintaining confidentiality *even if* participants say they want their identities to be known. Critical social research can unfold in unexpected ways, and maintaining confidentiality is a more prudent practice for the neophyte researcher.

At this stage in the research, where you are first contacting potential participants, anonymity and confidentiality issues come to the forefront. Potential participants may want a commitment from you to guarantee their anonymity or confidentiality. It can be of crucial importance to people who feel they may be at some risk if they participate. The researcher must know and be clear about what can be guaranteed and what cannot. For example, anonymity is easier to guarantee in noninteractive data gathering methods, such as questionnaires administered online or by mail. In interactive research methods, such as interviews and focus groups, confidentiality "is achieved when the researcher knows who said what but agrees never to divulge a respondent's identity" (Sedlack & Stanley, 1992, p. 273). Confidentiality means that readers of the research or other participants will be unable to identify participants by name, experiences being described, or location. The link between an identity and particular data needs to be protected, not only to maintain your promise of confidentiality, but also because the data recorded may be sensitive in nature or might involve some risk to participants if their participation in the research became known. While it is imperative that the voices of the participants come through in the writing and that the research participants be able to identify their own quotations, confidentiality must be maintained. Participants must be able to see themselves and their experiences in the research reports, but at the same time every attempt must be made to ensure no one else can.

The promise of confidentiality in a focus group or expert group (Morgan, 2004) needs to be made with caution. In this instance, you may ask the group to maintain confidentiality and not reveal the identity of participants or their comments. However, any group discussion can be considered a public forum. As the researcher you have no control over group members' adherence to the promise of confidentiality, which means that you cannot guarantee it (see Chapter 6 for more on focus groups). Another example is that of data gathering through interviews and participant observation with prominent individuals. It is hard to bury the identities of well-known and easily identifiable people. If such participants want confidentiality, you must either figure out a suitable way to meet the promise or tell the participants that it is impossible to guarantee. Some protective measures may be sufficient for them, but if not you may not be capable of reaching agreement for participation.

There are a number of other ways to make confidentiality and anonymity guarantees work. First, the consent form outlines the confidentiality and anonymity guarantees to prospective participants. Once these are signed by participants, or verbally agreed upon,[2] they become *the agreement* between the researcher and the participant. You are bound to uphold the promises made in the agreement. Second, research ethics boards (see Chapter 3) can assist researchers with general guidelines for protecting anonymity and confidentiality and with establishing better practices for meeting the guarantees. Third, before data are recorded you need to determine who else might have access to it. For example, if someone other than the researcher transcribes the interviews, or if collaboration with others during the analysis is planned, get permission from the participant for this kind of access. Fourth, names and places can be changed. Pseudonyms or participant numbers replace individuals' names. If necessary, places of work or types of work, age, and sex can be altered if changing these elements does not undermine the focus of the research study. Names of friends or relatives can be left out entirely or pseudonyms or different initials can be used. You may alter some or all of the situation, experience, personal identity, and timeframe in an effort to provide confidentiality with minimal change to the context and meaning of the participant's experience. Finally, ensure that participants' identifying information (such as the face sheet data and the document that links pseudonyms to participants' real identities) is securely stored for the duration of the research until it is destroyed.

In general, researchers maintain an identity file, the face sheets of information about each participant's demographics, each contact between the researcher and the participant and the nature of that contact, and any promises made that the researcher must keep track of. The identity file is always kept secure and separate from any of the data files. The use of identity files is discussed in more depth later in this chapter.

....

2 According to the Tri-Council Policy Statement (Panel on Research Ethics, 2014, p. 46), "there are means of providing consent that are equally ethical to a signed consent form. In some types of research, and for some groups or individuals, written signed consent may be perceived as an attempt to legalize or formalize the consent process and may therefore be interpreted by the participant as a lack of trust on the part of the researcher. In these cases, oral consent, a verbal agreement, or a handshake may be required rather than signing a consent form. In some cultures, the giving and receiving of gifts symbolizes the establishment of a relationship comparable to consent."

Stage 3: Arranging for and Conducting Data Collection

You are now ready to gather your data. The process of gathering data is a dynamic experience. Just as the process settles into a pattern, a new problem will arise and your plan may alter. Be flexible, record what you need, and stay attentive to participants in the research setting. In this section we provide some helpful pointers to assist with the data gathering process.

Be Attentive and Ready to Record Information throughout the Research Process. In some data gathering approaches (e.g., interviews, observations, case studies) you must be ready to collect data at any time. Despite your best plans you may find yourself having to gather useful data at inconvenient times. Also, data come from a variety of sources. Fragments of conversations from outside the data gathering process itself and information that may appear to have no immediate meaning can subsequently become central to the analysis. Since such information comes to you outside the scope of your ethical approval, it can only be used as part of the general contextual information supporting your analysis. Whether you are concluding an interview, tabulating survey results, or laboriously combing through documents, some discussions or events around you can provide new directions for research and breathe new life into old material. Be ready to pay attention to all types of information that emerge.

Follow Your Instincts. There is little room for indecision in research. If you think useful information is still untapped, you may have to alter the research plan to gather it. For example, if you realize that you have inadvertently forgotten to ask some participants one of the key probing questions on the interview guide, you may decide to contact participants again to ask that question. Aside from providing a good rationale for deviating from the research plan, the same consent issues apply.

Ask Good Questions. Good questions are the hallmark of good research. Even before data gathering, you will have opportunities to collect information useful to the context of your work. You can be more ready if you have thought about such opportunities in advance. Such questions should relate to the topic and theories that guide your work. During the data gathering phase, the way you ask the questions is equally as important as the order and focus of the questions and the overall interview setup. The interview guide is a series of questions organized around the research question, but you might be able to raise the quality of the interview by listening closely to the research participant and honing in on the right questions to be asked at just the right time. Generally, questions that are deemed easier to answer are placed early in interview guides. More complex or sensitive questions usually work best a little later in the process.

And participants always have the option of not responding or of not having their response recorded.

Begin Where You Are and Be Flexible. Where data gathering begins is dependent on such things as your familiarity and comfort with the topic, the types of questions developed, and what kind of access to information you have. Use your fieldnotes to monitor participants' questions and perceptions as the research progresses. Be disciplined and organized, but also be flexible when it concerns things you cannot control, like other people's schedules or their differing analyses.

Occasionally a research participant will ask to see the interview guide before an interview or the research plan before a participant observation. In more traditional research approaches such requests are usually denied. In our view, however, the researcher can choose to consider the request and negotiate with the participant. If it is important for all participants to be treated similarly, then this option would need to be presented to all participants. This may be desirable, because it may allow participants to more deeply consider the interview questions prior to the interview, and it may benefit participants in terms of managing their expectations or uncertainties about the research process. If the request comes from several participants, it may suggest that you overlooked some key aspect of the process. If initial interviews elicit saturation on some kinds of information but open up other areas for exploration, you may want to create room in the research protocol for the emergence of new questions.

Learn to Listen. Good research has as much to do with good listening as with good questions. When you are asking questions, the silence of others that sometimes follows is just thinking time. Listen to what is said and to what is not said. Developing your listening skills will ensure that you are able to fully hear and understand what is being shared with you. A skilled interviewer will bring her or his attention to what is being said and what can be probed in that moment, rather than focusing on the next question. In a semi-structured interview, for example, this might involve pausing between questions to assess where you are and what has been covered. It might also mean jotting down interesting notes or phrases that you want to pick up on later. But always focus on the participant's words rather than thinking ahead.

There are often distortions and inaccuracies in information and you will need to decide whether to check the information you receive from participants or not. In general, it is the participants' understanding of their social reality that we are recording—their truth is what we are after. So we recommend that you be prepared to listen to and really hear participants' stories as *their understanding* of their realities. Nevertheless, if they are referring to public facts or events, it will be important for you to verify those items if you are going to use them in your report.

Ensure That Asking Back Can Occur. Research can be a dynamic and social enterprise. While it is difficult to make absolute promises about, for example, the management of material or the way in which someone's voice will appear in the analysis, the rapport you establish with participants involves social interaction. You are learning about them, and they are learning a little about you. "Asking back" (Briggs, 2007; hooks, 1992) is when participants have opportunities throughout the research process, including data gathering, to make inquiries about the research or the researcher. For example, in research on pay equity, a participant may raise questions about how the researcher views race and sex inequities in the workplace. Or in response to a researcher's question about areas missed during an interview, a participant may seek personal advice or ask for the personal opinion of the researcher. There is an optimal level of asking back that frequently leads to a richer and more meaningful description of the purposes of the project and the participants' experiences. Too much asking back may create a lack of focus in the research or mean straying from the original purpose of data gathering. Too little asking back may mean that the rapport between researcher and participant is one-sided and the data gathering experience is a somewhat stilted experience for both. Make clear to participants that any questions they have are important and that you will try to answer them.

Pre-existing Relationships Can Be Challenging for the Researcher. Many researchers have difficulty in one-on-one research encounters with people they know. Researchers are gathering information, yet the tendency is for familiar individuals to fall back on familiar interaction patterns—patterns that can be counterproductive to data gathering. Indeed, after a research relationship is developed, neither will be able to return exactly to the prior interaction pattern. Other than avoiding interviews with familiar individuals, the best approach is to address the issue head-on at the beginning of the interview and agree that, during the interview, you will both attempt to stay on task. After it is concluded, you must treat both the information and the participant in the same manner as the other interviews.

While the familiarity between the researcher and the participant may not be problematic, familiarity between participants may be or may become so. Participants may know each other prior to the research. Imagine if more than one research participant is interviewed simultaneously (e.g., in a focus group or expert group)—the interaction between participants has existed, exists, and will continue to exist independently of the researcher. Participants may get to know each other quite well and, in a spirit of friendliness (or unfriendliness) that has nothing to do with the research, find they readily share information in the group setting that they would otherwise not normally share. You must be mindful of such group influences and make sure that the participants feel they have control over how much they want to say and to whom. As the researcher, it is important to consistently remind participants that their words and interactions "count" as data.

Get Close to the Data. In critical social research we contend that researchers invest their own experience and self in the research enterprise. If you have learned more traditional research methods, this may not come naturally. Do not be afraid to incorporate yourself, your emotions, and your experiences into the research process. Make sure you account for these in your research journal and fieldnotes.

Take Care of Yourself. Brackenridge (1999), who does sensitive research on sexual harassment and abuse of athletes, ensures that she is prepared for research by allowing herself a method of debriefing. With appropriate ethics approvals in place, she has one person with whom she arranges regular debriefing meetings for the purpose of personal support. The person has signed confidentiality agreements, remains outside Brackenridge's normal social contacts, and is not a co-researcher. Bringer (2002), originally one of Brackenridge's Ph.D. students, writes the following:

> I was aware of the possibility of hostility and physical threats, emotional exhaustion, feelings of helplessness, and emotional trauma. To protect myself against physical threats, I did not give out my home phone number . . . I used my mobile phone for all contacts. When I conducted the individual interviews, at least one (other) knew my location . . . in case something went amiss. (pp. 199–200)

There are other ways to ensure that your health and well-being are attended to during the research process. It can be helpful to consider, prior to conducting research, strategies for maintaining your own safety and boundaries. Strictly adhere to research tasks so that you do not inadvertently find yourself in the role of counsellor, job finder, or confidante to the participants. Other forms of stress relief might be regular journaling or participation in non-research-related but cathartic activities, such as recreational activities.

Continue Reviewing the Literature. The literature review can continue throughout the research process. Although data collection can be very time consuming, taking some time to find new articles or re-read ones you have already reviewed can provide new insights and "a-ha" moments. Once you are collecting data you will develop new understandings of your research question, and interacting with the literature will deepen your thinking about what you are hearing and seeing. Record your insights in your fieldnotes and make notes to yourself so that you can pick up on them when you begin data analysis.

Celebrate Researching. Research is about the creation of new knowledge. Critical social research is intended to make positive changes for people. Such creation is worth celebrating for researchers, participants, and those in the communities of people affected by the research outcomes. We recommend that time be taken by all to note and appreciate the research progress. We also recommend that you (and the participants, if feasible) take time to take stock at several points along the way to see what has been gained, to identify areas where improvements are needed, and to applaud yourselves. Much of the momentum for a research enterprise is dependent on your energy. Near the end of the research, particularly if the research is a collaborative effort, plan a time for bringing the research efforts to a close in a celebration of common effort and achievement. Share and celebrate your new knowledge and success.

Analytical Schema

The analytical schema spans from collecting data to the final analysis and presentation of your research findings. Since data gathered can include information that is numeric or text, the steps for collection, management, and analysis of data have to be comprehensive enough to allow room for such varieties of information to be handled. The overall analytical schema that we have found useful is shown in Table 8.1 (page 222).

Prepare, File, and Manage Data (KFP System)

As the researcher, you have two key parallel recording responsibilities. The first is to ensure that all data are accurately and thoroughly prepared for analysis. The second is to ensure that the data are filed and stored in ways that meet the ethical standards agreed to in the ethics review process.

Prepare the Data. Data can range from complex spreadsheets of mathematical notations, to diagrams and brief notes on dated scraps of paper, to complete verbatim transcripts. Data can also consist of audio and video recordings, descriptions of settings and observations, and public and private documents. Overall, data need to be recorded consistently, accurately, and with as little

TABLE 8.1 Analytical Schema

Prepare, file, and manage data (KFP system)	1. Prepare the data (transcriptions, data spreadsheet, other documentation)
	  – Name, file, and protect data according to KFP system
	  – Review data for accuracy
	  – Member-check data
	2. Organize the data

Analyze data	1. Descriptively code all primary documents 2. Make connections between codes 3. Organize codes into themes 4. Describe the themes analytically 5. Test codes and themes—cross-checking, double-checking, negative instances 6. Bring forward the literature review 7. Live with the data and engage in hurricane thinking 8. Search for alternative explanations 9. Complete the analysis by answering the research question 10. Record the process
Develop knowledge transfer plans	1. Present the data (e.g., research report, conference presentation, community report) 2. Develop policy implications, plans for action, and ideas for future research

interpretation as possible. If more than one researcher is involved, a constant checking back with the research team members will help ensure quality control. Though it is recommended that researchers resist the temptation to interpret material at the very early stages of data gathering, there are important moments of awareness or insight that you do not want to lose. To this end, each time potential interpretations emerge, no matter how temporary or timid they may be, record them in your fieldnotes. That way the emergent analysis is always accounted for in the research records and no ideas are lost. This means researchers have their fieldnotes at hand at all times and are diligent about keeping dated records of the research in progress. As the researcher this is how you live with the data.

Unless you are using a statistical program for quantitative data analysis, numerical data are input on a spreadsheet with a question-by-question tabulation of written answers to open-ended questions. These need to be checked several times for accuracy (this is called *cleaning the data*), particularly when the questionnaire is large. Cleaning the data also means gaining a sense of how complete the questionnaires are. (Preparing the spreadsheet and cleaning the data are discussed in more detail in Chapter 9.) Though a nuisance, incomplete questionnaires still contribute useful insight as long as samples and percentages are calculated on a question-by-question basis. The fact that a respondent fails to answer all the questions in a questionnaire in no way diminishes the value

Questions:	Q1	Q2	Q3	Q4	Q5	Q6	....
Participants							
1	5	4	4	3	2	5	
2	6	3	6	3	5	2	
3	4	3	3	3	4	5	
4	5	5	6	2	2	5	
5	3	3	6	2	2	4	
6	6	3	5	2	3	4	

Tabulation of answers of the six respondents to the 7th question

Question 7: Issue: One-fifth of Canadian children live in poverty

1—I don't think it is an issue. I have not heard anyone say that to me.

2—It has never come up. Why, I just don't know.

3—My grandfather thought it was important and tried to get us all to think the same way. My mother tried to show us just by example that we should try to help others—sort of to be like her. If we couldn't help poor people directly, we could help them indirectly by not consuming everything in sight and by giving our weekly allowance to the church . . . things like that.

4—The world would be a better place if we all were more serious about what was happening in other places in the world. I think it is an issue, but it never comes up amongst my friends. They don't think about it, I guess.

5—Of course it is an issue . . . but just for the older people. We didn't cause it so I don't think we have to fix it.

6—No, I don't think it is an issue. It's an obligation and I think we all should be doing something about it.

FIGURE 8.4: Sample Data Spreadsheet

of the feedback they provide (Johnson, 2013). Figure 8.4 shows the responses to a set of six questions (across top) by six participants (down the left side).

Notice that all responses inputted for questions 1 to 6 are numeric. Questionnaires may include text responses that then have to be converted to a numeric value for data entry. For Likert scale questions, the final score for the respondent on the scale is the sum of their ratings for all of the items. On some scales, you will have items that are reversed in meaning from the overall direction of the scale. These are called *reversal items*. You will need to reverse the response value for each of these items before summing for the total. That is, if it is a 1 to 5 scale and the respondent gave a 1, you make it a 5; if they gave a 2 you make it a 4; likewise, 3 = 3, 4 = 2, and 5 = 1. Also note that participants are identified already by number rather than by name, though it may be that names were never collected, in which case you can promise anonymity.

It can take a few attempts to determine how you want to set up your spreadsheet and input your data. Similar to many aspects of research, this is a practical as well as a conceptual exercise. Consider how you want to look at the data and what makes most sense to you. It is helpful to have some basic skills in data spreadsheet management in programs such as Microsoft Excel, SSuite Accel, Gnumeric, GS-Calc, KSpread, LibreOffice Calc, OpenOffice, or Pyspread.

In the case of interviews or records of interactive observations, you generally record two things: reflections immediately after each interview (process fieldnotes) and a transcript that is a verbatim account of exactly what was said during the interaction. For the reflections, identify the physical location, how you experienced the process (tensions, connections, or insights), and any data in comments after the audio recording was turned off. Although these comments cannot be directly quoted, they frequently offer rich insights about the research. You can also note any changes in your data gathering plan, questions that were reordered or omitted, probes that were particularly effective, and any successful new questions. As noted earlier in the chapter and in Chapter 7, you can also prepare a face sheet for each participant, which is a good strategy for ensuring that identical demographic information is gathered from all participants and that it is all in one place (see Chapter 7 for examples). Sometimes a summative statement about the participant will serve you well later when you want to describe, in general, your research participants.

The transcription is a written record of the interview. Researchers develop their own ways of transcribing, but all believe that how the transcription is done is important. Increasingly, digitally recorded interviews are uploaded directly onto a computer and transcribed with software such as Dragon. While the use of this kind of software can save time, it remains necessary to review the transcription for accuracy. Note that transcribing software does not document pauses in speech or intonations. Also, software cannot recognize different voices or decipher two people speaking at the same time, such as in focus groups or expert group interviews.

The method of transcribing depends on the purpose of the transcription. For example, there can be verbatim transcription, purposive description, or narrative transcription. *Verbatim transcription* is where accuracy is vital, for example in a medical or legal transcription, and one must be as precise as possible. For most of us, recording every nuance and bit of detail would be counterproductive. If you are transcribing without voice recognition software, you need to make preliminary decisions about what to do with repetitions, pauses, and filler comments. We want to reinforce the importance of checking transcripts by reading them on the screen while listening to the recording. Many typographical errors and misheard words can be caught this way. Also, we recommend that wherever possible the transcriptions maintain the original

CR: Would you say that there's a connection between your living situation, your social support networks and those kinds of things, and your financial situation? Do you see there's a connection between those things and your health?

E: Oh sure. Definitely.

CR: Can you talk a bit about that?

E: Like when you're going through all the bureaucratic BS that you have to jump through all the time, oh . . . you get such a headache, you know, you get passed around so much. I tried once to connect with a social worker. I tried for three weeks and could not get a person. You know modern technology's great, but you can't get a person anymore. And then they never return your calls and then. . . a big problem when I first moved in here, like I can see it from their point of view. But because I'm lucky enough to finally be in low housing, it's almost like you're being penalized. Like my rent is 30 per cent of my income, so that works out to $199 a month, and I put in for them to pay for that directly and they pay my hydro directly so they take care of that and that. And then I get $329 a month. That's everything. And they're like "that's all you're entitled to." And I just thought that was so unfair. I'm supposed to do everything with $329. "Well you still get your child tax for $200." So we're up to $500 to do everything for my son and myself. It's just. They're supposed to be forcing the ex to pay child support. But like you'll ever see that, right?

CR: And that is such a problem, right?

E: Oh, it's hideous [pause]. I'm like, ahhh, it used to always be a hundred that you can earn a month. I don't see the logic in that. Most people get $200 a month for their kid. So you can have a hundred of that but then you're penalized because you're getting an extra hundred? How is that fair? How are you supposed to support your child? So someone told me it went up to $200. OK, so whoopee we get all of our child tax benefit without being punished. And my worker got all mad and says, "Why do you say punished and penalized?" 'Cause that's what it's like. You know [pause]. I'm not saying you're allowed to live in the lap of luxury when you're on income assistance, but I mean you shouldn't have to be struggling quite so hard.

FIGURE 8.5: A Transcription

flow and wording given by the participants and that no effort be made to force their spoken words into grammatically correct forms that might "fit better."

The transcription in Figure 8.5 shows the researcher's voice using the researcher's initials (CR) followed by the participant's responses (E).

In this transcription, it is possible to see where turns of speech, pauses, and "uh" fillers occur. A purposive transcription is more expedient because the researcher does not transcribe all parts of the interview or interaction with the same precision. One might transcribe the whole interview somewhat generally and then pay precise attention to particular segments of interest by going over interview segments and retranscribing them in detail. A *narrative transcription* is where the account or story being told has its own flow and rhythm and the transcription follows the story in very close detail as communicated by the participant. This way the researcher is able to show both the story and how the story is told. Ultimately, the transcription process used should fit the purposes of the research and be easily rationalized.

The audio recording of an interview is "an artifact." The transcript is a mediated version of the data because it is one step away from the original interaction between the interviewer and interviewee—a transcription of the record selectively interpreted or mediated by you, the researcher. Merely letting the audio recorder run and presenting the respondent's voice (in transcript form) does not overcome the problem of representation, because the respondent's comments are already mediated by the questions in the interview (Lewis, 1991). Transcripts are not "voices in the raw"; rather, they are one step away in accuracy and authentic voice from the original data (Fine & Weis, 2003). Nevertheless, transcriptions serve to remind you of the information gathered in the interview or observation interaction and, with fieldnotes, can help you recall additional things of interest such as the voice, nuances of expression, and body language of the participant. We have frequently heard researchers say that by the time they have finished transcribing, they know the transcription almost by memory and can actually hear the voice of the participant speaking most parts of it. With this in mind, it is easy to see how the transcription itself can never replace the actual voice of the participant but is only an imperfect representation.

There are numerous other forms of data recordings than the spreadsheet and transcript versions provided so far. Figure 8.6 provides an example of fieldnotes from a participant observation and Figure 8.7 an example of content analysis.

"Member-checks" are optional and may be done once transcriptions are complete. To do this, circulate the completed transcript to the participants and ask them to check it for accuracy. This provides participants with an opportunity to view what they said and make changes if they wish. Usually inaccuracies are corrected and clarifications are added. It is also possible that new issues arise. All participants have the right to withdraw at any time,

Jan. 14. In the field (School XT, 4th observations visit with Leader AT).

Another aspect of group behaviour caught my attention. I saw it
again this morning. Action: As soon as one student started to strip a lighter
and put it in the sidewalk crack, others would gather around and cheer,
but quietly. It was as if they were in on the game too! Body language: a bit
furtive . . . they stood in such a way that they effectively blocked off any
chance that a teacher might catch a glimpse of what was going on from
the staff room window. Action: When the stripped-down lighter was then
lit, it was like a Roman candle—whoosh and then it was over. The group
forming the barrier then dispersed. I only saw this happen twice before this
morning, but apparently it has gone on for several recesses in a row
(student JB confided this morning). In my notes yesterday, as an aside, I
wondered when Leader AT would know and do something about this
behaviour. Today, it all came to a head.

Unfortunately no one had paid attention to the smoldering grass
underneath the sidewalk slabs and it was only when the smoke started to
drift about that a teacher caught on to what was going on. Teacher M
called in the fire alarm at about 11:30 and the fire trucks arrived promptly
and to the great excitement of all the students. The students I have seen
playing with the lighters this morning stayed apart from the other students,
standing up on the hill, a bit separated from the rest. Leader AT said early
this afternoon that the fire inside the west wall of the school was not really
about bad kids doing bad things, but was about a lot of kids doing
somethinga little bit dangerous but not intended to hurt anything or
anyone. It really was an accident in his view, and he thought the students
now understood the dangers of playing with lighters in this way and would
soon find other less costly diversions. I saidI was very impressed with this
approach and asked how he was going to convey this to the students. He
thought that he would just put out a quiet word through one or two
students and the ones who had been playing with the lighters would
maybe come to see him in private. That's how he wanted it done. No
wonder the school has such a good reputation in the community. This
appears to be thoughtful role-modelling and excellent leadership.

FIGURE 8.6: Fieldnotes from a Participant Observation

including withdrawing information from the transcript. If they add further
information, accept it gracefully. An invitation to member-check (letter) is
shown in Figure 8.8.

Most researchers strive to complete their initial reflections on the participant
interactions and get the transcriptions done almost immediately after the data gathering. The longer the delay, the more information and detail on the impressions and

Frequency of subtopics within meta-categories	
Health care: Management and regulation (n = 2,189)	
Private health funding	133
Public health funding	455
Public health sector management	627
Government health care regulation	501
Judicial health regulation	296
Health ethical review	99
Other management and regulation	78
Health care: Service provision and delivery (n = 886)	
Prevention	76
Diagnosis	75
Treatment/management	229
Alternative/complementary	57
Education/training	104
Error or malpractice	95
Advances	217
Other service of provision	33
Physical environment (n = 596)	
Natural environment hazards	50
Manmade environment hazards	215
Built environment	78
Animal hazards	60
Infectious disease	151
Other physical	42
Socioeconomic environment (n = 282)	
Income	9
Education/literacy/numeracy	2
Employment	36
Self	49
Social support	65
Social violence	96
Other social	25

FIGURE 8.7: Content Analysis of Data Records

beginnings of analysis are lost. We recommend that you record (in writing or on audio tape) your reflections immediately after data gathering rather than after long delays.

Organize Data

Here we briefly describe one way to organize the qualitative data to facilitate the coding, descriptive, and explanatory steps. Whether a computer program or a paper process is used, this way of organizing the data is useful. Organizing data is really about "housekeeping," or getting organized. Once all the materials

Dear _____,

Thank you so much for participating in both the interview and questionnaire portions of the research about Chemosabi dragon boat paddlers. Attached is a verbatim transcript of the interview with you. As we indicated earlier, we are sending it for you to review it for accuracy of the information. If there is anything here that you do not want to be included in the research or you would like to have recorded differently, please contact me by phone [include office number] or email [include email address] by August 30. A final report will be available by mid-October and will be printed in the Chemosabi national newsletter shortly afterwards. Thank you again for your thoughtful participation in this research.

Sincerely,
Jasmine Willard

FIGURE 8.8: Sample Member-Check Invitation

are organized, not only do you have a renewed familiarity with them, but they are easy to keep orderly and to access. Organizing data means keeping different types of information in different places.

Step 1: Divide *original* material into two folders: content and process.

The purpose of original folders is to keep the first or earliest material intact and secure yet available should any part need to be reanalyzed or reconstructed. Despite the various ways in which data are collected and recorded, all original information related to the substance or content of the research can be placed in an "original content" folder. This includes records of original research materials such as transcripts, completed questionnaires, fieldnotes, documents (articles, books, letters, diaries, periodicals, clippings, review of literature, etc.). Subfolders may be organized as follows: (a) documents for analysis, such as transcripts, observations, completed questionnaires, content for content analysis; (b) chronological fieldnotes;[3] (c) raw data, including audio files, photographs, video clips;[4] and (d) other materials. This original content

....

3 Reflections on content begin the evolving analysis as your thoughts become more focused on what the data mean and which themes run through the data. The focus on the content is very specific. Reflections recorded beside particular content often would not make sense if they were removed from the immediate context. Such reflections are data specific and substantive in nature.

4 This folder contains original video or audio tape recordings. These are to be coded by number rather than name (e.g., AUD #017), and the key coding sheet is housed in the identity file so that confidentiality is preserved.

file contains all dated original research materials. It is advisable to keep documents gathered for the literature review, such as PDFs of articles and notes, in a separate folder.

A second folder entitled "original process" contains a separate and secure identity file, including the face sheets for each participant, original material on matters relating to plans and data gathering, reflections on this, and field-notes related to the process. You can organize this as a "logbook" (Esterberg, 2002). Refer to Chapter 4 for a description of maintaining a logbook. We manage the process data in a similar way to that of the substantive data about the research question. The purpose of the "original process" folder is to have enough information in enough detail about the organization of methods and data gathering that you could reconstruct the entire process if required. All process information in this file should be chronologically ordered and include all reflections and feedback you have received on the process.

Researchers keep meticulous records to allow for the reconstruction of the step-by-step process used for preparation, data gathering, and analysis. This folder contains the record of all decision making about the research focus, early refinements of the research question, final data gathering instruments (e.g., interview guide, questionnaire, criteria for content analysis), and final copies of the data gathering packages, ethics forms, and cover letters. Any steps taken to ensure better return rates or identification of potential research participants are also included here. Notes about the process taken during data gathering (jottings, keywords, points to question, landmarks) and post–data gathering comments go in this file as well. Finally, reflections on how you progressed, problems you faced, and how you solved them are also located in the file. If the files are kept electronically, the original format can be relatively easily altered as a structural framework around the process information is developed. Guidelines for creating a keep, file, protect (KFP) system that works for your project are provided in Chapter 4. All decisions made or actions taken in the research process are documented. Here is a summary of what the "original process" folder contains:

- Identity file (separate and secure)
- Meeting dates and minutes
- Dated contacts with potential collaborators and participants
- Ethics forms, including consent forms and information letters
- Information about the nature of contacts with participants
- Information about prospective data sites
- Steps taken to develop data gathering instruments
- A copy of all data gathering instruments (e.g., interview guide, questionnaire, criteria for content analysis)
- Steps taken to pilot the data gathering instruments and changes made

- Descriptions of the data gathering process
- Steps taken for member-checking
- Steps taken for data management and analysis
- Reflections on all of the above

The purpose of setting up these two folders is to (a) separate the data for analysis from the data that document the research process and (b) maintain an untouched copy of all raw data. Note that these two folders should be clearly named, saved, and protected. These folders remain untouched throughout the rest of the analysis process.

Step 2: Create three *copy files* for analysis: a copy of the identity file with identifiers removed and codes in place, a "copy content" file, and a "copy process" file.

The copy files are your *working files*. Materials may be moved about, analyzed, removed, replaced, and so on. Importantly, all data in the working files must be stripped of identifying information, which is replaced with pseudonyms or participant numbers. Once you begin working with your data, you must adhere to all ethical promises made in your ethics forms. As well, if you have data that have been translated you will work with the translated documents in the working files (in this case the original files should include both the original transcript and the translated transcript).

The original files, untouched, always form the backdrop that you can rely on if you need to recover or re-create from the originals. Folder 1, the "identity folder," contains one or several files that contain information about your participants, contacts, contact person(s), promises, comments, and so on. There are three purposes here: (a) to store the "key" for linking participants' real identities with their participant numbers or pseudonyms, (b) to track each contact with each participant and the demographic information associated with individual participants, and (c) to house all demographic information collected from participants. The example in Figure 8.9 is a key that links participant identities with their participant number and pseudonym.

A001   Jon Monteiro, Toronto—called Jo
A002   Sui Yi Alga, Regina—called Suza
C001   Alicia Greenberg, Guelph—called Lisa
C002   Liesel Bebber, Ft. St. John—called Elly
A003   Guylaine Renault, La Salle—called Gaetan
C003   Daniel Horne, St. John's—called A.J.

FIGURE 8.9: Sample Key

Participant #A002	Date:
First contact time:	Place:

Contact information (telephone and/or email):   Best way to contact?   Participant criteria for selection (gender, age, ethnicity/race, etc.):   Other information relevant to research arrangements: List of each contact/date and any decisions made:

FIGURE 8.10: Sample Contact Sheet

The second file should contain information that provides, at a glance, a snapshot of all contacts with the individual and information that facilitated the research process. Information from the face sheets are entered here. Figure 8.10 shows a sample contact sheet.

For ethical reasons, the participant code "key" and contact sheet must be kept separate from any files where content is housed so that participants' true identities are separate from the content. Also, consider the storage and security issues together. How are you guaranteeing confidentiality when you use your computer, access online storage, and share files with colleagues or team members? These files must only be accessible to people whose approval has been granted through the ethics review process, and file sharing must be done with adequate security provisions.

The third file contains all participant information together. Essentially, this file provides a snapshot of your research participants (see Figure 8.11). This snapshot is a useful document to review and return to over the course of your project.

Folder 2, the "content copy" folder, contains exact copies of data from the "original content" folder. This folder contains all raw data, reflections on this, and all fieldnotes related to content. When data gathering is complete, original records of data are copied to this file. Be sure to use your file naming system so that you can differentiate the kinds of data and date based on the name of the document. This is the folder you will use for data analysis. In addition to copies of all folders and documents saved in the "original content" folder, the "content copy" folder also contains copies of coded sections of data, analytical memos, and other documents used for data analysis (see Chapter 9).

Folder 3, the "process copy" folder, contains exact copies of data from the "original process" folder. This folder contains all matter relating to plans and

Participant #	Age	Gender	Language	Education	Employment Status	Living Situation	Domestic Status	Income
1	65	Female	English	Some college or university	Part-time volunteering; pension	Alone	Single, divorced	$11,000 15,000
2	61	Male	English	Some college or university	PWD; volunteering	Alone	Single	Less than $10,000
3	58	Male	English	Some college or university	PWD; volunteering	Alone	Single	Less than $10,000
4	50s	Female	English	University degree	Pension; volunteering	Alone	Single, divorced	Less than $10,000
5	52	Male	English	Some high school	PWD; volunteering	With family	Single	Less than $10,000
6	59	Female	English	Some college or university	Volunteering	With partner	Married	Less than $10,000
7	27	Male	Cantonese	Diploma or certificate	PWD; social assistance	With family	Single	$11,000 15,000
8	51	Female	English	Diploma or certificate	PWD; CPP	With family	Married	$26,000 or higher
9	50	Male	English	Some college or university	CPP; volunteering	Alone	Single	$11,000 15,000
10	64	Female	English	Diploma or certificate	PWD	Alone	Widow	$11,000 15,000

FIGURE 8.11: Snapshot of Research Participants

TABLE 8.2 Folder and Filing System

PURPOSE	FOLDER NAME	CONTAINS
Contains documents for storage and backup; saved, protected, and untouched; not used for analysis	Original content	- Subfolder 1—transcripts, observations, completed questionnaires, content for content analysis - Subfolder 2—chronological fieldnotes - Subfolder 3—raw data, including audio files, photographs, video clips - Subfolder 4—other materials
	Original process	Fieldnotes and logbook with the following: - Identity file, including face sheets - Dates of meetings and minutes - Dated contacts with potential collaborators and participants - Ethics forms, including consent forms and information letters - Information about the nature of contacts with participants - Information about prospective data sites - Steps taken to develop data gathering instruments - A copy of all data gathering instruments (e.g., interview guide, questionnaire, criteria for content analysis) - Steps taken to pilot the data gathering instruments and changes made - Descriptions of the data gathering process - Steps taken for member-checking - Steps taken for data management and analysis - Reflections on all of the above
Contains documents for coding and analysis	Copy Identity	- File 1—key - File 2—participant contact sheet - File 3—participant demographics
	Copy content	Exact copy of "original content" folder that is used for analysis *as well as* coded sections of data, analytical memos, and other documents used for data analysis
	Copy process	Exact copy of "original process" folder that is used for analysis. You will *add* to this folder as you move through data analysis

data gathering, reflections on this, and all fieldnotes related to the process. This includes a record of all steps taken in doing the research, chronologically organized, and all reflections and feedback related to the process. Again, this folder contains a copy of all decisions made and actions taken in the research process.

At the end of the organizing step, all information that has been collected should be housed in both the original and copy folders. Though this does not mean that data gathering is completely finished, the process of analysis can begin. As data gathering concludes, the information can simply be added to the appropriate files and copied to the working files. Continuing to reflect on the research process enables researchers to become more skillful and intuitive.

As an overview, the folder system you set up should look something like Table 8.2.

All content and process data should now be sequentially organized to be ready for analysis. All the originals should now be safe and secure. You are ready to do further analytical work on copies made from these folders.

Summary

In this chapter we have provided checklists to prepare you to gather different kinds of data, ranging from observations, interviews, focus groups, and questionnaires to case studies, life histories, and discourse and content analysis. Along with this we gave some final advice for you to consider prior to collecting data in terms of your health and boundaries and remaining aware of yourself and your research participants when you are gathering data. Similar to other stages of research, data collection and management are both practical and conceptual exercises. As you gather data you need to think carefully about how to prepare it so that it can be analyzed. We described strategies for preparing, organizing, and managing the data that you collect. Creating a folder, subfolder, and file system will help immensely as you move forward toward data analysis.

Questions for Discussion

1. Why do you need to keep some information secure and separate?
2. How will the data be recorded? Are there data that you have been unable to record? Why? How can you correct that?
3. Why is it important to write up interview experiences immediately after they are completed?
4. Why is it necessary to reflect on the content of what is gathered and on the process of researching?
5. How can you account for yourself in the data gathering process?
6. What is the difference between original and copy folders, and what are their purposes?

Our Recommended Readings

Babbie, E., & Benaquisto, L. (2010). *Fundamentals of social research* (2nd ed.). Toronto: Nelson Education.

Briggs, C. L. (2007). *Learning how to ask: A sociolinguistic appraisal of the role of the interview in social science research.* Cambridge: Cambridge University Press.

Johnson, J. C., & Weller, S. C. (2001). Elicitation techniques for interviewing. In J. F. Gubrium & J. A. Holstein (Eds.), *Handbook of interview research: Context & method* (pp. 491–514). Thousand Oaks: Sage. http://dx.doi.org/10.4135/9781412973588.d30

Poland, B. D. (2001). Transcription quality. In J. F. Gubrium & J. A. Holstein (Eds.), *Handbook of interview research: Context & method* (pp. 628–650). Thousand Oaks: Sage. http://dx.doi.org/10.4135/9781412973588.d36

CHAPTER 9

ANALYZING DATA

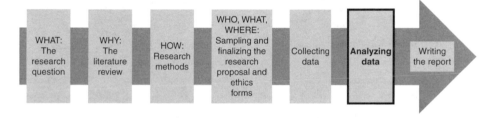

FIGURE 9.1: The Research Process

In this chapter we provide a step-by-step description of data analysis. Although there are many ways to analyze data, we concentrate on analytical approaches common to descriptive, inductive, and emergent research. But before getting into the step-by-step description of the analysis process, it is useful to understand the "big picture" of data analysis in critical social research. The analytical ladder (Carney, 1983) or, as we have adapted it, a series of embedded circles (see Figure 9.2), represents how both inductive and deductive thinking are important in the analysis process.

Until this point, you have mostly been guided inductively, in terms of "What do my participants have to say about x, y, and z?" While it is possible that your research question came directly from the literature, it is more likely that it came from some combination of your own observations, life experience, and curiosities and was reinforced or modified by reading the literature. We have encouraged you to think inductively by asking you to be reflexive, to understand yourself as the researcher, and to identify a research question that is meaningful and important to you.

As a critical social researcher poised to engage in data analysis, it is important to appreciate that in the analysis process you will cycle between inductive and deductive thinking. Working entirely inductively, as in "What do the data tell me

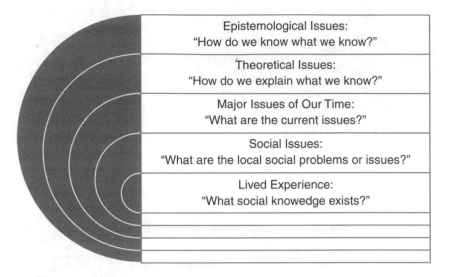

FIGURE 9.2: Analytical Circles

about my research question?" could lead you to neglect a vast body of literature where the issue has been discussed, debated, and contextualized more broadly. Conversely, working entirely deductively could lead you to mould your data into pre-existing analyses, theories, or models where you don't have anything original or new to report. Our version of the analytical ladder, adapted into a series of embedded circles (see Figure 9.2), demonstrates the connections that exist between broad epistemological issues and lived experience. The data that you have gathered are linked directly to the question "How do we know what we know?"

Data analysis is an iterative or "back-and-forth" building process. where researchers make sense of new data, information, or knowledge and in the creation of theory constantly refer back to the data to develop the analysis. Each informs the other: Data inform theory and, in turn, theory informs data. The circles demonstrate how data analysis builds and is directly linked to and contextually supported by the social issues of the day. These are, in turn, connected with current sociocultural forces, theoretical views of the world, and even to epistemological issues in the social world.

The Data Analysis Process

Fundamentally, when we analyze data we are answering the questions "What do the data say?" and "How are the data related or not related to each other?" Before we can answer these questions we give priority to three essential components of critical social research: intersubjectivity, the researcher's role, and critical edge.

Intersubjectivity was defined in Chapter 3 as an authentic dialogue between all participants in the research process in which all are respected as equally knowing subjects. One important aspect of intersubjectivity is "when two different researchers, studying the same problem, arrive at the same conclusion" (Babbie, 1998, p. G5). The outcomes are valid if researchers with different orientations come to the same conclusions. If you are a lone researcher, it is advisable to confirm your analysis through a combination of checking back with participants to ask "Have I got it right?" and inquiring of other researchers "Would you get this result too?" A research "buddy" can be useful in the stage of data analysis.

The analysis of critical social research data reveals how people make sense of their lived experiences and their everyday lives within their social contexts. Critical social research requires interaction or dialogue with participants (e.g., interviews, some forms of observation, case studies), between participants (e.g., focus groups, narratives with audience), and with researchers communicating (e.g., in analytical and confirmatory activities). Data gathered are thus both an individual representation and, as the analysis progresses, a collective representation of the information of all participants and researcher(s).

For each bit of data to be given equal opportunity to be part of the analysis does not mean that each person's information takes equal space in the analysis. As you move through the analytical steps, particular information may take more space and some information may disappear. Not all information will need to be selected. This also points to the importance of "narrated realities" (Miller & Glassner, 2004) and the cultural embeddedness of meanings people assign to experience. At the end of the research, we should be able to demonstrate that the analysis is a percolation of all the information gathered in the research.

As the researcher, you are an instrument in the research process. Throughout the analytical process, part of the iterative process is in each researcher's effort to live with the data and make sense of it. To do this, researchers must constantly reflect on both the data and the analytical process. Researchers move back and forth between data and concepts, among concepts, and between individual ideas and research explanations to build the analysis. *Iterativity* is the building process resulting from this repetition of analytical steps, coming at the data from different directions, with different researchers, and over different "cuts of the data" until nothing new emerges and the overall analytical pattern "steadies" or ceases to shift as new parts of the analysis are added. One way to think about this is that the analysis becomes saturated and the data have spoken. It also means moving up and down the analytical ladder (or in and out of the analytical circles; see Figure 9.2), demanding that the researcher think both inductively and deductively. Throughout this process researchers remain vigilant for new insights at all analytical points to fully describe and explain what is being researched. Such insights can come from focused attention to the analysis of communication between and among research team members (intersubjectivity) or from focused interactions with participants, collaborators, and knowledgeable others.

Finally, research requires a *critical edge*. Critical reflection is "an examination of the social reality within which people exist and out of which they are functioning" (Finson, 1985, p. 117), for that is the "real, concrete context of facts" (Freire, 1985, p. 51). In other words, social context is the structure in which participants' experiences have occurred. It makes sense that if we are to fully understand the data and use it to effect change, we must understand contextual patterns and how they are sustained and controlled. Having a critical edge may mean putting the data and the research question in social context and interrogating the assumptions about social structures, social status, equity, and ideological positions that surround the issue. Some of the approaches in Chapter 2 will help in thinking through and becoming more critical of the data. It may mean evaluating the strengths and weaknesses of the data to strengthen the resulting analysis and increase your confidence. If the data themselves are strong, comprehensive, and representative of the participants' experiences, you will have more to say and a stronger basis for action. This critical edge is *extremely important* as it reflects the reasoning process you use to understand the meaning and social context of people's experience.

In critical social research, a large volume of data can be gathered in a short time. Some researchers do their analysis at the conclusion of the data gathering when all the data are in one location and attention can be focused on finding the answer to the research question(s). Others analyze as the data are gathered. The latter approach is called a *progressive analysis* and means writing preliminary results at the same time as you are data gathering. Either way, we recommend that you begin writing about your preliminary thinking (or analysis) as soon as you can. Whatever approach is taken, analysis plus the report writing take about a third of the total research time allotment. This is the time to live with the data, get comfortable with what they have to say, and discover larger, more holistic understandings through identifying patterns or arrangements. It takes time to think, so allow enough time to be thorough and clear your mind before completing the final analysis. Also, in the analytical stages, continue with reflections in your research journal to keep your intuitive and analytical edges well honed.

In this chapter we move through the data analysis process to enable you to make sense of your data set. You may have text data, numerical data, or some combination of the two. Figure 9.3 depicts the data analysis process. First we discuss the description and analysis stages for qualitative (text) data, then we discuss these stages for quantitative (numerical) data. In the "analyze the process file," "interpretation," and "credibility" stages of analysis we bring both kinds of data together since the same principles and processes apply to these data and many data sets contain both numerical and text data.

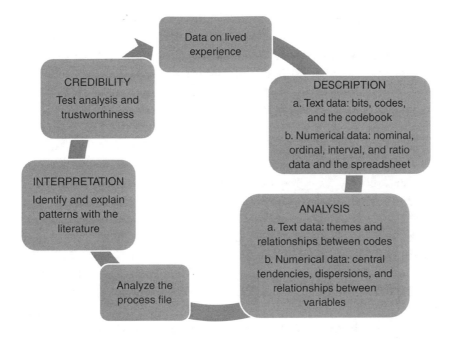

FIGURE 9.3: The Data Analysis Process

Here data analysis is depicted as an iterative process (spiralling, circular, and building) that ends with reaffirming the analysis by checking back on the data that were collected. As you move from analysis to interpretation it is necessary to go back to the data to ensure the accuracy of your interpretations. In other words, as you move higher up the analytical ladder (or more closely to the outside of the analytical circles), you need to cycle back to the inner circle to ensure that the analysis, which often becomes increasingly more theoretical, is trustworthy and grounded in the data you have collected.

Analyzing Text Data: Description and Analysis

Qualitative data analysis has been widely studied in the past few decades. There are now many methodological and theoretical approaches to analysis. Our approach to analysis is generally consistent with grounded theory (Bernard, 2006; Glaser & Strauss, 1967). While we draw on the basic tenets of grounded theory, we present data analysis as an inductive and deductive process that moves from understanding to description to explanation and that uses theory and literature to help answer the research question(s).

If you have different kinds of data, such as interview transcripts and fieldnotes from observations, you need to consider how you will treat these data sources. We recommend identifying one data source as "primary" and beginning data analysis focusing only on that data source. Once that analysis is nearly complete you can then begin analysis of the second data source. Multiple data sources and strategies for triangulation are discussed later in this chapter. Alternatively, you may have two or three data sources that all contribute to the analysis but in different ways. For instance, questionnaire data may answer one of your research questions and interview data may answer a second research question. Should this be the case, then you will need to analyze the data sources separately (to start) and then consider how they can or should be integrated. We briefly discuss the nature of your data set here because it may determine how you wish to organize and manoeuvre through your data files and folders.

By now you have prepared, organized, and managed your data, which involves transcribing and reviewing transcripts, stripping text data of identifying information, inputting numerical data into a spreadsheet, and so on. Although this work can be tedious and time consuming, it is valuable in increasing your familiarity with the data and your data management system.

1a. Description: Bits, Codes, and the Codebook

You have already spent time organizing and managing your data. This is time well spent as the process of understanding and describing your data relies on your intimate familiarity with it. Before engaging in any formal analysis process, spend time reading and re-reading your data, keeping notes in the margins or in memos, and allowing yourself to be curious about interesting things that pop up.

The first "formal" step of analysis is descriptive coding. In qualitative research, *coding* means assigning a word or a phrase that summarizes a section of text data. It can capture whatever is salient, the essence of what is in the section, or it can be an evocative attribute (Marelli, 2016). The portions of text that are coded can be referred to as data "bits" or "bits" of text. *Bits* are freestanding portions of data. Coding bits of data is the process of dividing the mass of data into portions that are manageable. Descriptive codes that include several bits of data are the initial bases or units of analysis.

- *Bit:* A freestanding portion of data that makes sense even when separated from its data gathering context. It can be a segment of a transcript, a piece of information from fieldnotes, a section of a document, or a snippet of conversation recorded on a scrap of paper that can stand on its own.

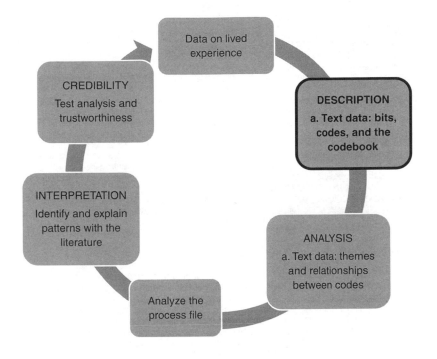

FIGURE 9.4: Text Data: Description

- *Code:* A characteristic of a bit. It is a grouping of bits of data with a common attribute, identifier, description, or definition. A bit may have more than one code.

The bit of text can be descriptively coded with a name you assign related to the interview question. For example, if you used a structured interview format it may be desirable to analyze how all participants answered each individual question. If the interviews were semi-structured or unstructured, it is more difficult to code in this way. In these instances you will code descriptively around a given topic, for example, how each participant defined a concept (Reid, Brief, & LeDrew, 2009). Figure 9.5 shows an example of a coded document and the bits of data that are extracted for the codes.

Note that the transcript is named "ITES 20150305": This signifies that it is an interview transcript (IT), followed by the participant's initials (ES) and the date of the interview. It is saved and filed under this signifier. All bits of data that are coded have this identifier beside it, as well as the location tag, in this case 05/E and 06/E (participant initial [E] and line number [05 or 06]). It is important to provide each bit of coded data with a "home address" or "relocation tag."

	CODES
R: Can you talk a bit about the connection between your living situation, your social support networks, and your financial situation? (04/R)	
E: Like, when you're going through all the bureaucratic BS that you have to jump through all the time, oh . . . you get such a headache, you know, you get passed around so much. I tried once to connect with a social worker. I tried for three weeks and could not get a person. You know, modern technology's great but you can't get a person anymore. And then they never return your calls and then . . . a big problem when I first moved in here, like I can see it from their point of view. But because I'm lucky enough to finally be in low housing, it's almost like you're being penalized. Like my rent is 30% of my income, so that works out to $199 a month, and I put in for them to pay for that directly and they pay my hydro directly so they take care of that and that. And then I get $329 a month. That's everything. And they're like "that's all you're entitled to." And I just thought that was so unfair. I'm supposed to do everything with $329. "Well you still get your child tax for $200." So we're up to $500 to do everything for my son and myself. . . . They're supposed to be forcing the ex to pay child support. But like you'll ever see that, right? (05/E)	Bureaucracy Social workers Social assistance—rules Finances—monthly Social assistance—rules Child support
R: And that is such a problem right? (05/R)	
E: Oh, it's hideous, I'm like, it used to always be a hundred that you can earn a month. I don't see the logic in that. Most people get 200 a month for their kid. So you can have a hundred of that but then you're penalized because you're getting an extra hundred? How is that fair? How are you supposed to support your child? So someone told me it went up to $200. Ok, so whoopee we get all of our child tax benefit without being punished. And my worker got all mad and says, "Why do you say punished and penalized?" Cause that's what it's like. You know. And I'm not saying you're allowed to live in the lap of luxury when you're on income assistance, but I mean you shouldn't have to be struggling quite so hard. (06/E)	Finances—monthly Social workers Social assistance—rules Finances—concerns

FIGURE 9.5: Example: Coded Transcript (ITES 20150305)

We were all waiting at the Legion for like 45 minutes and she didn't arrive. I know we said the front door and well, with Carole, Carole knows . . . but she forgets most everything you tell her. It is the MS. She's smart, just that you can drive a truck through her memory. Vi said that chances are Carole forgot what time to come and maybe told the taxi driver the wrong door. Well, I did the circuit of the building and there she was, sitting in her wheelchair in the rain in the alley because the driver didn't knock on the door for her. What a way to begin Dad's memorial service! (1 02 / S)

The researcher tagged the data example above bit to indicate that it came from data source 1, page 2, and "S" is the participant. Whatever tagging codes are used, the researcher must always be able to recontextualize the data bit quickly and efficiently. Often this means putting a page number or line number beside the bit of data. Much like the practice of citing references in the literature review, the bits of data that are coded for the analysis must always be referenced. As you move through

Code	Data Bits
Bureaucracy	When you're going through all the bureaucratic BS that you have to jump through all the time, oh . . . you get such a headache, you know, you get passed around so much (ITES 20150305 – 05/E)
Social workers	I tried once to connect with a social worker . . . I tried for three weeks and could not get a person . . . And then they never return your calls (ITES 20150305– 05/E)

Most people get 200 a month for their kid. So you can have a hundred of that but then you're penalized because you're getting an extra hundred? How is that fair? How are you supposed to support your child? So someone told me it went up to $200. Ok, so whoopee we get all of our child tax benefit without being punished. And my worker got all mad and says, "Why do you say punished and penalized?" Cause that's what it's like. (ITES 20150305– 06/E) |
| Social assistance—rules | But because I'm lucky enough to finally be in low housing, it's almost like you're being penalized. Like my rent is 30% of my income, so that works out to $199 a month, and I put in for them to pay for that directly and they pay my hydro directly so they take care of that and that. And then I get $329 a month. That's everything. And they're like "that's all you're entitled to." And I just thought that was so unfair. I'm supposed to do everything with $329. "Well you still get your child tax for $200." So we're up to $500 to do everything for my son and myself. (ITES 20150305– 05/E)

They're supposed to be forcing the ex to pay child support. (ITES 20150305– 05/E)

Most people get 200 a month for their kid. So you can have a hundred of that but then you're penalized because you're getting an extra hundred? How is that fair? How are you supposed to support your child? So someone told me it went up to $200. Ok, so whoopee we get all of our child tax benefit without being punished. And my worker got all mad and says, "Why do you say punished and penalized?" Cause that's what it's like. (ITES 20150305– 06/E) |
| Finances—monthly | But because I'm lucky enough to finally be in low housing, it's almost like you're being penalized. Like my rent is 30% of my income, so that works out to $199 a month, and I put in for them to pay for that directly and they pay my hydro directly so they take care of that and that. And then I get $329 a month. That's everything. And they're like "that's all you're entitled to." And I just thought that was so unfair. I'm supposed to do everything with $329. "Well you still get your child tax for $200." So we're up to $500 to do everything for my son and myself. (ITES 20150305– 05/E)

I'm like, it used to always be a hundred that you can earn a month. (ITES 20150305– 06/E) |
| Finances—concerns | And I'm not saying you're allowed to live in the lap of luxury when you're on income assistance, but I mean you shouldn't have to be struggling quite so hard. (ITES 20150305(ITES 20150305– 06/E)) |
| Child support | They're supposed to be forcing the ex to pay child support. But like you'll ever see that, right? (ITES 20150305-05/E) |

FIGURE 9.5: Coded Transcript (ITES 20150305) (Continued)

the analysis you must always be able to trace every bit of data back to its original source. Qualitative data analysis computer software programs have linking functions that enable you to colour code, number, or mark bits to ensure relocation.

Descriptive coding is the process of assembling data that look, sound, act, or feel similar. Data that are dissimilar belong in separate or distinct codes. The code can be inductive (it emerges from the data or is "*in vivo*") or deductive (it is imposed from existing concepts in the literature or is "researcher defined")

(Bernard, 2006; Bringer, 2002). As the researcher codes data, she or he methodically labels and groups events, behaviours, structures, and experiences for further analysis. Whether or not you are using a computer data analysis software program, the researcher is the essential element of the coding activity. According to Bernard (2006):

> You can't go wrong by just reading the texts and underlining or highlighting things as you go . . . when you start to work with a text, just read it and if you see something that you think might be important, highlight it . . . Strauss and Corbin (1990, p. 68) recommend explicitly using actual phrases in your text—the words of real people— to name themes, a technique they call *in vivo* coding. (p. 493)

Figure 9.6 presents another example of a coded transcript. In this example, the research question was about how a sexually harassing relationship begins. When you look closely at a section of transcript such as the one above with the research question in your mind, the important codes will emerge. The codes bring at least two analytical points forward: the young age of the athlete and question of vulnerability, and the age difference between the athlete and the coach.

Richards and Richards (1994) refer to coding as "working up from the data" (p. 446). The result is denser descriptions of information, new or enhanced concepts to explain data, and possibly some theoretical findings based on the data that were collected. In comparison to quantitative research, qualitative approaches are less likely to impose restrictive classifications on the analysis of data, as the research is less driven by specific hypotheses and more concerned with emergent themes (Symon & Cassell, 2012).

The code names are developed by the researcher. Code names may expand, contract, or even shift dramatically as the material in the code collects and expands. If the distinctions between two or more codes become blurred because they show an affinity for one another or have common content, an amalgamation of data bits may occur. If, on the other hand, a code becomes too large and many bits are assigned to it, that code may need to be split into two (or more) distinct codes. The longer a researcher lives with the codes, the more settled and clear they become in the researcher's mind. At some point you will have to demonstrate and provide a rationale for the final version of the codes used in the analysis.

As you descriptively code your text data you must assemble a *codebook,* which is a document used for gathering and storing codes. The use of a codebook ensures that coding is consistent within and across researchers. Every

A1:3	Hmmm, I . . . find um . . . this difficult to talk about. My . . . um . . . background is something I don't talk about very often and no one really knows this part of my history.	Secret
SK03	Uh, hmm . . . do you think you can talk about it now with . . .	
A1:4	. . . with anonymity, for sure . . .	Ethics
SK04	Yes, with anonymity—and maybe if you feel safer now than before.	
A1:5	Shall I just start at the beginning where . . . (pause)	
SK05	Yes, starting at the beginning is fine. When was the beginning?	
A1:6	Well, I was 14 and had just been selected to attend the music camp in London and I thought my dreams were coming true. I finally felt like the goals were in my reach and that I had the talent to make it to . . . well maybe even the uh, uh highest levels. It was like the first time I really thought I could see the light there at the end of the tunnel. I could see it and I thought I could get there. It was like I was grown up and I could really stand on my own—and then I, uh . . . Ok, I uh ran, ah ran . . . ran into the problem.	Penultimate goal Problem
SK06	Can you tell me specifically what the problem was?	
A1:7	The problem? The problem was that I, uh, well I, I . . . fell in love with the music director. But he was married and had two children and well, now I see it for what it was, but then, I just felt so special that he and I had found each other and that he was part of my music world too. It was so secret and so perfect too.	
SK07	What was the age difference between you? Was it a lot?	
A1: 8	Not a lot, about 16 years. The age was not the issue. I remember the issue being that he was in a marriage with a woman he didn't love and he loved me. We had to be quiet about it, but I knew that he loved me and he promised to marry me as soon as I was old enough. Now I know that he said that to all the girls, but at the time he was the only star in my heaven and . . . I was in love, really in grown up love for the first time in my life.	Age Age difference Love/marriage
SK08	Did you feel that you were alone, the only . . . ?	
A1:9	. . . I thought I was. But I found out much later that other girls in the camp had the same kind of problem. We just didn't know about each other until much later. I wish I had known about them earlier. I would have maybe been, you know, less damaged by it all.	Only one Damage

FIGURE 9.6: Example! Coded Transcript #2

code must be defined such that it is clear to the researcher (and co-researchers) what is included in and excluded from that particular code. Similar to the entire analysis process, coding is iterative, and the codes and their definitions change as you move through the analysis. The "first draft" codes often come from the questions posed in the interview or focus group or the specific things that were focused upon during the observations. Depending on the nature of the project and research question, there may be many or just a few changes to the codebook as coding progresses. Below are two examples of codebooks from very different projects.

Example: Codebook #1

This is an excerpt of a codebook from a photovoice project that examined experiences of community inclusion for individuals with lived experience of mental illness. The data included focus group transcripts, one-on-one interviews, and photographs. This version of the codebook was generated from the analysis of focus group transcripts and photographs, which were considered to be the primary documents for analysis.

The codebook for this project was six pages long. In the excerpt above the codes are defined in detail. As the researchers code they add to the definitions, find

Code	Definition	Representative photos	Analytical memo
Exclusion	Any reference to - Feeling excluded from society - Feeling excluded due to ethnicity, gender, language, migrant status - Having few choices d/t exclusion - Being an outsider	P3-Ph1-Mon1-PV5	Strong links to poverty
Stigma—Self	Any references to - Judging oneself - Subconscious comparison to others - Expectations of self - Fear of being "discovered" - Low self-esteem, self-worth - Overcoming self-stigma	P8-PH1-Mon2-PV5	Believing that because of mental health diagnosis and symptomology they are not normal and do not belong
Stigma—Society	Any reference to - Societal pressures—media, greed, jealousy, family, friends - Ignorance, intolerance - Others' negative feelings or fears re. mental illness	P2-PH1-Mon2-PV5	People with mental illness are restricted in the ways they can operate in society. Variable: depends on time and location
Hope	Any reference to - The importance of hope in one's life - Definition of hope - Things that provide a feeling of hopefulness—being heard, supported, etc. - Hope and recovery - Experiencing success and feeling hopeful - Having the will or energy to be hopeful	P33-PH1-Thur3-PV7	One needs more than feeling positive and hopeful. "To survive in society" one needs skills, resources, supports—"skills and armour." Societal expectation that you are "cured" if one day you look well.
Inclusion	Any reference to - Things that make people feel included - What people do to feel included—strategies - Belonging and being "known" - Places of inclusion - Barriers to inclusion	P34-PH3-Th4-PV6	Link to income, poverty. Price of inclusion re. what you have to be able to afford or how much you have to compromise of who you are to "fit in"

FIGURE 9.7: A Longer Codebook

areas of overlap, and reorganize as needed. There is a column for "Representative photos," which, in this case, are photographs taken by the participants that exemplify the code. Through the coding process the researchers add photos to this list. Finally, the far right column entitled "Analytical memo" is where the researchers document their emerging and evolving analysis of the code, links between codes, and direct quotations that exemplify the code.

Example: Codebook #2

This is one of several codebooks generated to analyze text data from an online questionnaire. The questionnaire was administered to therapeutic recreation practitioners to gain a better understanding of their role as an allied health professional. The questionnaire had several open-ended questions, and for each of these questions the research team developed a codebook. The header for each codebook contains the question, the question's location on the questionnaire, and the response count. Frequencies for each code are also tallied.

Page 4, Q3 (19) "How do other professionals you work with view your work as a therapeutic recreation (TR) practitioner?" Response Count: 82 Answered question: 82 Skipped questions: 2		
Frequency	Code	Definition
63	Important (I)	Any reference to • Being valued, important, respected, or useful • Other professionals as being supportive, curious, or interested in TR • Other professionals understanding and appreciating TR • Having a sound practice
28	Undervalued (U)	Any reference to • Not being considered high priority, necessary, essential, or useful • Not being recognized as an allied health profession • Other professionals undervaluing/being ignorant about TR
21	Varies (V)	Any reference to • Some, majority, most • Sometimes—differences in perception related to population served, work environment, professional group, levels of knowledge of TR
15	Lack of Understanding (LU)	Any reference to • Other professionals not knowing/having no idea • Need for advocacy

FIGURE 9.8: A Codebook

So far we have discussed grouping data that are similar. Data that are dissimilar with no apparent relationships are called satellites, and they also need to be tracked in your analysis. *Satellites* are bits that are freestanding that have no obvious relationship to other bits. Satellites are difficult to code because they do not fit the coding scheme but intuitively the researcher knows they are important to the analysis. Satellites can indicate areas for further analysis or future research.

When enough bits are present together in a code and when there is relatively strong coherence among them, the code is saturated. *Saturation* occurs when added information does not reveal new understanding and when the addition of new bits does not alter its complexion or add to the richness and density of the code description. When codes are saturated, there is enough information to make statements with a comfortable degree of certainty. When no new links between codes emerge, the analytical development is exhausted. If no saturation occurs, only statements about tendencies within codes or links between codes can be made.

In the past researchers used pen and paper, cue cards, highlighters, white boards, or Post-its to "cut and paste" the bits of data into descriptive codes. Now there are a number of computer software programs that can facilitate this process. Qualitative data analysis software programs, such as NVivo or ATLAS.ti (briefly described in Chapter 4) are designed to do this and have the capacity to store code definitions and analytical memos, track participant responses, and so on. These programs have other useful features such as auto-coding, where a phrase or combination of phrases can be searched in all of the data and pasted into a new code. While the use of a program can help you organize your analysis process and be more efficient, such programs do not do the analysis for you. As the researcher you must conceptualize, drive, and manage data analysis.

Search and find and auto-coding functions can be used to confirm the saturation or nonsaturation of a code. While you may have been diligent in your coding efforts, it is still possible to miss some references to key concepts or ideas. Consider all of the ways that participants spoke about a specific topic and then search systematically through your data by using these functions. See what emerges—often this extra step will affirm your analysis and can be used as an indication of the rigour of your coding, while at other times new bits of data come to the surface that reshape or strengthen the code.

2a. Analysis: Identify Themes and Trends within and between Codes

The steps of qualitative data analysis that have been discussed so far include:

- Identify all *bits* (segments, bites, pieces of data that still make sense separated from their context) and label them in such a way with relocation tags so that you can return them to their original context.

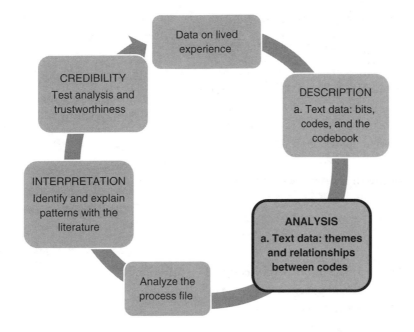

FIGURE 9.9: Text Data: Analysis

- Organize data bits into *descriptively defined codes* or separate them out because of their uniqueness (stand-alone satellites).
- Tighten and hone code definitions with descriptions of what counts as the code and what does not count in a *codebook*. Code definitions can be thought of as common or shared properties among bits of data. Satellites, the stand-alone bits, may be "unpopular" but are still important for the research outcomes. Attach a tentative label to each of these thinly populated or stand-alone groups of data.[1]

The next step of analysis is to identify themes or trends within and between codes. To develop *themes* we move away from the data somewhat and work more directly with the codes themselves. Look at which codes seem to be attracted to other codes. Why do some codes need to be grouped together and what do they say together? How strongly (or with how much confidence) can you demonstrate the overlaps or links among codes? What explanations exist to show why the overlaps exist? In addition, which codes seem to be repelled by other codes and why?

....

1 Sometimes is it difficult to name satellite codes. In such cases, Colleen uses a catch-all code entitled "zzz— important data" and will return to these data periodically throughout the analysis. Most often these data help fill in gaps in the analysis. They may be integrated into already existing codes or they may become a new code. Or they may represent a broader theme. Occasionally some of these data are eventually disregarded.

Going back to a previous example from the study that examined women's experiences of poverty (see the coded transcript and data bits in Figure 9.5), the codes generated from coding 24 one-on-one interviews are then reorganized into themes:

Theme 1: Daily challenges of living in poverty
- finances—monthly (code)
- finances—concerns (code)
- living conditions (code)

Theme 2: Difficulties with social assistance and social workers
- bureaucracy (code)
- social assistance—rules (code)
- social workers (code)

Theme 3: Issues with services and entitlements
- services and policies—general (code)
- transportation (code)
- food banks (code)
- child support (code)

Reorganizing the codes and aligning them thematically can take some time. Sometimes it requires moving codes around to determine how they best fit together, which ones continue to stand alone, and how they need to be sequenced to make sense of the findings. Another way to think of it is that the themes represent a higher level of analysis or a more comprehensive "answer" to your research question. As data with similar properties are grouped together, themes develop and emerge from the data. Look for codes that belong together by cross-referencing the codes.

In the sexual harassment example from Figure 9.6, the bits of data from two codes, *love* and *damage*, are double-coded. These are clues to possible patterns. If many of the bits in a code have a similar pattern of cross-referencing or double-coding (i.e., those same bits are also coded with a different code name), it may indicate a strong pattern. Similarly, if bits in a code do not cross-reference with any other codes (meaning they stand alone), there is a pattern there as well. It might be that a single code becomes a theme because of its strength and the fact that its data bits are not double-coded. On the other hand, another theme might be generated by bringing together two or more codes that are cross-referenced or relate in some way. As the codes are brought into proximity with each other, look for trends, matchings, or obvious mis-matchings. These patterns are the beginning of creating themes and concept building.

TABLE 9.1 Tracking Process

THEME	CODES	NUMBER OF PARTICIPANTS WHO IDENTIFIED THIS ($n = 24$)	PARTICIPANT IDENTIFIER/ PSEUDONYM	TRENDS OR PATTERNS
Daily challenges of living in poverty	finances—monthly	22	[list participant numbers for each code]	
	finances—concerns	24		
	living conditions	21		
Difficulties with social assistance and social workers	bureaucracy	20		
	social assistance— rules	19		
	social workers	15		
Issues with services and entitlements	services and policies—general	21		
	transportation	18		
	food banks	10		
	child support	12		

As you identify the structural themes, it is important to maintain a record of the "weight" or dominance of the themes. A tracking process can be helpful, as that shown in Table 9.1.

As you track the themes, the weight of the evidence becomes clear. In the example above, the "daily challenges of living in poverty" is a dominant theme shared by most participants, whereas "issues with services and entitlements" was somewhat less common or dominant. The "Trends or Patterns" column can be used to identify where double-coding occurred (did all participants who mentioned monthly finances also mention finances—concerns?) and where you begin to notice trends in participant responses. Chronicling the participant identifier or pseudonym will allow you to refer back to the demographic data (collected with the face sheet; see Chapter 8) and determine precisely if the number of participants who cited a particular code or theme had anything in common. Some connections will be obvious (e.g., all participants who spoke about child support had children), whereas other connections may elicit new and interesting understandings (e.g., all participants who spoke of transportation were on disability benefits).

Once the codes are reorganized into themes and the weight of the themes is determined, write a *descriptive paragraph* to describe each theme that contains the codes and their definitions. Consider themes as a higher level of analysis or organization for your data—they hold together coherent and multiple bits of data and, most often, multiple codes. The more bits in the codes and theme, the stronger the description and the more confident you can be of its accuracy and support. The themes with higher numbers of bits and greatest coherence can be considered "dominant." At the same time, describe aspects of the codes' definitions that are uncommon or less dominant. Here the researcher's confidence in the codes and theme is weaker because there are less data and less uniformity among the data; it is not as "popular" and, hence, not as convincing. Finally, describe the properties of those bits that remain alone, unique, and unshared. The researcher cannot be at all confident in drawing conclusions based on single and unique bits, but these often point to important directions for further research.

How many themes are appropriate? The number depends on the data and the researcher's insight into what the data indicate. Some codebooks can be pages long and result in several dominant themes. Other codebooks are simpler with only five or six codes and one or two themes emerging. The number of codes and themes depends on the research question, the data gathering method, the skill of the researcher, and the willingness of participants to share their stories.

An initial number of themes may be identified, though you may consolidate or expand the themes or content of the themes at any time. Although the number of themes could be quite high, it is important to remember that themes are used to bring bits of data into proximity with each other. Too many themes can be counterproductive to the analysis because they will likely be too narrow to be useful yet not distinct or saturated enough to be freestanding as themes with "something to say." You will not know if you have too many themes until they become unwieldy in number and your instincts tell you to group some of them together because their similarities are stronger than their dissimilarities. If there are not enough data in a theme, then the theme may not come close to saturation, making analysis of the content difficult and, ultimately, weak. Themes overloaded with *dissimilar* data are equally counterproductive. Too few themes can lead to thick files where only peripherally related bits are located side by side.

Analyzing Numerical Data: Description and Analysis

To answer the research question, the analysis may need some combination of qualitative and quantitative analyses. While numerical data are typically not considered qualitative, we use many of the same analytical strategies with numbers that describe a particular phenomenon. It is important to note that numerical data are not used in this context for determining causation or generalizability as would be done in research within the positivist paradigm. But we can employ quasi- or descriptive statistics that are "primarily used in mixed-method techniques to expand the scope and improve the analytic power" (Sandelowski, 2000). If the data include numerical information (e.g., counting things, choosing categories, demographic characteristics), quasi- or descriptive statistics can be used. Here we use the term "quasi" because the principles of statistics, including random sampling, setting hypotheses, and testing the relationship between a dependent variable and an independent variable, generally *do not* apply to qualitative and most mixed-method approaches. Although it can be difficult to mix textual and numerical data analysis (Morse, 2010), simple descriptive statistics can provide an understanding of disparity (difference or sameness) of data while the qualitative analysis provides an interpretation of meaning (Hesse-Biber, 2010). In this way, numerical and textual data can interact.

To draw quantitative conclusions we use mathematical principles to determine what counts, relationships between variables, and what is significant enough to report. In computer-assisted *qualitative* packages, the data are normally left intact—contextualized and coded *in situ*. Conclusions are drawn based on the strength of the data categories, the links between concepts, and the overall mapping that is used to explain, in a comprehensive way, the study outcomes or results. On the other hand, if we use *quantitative* analyses, the data are categorized, coded, removed from their context, and then analyzed. Broadly speaking, this can produce either descriptive statistics or nonparametric statistics. We discuss both below.

1b. Description: Nominal, Ordinal, Interval, and Ratio Data and the Spreadsheet

When some of your data are represented by numbers, you must first determine the type of data (nominal, ordinal, interval, or ratio) and then identify which measures of central tendency (mode, median, mean) and dispersion (range) are useful to describe, display, and analyze the data. Depending on the type of numerical data, descriptive statistics can be used to provide a picture of central tendency and dispersion. *Central tendency* is how well (or not) the data are grouped toward the centre and *dispersion* is how far apart the data are. Descriptive statistics measure the mean (average), the mode (most frequent score), the median (the score at which 50 per cent of the scores are below and 50 per cent of the scores are above), the range (the distance between the highest and lowest score), and the standard deviation (the difference between the score and the mean distribution).

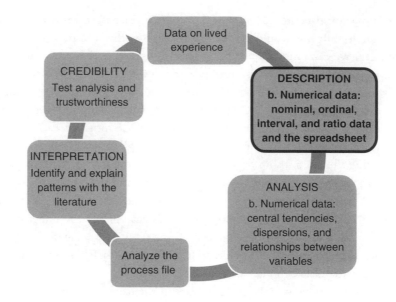

FIGURE 9.10: Numerical Data Analysis: Description

To use descriptive statistics, we need to know something about the data, that is, is it nominal, ordinal, interval, or ratio data? *Nominal data* look like frequency counts of distinct groups of information (smokers and nonsmokers; apples, oranges, and tomatoes; see Table 9.2).

For such nominal data, it makes sense here to ask how many or what kind or even what percentage of each grouping, but it does not make sense to calculate an average or range.

TABLE 9.2 Nominal Data and Percentages

	MEMBERSHIP FREQUENCY	PERCENTAGE
Smokers	17	55
Nonsmokers	14	45
Total	31	100

Ordinal data are data that can be ranked or ordered, but there is no assumption that the differences between the data are equal. A good example is the numbers on the jerseys of the Canadian women's World Cup soccer team of 2015, shown in Figure 9.11. The jerseys can be ordered from lowest to highest, but the numbers do not bear analysis beyond that simple ordering. The player in the number 12 jersey, Christine Sinclair, a striker, is not four times

FIGURE 9.11: Ordinal Data

more valuable than the player in the number 3 jersey, Kadeisha Buchanan, a defensive player.

In the example in Table 9.3, it makes sense to order the data but the mathematical distance between "Very Good" and "Good" may have absolutely no relation to the distance between "Good" and "Poor," hence these are still discrete categories of data, but ordered or ordinal.

Data on a Likert scale are usually based on an odd-numbered scale. In Table 9.4, this is a 5-point scale on musician preparedness, from "Not prepared" to "Really well prepared." Ordinal data are good for scales (e.g., a housing quality scale) and for frequency of occurrence (e.g., sometimes, rarely, not at all). The data can be ordered, and the mode (most frequent score) can be identified.

TABLE 9.3 Ordinal Data

QUALITY OF HOUSING IN THE NEIGHBOURHOOD		
SCORE	NUMBER	PERCENTAGE
Very Good	13	41
Good	11	34
Poor	8	25
Total	**32**	**100**

TABLE 9.4 Performance: Ordinal Data on a Likert Scale

	MUSICIAN PERFORMANCE READINESS 24 HOURS PRE-PERFORMANCE					
LIKERT SCALE	1	2	3	4	5	TOTAL
	Not prepared	Partly prepared	Prepared	Well prepared	Really well prepared	
Musician Performance Readiness	1	3	7	17	6	34

Sometimes numerical values are assigned and a quasi-analysis occurs, showing a weight of evidence (frequency times assigned value). In a Likert scale, for example, we give a numerical value to the data and use that as if the distance between each of the categories is equal, as in Table 9.5.

This allows us to show that the mean is 3.14 (even though there is no category of 3.14). The mode is the score of 3, or "Good." The median or midpoint is the twenty-second of 43 scores, or one specific score within the group of "Good." The range 1 to 5 (or Poor to Excellent) is a range of 4. As is evident by the mean of 3.14 and the range of 4, we are forcing the data by applying statistical measures. In mathematical terms, the 3.14 and 4 make sense, but in the categories or actual terms they do not. The 3.14 is not a category, so in reality it does not exist. Similarly, the number 4 is a category but cannot stand as a range (high–low score) since the distances between points on the scale are not determined as equal.

Interval data fall on a continuous scale with no true zero. Examples commonly used to illustrate this are IQ and temperature. IQ, or intelligence quotient, is usually measured by some version of mental skill divided by chronological

TABLE 9.5 Ordinal Data on a Likert Scale: Frequency × Assigned Value

	QUALITY OF HOUSING		
	FREQUENCY	VALUE × *f*	PERCENTAGE
Excellent	7	5 × 7	26
Very Good	9	4 × 9	27
Good	13	3 × 13	29
Fair	11	2 × 11	16
Poor	3	1 × 3	2
Total	**43**	**135**	**100**

age and scaled. Standard deviations are used to distinguish interval data. For example, it may be that one standard deviation is 15, two standard deviations are 30, and so on. However, this does not suggest that a person with an IQ of 50 has half the mental ability of someone with an IQ of 100. With interval data, such as IQ points, there are no percentages.

It is clear that the more sophisticated the data, the more that descriptive statistics can be used. On IQ data, the full range of descriptive statistics can be used, though interpretation must ensure that in the absence of a true zero, one person cannot be considered twice as intelligent as another who had half the score (see Table 9.6).

TABLE 9.6 Interval Data

IQ SCORES: GRADE 4 CLASSES AT ELMPARK ELEMENTARY SCHOOL, 2015					
IQ SCORE	NUMBER OF STUDENTS	CATEGORY	FREQUENCY	CENTRAL TENDENCY AND DISPERSION	
91					
92	1				
93		91–95	3		
94	2				
95					
96				MODE	101–105
97					calc = 103 IQ points
98	3	96–100	10		
99				MEDIAN	101–105
100	7				calc = 101.9 IQ points
101	2				
102				MEAN	calc = 104.5 IQ points
103	9	101–105	13		$3 \times 93 = 279$
104	1				$10 \times 98 = 980$
105	1				$13 \times 103 = 1339$

(continued)

TABLE 9.6 Interval Data (Continued)

IQ SCORES: GRADE 4 CLASSES AT ELMPARK ELEMENTARY SCHOOL, 2015					
IQ SCORE	NUMBER OF STUDENTS	CATEGORY	FREQUENCY		CENTRAL TENDENCY AND DISPERSION
106					10 × 108 = 1080
107	8				7 × 113 = 791
108		106–110	10		3 × 118 = 354
109	2				Total = 4,823
110					4,823/46 = 101.9 IQ points
111	1				
112	5				
113	1	111–115	7	RANGE	25 IQ points
114					calc 118 – 93 = 25
115					calc using raw scores
116					
117	2				
118		116–120	3		
119					
120	1				
Total	46		46		

When categories are used, in this case groups of five IQ scores, the midpoint of each category is used to calculate the measure of central tendency. This is based on the assumption that all the scores in the category are equally spaced across the category. Also assumed is that the distance between each IQ score is exactly the same, so that 101 to 102 is the same as 102 to 103, so each category covers the same point spread and is comparable to each other category.

Similar to interval data, *ratio data* are also continuous. All descriptive statistics and inferential statistics may be used. Ratio data are interval data with a true zero. Examples might include the amount of money one has, or a measure for distance or a scale for time; see Table 9.7.

TABLE 9.7 Ratio Data: Students' Commute from University

	FREQUENCY	PERCENTAGE	VALUE/ MID	F X MID	MEAN	MODE	MEDIAN
			DISTANCE FROM CITY CENTRE				
0–4 km	7	16	2 km	14			
5–9 km	9	21	7 km	63			
10–14 km	13	30	12 km	157			
15–19 km	11	26	17 km	187			
20–24 km	3	7	22 km	66			
Total	43	100		483	483/43 = 11	12 km	22 – 2 = 20 km

With the true zero, it is possible to say someone lives twice the distance from the city centre than someone else, or that one has only half the amount of money needed for a purchase. All measures of central tendency and dispersion apply.

Creating the Spreadsheet. Although it is beyond the purview of this book to present a full section on quantitative analysis,[2] it is appropriate to provide a brief introduction to the foundations of parametric analysis—that is, whether any difference (variance) can be determined from what does or might exist in an entire population. Data entry is usually presented in a spreadsheet or code-book format, with data on each variable presented in the same order for each case. (The data spreadsheet was introduced in Chapter 8, but here we revisit it as some revisions may be necessary now that you have a better understanding of the different kinds of data in your data set.) Each row is for a single case, and the columns are for the data for that case across the variables being measured. For computer-assisted analysis packages, the spreadsheet entry is a built-in feature. Table 9.8 presents a data set example.

The cases, or research participants, are numbered 1, 2, 3, and so on down the far left column. The variables with data are VAR 1, VAR 2, and so on. If you are collecting data by using completed questionnaires, this kind of spreadsheet can be easily created in Excel (or similar spreadsheet programs). Online

....

2 For computer-assisted analysis (e.g., SPSS, SAS, S-PLUS, Stata, STATISTICA), researchers need to display data in the form of variables, attributes, and numerical representations of responses. Some startup effort is required to learn the language of these programs, but this time commitment is quickly offset by the wide variety of data entry and analyses possible in a "point and click" format. If you are using these for the first time, you will likely make heavy use of the online Help function. For statistical analyses, the programs SPSS and SAS are most commonly available to students in undergraduate (nonstatistics) studies. (See Afifi, May, & Clarke, 2011.)

TABLE 9.8 Spreadsheet with Data: Variable Numbers

DATA SET A							
VAR 1	VAR 2	VAR 3	VAR 4	VAR 5	VAR 6	VAR 7	VAR 8
1	F	27	4	4	3	4	4
2	M	52	4	5	2	2	3
3	M	46	2	4	2	2	3
4	TF	48	2	3	3	2	2
5	F	29	3	4	3	3	3
6	M	33	3	1	3	2	2
7	TM	59	2	2	1	2	2
8	F	63	1	1	1	2	1
9	M	73	3	3	4	3	3
10	Undiscl	19	3	4	4	4	4
11	M	20	3	4	4	3	3
12	F	42	2	2	2	2	2

survey tools such as FluidSurveys and SurveyMonkey will export question-naire data into an Excel spreadsheet for you. Here are some tips for data entry:

- Code using numbers rather than the alphabet.
- Put all the information you can into the spreadsheet (it can be cleaned and categorized later).
- Eliminate the extreme values if needed (outliers, accuracy check).
- Keep a backup of the original data files.
- Make sure there is a code used for missing values (e.g., NR = nonresponse). In the example above the "undiscl" under VAR 1 for case 10 may be an NR or a useful piece of information from someone who is not ready to disclose his or her identity.

The more complete the spreadsheet data file, the easier the subsequent analysis will be.

Next for your spreadsheet, you will need to make the data set understand-able to all users. In this data set, the variable names are as follows: VAR 1 is

TABLE 9.9 Spreadsheet with Data: Variable Names

			DATA SET A				
ID	SEX	AGE	HEALTH CAT*	EXERCISE CAT*	EDUCATION CAT*	SOCIAL CAT*	FUNCTION CAT*
1	F	27	4	4	3	4	4
2	M	52	4	5	2	2	3
3	M	46	2	4	2	2	3
4	TF	48	2	3	3	2	2
5	F	29	3	4	3	3	3
6	M	33	3	1	3	2	2
7	TM	59	2	2	1	2	2
8	F	63	1	1	1	2	1
9	M	73	3	3	4	3	3
10	Undiscl	19	3	4	4	4	4
11	M	20	3	4	4	3	3
12	F	42	2	2	2	2	2
	T = trans		1 = high	1 = high	1 = grad deg	1 = high	1 = high

participant ID, VAR 2 is Sex, VAR 3 is Age, VAR 4 is Health Category (1–5), VAR 5 is Exercise Category (1–5), VAR 6 is Education Category (1–5), VAR 7 is Social Category (1–5), and VAR 8 is Function Category. Table 9.9 shows the same data set with variable descriptions, which are a straightforward listing of the attributes: Sex is M, F, TM, TF, undisclosed; Health is on a scale of 1 to 5, with 1 being the high score and 5 being the low score; and so on.

Now the data set can be analyzed with VAR 1–3 as the demographic variables and VAR 4–8 as the overall well-being variables.

2b. Analysis: Central Tendencies, Dispersions, and Relationships between Variables

Before analysis, the data need to be cleaned, which includes taking simple steps to ensure that the analysis does not get "hung up" on something and that the outcomes make sense. (As a reminder, you will first want to make a backup

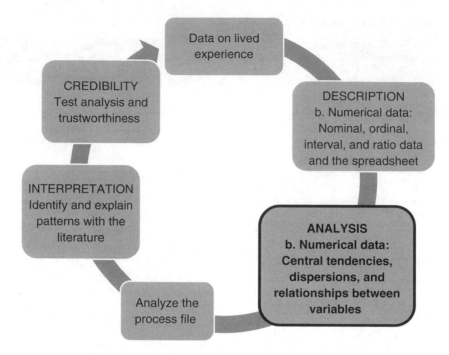

FIGURE 9.12: Data Text: Analysis

copy of the spreadsheet(s) before you go further.) Cleaning the spreadsheet includes checking for spelling errors, removing any duplicate rows, making sure that the appropriate upper and lower cases are used for the words, removing any characters and spaces that are unnecessary, double checking the accuracy of the scores, ensuring that the case (ID, far left column) matches the data for that case, and ensuring any rows or columns that were changed are correct. Establish new columns next to each existing column and make the changes there. Once completed, you can delete each original column and the cleaned columns take their place. This keeps your eyes on one spreadsheet and not moving between two or three documents at the same time, thus decreasing your chance of making an error.

We can determine the type of numerical data. For Data Set A in Tables 9.8 and 9.9, VAR 1 and 2 are nominal, whereas VAR 3–8 are interval data. We can produce graphs and charts to represent the data. For the nominal data, bar and pie charts are good graphics to use. For the ordinal, interval, or ratio data, histograms (normal curves and probability charts) can be used. Figure 9.13 shows a histogram with a skewed right (positive) distribution.

A plot of, for example, VAR 3 by VAR 5 would give us an Age versus Exercise relationship, which we could put that on a graph with Age on the x-axis and Exercise on the y-axis, as in Figure 9.14.

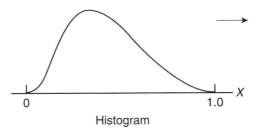

Histogram

FIGURE 9.13: Example of a Positive Skew

This is a normal probability plot—that is, we can use this to predict that as VAR 3 Age increases (horizontal *x*-axis), the VAR 5 Exercise Cat (vertical *y*-axis) also increases. Note that all the statistical packages we identified earlier have the capacity to produce these types of box plots. Then we can do further statistical analyses to discover if there is a symmetric distribution around the mean of each VAR, and if so whether the scores gather closely around the slope line on the graph—that is, whether there is a "goodness of fit" for the data when we compare it. We address this more fully later in the chapter. There is limited interpretation of the data possible with statistics, but in combination with reference to how the participants give meaning to the data the analysis can really come to life. You can answer how much or what kind of data or outcome is present, how the data are similar to or different from each other, and perhaps even where there are (or are not) associations between data groups.

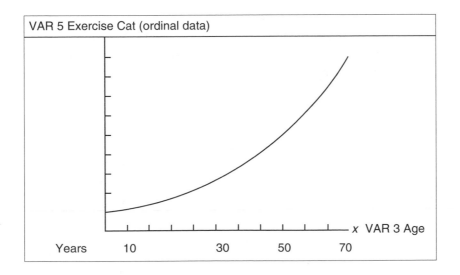

FIGURE 9.14: The Relationship between Two Variables

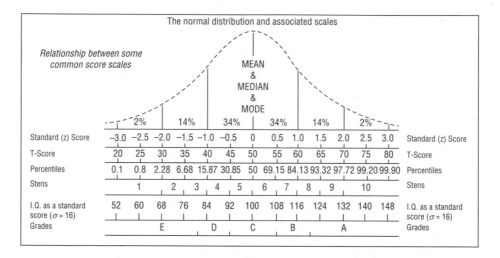

FIGURE 9.15: The Normal or Bell-Shaped Curve

If we use the demographic data from Data Set A, we may want to know the central tendency and dispersion for VAR 2 (Sex) and VAR 3 (Age). VAR 2 is nominal data, so all that can be said is that of the 12 cases, 3 are females, 5 are males, 2 are trans females, 1 is trans male, and 1 is undisclosed; the mode (or most frequent choice) is male (5). For VAR 3, the data are interval with a range (19 to 73, or 54 years), mode (none), median (between 42 and 46 years), and mean (42.58 years). Because there are only 12 cases, it is unlikely that further numerical analysis would be used on the demographics.

There is often a need to look at a statistical description of how the numerical data are spread out, and this is done with reference to the normal curve. Normal curve distributions are based on data that are sampled randomly. The normal curve is used to assist with determining how strong your data are and how much you can say about it with confidence. If the data are sampled nonrandomly or purposively, as is the case with qualitative questionnaires, the normal curve can still be used, but you will be necessarily less confident in the results.[3]

From the range on larger data sets (the distance between the high and the low point), you may also want to know if the data are normally distributed (see Figure 9.15) or skewed positively (more weight to the left of the curve) or negatively (more weight to the right of the curve). Distributions with positive skews occur more

....

3 How close the sampling is to a random sample becomes quite important. For random sampling—where all data have an equal chance of being selected—you can be very confident. With purposive sampling, you cannot be as confident in the outcomes as with random sampling. With representative sampling, where you have tried to balance the overall sample so that it looks proportionately like the population, you can be less confident still.

Data set: 7, 11, 13, 18, 19, 21 kilometres from university
Mean ($\bar{X}$) ≥ sum of all scores/number of scores = 14.83 km
Standard deviation calculation (SD for a sample, rho for a population)

$$\sigma = \sqrt{\frac{\sum\left(x_i - \bar{X}\right)^2}{n-1}}$$

The standard deviation is the average distance of each score from the mean, squared and summed (144.83). This is then divided by the number of scores minus 1 (6 − 1 = 5).
Then the square root is calculated (5.38).
SD (σ) ≈ 5.38 km²
Skewness is calculated as follows:

$$Skewness = \frac{\sum\left(x_i - \bar{X}\right)^3}{(n-1)\cdot\sigma^3}$$

Skewness = −0.2624

FIGURE 9.16: Small Data Set Example of Interval Data

frequently than those with negative skews. A positive skew distribution usually has different scores for the mode, median, and mean, with the mode being the lowest score. Also, the mean is pulled by extreme scores, so it is always important to look at the actual score distribution to describe central tendency and dispersion.

Since a normal curve is defined by the mean, median, and mode all being identical, if there is a skew it tells you something interesting about the data. This simple look at the curve can tell you if the data are distributed "by chance," which would likely be on a normal curve, or if something is pushing or influencing the data curve to "lean" one way or another. Online calculations can be used for any preliminary analysis (see Figure 9.16).

By using an online calculator (e.g., www.mathportal.org/calculators/statistics-calculator/standard-deviation-calculator.php), it is possible to determine that the skew in Figure 9.16 is negative (−0.2624), meaning that there is less weight than expected on the left side of the normal curve.

More advanced statistical measures are beyond the scope of this chapter, but it is important to note that as you move from descriptive statistics to parametric or inferential statistics you are simply using mathematics to determine whether you can predict something on the basis of the sample results you have. In the Appendix to this chapter we have provided explanations of determining the chi-square or "goodness of fit."

What does moving from spreadsheets to calculations look like? For this, we will go back to Data Set A from Table 9.9. Similar to qualitative analysis, you will want to look for patterns and themes and the relative strengths of these. You may also want to look at overlaps among the data and even some predictability. What decisions do you need to make at this point? With 12 cases and lots of variation in gender and age, you will want to go back to the research question that prompted the data gathering in the first place. For example, if you wanted to mine the data, you could look for whatever patterns or themes emerged. For the five cases of men, what exercise levels did they have (4, 2, 3, 3, and 3) and is there a pattern there? With five cases, you can describe this. With 100 cases, you can begin to use statistics to give some power to your analysis.

First, from your cleaned spreadsheet, check to see what kinds of variables you have. In Data Set A, Sex is nominal and Age is interval. All the categorical data are on Likert scales of 5 points, so we can cautiously use the ordinal data as interval data. For demographic analysis, we ask about the participants (ID, Sex, and Age) and we describe and display what we have found. Age ranges from 20 to 73, and we can calculate the average. The Sex variable tells us that we have considerable variety and unevenness because no category is the same size. In describing the participants, some reference should be made to the research question and how these participants contributed to answer it while remaining mindful of confidentiality.

Next you will want to describe the other categories, likely in the same pattern. For example, the Health Category shows scores ranging from 2 to 4; there are no high and low scores. Looking at the data column will tell you what is needed: How many 2s are there, how many 3s, and how many 4s? What is the pattern? What is the average (add them all up and divide by 12)? Do the same for all columns. If you have a large data set, you will go through exactly the same process but with computational assistance. You will analyze the frequency with which each score was selected and, if you want to compare to the total, you would calculate percentages on each column. Also, if you have a number of scores in a larger data set, you might want to look at each of those scores in relation to the complete data set. As an example, what did I get on the test? What did everyone else get? Where do I stand in relation to the others? Are the scores normally distributed on a curve? For this you would be using standard deviation and z-scores. These measures will tell you about the position of the score or the position of the sample in relation to all the data collected. Further, it will tell you the relation of that score to the others and the proportion of the scores above and below the mean (average) score as well as the distance of the scores from the mean score. The z-score describes the area of the curve that is to the left and to the right of a particular score, and by doing so it indicates the proportion of the scores above and below a particular score. Roughly 68 per cent of all scores on a normal curve fall between one z-score above and one z-score below the mean. Only 2.5 per cent of all scores on a normal curve will be outside the z-scores of $+2$ and -2.

You could do the same analysis with a collection of samples that together make up a large data set. What did our class score? How does that compare to all the other classes and the total scored by all who wrote the test? If you want to know more about the position of a particular score or groups of scores (i.e., the measures of standard deviation and z-scores), use the area above and below the score to help you.[4] With a larger data set you may want to display the data using the measures of central tendency, bar charts, and histograms. You will want to say something about the skew pattern (do the data fall on a normal curve pattern or are they skewed in one direction, and if so, why?) Using Excel spreadsheets to produce these graphs and charts is easily done, and you will get better at doing so with practice.

Let's go back to Data Set A. Once you have a description of all the columns (demographics plus the five categories), you will want to know what patterns are evident. What does comparing the data on Sex to Health Category show? Here is a description of the data: males (2–4, average = 3) and females (1–4, average 2.7). Are females less healthy than males? Similarly, if we have 100 cases, we can compute the measures of central tendency to produce range, mode, mean, and median. Then we would run a comparison between Sex and Health Category (Sex × Health) to see if a pattern emerged. We would do the same through all the variables in the data set. Remember that these comparisons between variables are still descriptive in nature, though the size and complexity of the data sets can make us lose sight of that.

For our purposes, it is likely that you will stop here. If you have not used probability or random sampling your analysis will become increasingly weak the further down the statistical path you go.[5] Data descriptions, however complex, may be all you need to answer your research question.

....

4 Earlier in the chapter we provided names of some of the more common statistical packages that might be useful for these purposes. All statistics books have details on how to go about these analyses, and many will show you how to calculate them by hand as well.

5 If your research question and data are capable of inference and prediction, then more advanced parametric statistics can be used, such as bivariate and multivariate statistics (confidence intervals, t-tests, chi-squares, ANOVAs, and correlations). Questions we might ask here are, What make my two sample scores different? How much difference is there? What is the likelihood that two groups would get the same score (probability)? Is the association between these variables strong, and if so how strong? and so on. Chi-square can be used for the "goodness of fit." It also allows us to infer a relationship between variables based on what we anticipated earlier (i.e., a null or alternative hypothesis). Moving into multivariate analysis requires us to have dependent, independent, and control variables.

AN EXAMPLE OF ANALYSIS

On the following pages we show an example of data analysis for one question contained in a data set that is mostly numerical from the study "Using Community-Based Research to Explore Common Language and Shared Identity in the Therapeutic Recreation Profession in British Columbia, Canada" (Reid, Leon, & Landy, 2013).

Question 18: What is your highest educational qualification? (one answer only)
☐   Postsecondary
☐   Certificate, name:
☐   Diploma, name:
☐   Undergraduate degree (name degree and discipline):
☐   Graduate degree (name degree and discipline):
☐   Other:

FIGURE 9.17: Analysis of Numerical Data: Question 18

The data set for question 18 is shown in Table 9.10.

TABLE 9.10 Data Set for Question 18

ANSWER OPTIONS	WHAT IS YOUR HIGHEST EDUCATIONAL QUALIFICATION?							RESPONSE PERCENT	RESPONSE COUNT
	<1–3	4–6	7–10	11–14	15–20	21–25	>25		
High School	0	0	0	0	0	0	0	0.0	0
Certificate	0	1	0	0	1	0	0	2.4	2
Diploma	1	3	1	3	11	4	6	34.5	29
Undergraduate Degree	9	10	6	5	3	3	3	46.4	39
Graduate Degree	3	3	0	1	1	2	4	16.7	14
Answered question									84
Skipped question									0

From this, we see the educational qualification levels for respondents with 1–3 years' experience, 4–6 years' experience, and so on. Then, the nominal data (school achievement) versus nominal data (years' experience) produced the bar chart shown in Figure 9.18.

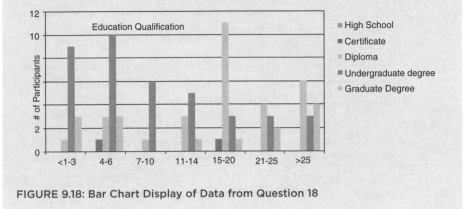

FIGURE 9.18: Bar Chart Display of Data from Question 18

3. Analyze the Process File

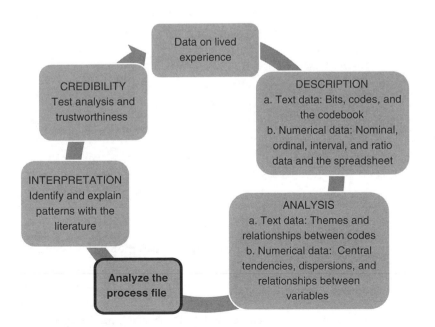

FIGURE 9.19: Data Analysis Process: Process File

You now need to bring information on your research process into the analysis. Process files contain information about how the steps of research were planned, undertaken, and perhaps altered along the way. Similar to the treatment of data bits, information and reflections about doing the research are also coded and placed in appropriately named files. Common themes for the process files might, for example, include rapport, analysis, problems in data gathering, time, check-off lists, interview strategies, coding strategies, or general reflections on the research process.

Some of the process data lend itself to chronological ordering. Other bits are more thematic reflections on the research process. Here are some sample bits from the process files of two researchers:

> *FN Josef:* Doing my reflections is easy. Writing is easy, so easy in fact that the more I write, the more I feel compelled to write. I was spending too much time on my own thoughts about the data and not enough on making sense of the data. So I had to sit back for a couple of days and reacquaint myself with the data. So I know what is so intriguing about this research. Now, with a clear head, I have been able to go through each category and have it really make sense to me. To write the paragraph on top of each category was good and some were really, really good. I had to keep myself from cross-referencing too soon. I am just taking my time and doing a good job. The cross-referencing will just flow because I can see all the links already. I need to walk instead of vaulting into the analysis.

> *FN Simone:* I am not good at keeping procedure memos. Lots of thoughts. Lots of promises to write it down later. I never did. I'm not lazy, just don't want people to find my notes, or maybe I am just too busy to be thorough. I really thought I would remember stuff. Now it's too late. I have to put this report together and I can't remember details like why I contacted the head honcho and when I was at her office. I can't think of why I coded the two big files the way I did. I am tempted to make it up out of what I do remember, but that's foolish.

Josef writes about reacquainting himself with the data and cross-referencing for his analysis. The struggle is to do what is needed as thoroughly as possible and not get ahead of himself on the analysis, exciting though it may be to do so. Simone, on the other hand, was uncomfortable with the discipline of fieldnotes and struggled to maintain them. There is no judgment implied here—it can be difficult to be disciplined with recording process fieldnotes. Simone's awareness indicates her understanding of their importance. Were she to do more research, she would likely pay more attention to the discipline of recording dated notes along the way.

Here are comments from a process file from researchers engaged in data analysis:

Handling the data:

- The more voices—either diversity of people or diversity of experiences—I hear, the better I understand the meaning of what they are telling me.
- I wanted to gather every little bit of data. I had to make myself stop. I was living inside the data and couldn't get enough distance from it to actually hear what it had to say to me.
- I interviewed myself to get the fieldnotes recorded. I made a file on myself and loved it. I was scared a bit, though, because I didn't know how to do the write-up. But I really learned a lot from the participants and a lot about myself.
- I decided to use code words and do a search on each one, or a phrase with that word in it. It was quite easy and it went quickly. I ended up with a page on each code with a list of pertinent quotes. For a superficial run at the data, this worked. I then re-read all the data and began to code in earnest with themes that kept emerging after that initial scan.

The researcher distancing her/himself from the data:

- I needed to distance myself from the data. This distance resulted in an inability to write down my reflections concerning the data that I had collected. My reflections were limited by what I was able to allow in at one time because I knew my life would be changing from this experience.

Coding and recoding:

- Some of my coding I did as mapping instead. I could see the relationships and figure out what events went with what. I got the chronology down early and that really helped.
- I had to think about what I could include in the code and what it did not include—and then stick to it.
- I printed out the coded sections and then I shuffled them like a deck of cards. Each shuffle meant that some new possibilities for links poked their heads up. I had to do some recoding when I found that some of the categories weren't as strong as I thought.

- I couldn't keep all the codes in my head as they developed. So I decided to go through all my data with only three or four codes at a time and find everything related to them. Then I repeated it with three or four other themes . . . until I was exhausted and I think I had everything coded pretty well.
- My way of coding was to ask questions of the data. "What event is this?" "What theme do you belong to?" "What does this mean?" "What is being done here?" "How does this happen?" The more of these I answered, the better I was able to describe what was going on in the data.
- How do I separate my reflections from the data? I don't want to be interpreting what they are saying to me. I want to give their voices priority.

Making sense of the data:

- I find that the research question I was asking was not what I really got at. They were telling me about what kinds at choices they made and I was asking about how they made them.

As shown above, the coding of process is vital to all further analytical work. Just as all content is eligible for coding, so too are materials in the process file. Here the analysis is heavily influenced by the amount of information collected. In all likelihood, a thematic approach to analysis will work, where you account for process with sections such as chronology of research activities, method choices, rationales for choices, relations with participants, recommendations, or things to improve upon.

Once you become relatively content with the themes, then interpretation begins in earnest. "Settling" means that the themes become stable, the data no longer move in and out of them, and the code(s) accurately reflect what is contained within the theme. At this stage of the research process you can bring all themes (saturated and unsaturated) together to identify where the links exist among them. It is the data that determine what analysis is possible and what experiences and concepts can ultimately be described.

4. Interpretation: Identify Patterns and Explanations

The approach to identifying patterns and explanations involves examining each theme for a thorough description and explanation. By description we mean what characteristics the theme exhibits. What is occurring and how is it occurring? By explanation we mean how it makes sense in relation to the research

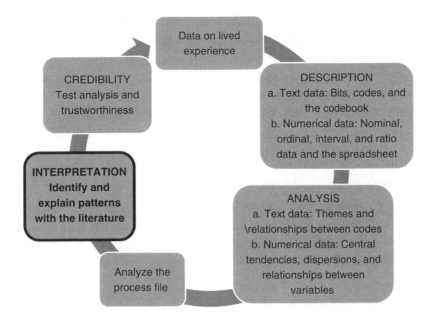

FIGURE 9.20: Data Analysis Process: Interpretation

question. When each theme's description and explanation are complete, examine the relationship between them. A systematic comparison across themes or cases is then used to identify patterns and their strengths.

Bring Forward the Literature Review

Once most data are accounted for in the analysis and there is some stability in your themes, explanations, and overall patterns and interconnections, you will need to draw on the concepts and theories identified in the literature review. In some emergent research there may appear to be little to bring forward because of the newness of the field of study or the particularity of the data gathered. Regardless it is important to draw on the literature, or even related literatures, to properly contextualize your results. Once the thematic descriptions are in place, the researcher needs to return to the original review of the literature and to the fieldnotes to draw out ideas, theories, and potential explanations that might be useful in the data analysis.

In approaches to analysis that are less inductive, you may also consider applying existing theories to your research themes to determine whether those theories can explain your research outcomes. To do this, a set of potentially applicable theories would have already been covered in the review of the literature. These need to then be applied to the data. The task is to see if the theories apply, and if not what other theories may apply instead. A theory is only as good as its ability to explain the data. If the theory does not offer explanatory power, you will have to search for another theory to explain the data or create one. You always use a theoretical paradigm approach if you are testing theory.

Theory Building

But if you were researching a new area or attempting to develop new theory, you need to take a different approach. Theory building is hard work, the work of "conceiving or intuiting ideas (concepts) and formulating them into logical, systematic and explanatory schemes" (Strauss & Corbin, 1988, p. 22). Glaser and Strauss (1967) and later Strauss and Corbin (1988) conceptualize analysis as "doing the theory." Theory exists because we create it, live it, use it, and sometimes discard it as no longer useful. "Doing theory" is largely an inductive process where, in an iterative fashion, we develop concepts and then check back to see if they have support from the data. If support is lacking we look for new explanations. If support is present we look for broader support and application.

DERIVING THEORY

Lorraine developed a theory of women's smoking based on her qualitative research with a range of women in Australia and Canada. As mentioned in Chapter 6, this research was designed to investigate the meanings that women ascribed to (their own) smoking and included women who were self- described feminists and women who were in women's shelters, having experienced abuse. These groups were chosen to investigate varied interpretations of smoking, ranging from "liberating" to "rebellious" to adaptive and addicting. Lorraine concluded her study by deriving a theory of women's smoking, summarized as follows:

> Smoking may be a means through which women control and adapt to external and internal realities. It mediates between the world of emotions and outside circumstances. It is both a means of reacting to and/or acting upon social reality, and a significant route to self-definition. (Greaves, 1996, p. 107)

This paragraph introduced a longer discussion of elements of the theory and set the stage for a new approach to thinking about women's smoking, its symbolism, its various contradictory elements, its role in women's lives, and ultimately its prevention and treatment. This theory building introduced a gendered approach to understanding smoking and ultimately encouraged the tobacco control movement to confront sex, gender, and equity considerations in tobacco use.

Theory is based on the strength of the data, so if the data are strong enough the theory will be cohesive in its ability to explain it. Challenging the developing theory with negative cases (negative case analysis) and ensuring that weak (unsaturated) or satellite (unique in character) data are not at the centre of the theory are useful strategies. The researchers can rely on theory built from saturated data but cannot rely on theory based on weak and unsubstantiated data. Overall, developing themes is also called the development of substantive theory—theory that is close to the substance or content of the research. Moving through the analysis process we link the new way of explaining something that has not been explained or analyzed before. In our experience, one of the joys of research is the discovery of new ways of knowing.

The iterative or ongoing back-and-forth nature of analysis ultimately strengthens it; when complete, it means we can speak with considerable confidence about our theories and the breadth and depth of the data supporting them. Theory and data remain close, and theory is created from thematic data. Themes and their relationships form the base of theory. Writing memos and coding are large parts of the process, as previously described. We search for what is "shared in common" or "unique" and what is saturated or too weak to stand alone as a theme. As we look for overlap between bits of data, codes, and themes, we are engaging in the development of theory.

Below is an example of a content analysis and the framework established by Pawlychka (2010) to determine how restorative justice was presented in educational, informational, and training films. It illustrates how comprehensive coding can make visible the themes and intentions of the creators to broaden the appeal and implementation of restorative justice.

EXAMPLE: FRAME ANALYSIS

In my master's thesis, I examined the presentation of restorative justice (RJ) in educational, informational, and training films and its potential impact on acceptance, implementation, and practice. Specifically, contemporary restorative justice, as a social movement, uses framing tactics in a constant attempt to broaden its appeal and advance its acceptance and implementation within a culture of crime control, where retribution and punishment dominate.

I collected internationally, nationally, and locally produced films from various sources, including conferences, practitioner training and/or educational settings, the International Institute for Restorative Practices website, the University of Winnipeg, the University of Manitoba, Menno Simons College, Canadian Mennonite University, and Mediation Services. From films collected, 11 films met the selection criteria, which included date of production (1995 or later); promotes practice of RJ; intended audience of RJ participants, potential participants, stakeholders, funders, politicians, or general public; presents topics including mediation, victim–offender mediation, and/or conferencing; and availability. A total of 528 minutes of film, including offences ranging from minor conflict/crime (break and enter or school conflict) to serious crime (murder, sexual assault), were analyzed.

To conduct the content analysis, films were analyzed in three ways. They were viewed without audio to focus on visual characteristics; listened to without visual to focus on voice, language, keywords/terms, intonation, and pauses; and viewed with both audio and visual. The framework developed was based on framing (Goffman, 1974), framing tasks (Snow, Rochford, Worden, & Benford, 1986), and frame alignment processes (Snow & Benford, 1988). Table 9.11 shows the framework used for content analysis.

TABLE 9.11 Framework for Content Analysis

FRAMING TASKS	EXAMPLE	DEMONSTRATED IN FILM THROUGH:
Problem identification and cause of problem (Diagnostic Framing)	• Crime in society is not currently effectively addressed • Causes of crime: residential schools, lack of community, courts ineffective/inefficient • Consistency/agreement as to causality	• Images of courthouses and angry citizens, victims weeping • Discussion of breakdown of community in contemporary society • Newscasts of crime statistics
Identification of strategies to address cause of problem (Prognostic Framing)	• Increased use of dialogue: mediation, conferencing, or circle processes within current system • Increased community responsibility • Increased focus on healing (of all parties) • Complete paradigm shift to RJ	• Modelling of RJ process • Emphasize healing as primary strategy for addressing crime • Draw attention to need for healing of impacts of residential and mission schools • Images of teachers mingling with students informally
"Call to Action" to motivate potential participants (Motivational Framing)	• Moral inducements • Material inducements • Status inducements	• Adult and community responsibility for and to youth • Current system employs ethnocentric methods • Cost of current system, financial efficiency of RJ (material) • Expertise in scientific field (neurological impact of trauma, shame on behaviour) • Statistics of effectiveness of RJ (captions, images, discussion)

FRAMING TASKS	EXAMPLE	DEMONSTRATED IN FILM THROUGH:
Dissemination of information to potential participants in RJ movement (Bridging Process)	• How is film used as a mechanism to disseminate information to stakeholders, third parties, governing authorities through inclusion of various parties?	• Direct film at specific stakeholders • Engage dialogue with academics, practitioners, volunteers, youth educators, victims, offenders, criminal justice system staff and professionals, police-led conferences • Use of casual environment and practical language (rather than technical or highly specialized) • Emphasize effectiveness across a variety of offences
Clarification of values and beliefs (Frame Amplification)	• What values are amplified in films? How? • Are values of both systems (CJS & RJ) amplified? How? What are they?	• Respect: importance of respect, which includes physical and emotional safety at all times, emphasized as an RJ "ground rule at all times" in various films • CJS belief: responsibility = assignment of guilt; accountability = length of sentence, amount of fine • RJ belief: responsibility = assume blame; accountability = repair harm, provide apology and explanation • Beliefs include seriousness of problem: "Canadian Aboriginal population 4% but 16% of prison population."
Extension of primary frameworks to include points of view/interests important to potential participants but incidental to movement (Frame Extension)	• How do films demonstrate that interests/views important to the old system are also important and addressed under RJ processes? • Emphasis on "tough on crime" • Connection of shame and criminal behaviours	• "Come watch serious butt being kicked . . ." • Direct statements about arduous nature of RJ process • Contradict myths (RJ is soft on crime) • Challenge prison as tough ("insulates offenders from facing impact/harm to victims") • Images of offenders pacing nervously prior to RJ process
Reframe old values and understandings so that old values become seen by participants as "something quite else" (Frame Transformation)	• How do films "reframe" values and understandings? What values are transformed? How? • How do films promote old methods as "unjust" by (a) altering participant perspectives—old view becomes inexcusable, unjust and (b) provoking shift in cause of problem to structural/systemic blame? • How do films connect values of old/dominant (CJS) system to values and processes of new (RJ) system	• Insulating offenders is unjust and immoral; RJ requires them to take responsibility, face victims, and be held accountable • Redefines "justice" as meeting needs of all parties, holding offenders accountable; in doing so all parties heal and future crime is reduced; justice = healing

Through the use of this framework, it became evident that some films engaged in a number of framing tasks and processes while others engaged in fewer tasks to greater depth. Connecting these processes to the literature on restorative justice allowed clarification of RJ values as well as to challenges to acceptance and implementation. It was particularly informative insofar as inconsistent presentations and practices are concerned and risk of conflating the identity of restorative justice, as well as avenues through which the movement is enhanced and facilitates acceptance and implementation in an internationally dominant punitive society. (Pawlychka, 2010)

Final Steps

For the researcher, living with the analysis for a period of time is a way to ensure that the analysis is solid, steady, and unlikely to change. This means that the researcher has to retreat from the analysis (Lofland & Lofland, 1995) to get some distance from it and reflect on it. After a period of time has passed (a day, a week, a month on bigger projects), the researcher returns to the analysis with a fresh outlook. Time for reflection on the data and the analysis is a good thing to do after data gathering and management. Co-researchers, peers, or project supervisors may be called upon at this stage, or the reflection can be done alone.

It is also time to review the early fieldnotes for hunches, queries, and concerns. This retreating or temporary distancing can respark some of the original excitement in the research question and can highlight possible connections and solutions to complex relationships that have not been clarified. Often, stepping away from the detail can open you to the ebb and flow of explanations. The researcher is then able to use this distance to gain a different perspective on the data. The researcher's length of time away depends on such things as the researcher's needs, competing obligations, and the complexity of the analysis. When the swirling maps start to settle into a pattern that makes sense, it is time to go back to the research and commit to the analysis and findings.

5. Credibility: Test Analysis and Trustworthiness

To do analysis the data must have been originally divided into manageable portions and the labelling done diligently and consistently. *Inductive labelling* means that each label grows out of the material in each bit, rather than being applied to a bit from some preconceived notion of what groups of data will appear. Thus, by using coding as our labelling strategy, similarly labelled segments are grouped together and a continuous process of comparison helps researchers understand the specific and overall properties, patterns, and relationships

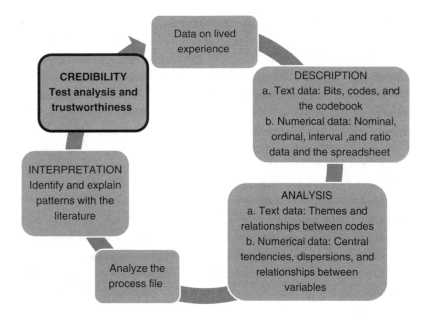

FIGURE 9.21: Data Analysis Process: Credibility

between portions of data and between groups of data. If we have remained attentive, the coding and recoding will bring increasing clarity and stability to analytical themes. It can then be said that our analysis is nearing completion.

In qualitative research a major concern is obtaining in-depth, rich description and explanation of a particular phenomenon. While quantitative researchers focus on the generalizability and external validity of their results, qualitative researchers are more concerned with obtaining a comprehensive and truthful representation of a particular question or context (DePoy & Gitlin, 2011). As you near completion of the analysis it is now necessary to examine it for its trustworthiness. The primary concern in establishing the trustworthiness of the analysis is whether the same findings would have emerged if another researcher had conducted the identical research project. Two questions are asked to establish the trustworthiness or credibility of the findings:

1. To what extent are the biases and personal perspectives of the researcher identified and considered in the data analysis and interpretation?
2. What actions has the researcher taken to enhance the credibility of the research? (DePoy & Gitlin, 2011, p. 279)

Below we describe eight strategies to enhance the accuracy of representation of data and the credibility of interpretation: (1) negative case analysis; (2) triangulation; (3) saturation; (4) member-checking; (5) reflexivity; (6) descriptive statistics; (7) audit trail; and (8) peer debriefing (DePoy & Gitlin, 2011).

Negative Case Analysis

As previously described, satellites are data bits that are free standing and have no obvious relationships with other bits. Satellites can act as areas for further analysis or areas for future research. Satellites can also be referred to as outliers—data, people, behaviours, or events that do not fit. If you have been continually referring back to the satellites in your data, you may have found instances where they fit the analysis as it has emerged and evolved over time. However, some satellites may simply not fit and remain stand-alone. You need to thoroughly search for and discuss these elements of the data that do not support or appear to contradict patterns or explanations that are emerging.

Deviant or *negative case analysis* is a process for refining an analysis until it can explain or account for a majority of cases. Analysis of deviant cases may revise, broaden, and confirm the patterns emerging from data analysis. Sometimes you will need to find ways of gathering more data to understand these negative instances. Usually this leads to deeper clarification or even alteration of the analysis (Creswell, 1998; Lincoln & Guba, 2005; Marshall & Rossman, 2016; Mays & Pope, 2000; Patton, 1999, 2001).

Triangulation

Denzin (1988) defined triangulation as using different research protocols or procedures to gather information from the same or similar groups of participants. Triangulation enables the researcher to validate a particular finding by examining whether different sources provide convergent information (DePoy & Gitlin, 2011, p. 280). This demands that the researcher have a greater variety of analytical skills to deal with different forms of data and also the tenacity to stay within each method to do a complete analysis.

Where two or more methods of data gathering are used, the researcher first independently analyzes data within each protocol, and only when those descriptions and explanations are complete does she or he analyze the relationship between protocols. The within-method analyses are then overlapped with each other to check and cross-check the emergent substantive patterns. A triangulated analysis is considered strongest if the whole or final analysis (the big picture) is confirmed first by each of the within-methods analyses and then across the methods.

When triangulating, data analysis is done by each researcher rigorously and systematically compiling the codebook with exhaustive code definitions and analytical memos. Then, inter-researcher results are examined on such points as agreement and clarity, ambiguity, deficiencies and gaps, and disagreement. As agreement and clarity accumulate across researchers, these triangulated results will have stronger credibility. Depending on the composition and working relationships of research team members, triangulation can happen during the analysis of the first few data files, periodically over the course of the analysis, or collaboratively throughout the analysis. If you uncover discrepancies in your efforts to triangulate data sources or among different researchers, it will be necessary to reflect on your research choices and approaches, for example, computer-assisted analysis and analysis done "by hand," qualitative and quantitative approaches, and researchers of different experiential and disciplinary backgrounds.

Saturation

Saturation refers to the point at which data obtained from fieldwork provide no new insights or understandings. When saturation occurs the researcher can be confident in the solidity and correctness of the analysis. There are two reasons why saturation may not occur: (a) participants' inclusion criteria are too broad, resulting in little uniformity among them and therefore little uniformity in the findings; or (b) the sample size is too small, resulting in too little data to achieve saturation. A "higher level" analysis, or theory development, is based on saturated categories, and the links between them are based on overlapping data between themes.

Member-Checking

Member-checking involves bringing the analysis to one or several research participants to verify its accuracy. Is the analysis salient and plausible? Does it make sense to the participants? Can the participants see their own experiences within the overall analysis? We recommended the use of member-checking after transcribing and checking interview transcripts (see Chapter 8). Member-checking can occur throughout the analysis process and be a tool for ensuring credible analyses. At the very least, member-checking should be conducted at the end stages of formal analysis to "confirm the truth value of specific accounts" and researcher impressions (DePoy & Gitlin, 2011, p. 280).

Reflexivity

In the final report the researcher must discuss how her or his own biases, assumptions, and worldviews shaped the research process. In Chapter 3 we discussed at length positionality and reflexivity, and in Chapter 4 we provided tools for engaging in a reflexive practice, such as maintaining a research journal and documenting "process" fieldnotes. In this final stage, the researcher must reflect on how her or his positionality may have influenced "not only what is learned but also how it is learned" (DePoy & Gitlin, 2011, p. 280).

Descriptive and Inferential Statistics

In this chapter, we have discussed the use of statistics above. Almost all data can be counted in some way, even if it comes from the face sheet. The use of numeric data to support a text analysis will strengthen it, particularly when saturation occurs (e.g., all respondents with incomes lower than $10,000/per year said X and Y).

For data sets from questionnaires, more advanced statistics can also be used. The appropriate use of basic mathematical statistics—such as central tendency measures and dispersion—alongside a good understanding of the strength of the data set itself will increase the credibility of the analysis.

Audit Trail

As described in Chapter 4, an audit trail is a transparent description of the research steps taken from the start of a research project to the development and reporting of findings. It is important to keep an audit trail because there are a range of approaches that can be used in data analysis, and the decisions you make need to be visible and clear. Researchers should leave a path of their thinking and coding decisions so that others can review the logic and decision making that was followed (Denzin & Lincoln, 2003). As the researcher, you must be able to articulate clearly the analytical pathways so that others can agree or disagree or question the decisions that were made. The disciplined practice of maintaining a logbook will lead to a clear and transparent representation of the research process.

Peer Debriefing

Involving peers in the analytical process is another strategy that can be used to affirm emerging interpretations. A debriefing process can involve peers reviewing the audit trail and decision making that occurred throughout the research process, or peers can engage independently in analysis to verify codes and themes and identify areas of agreement and disagreement. This allows for reflection on possible competing interpretations of the data. Peer debriefing is particularly useful in the classroom or graduate school contexts. Engaging in a continuous peer debriefing process can be instructive for everyone and lead to greater insights and learning.

Summary

In this chapter we have described the process of data analysis, including both qualitative and quantitative elements. We began with a discussion of intersubjectivity to remind you about your role and responsibilities as the researcher who is making sense of the lived experiences of participants throughout the analytical process. We ended with suggestions about how to verify your analysis of the data, again to enhance your work and fulfill your responsibilities. While many may think generally about "analysis," we broke this process into three major stages: description, analysis, and interpretation.

All of these stages require diligent attention to the organization and management of data and to checking and rechecking your assumptions. Once you have moved through these stages of analysis you are then ready to "test" the credibility of your analysis by using a range of strategies, including negative case analysis, triangulation, saturation, member-checking, reflexivity, descriptive statistics, audit trail, and peer debriefing (DePoy & Gitlin, 2011).

Questions for Discussion

1. What are the steps for describing textual data and numerical data?
2. Why should you check if your coding is thorough and comprehensive? How do you know if you are finished coding? What is cross-referencing of bits?
3. What are the steps for analyzing textual data and numerical data?
4. After completing the analysis, why must we live with the analysis for a while?
5. How do you derive a theory?

Our Recommended Readings

Bernard, H. R. (2006). *Research methods in anthropology: Qualitative and quantitative approaches* (4th ed.). Lanham: Altamira Press.

DeCuir-Gunby, J. T., Marshall, P. L., & McCulloch, A. W. (2011). Developing and using a codebook for the analysis of interview data: An example from a professional development research project. *Field Methods, 23*(2), 136–155. http://dx.doi.org/10.1177/1525822X10388468

Hesse-Biber, S. (2010). Qualitative approaches to mixed methods practice. *Qualitative Inquiry, 16*(6), 455–468. http://dx.doi.org/10.1177/1077800410364611

Huberman, A. M., & Miles, M. B. (2004). Data management and analysis methods. In N. Denzin & Y. Lincoln (Eds.), *Handbook of qualitative research* (pp. 428–444). London: Sage.

Morse, J. (2010). Simultaneous and sequential qualitative mixed methods designs. *Qualitative Inquiry, 16*(6), 483–491.

Saldana, J. (2009). *The coding manual for qualitative researchers.* London: Sage.

Sandelowski, M. (2000). Combining qualitative and quantitative sampling, data collection, and analysis techniques in mixed-method studies. *Research in Nursing & Health, 23*(3), 246–255. http://dx.doi.org/10.1002/1098-240X(200006)23:3<246::AID-NUR9>3.0.CO;2-H Medline:10871540

Shenton, A. K. (2004). Strategies for ensuring trustworthiness in qualitative inquiries. *Education for Information, 22,* 63–75.

Appendix: Parametric Tests

Parametric tests are those that allow us to compare the data we have gathered against a population of data, even if that population data is unknown. We also use hypotheses to articulate whether we anticipate that our results (means) will be the same as or different than the mean for an entire population, the null (H_o), and alternative hypotheses (H_a), respectively. Here we can use calculations such as the percentile and the *t*-test to calculate what the chances are (confidence) that our sample mean is the same as or different than the population mean—that our H_o or H_a is correct.

Percentiles: Looking at the percentiles line on the normal curve example (50 per cent), what proportion of the scores would fall above or below the centre line? Using our IQ score example, if an IQ score is 116, fully one standard deviation above the mean (see the normal curve depiction in Figure 9.15), it means that the percentile is 84.13, which literally means that 84.13 per cent of the IQ scores will be below that 116 IQ score. Calculating percentiles will show that, for example, at the seventy-fifth percentile, 75 per cent of the IQ scores fall at or below the IQ score of 112.

Standard Deviations: With data gathered using a random sampling format, if the collected data are organized as either raw scores or groups of means (a number of different groups of data for which you have calculated means), then chance would suggest that 68 per cent of the scores/means should fall within one standard deviation (SD) of the highest point (mean, median, and mode) of the normal curve. For the IQ scores referred to earlier, the calculated standard deviation is already known—16 IQ points—which means that 34 per cent of a population will have scores from 86 to 100 and another 34 per cent will have scores between 100 and 116. Approximately 95 per cent of all scores (or means of scores) will by chance fall between 2 SD to the left and 2 SD to the right of that centre line. Following along with the IQ example, one would have only a 2.5 per cent chance of scoring below 68 IQ points or above 132 IQ points. That 95 per cent also can tell you that you can have only a 5 per cent chance of being incorrect if you say your data falls between $+/-$ 2 SD from the centre line. That is, you can have 95 per cent confidence that your outcome is accurate. If your data falls within 3 SD of the centre line, then you can have 99 per cent confidence and only 1 per cent lack of confidence in your outcome.

A *t*-test can determine if a small sample comes from a parent population with a specific mean—a "goodness of fit." This may be important if we don't know the values of the population mean exactly. In the example shown in Figure 9.16: Small Data Set Example (Interval Data), suppose the scores represent the test results on a math skills examination. The provincial average is thought to be ~15. The *t*-test will determine if our scores differ from that provincial average. Note: To conduct *t*-tests, the data have to be continuous (interval data), independent (each score is independent of the others), with no significant outliers (true), and approximately normally distributed (sort of). By using SPSS statistics, it is possible to follow the step-by-step procedure guidelines (Analyze → Compare Means → One-Sample *t*-test → choose the CI Percentage of 95 per cent; Laerd Statistics, 2013).

The **chi-square** calculation is a measure of how well the scores obtained fit or don't fit with a random distribution. If they fall as random scores should fall, there is no difference from the expected result. If there is some difference, then something is different about the observed results of our sample. For example, if we toss a coin 100 times, the expected result is that it should be heads 50 per cent of the time and tails 50 per cent of the time. If in our sample we got 10 heads and 90 tails, those observed results don't fit well with what is expected. You might ask, then, how important is that outcome? Chi-square calculations tell us that.

Chi-square is a particularly good test if we want to calculate the chi-square for a larger sample—say, from more than 100 cases. In the example in Table A.1, the Sex variable, with its two listed attributes (M and F), can be compared to the Attending University Orientation variable with its two categories of data (Attend, Did Not Attend). Both variables are nominal. We anticipate that proportionately fewer males (about 40 per cent) would attend orientation (past experience) compared to females at about 60 per cent. Now we want to determine if there is something other than chance that might explain why the observed scores do not match the expected scores. By using the chi-square formula, we can calculate that the chi-square for this sample is 6.533 and the degrees of freedom $(r-1)(c-1) = 1$ (see Table A.2).

TABLE A.1 Goodness of Fit or the Chi-Square

	OBSERVATION SEX BY ATTENDING (UNIVERSITY ORIENTATION)				EXPECTED SEX BY ATTENDING (UNIVERSITY ORIENTATION)		
	ATTENDED	DID NOT ATTEND	TOTAL		ATTENDED	DID NOT ATTEND	TOTAL
Male	18	28	46	Male	20	30	50
Female	24	30	54	Female	30	20	50
Total	42	58	100	Total	50	50	100
n = 100				p = .01			
df = 1				Significant at p = .01			
Chi-square = 6.533							

We can be 99% confident that these results are due to something other than chance.

TABLE A.2. Percentage Points of the Chi-Square Distribution

DEGREES OF FREEDOM	PROBABILITY OF A LARGER VALUE OF X^2								
	0.99	0.95	0.90	0.75	0.50	0.25	0.10	0.05	0.01
1	0.000	0.004	0.016	0.102	0.455	1.32	2.71	3.84	6.63
2	0.020	0.103	0.211	0.575	1.386	2.77	4.61	5.99	9.21
3	0.115	0.352	0.584	1.212	2.366	4.11	6.25	7.81	11.34
4	0.297	0.711	10.64	1.923	3.357	5.39	7.78	9.49	13.28
5	0.554	1.145	1.610	2.675	4.351	6.63	9.24	11.07	15.09
6	0.872	1.635	2.204	3.455	5.348	7.84	10.64	12.59	16.81
7	1.237	2.167	2.833	4.255	6.346	9.04	12.02	14.07	18.48

If you are working with hypotheses and variables (with their attributes), you may want to analyze a relationship between variables and what might explain such a relationship. Or you may want to compare some difference between settings or among individuals. Or you may want to ask how similar or different the data you gathered are from the population overall. In all those cases, parametric tests may help.

CHAPTER 10

WRITING THE REPORT

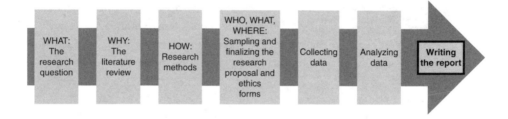

FIGURE 10.1: The Research Process

In this chapter we discuss strategies for writing the final report. Learning to write well is an ongoing process. With practice, skills can be acquired to make your writing clear and effective. Here we break it down into manageable steps so that you can move smoothly from the analysis to the final research report. We also discuss some of the challenges researchers may experience in writing the final report. Throughout we provide many examples from research projects to illustrate this process.

Why Write? The Purpose of a Written Report

All research activities conclude with some sort of reporting. Although the presentation of the information may take a number of forms depending on what is to be reported and to whom, a written document usually accompanies such presentations in almost any format. Written reports serve as a public record of the research. Writing a report or other knowledge product can be an important way to get the word out to those who share similar experiences or questions or to influence policy or program development. Reporting can take the form of a formal research report, a short article, a briefing note, a picture journal, a photo exhibit, a film, a brochure, or a list of points, such as a set of presentation notes. Writing underpins all of these formats. Before presenting the data, first ask, "Who am I presenting to and for what purpose?" The process and format of presenting the research should then fall into place. For example, academic audiences expect different kinds of presentations than practitioners or policymakers, research participants, or the general public. We explore practices and products of knowledge transfer and translation in more depth in Chapter 11.

As an undergraduate or graduate student, it is likely that a written report is required to complete your research course or thesis project. Whether or not you are a student or have plans to present your findings to a specific audience, a research report is an important and necessary first step. First, going through the process of writing a final report will help you pull your data together in a comprehensive manner and complete the analysis. Second, with a written report you can refer back to it as you work at developing other products from your research that are intended to reach different audiences (e.g., the public, the media, a thesis examination committee, a policymaker, a student seminar, or a conference presentation). Finally, a written report can represent the formal completion of the project and can be used and referenced by others (e.g., a publication in a refereed journal, on a website, in a local publication, or in an agency report). Ultimately, this report will contribute to the body of knowledge on your topic and may be used by others to inform their future research endeavours. This is a key goal of any research!

Presenting the data always takes place in a dynamic context. That is, writing is an ongoing part of your analysis, and the receptivity of your audience(s) changes according to other events and emergent knowledge. Also, as you write, the interplay between you and the data continues as you go back and forth, iteratively, from data to analysis: "As you make interpretations, the remaining data are examined to see if and how they corroborate or refute the ongoing analysis" (Reinharz, 1983, p. 183). A clear articulation of your findings through identifying and refining codes and themes is sure to excite new interest in further research about your topic, both in yourself and in others. As the presentation or report takes shape, you can build your writing confidence by sharing drafts with others to see if the analysis holds true and is regarded as credible by others.

While your own words are the glue that hold the report or presentation together, they must reflect the experiences and therefore the voices of the participants. This means that ample room has to be given to their voices in a well-integrated account. Qualitative research reports are difficult to condense (Neuman, 2004) because data are often described and explained in some detail.

The evidence for your interpretation, analysis, and conclusions is housed in their voices, pictures, descriptions, and examples. You are providing a forum for the expression of the experiences and thoughts of the participants and an analysis to frame them. Since the research is concerned with evaluating the data, not the participants, your words must be free of judgment and rhetoric. Think about these issues as you find the writing style that is most appropriate for the data and your anticipated audience and begin.

Components of a Research Report

There are some essential elements to any report that document the process of research and discovery. These include (a) an introduction to the research, (b) research goals and the researcher's orientation to the research, (c) a review of the literature and formation of the research focus and question, (d) the research methodology, (e) the research participants and sampling techniques, (f) methods and an account of data gathering, (g) the data management and analytical processes, (h) the research findings, (i) the links between the findings and the literature, and (j) the implications and/or recommendations. Consistent with our stance that critical social research adopts a social change or political stance, we add to the list (k) the plan for action and (l) the author's reflections on the research.

We recommend preparing a general outline. An overall outline will likely parallel the manner in which the research process unfolds. In Chapter 7 we provided a detailed outline of a research proposal and a final report. As you write your report, refer back to the questions posed in Table 7.1 to ensure that you have covered all necessary material. As the author and researcher, you make the final decisions about how you will organize and present the data. It will help to consider the questions in Table 7.1 and reflect on your own research processes and decisions before you begin writing—and referring back to your research journal and fieldnotes will help tremendously. Decide on the tone and format of your reporting. If the audience or data demand different modes or formats of reporting, make that decision before your start. This depends on a number of factors, including your preferred writing style, the kinds of data to be reported, the placement of any personal accounts (the researcher's or participants'), and the role of textual accounting, among other considerations (Esterberg, 2002).

Steps in the Writing Process

While there are different ways to approach writing a research report, most often we follow the steps outlined below as we move from analysis to writing.

Step 1: Create an Outline

An outline will help you organize where the various pieces will fit in relation to each other. Typically, the findings section of a final report is organized thematically, with subthemes (groupings of codes) that illustrate each major theme. Create an outline and consider how the themes need to be ordered. Most often the major or dominant theme should be presented first. At this stage, writing a purpose or a "so what?" statement for each theme is a useful strategy. In essence, in such a statement you ask and answer the following questions: Why am I presenting this here? How does this answer my research question? Why is this important? Formulating a clear statement about each theme will help you decide on what you are including and excluding in each section. If you find it difficult to write these purpose or "so what?" statements, then the thematic structure of your findings section may need to be revised. Here is one example of an early working outline for a comparative work on racism and homophobia in sport:

EXAMPLE: RACIAL AND HOMOPHOBIC DISCRIMINATION

Partial outline, taken from Kirby, S. L. (2015). Racism and homophobia: How is it experienced in sport? Unpublished report.

RACIAL DISCRIMINATION

Definition and types

Indicators (signs and symptoms)

- Racist stereotypes
- Forms of racial discrimination
- Individual athletes may experience various forms of racial discrimination and abuse

It is complacency? [Possible side question]

From the literature review

- Individual cases of or accusations of discrimination, racism
- Harm to the athletes (short term, long term, how do they talk about it?)
- What do they do about it, if anything, and to what end?
- From the athletes' perspectives, what does the sport system know about this?

HOMOPHOBIC DISCRIMINATION

Definition and types

- Homophobia
- Discrimination
- Multiple discriminations

- International spectrum: LGBT, LGBTQ, LGBTQA, TBLG where
  L = lesbian, G = gay, B = bisexual, T = transgender or transsexual,
  Q = queer or questioning, A = asexual or ally
- Discrimination and homophobia against LGB people in sport

From the literature review

- Individual cases or accusations of discrimination, homophobia
- Harm to the athletes (short term, long term, how do they talk
  about it?)
- What do they do about it, if anything, and to what end?
- From the athletes' perspectives, what does the sport system know
  about this?

Step 2: Gather Data for Each Theme and Subtheme

Once the themes and subthemes have been organized and form a coherent picture of the overall research findings, re-read the quotations that were assigned to each code within the themes and subthemes and highlight the quotations that best illustrate the theme or subtheme. At this point the highlighted quotations can be inserted into the relevant sections of the draft outline and organized in a way that makes sense. The results of this process provide the starting point for writing each section. Typically there are more quotations available than are required to make the point of each individual section. You do not need to include them all, since it is your task to summarize and discuss the findings more generally. As a guideline, often only two to four quotations are required to illustrate one subtheme. Selecting which quotations to include may require another round of decision making:

- Which quotations make the point in the strongest manner?
- Does one quotation better capture the nuances of this argument?
- Which quotations capture the sentiments or experiences of several participants?
- Is the number of quotations used per participant balanced? (Try to avoid using too many quotations from one particularly articulate participant.)
- Does one quotation help transition or link to the next point in the argument or report?

EXAMPLE: RETRIEVING QUOTATIONS FOR EACH THEME AND SUBTHEME

In Chapter 9 we referred to a study that examined women's experiences of poverty (see Figure 9.5, coded transcript and data bits ITES 20150305, p. 244-245) to illustrate coding and the development of themes. Here we pick up that example to demonstrate how data are then grouped for each theme.

Theme 1: Daily Challenges of Living in Poverty

Financial Concerns—*Having Little Money*

There have been occasions where I have not had enough money to eat myself so that my children could. You know, and I've had medical situations that I couldn't get help with and I have to pay these things so. So therefore I starve . . . last month I lost almost fifteen pounds in one month (Lenora, interview1).

If you don't have any money, you can't get there and you can't, you can't do anything if you don't have any money. You have to have money. When you're a single parent and you didn't invest anything cause you spent everything and it's all gone. But you need money to get there. You need money to buy tickets. You need money to have proper apparel. If it's summer, winter, spring, or fall, if you don't have nice warm coat and winter boots in the winter, you can't get there. You just can't (Cationa, interview2).

[I] went to the welfare office because I lived on $730 [a month], I had no medical, no dental, none of the extras that you don't think of as extras but they are when you don't have them (Wanda, focus group1).

Financial Concerns—*Budgeting and Paying the Bills*

I get $359 and that's to cover everything. I get child welfare and that brings it up $200 (Elizabeth, focus group1).

If anybody can stick on a budget it's someone on assistance, because you have to feed the kids, you have to eat, and you may not have enough, but you take care of that budget as good as you can (Susie, focus group1).

Well you have a car or whatever you need for transportation, I separate the bills between car, the tune-up, and the food, and then pay half of the utilities, you juggle. You're always juggling, you never sit down and say "all of my bills are paid." Food and house for the month, I'm a-ok—you never do that (Adele, focus group1).

You get paid for your welfare and then you get your child tax every month. And it's just like oh my god . . . I don't get paid now until the twentieth again. Like that's a long ways to go with. You know you got to budget

> your money. Or you got, you know, milk and bread and fresh fruit and veg-
> etables in the house you know like. It's hard man (Diane, interview2).
>
> And it never stops, you're always thinking of how can I do this, how can
> I do that. Who can I not pay this month, who do I have to pay? (Eve, focus
> group2)

For qualitative questionnaires, the process is similar. In the following example, Katryna gathered data from different parts of her questionnaire to provide a complete explanation of the first theme, "The need to improve awareness of campus activities":

EXAMPLE: BRINGING NUMERIC DATA INTO THEMATIC ORGANIZATION OF THE REPORT (KATRYNA KOENIG)

Theme 1 The need to improve awareness of campus activities

CODES: FOUND IN:		FREQUENCY:	RATIONALE:
Lack of information	Q3.3	29%	Directly related to why students did not participate. This is a reported barrier to participation.
I don't know anyone going	Q3.3	36%	Lack of peer awareness resulting in low peer involvement prevents students from participating.
Improved advertising	Q4.1	52%	This is a reported recommendation for enabling the students themselves to participate.
More information available	Q4.1	11%	This is a reported recommendation for enabling the students themselves to participate. By increasing the information available, you increase access to improved awareness.
Increase advertising	Q4.2	58%	This is a reported recommendation for enabling all students to participate.

Step 3: Write about the Quotations

Once you have placed the quotations and/or numeric data within the draft outline, begin writing. This can be the most challenging and rewarding aspect of the entire research process. Remember to distinguish between what you may *want* to say about the research findings and what you *can* say about the findings. Begin by writing descriptively—what was said about a particular theme and its subthemes? Essentially, the participant speaks for her or himself through the quotation, and you, the author, offer more insight, explanation, and possibly conclusions. For example: "When Anne was asked about employment when her children were young, she explained the difficulties in obtaining affordable childcare. She said 'insert selected quotation.' Her response illustrates that minimum wage does not afford women the luxury of paying for childcare" (Reid, Brief, & LeDrew, 2009).

At this stage of writing, think about writing a first draft rather than the finished product. This will help with the flow of writing. It will be necessary to return to this first draft to fine-tune the content, move some sections, and re-evaluate the overall importance or weight of some themes and subthemes. At a later stage you may want to return to each section and begin to deepen the analysis. Expanding on the example provided above, it might be desirable to further discuss the problems of minimum wage in the current socioeconomic environment and the gendered nature of childcare. Or, to pick up on the example from the study on women's experiences of poverty, one written section could look like this:

EXAMPLE: WRITING WITH TEXT DATA

Daily Challenges of Living in Poverty: Financial Concerns
All of the women spoke at length about their financial concerns and the challenges of budgeting and paying for food, housing, clothing, and transportation. After Elizabeth paid her rent, "I get $359 and that's to cover everything. I get child welfare and that brings it up $200" (Elizabeth, focus group1). Wanda, who was on a seniors' pension, "went to the welfare office because I lived on $730 [a month], I had no medical, no dental, none of the extras that you don't think of as extras but they are when you don't have them" (Wanda, focus group1). The women's material deprivation was so severe that they were never able to pay all of their bills "and it never stops, you're always thinking of how can I do this, how can I do that? Who can I not pay this month, who do I have to pay?" (Eve, focus group2).

As you integrate text data into your writing, consistently use the following guidelines:

- Direct quotations from qualitative text data require "sourcing" or a tag (i.e., a pseudonym or participant number, kind of data, date). This can be the "tag" or a more general identifier that helps separate the bits of data from one another. For example, the reader will want to know if the same person is quoted throughout your report or if it's a range of respondents, as well as if the quotations all come from one kind of data rather than from the entire data set from your project.

- Direct quotations that are longer than three lines require indenting *without* quotation marks.
- Direct quotations shorter than three lines are integrated in the text *with* quotation marks.
- Direct quotations can be edited for readability, using ellipses (. . .) to move between parts of sentences or square brackets [place of employment] to fill in pieces of information that are deleted for confidentiality reasons or that will help with readability. "Uhms," "ahs," "so you know" can all be deleted for improved flow of the text.

You may have text data, numeric data, or some combination of the two. Even if you have only text data you can use numbers to provide a clearer presentation of the weighting of the findings.

EXAMPLE: WRITING WITH NUMERICAL DATA (CHERA YELLEN)

In the following example Chera used numbers (frequencies) to speak to the strength of qualitative text findings:

Research findings in the cognitive domain indicated that four of the six participants reported some memory loss and difficulty concentrating since caring for their parent. These same participants also reported a difference in their ability to fulfill expected work duties since caring for their parent. They indicated managing medical appointments; feeling distracted, overwhelmed, and tired; and having a busy mind as reasons for their cognitive decline. The two participants who did not report any cognitive impacts . . .

Words such as "some," "many," "several," and "few" are less precise and are therefore open to interpretation. When possible, provide the exact number. Methodologically, if you used the same method and process with each participant and analyzed your data systematically, precise response numbers should be possible for all themes.

When reporting numeric findings, follow these guidelines:

- Use a consistent strategy for reporting numbers and remember that percentages can be misleading when participant numbers are low. Generally, use the following strategy, "Five of the seven participants said . . ." (versus 71 per cent).

- When your participant number exceeds 75, you can more confidently use percentages to report the findings.[1] Unless you are running a statistical analysis with a program such as SPSS, it is preferable to use both the percentage and absolute number of responses, for instance, "Fifty-seven per cent (n = 47) of respondents worked with older adults, 32 per cent (n = 27) in mental health, 8 per cent (n = 7) in physical rehabilitation and disabilities, 2 per cent (n = 2) with children and their families, and 1 per cent (n = 1) in forensics" (Reid, Landy, & Leon, 2013).

- In cases where the total number of responses varies in the data, as is often the case in questionnaire data when respondents skip some questions, it is necessary to provide the total number of responses. For instance, "Ninety-two per cent (60 of 65 participants) indicated that they felt supported in their work."

- If you have numeric and text data for a particular theme or finding, it is typical to start with the numeric data and follow-up with a quotation. Bear in mind that the quotation can be from a different kind of data (e.g., interviews) or from an open-ended question in a questionnaire. The methods section of your report will have the kinds of data you are reporting clearly outlined, so this information does not need to be repeated in the findings section.

- If you have a large amount of data and the body of the findings section begins to feel repetitive, a table can often help provide a "bird's-eye view" of the data and be more readable for the reader. Table 10.1 is an example of a table that pulls together both numeric and text data from a questionnaire.

- As you are writing about the quotations or numeric data, *describe* and then *explain*.

Some of the more saturated themes will take some time to describe thoroughly, while others will need only a sentence or two. You will probably want to start by describing the themes that are saturated. Include the main points, two or three sample quotations (depending on the type of data), and an evaluative comment

....

1 The sample size is a calculation based on the number of respondents we need as a proportion of the population size. For example, if the population is 500, a sample of 220 will give you confidence to plus or minus 5 per cent, while sample of 80 will only give you a plus or minus 10 per cent. In reporting outcomes, if you have 10 responses, 10 per cent = 1 response, therefore percentages should not be used. As a rough estimate, a minimum of 75 respondents is needed to report with percentages.

TABLE 10.1 Reporting Numeric Findings by Frequency and Percentage

| | | RECREATION THERAPISTS' IDENTITY | | |
THEME	FREQUENCY	PERCENTAGE	DEFINITION	REPRESENTATIVE QUOTATIONS
Knowledge	41	35	References to formal education; knowledge; experience; professional skills and training	"getting my degree in RT" "very resourceful, good communication skills" "using therapeutic programs to create change within the individual" "vast knowledge of benefits of leisure and recreation participation" "my specialized training"
Desire to Help Others	30	25.5	References to personality traits such as caring, loving, compassionate, empathic; desire to empower, help, motivate, or support others; advocacy	"the love of making people happy" "commitment to support and advocate for my clients" "be helpful, love working with seniors, being supportive" "love of people, compassion, and ability to engage"
Passion for Leisure and the RT Profession	30	25.5	References to leisure lifestyle; leisure and recreation as a component of health and wellness; right to leisure; RT profession and philosophy; professionalism	"healthy living and the idea that you have a choice in your leisure" "passion for the field of RT" "belief in the value of leisure" "passion for leisure and [I am] someone who walks the talk in participating in all domains of leisure and people know that about me"
Holistic, Person-Centred, and Strengths-Based Approach	16	14	References to the "whole" person and domains of wellness' person-centred/individualized care; clients' strengths and abilities; seeing people beyond their disability	"seeing the person as a whole and not what's wrong with them but what's positive" "looks at big picture, identifies individual's strengths and abilities" "[helping] others maintain their quality of life in all domains of their well-being" "I maintain their [clients'] dignity by setting them up for success. I give choices with boundaries to enable positive results"

INTEGRATING NUMERIC FINDINGS AND EXPLAINING THE FINDINGS
(DEVIN CARLSON)

Intrinsic-based reasons for playing hockey: The intrinsic value of the game of hockey for adult men was found to be particularly important in regards to their reasons for participation. The most unanimous response among all respondents was that fun was an extremely important reason for playing hockey. This correlates with previous research that suggests fun as a significant reason for adult male participation in sport. Ninety per cent of respondents said that they looked forward to their hockey game all week. In addition, 70 per cent of respondents rated the statement "my life would be less enjoyable if I didn't play hockey" as extremely accurate. These findings suggest that many adult men find participation in recreation-league hockey intrinsically valuable and that participation adds significant value to their lives. The feeling of total engagement with an activity and the ability to forget about problems when playing hockey were also reported as important reasons for participation. Both of these factors can be strongly associated with the concept of flow.

about the degree of saturation. For less-saturated categories, the description is more tentative. Remember that both content and process files need to be described. Free-standing pieces of information that are considered unique may have no known similarities to other bits of data. But as you write, sometimes the similarities become evident. At other times, there are simply no recognizable overlaps or links. In these situations, these data need to be described by their uncommon features and you can then comment on any questions these outliers may raise.

Step 4: Prepare a First Draft of the Findings Section

It may take some time to organize your data in the outline of the findings section, and some themes and subthemes will be easier to write about than others. Take your time to organize and reorganize your themes. Once you have everything in place and have roughly drafted each section, you are ready to prepare a full first draft. Get all of the ideas down on paper. Do not worry yet about the quality of your writing. The act of writing can spark new ideas; revisions, however extensive, can be made later for the final version of the report. The point here is to write blocks of material. It is not necessary to have it ordered perfectly this too can be done later. For each section, ask yourself if you have written enough so that someone else would have enough information to fully understand the research. And remember, *describe* and *explain* each theme and subtheme. As you write you will need to be flexible. Be prepared for sudden insights that bring you to a new understanding.

Step 5: Reorder and Edit Your Writing

Once you have a first draft of most sections of your findings, you can begin reordering and editing your work. Ask yourself the following questions:

- How have I answered the research question?
- Are things in the right order and is there a progression that makes sense?
- Have I adequately described the data? Have I included explanations throughout? Is there a balance between description and analysis?
- Should I organize by theme (usually grounded research, theoretical research, or field research), chronology (reporting on events or life histories), or focused questioning?
- Which aspects of the analysis should I "zoom in on" to best communicate my findings?
- Have I accounted for myself in the write-up? How much of my own involvement should I detail?

In the following example, Samantha determined that her exploration of chronic pain required the theme "description of pain" and that within this theme the subtheme "pain at its best and worst" could provide greater clarification. She also determined that "description of pain" needed to be the first theme to appear since it was broad and spoke to all participants' experiences.

EXAMPLE: CREATING A STRUCTURE THAT MAKES SENSE
(Samantha Bertolone)

Description of Pain

All of the women spoke at length about their experiences of living with chronic pain, including in-depth discussions about how they describe their pain at its best and worst, the most challenging component of living with pain, and lastly how their pain has directly impacted their ability to participate in activities (including activities of daily living and leisure and recreational pursuits).

Pain at its best and worst

When the women were asked about their pain when it is in remission/less severe than usual, all responded with a general sense of relief. One woman stated:

> I feel like I can be a normal person and I can do things like everyone else can do . . . I can bake cookies, I can run to the store, I can do whatever I need to do . . . yeah, I feel like I can be a normal person. (Annie, 2012)

Of the five participants, three admitted their pain was never gone, just reduced and more bearable. One participant stated: "It's never gone. It's always there" (Minnie, 2012). All of the women who indicated that their pain was never gone had fibromyalgia. For this reason it is possible that they experienced a different kind of pain than the other two participants in this study.

When the participants were asked to explain their pain at its very worst, three of them began to cry. Annie stated that "[I] probably would have committed suicide if [I] hadn't had [my] kids at its very very worst" (Annie, 2012). She further states that the pain is more than she "can possibly bear" (Annie, 2012). Ginger discussed her feelings of limited motivation and frustration by being able to function. She stated:

I feel like I can't function, and I have to try to function and try to carry on . . . I just feel overall pain throughout my whole body, well I just have no energy and I have no motivation to do anything because it kind of brings me down. (Ginger, 2012)

As you edit and reorganize the writing, it may be advantageous to involve others. With large amounts of data, many interpretations and lines of analysis are possible. The more access you have to possible interpretations offered by research participants or other collaborators or peers, the more complete your analysis can be. The pursuit of alternative interpretations can be consciously undertaken on your own or in conjunction with others. It often turns up one or two good alternatives. Also, remember your audience. If the participants are the first to see a draft, they should be able to locate their own experience in the document. The final report should be written in such a way as to make it accessible for its anticipated audience(s). As you are writing, new questions will emerge from the analysis, some of which show directions for further research and actions while others require that you return to the original research focus for a new layer of reflection and analysis. Keep track of these for the final section of the report.

Step 6: Critically Evaluate Your Analysis

Acknowledge the shortcomings of your work. Point out where the data are too weak to provide direction or where conflicting interpretations exist. Make notes on how you will assess and describe the limitations of your sample or your methods. This helps to situate your audience, letting them understand that you are not selling them on the conclusions but inviting their understanding of what you found, with what group of respondents, and how you found it. When you are preparing the draft, you may struggle with some of the following:

- *The agony of omitting* (Lofland & Lofland, 1995). Think about not presenting all your descriptions and explanations (Tom, 2005). Data reduction is necessary in analysis. Every single bit is important, but there is not room for it all in the report. Choose the best examples, descriptors, and concepts and indirectly convey the rest.

- *The difficulty of guaranteeing equal weight to each bit, each saturated category, each link in the analysis.* It is impossible to give equal weight. What you *can* guarantee is giving all information an equal opportunity to become and remain visible within the research. No information is intentionally

- excluded. The analytical process is an open and inclusive one. Just carefully describe the data and provide examples of your analytical steps.

- *The concern about forcing the data analysis.* If you choose to include something even though it does not fit because you think it is somehow important, simply account for why you are including it. Or the concept might have emerged from unsaturated categories. Write about it as tentative or perhaps indicative of a trend . . . and move on to the next point. Do not dwell on the weaknesses. There is a section of the final report where you can reflect on "study limitations." Later, as you are writing the final report, "include a counterargument in the same paragraph to show how you are including (different) disciplines and viewpoints" (Tom, 2005, p. 6).

- *The risk of decontextualizing.* Because of the mobility of bits, codes, and themes, a piece of data can move about and become severed from its context. Keeping a file of original materials (Data File) and careful coding of material will always enable you to relocate the data in the ongoing analysis. Be a disciplined recorder and keep referring to the original copies of the data.

- *The risk of analyzing too quickly.* It takes time for the analytical schemas to gel. Avoid drawing conclusions too quickly to prevent leaving out potentially significant ideas. Take time to go methodically from description to the conceptual links between categories to theory. Then draw clear and explicit conclusions.

- *The risk of being generic.* In an effort to be profound and to draw a conclusion, we run the risk of condensing the research ideas too much. The emergent or imposed concepts for explaining the data need time to meld with the data. Reducing too much can mean that we actually lose the essence of our work with oversimplification.

- *The risk of appropriating the voices in the research report.* Each participant has his or her own voice. People participate in research for a purpose, and we respect their contribution (e.g., their voice, their experience) and protect it (through anonymity and confidentiality, contextualizing the statements, checking for accuracy and appropriateness). For example, the "Aboriginal voice must represent itself, or have thorough and respectful representation from non–Aboriginal researchers, especially in the policy arena" (Kenny, Faries, Fiske, & Voyageur, 2004, p. 13). This applies to all research. Member-checking is one of the techniques you can use to establish how data, evidence, narratives, and so on are to be written up and in whose voice. Being culturally, linguistically, and /or contextually sensitive is another.

- *The risk of confusing the voices in the research report.* There are a number of voices in the draft report: the researcher's, the participants', and the voices of those assisting with parts of the research or contributing secondary information. There are also the various authors whose contributions you recognize from the literature review. Similar to referencing ideas or direct quotes, the research report must include a reference or situating context for each voice. As *you* draw a concluding point, ensure the reader knows it is *your* analysis. When the conclusion actually comes from a particular participant, provide enough context to situate the information in the participant's reality without risking his or her confidentiality. The voices of the researcher and the participants differ in two main ways. First, the researcher is interested in expressing what a number of people think about a particular experience or topic, rather than concentrating on one individual's description. Second, the researcher is likely to be concerned with discussing how those ideas fit together and how well such patterns explain the topic being researched.

If desired, conclude the draft process by inviting participants to make comments about the material. You could call a small group of participants or other collabora-tors together to discuss the developing analysis and written account. Participants should be able to see themselves reflected in the research report, within the boundaries of the confidentiality that you have guaranteed. Questions address-ing specific areas where feedback would be helpful should be considered. For example, you may want their comments on the descriptions, explanations, and possible directions for social change. Organizations or research partners may orga-nize a group activity to discuss the report. Or you can talk the project through with others who are involved in similar areas to get their feedback on your work.

Step 7: Link the Review of the Literature with the Data Analysis

It is necessary to ensure that the relationship between your research and the existing literature is brought together both at the introduction and conclusion of your written report. These two sections show where your questions sit in the context of existing data and analysis, as well as the impact of your work on the field. However, we recommend that you first have a firm grasp of the data and data analysis before turning to secondary sources in the literature review to support your analysis. The rationale for this is that the emergent sense of the findings is difficult to maintain in front of the overwhelming weight of the authority of literature, even though weighty documents cannot substitute for the richness and denseness of description and explanation grounded in the original data. To maintain the integrity of the iterative nature of analysis, the researcher ensures that concepts that emerge from the data have priority over concepts existing in the literature. In the following example Shayna had a rough sense of her main findings and drafted what she was learning about each one. As she drafted the main findings she documented connections to the literature. This allowed her to return to these "links to the literature" when she was ready to write the discussion section of her research report. In Shayna's research, she wrote about her findings and then made connections to existing literature.

EXAMPLE: LINKING FINDINGS TO THE LITERATURE (SHAYNA DOLAN)

Many women report that they felt lonely, isolated, and depressed, which comes as no surprise. One respondent mentioned that she cries for days when her significant other leaves but holds it together so as not to upset him. Other women wrote that they enjoy their "me" time that the repeated absence provided them with, but would like a more consistent schedule. Many women reported that they worry about their children and have difficulty dealing with their significant other missing children's events, milestones, and losing quality time with the children. Other women reported that they feel the repeated absence has allowed them to form a special bond with their children, leading to more quality time with their kids. Some women were very "vocal" about their experience and wrote of the importance of taking time for yourself, having your own social network, and communicating with your spouse. In contrast, there were many responses that indicated women feel as if they can't complain because they made the choice to move to the community and the lifestyle allows them to pay their bills and have certain financial advantages. There is the notion that this lifestyle is all part and parcel of living in this community and that is just the way it is, as one respondent wrote when asked how she copes with stress in her life, "Get over it." Another reported, "We live in an area that spouses have to be in the bush; not all jobs make it possible for them to be home every night." Questions about their experience had many women writing about the effects of the situation on their significant other and the importance of supporting them . . .

Links to the literature:

- Lack of emotional and social support (Hubinger, Parker, & Clava-rino, 2002; Ulven et al., 2007)
- Husband's work-related absence has the potential to exacerbate wives pre-existing health conditions (Ulven, Omdal, Herlov-Neilsen, Irgens, & Dahl, 2007)
- Repeated absence and presence of romantic partners has been shown to negatively affect the sleeping patterns and stress hormone levels of both partners, but effects are increased in the partner that remains at home (Diamond, Hicks, & Otter-Henderson, 2008)
- Women report a lack of communication with their repeatedly absent husbands and often delay or avoid dealing with poten-tially conflicting relationship issues (Kaczmarek & Sibbel, 2008)

Typically, the "findings" and "discussion" sections are distinct (see the final report outline in Chapter 7). It might feel tempting to weave in the literature to the findings section, but we recommend that the findings section is strictly a description and explanation of the major themes. The discussion section is where the findings and the literature are brought together. It is important to remember that the literature review should cover all literature that is needed for the discussion, and the findings section should cover all data that will be reviewed in the discussion. Neither new literature nor data should be introduced in the discussion; rather, that is where "high-level" connections and integration occur. Assume that the reader has read the report from beginning to end, which means that you do not need to re-explain a particular concept that is covered in the literature review in the introduction of the report or restate a particular theme from the findings section. Finally, we recommend that you write the introduction last. It provides a high-level overview of the entire study—its rationale, relevance, and the "so what?" of your research.

As you write the discussion section, always treat your study as finished work. Refer to your study and literature in the past tense. Consider how your find-ings support what is in the literature or how your findings conflict with or contradict what has been written. Alternatively, it might be that your findings say something completely different or unique from what has been reported before. Explain all of your findings as much as possible. How and why did you arrive at these conclusions? Why did participants report a particular experi-ence? For a theme or finding that is not found in the literature, what can you say about what you are contributing to the body of knowledge? You can reflect on both the content of your findings as well as your methodology. Consider all angles and be prepared to write with insight and depth. Avoid a superficial interpretation that restates the findings. It is necessary to suggest why findings came out as they did. Try to offer alternative explanations if reasonable alternatives exist. When you refer to information, distinguish between data generated by your study and published information.

EXAMPLE: DISCUSSION SECTION OF A PUBLISHED MANUSCRIPT

Discussion

Our findings revealed that a diversity of individual and collective actions were meaningful for a group of women on low income and that individual actions sometimes led to collective efforts for more widespread change. The findings also revealed that although working collaboratively to change the conditions of one's life was important for this group of women on low income, challenges and risks arose in attempting to do that work. These findings indicate that action is complex and varied and needs to be understood on multiple levels and as being both beneficial and risky to marginalized individuals and groups. This may help explain why some women resist feminist research (Barazangi, 2004). Feminist researchers who fail to take these realities into account reduce the possibilities for actions that are relevant to the lives of women and may unintentionally promote actions that actually cause them harm (Brabeck, 2004; Williams & Lykes, 2003).

Current understandings of action, particularly as portrayed in the participatory and feminist action research literatures, need to be revised and expanded in order to understand action in all its complexity. The research participants' actions were tremendously diverse—they occurred on individual and collective levels and arose prior to, during, and after the FPAR project. Some actions were achieved, others led to different form of action outside of the FPAR context, and still other actions remained hopes for a broader action agenda. Action was also an integral part of each research participant's life . . . (Excerpted from Reid, Tom, & Frisby, 2006)

If you have a finding or theme that is not found in the literature, it is likely that it will need further study. This can be raised in your recommendations section. Finally, at the end of the discussion section you can include your own (author's) reflections on your research. Be sure to distinguish this from the discussion that integrates the major themes with the literature.

The Final Report

The final report is the document that ultimately represents the research. Babbie and Benaquisto (2010, p. 465) remind us that the report is the record of the research content, process, and analysis as reported by you, the researcher. It also serves as the scientific contribution you make to what is known about the social world. Further, since your research will answer some questions but raise others, the report also can act as a catalyst for further research.

Again, refer to Chapter 7 for an outline of the final report. Typically, you will have already written the introduction, literature review, and methodology sections for the research proposal. These sections will need to be revised to reflect the final, completed research study that you are presenting. As previously stated, it is likely that the literature review will require some additions or revisions. As well, the methodology section will need to reflect exactly what unfolded in your research process, in terms of participant selection and recruitment, data collection, management and analysis, trustworthiness, ethical issues, and so on. The report outline provides the specific questions you need to address. Remember that a full explanation of your methods allows the reader to understand and contextualize your research findings.[2]

While the content of the final report will be essentially the same for each audience, the emphasis on specific points and the way in which they are expressed will be different depending on the target audience. For example, if you are reporting to the general public, your final report will be different than if you report to a collective, a government funding agency, the media, or a group of peers who have participated in the research process. The main messages (content), style, language, length, and depth need to be tailored to the audience. For some audiences, a short descriptive summary, executive summary, or research brief may be what is wanted or needed. For other audiences, emphasis on the content may take precedence over any discussion of the method. Write each version in a way that conveys what is needed for the specific audience.

The final report should begin with an introduction that provides a short, high-level rationale for the project, the research question(s), and the importance of the work. The summary section provides a description and explanation of the new knowledge or unique contribution that this research makes. Not too much detail is needed here—simply answer the research questions and draw your conclusions. As research is an ongoing process, these will inform subsequent research projects in a variety of ways. The final report can suggest

....

2 In our experience, first-time researchers who submit research manuscripts for publication are most often told by reviewers that their methodology section is inadequately explained or rationalized. It is essential to include all details pertinent to your methods and outline specifically how data collection and analysis unfolded, and why.

some of the potential direction for further research and, in line with effecting social change, what kind of policy, initiative, or individual or group action might be supported or recommended.

Given all of that, the reader of the final report should be able to walk away from reading your research report with an answer to the "so what?" question. With this research, what do we know that we didn't know before? How does this research improve the world or the circumstances of a particular group of people? Tell the readers why it counts and why it is important. The answer to the "so what?" question is written first in the conclusion of the research and then, to ensure people get the message, it is repeated in the abstract and the introduction. It should also appear in any short (or executive) summary. Ultimately, the answer to the "so what?" question is the take-away message of your research.

The Importance of Proofreading

Proofreading is the next essential step in the writing process. Taking the time to properly proofread can make an enormous difference in the quality of the final written report. Poorly constructed sentences, inconsistent use of terminology, and grammatical, spelling, and typographical errors will distract the reader and negatively affect their overall impression. If you are completing the research project as a course or thesis project, these kinds of errors will undoubtedly affect your grade.

The first step is to ensure that you are ready to proofread. Be sure you've revised the larger aspects of your text. Don't try to make corrections at the sentence and word level if you still need to work on the focus, organization, and development of the whole paper, specific sections, or paragraphs. It is not advisable to begin proofreading right after completing the writing. Setting aside the text for a while (at least an hour, but ideally longer) will enable you to have some distance from the text and be sharper with your proofreading.

When you are ready to proofread, determine how your proofreading process will be most effective—with a printed copy that you can write on or on your computer screen? Then, as you begin proofreading, determine what you need to look for. You may know that you tend to make the same mistakes repeatedly, or your instructor (if you are a student) may have alerted you to common mistakes to avoid. For all writers, unnecessary words can be eliminated, and editing is always beneficial. Avoid feeling attached to your writing. Instead, aim for clear and concise writing. If the word(s) don't add anything to the overall message—or worse, if they obfuscate the point you are making—they need to be changed or eliminated. Proofreading strategies include the following:

- *Read out loud*. This is especially helpful for spotting run-on sentences, but you'll also hear other problems that you may not see when reading silently.

- *Use the search function to ensure absolute consistency throughout the text.* Inconsistencies will distract the reader, and more concerning, they are confusing. They will serve to discredit your findings. For example:
  - Did you always refer to the same number of participants in the same way?
  - Did you reference/tag your data similarly throughout?
  - Are your literature citations properly cited and cited according to the style required?
  - Are concepts used throughout the report referred to in the same way? Are they always spelled the same way (e.g., well-being versus wellbeing)?
  - Are the themes always named similarly?
  - Is the overall structure of your report (with the use of headings and subheadings) clear and coherent?
- *Use the search function of the computer to find mistakes you're likely to make.* For example, search for "it" if you tend to confuse "its" and "it's"; for "-ing" if dangling modifiers are a problem; for opening parentheses or quote marks if you tend to leave out the closing ones.
- *If you tend to make many mistakes, check separately for each kind of error.* Move from the most to the least important, and follow whatever technique works best for you to identify that kind of mistake. For instance, read through once (backwards, sentence by sentence) to check for fragments; read through again (forward) to be sure subjects and verbs agree, and again (perhaps using a computer search for "this," "it," and "they") to trace pronouns to antecedents.
- *End with a computer-based spelling and grammar check.* However, remember that a spelling and grammar check will not catch mistakes with homonyms (e.g., "they're," "their," "there") or certain typographical errors (like "he" for "the"; The Writing Centre at the University of Wisconsin—Madison, 2014). In addition, some words are not recognized by spell-checkers and may instigate queries or suggestions that will not make sense. However, using a spelling and grammar checker will alert you to run-on sentences, unclear paragraphs, simple spelling errors, and subject-verb disagreements.

Summary

In this chapter we moved from the last stages of data analysis to writing the final report. Writing can be challenging for a novice, but if you follow the specific steps as described in this chapter, writing your final report will be a much easier and less daunting task. It is important to remember that writing is the final stage of analysis, which means that as you write you may find that sections need to be moved, data reorganized, and so on. This is to be expected. Take your time and continue to "live with your data" through the writing process. Once you have a written report you are then positioned to develop other products from your project. In Chapter 11 we discuss the range of possibilities that might suit your purposes and meet the needs of your participants and the people who need to hear about your research project.

Questions for Discussion

1. What is the value of the written report?
2. What are the essential steps in moving from data analysis to writing?
3. Do the voices of the research participants have priority in the research report? Why or why not?
4. Why is it important for your report to be usable and readable?
5. What are the required parts of a draft report?
6. How and when should you share your draft report with research participants?
7. What is the final destination of your research report?

Our Recommended Readings

Bolker, J. (1998). Writing your dissertation in fifteen minutes a day: A guide to starting, revising, and finishing your doctoral thesis. New York: Owl Books.

Dundurn Press. (1997). *The Canadian style: A guide to writing and editing.* Toronto: Dundurn Press.

Marshall, J. (2008). Finding form in writing for action research. In P. Reason & H. Bradbury (Eds.), *The SAGE handbook of action research: Participative inquiry and practice* (2nd ed., pp. 682–694). Los Angeles: Sage. http://dx.doi.org/10.4135/9781848607934.n59

Pelias, R. J. (2011). Writing into position: Strategies for composition and evaluation. In N. K. Denzin & Y. S. Lincoln (Eds.), *The SAGE handbook of qualitative research* (4th ed., pp. 659–668). Los Angeles: Sage.

Richardson, L. (2004). Writing: A method of inquiry. In S. N. Hesse-Biber & P. Leavy (Eds.), *Approaches to qualitative research: A reader on theory and practice* (pp. 473–491). New York: Oxford University Press.

Social Change

CHAPTER 11

STRATEGIES AND APPROACHES FOR MAKING CHANGE AND THE ROLE OF THE RESEARCHER

So what are the purposes of critical social research? There are many goals: to generate new data describing social life, to spot trends or investigate certain experiences or issues more deeply, or to collect information and data to generate action. Sometimes the purposes include all of the above. This book has described many different approaches to generating data, but it has also stressed that using the results to make change is the ultimate and essential point of doing critical social research. This chapter discusses a range of ways of using research—from knowledge translation processes to influencing practice and policy development to shifting public opinion to generating large-scale social change by supporting activism and advocacy. All of these have merit but require different skills in the researcher. In this chapter we describe some of these approaches and how they work. It is important to think about your own project's utility and plan for or seek some of these options for your research results.

> "We don't receive wisdom: we must discover it for ourselves after a journey that no one can take for us or spare us." Marcel Proust

Knowledge Translation

In Chapter 2 we briefly discussed knowledge translation in the context of engagement and collaboration in critical social research practices. The basic idea of knowledge translation is to make sure the results of your research or the evidence you discovered gets used by relevant or interested audiences. Knowledge translation can be one way, meaning that researchers present their research at the end of their project to potential interested parties. On the other hand, knowledge translation can be integrated, meaning that potential or ultimate knowledge users are identified at the beginning of the research process and are involved throughout the project. While integrated knowledge translation is usually preferred, it is not always possible or appropriate due to timeframes or resources. Many student projects are in this category.

For more extensive research projects, some funding agencies are now demanding a knowledge translation plan as part of a research proposal. This is an excellent development in research practice because it means that researchers are now obligated to think about the eventual use of their research and to make some plans about how it might get used most effectively and how to engage with users. It also reflects the wishes of funders. For publicly funded agencies, taxpayers are paying the bill and deserve to have research results presented and used. For private foundations, donors with specific interests in research are paying the bill and want to know what effect the research they funded has had. Some funders, such as the Canadian Institutes of Health Research (CIHR), offer assistance and choices of knowledge translation approaches and even specific funding for knowledge translation of findings. See www.cihr-irsc.gc.ca/e/45321.html#a4 for the full guide on CIHR knowledge translation.

Some Terms and Definitions

There are many terms used to describe the transfer of research findings to practice. These include knowledge transfer, knowledge mobilization, knowledge dissemination, research uptake, implementation and diffusion, and so on. However, Graham et al. (2006) suggest that "knowledge translation" is the term gaining most prominence in Canada.

A definition of knowledge translation (KT) used by the CIHR stresses the ultimate uses of research to its area of interest, namely the health system and population health. Each research funder would have different goals that would be made explicit in their funding requirements.

> Knowledge translation is a dynamic and iterative process that includes synthesis, dissemination, exchange and ethically sound application of knowledge to improve the health of Canadians, provide more effective health services and products and strengthen the health care system. This process takes place within a complex system of interactions between researchers and knowledge users that may vary in intensity, complexity and level of engagement depending on the nature of the research and the findings as well as the needs of the particular knowledge user. (CIHR, 2012, p. 1)

The Social Sciences and Humanities Research Council (SSHRC) of Canada funds research in a range of social sciences and humanities topics. It aims to use such research to improve quality of life and foster innovation. Its approach to KT is encompassed in the following statement:

> Knowledge mobilization in the social sciences and humanities facilitates the multidirectional flow of research knowledge across academia and society as a whole, in order to inform Canadian and international research, debate, decisions and actions. Those who stand to benefit from publicly funded research results in the social sciences and humanities—diverse groups of researchers, policy-makers, business leaders, community groups, educators and the media—should, ideally, have the knowledge they need, when they need it, in useful form. (SSHRC, 2016)

There are at least two kinds of KT suggested by the CIHR: end-of-project knowledge translation and integrated knowledge translation. End-of-grant KT is often less involved and possibly didactic because it uses a research result as a basis for communicating findings without having had engagement from end users throughout. On the other hand:

> Integrated knowledge translation (iKT) is an approach to doing research that applies the principles of knowledge translation to the entire research process. The central premise of iKT is that involving knowledge users as equal partners alongside researchers will lead to research that is more relevant to, and more likely to be useful to, the knowledge users. Each stage in the research process is an opportunity for significant collaboration with knowledge users, including the development or refinement of the research questions, selection of the methodology, data collection and tools development, selection of outcome measures, interpretation of the findings, crafting of the message and dissemination of the results. (CIHR, 2012, p. 2)

Comparing these two approaches is useful and raises questions about the value of collaboration and engagement. It also raises questions about ways of learning and assimilating knowledge. Some believe that we must experience the process of acquiring knowledge in order to use and understand it properly.

Some believe that the essence of critical approaches to research that this book supports requires engagement and deep process and may lead to a resistance to doing KT in a formulaic manner: "Critical inquiry's essential features of critique, reflexivity, and action . . . are marked by tentativeness, openness, and focus on process, and therefore do not fit easily with the KT methods of 'packaging' knowledge for practice" (Reimer-Kirkham et al., 2009).

In either case, doing knowledge translation of some type is advisable, if not required, by many funders and foundations. In your own projects, it is always worth thinking about who could use the results of your research and for what purposes well before you have consolidated your plans for the project. This exercise will sharpen your focus and put you more in touch with existing evidence, practice, policy, or advocacy on your topic. Even more importantly, this exercise will force you to decide how your results might be useful and when and how you might seek input from end users to figure that out.

How Do You Translate Your Results?

The type of audience you are aiming to influence will have a great influence on how you translate your results. For example, if you are trying to reach the communities from whom the data were gathered, the reporting will take various forms to best communicate with them—for example, articles for local distribution, public presentations, websites and blogposts, or a script for a play based on the data. If you are trying to reach media representatives and attract the attention of journalists, there are "sound bites" that must be created—short messages that simplify your work and make it easy for the media to publicize your results. If you are trying to reach government policymakers in the interest of changing policies as a result of what you have found in your research, you would need a more detailed "brief," outlining the current state of policy, the evidence you found, and the preferred policy change.

If you are trying to influence the practices of professionals such as lawyers, city planners, health care providers, or social workers, you will need specific suggestions for "better practices" or guidance for professional associations to adopt. If you are trying to influence community groups or the general public, you might need to create information sheets, infographics, videos, or public service messages and make them easily available on the Internet or a website. Each situation or knowledge translation goal requires a careful plan to determine your goal and to fix on a form of communication. Again, consulting with end users can be critically important to this decision-making process. Sometimes you can create a resource that responds to all of these audiences based on the same research study.

Exercise 11.1 Who is the research audience?

Use the first table to consider the audiences or people who need to hear about your research findings. Then consider the communications tools that are available to you.

AUDIENCES	COMMUNICATIONS TOOLS

• Research participants
• People in the community who represent research participants
• The general public
• Organizations (nonprofits, community organizations, health authorities, etc.)
  – Practitioners or service providers
  – Managers or supervisors
  – Executive directors
  – Board members
• Policymakers/creators, at local, provincial, or federal levels
  – Municipal councils
  – Provincial and federal politicians
  – Bureaucrats at all levels of government
• Other?
	• Research report
	• Research brief or executive summary
	• Policy brief
	• Position paper, concept paper
	• Community forum or public discussion
	• Webinar or presentation
	• Website
	• Best practices
	• Blog posts
	• Newsletter article
	• Media release
	• Newspaper article
	• Poster
	• Pamphlet
	• Video or film
	• Photographs
	• Listserv
	• Social networking site
	• Other?

Questions to Consider

Which of these "audiences" needs to hear about your research?
Which ones can you reach or gain access to?

Which of these communications tools are within your reach or accessible to you?
What resources do you have at your disposal to pursue them?

Now select the audiences that are most relevant or important for knowledge translation from your project. Beside each audience, list the one or two communications tools that you feel would work best for them:

Audience #1   Communications tool(s):

Audience #2:   Communications tool(s):

Audience #3:   Communications tool(s):

Audience #4:   Communications tool(s):

What follows are examples from two very different research projects.

Greaves et al. (2011) did a systematic review of interventions on tobacco reduction and cessation during pregnancy that resulted in a range of KT products. A team of tobacco researchers conducted a best practices review to examine smoking cessation interventions tested with various populations of pregnant women. A best practices review uses a systematic review methodology and then contextualizes the results in the wider literature (in this case, women's health, women-centred care, and women's tobacco use), assesses feasibility, and makes recommendations for practice. The review underlined the importance of providing cessation/reduction advice and relapse prevention that is reflective of the social context and pregnancy-related biology, is sensitive to age and disadvantage, and is relevant, especially to young pregnant women, who have the highest rates of smoking during pregnancy.

In addition to writing a report, holding a webinar, and giving numerous conference presentations, the team created other forms of KT. Given the wide interest in practice recommendations for physicians and other health care providers who work with pregnant and postpartum girls and women, these researchers created a three-part website to translate the findings (www.expectingtoquit. ca). One part was designed for researchers and others interested in engaging with the evidence. Another section included materials for practitioners that offered resources for discussions with women and brief advice on "Five Ways to Change Your Practice." Finally, a section for pregnant women was designed that included resources for various stages of quitting or reducing smoking as well as digital narratives created by women with lived experience of this issue. An interesting result of this approach was that website analytics showed that all sections of the website were visited by researchers, practitioners, and women alike.

The next example demonstrates how the use of some research methods can become the main mechanisms for knowledge translation. Jennifer, a community-based researcher, engaged in digital storytelling with Indigenous youth because it was viewed as the most appropriate and effective method for engaging youth, answering the research question, and making change in the community.

DIGITAL STORYTELLING (JENNIFER MULLET)

A multiyear research project brought together Indigenous youth and Elders from Vancouver Island communities to learn the art of digital storytelling and to celebrate culture. It was initiated in response to the disproportionate number of First Nations individuals suffering from diabetes and chronic diseases. Through documentation of cultural knowledge of healthy eating and healthy lifestyles, the project aimed to increase awareness of some of the causal factors related to chronic disease while the process of the research created opportunities for intergenerational knowledge sharing. The product of the research was the preservation of historical cultural knowledge in new communications technologies.

Digital stories are a slideshow, or combination of movie clips and images that, when imported into a movie program (we used iMovie), can be transformed into a movie with narration, background music, and other visual effects. There are several advantages to digital stories: They provide an alternative to written expression, knowledge can be shared in a way that is readily accessible and current, and they provide wider access to ideas. In this project the digital storytelling method was seen as particularly relevant to working with Indigenous youth because it is engaging and allows participants to communicate meaning on multiple levels, it creates a legacy of traditional knowledge/community knowledge, and it celebrates expertise and gives voice to marginalized perspectives. It also is a unique way to bring attention to community concerns by creating objects of reflection that enable a community to examine issues in a different way. The story becomes "a thing to think with," and the creative process strengthens a sense of community and builds self-esteem in the authors.

A core group of five youth were trained as research assistants. These youth planned and facilitated a three-day workshop where they showed their digital stories, led team-building activities, coordinated knowledge sharing sessions by Elders, and taught other youth to prepare short mini-stories using digital cameras and storyboards. Participants were given digital cameras to take photos in their communities. They reconvened at Vancouver Island University's media lab a few months later to transform their photographs into digital stories, incorporating art, music, and other special effects. Stories were broadly focused on healthy lifestyles and connection to community.

A second digital stories workshop with the same format was held six months later in Cowichan, British Columbia, with a new group of youth. New technology on iPads and the availability of iMovie made the process much faster. As the project progressed, additional funding was received from the CIHR to train new youth as trainers, facilitators, and presenters. Mini-stories (short digital stories typically using six to eight images with voiceover) were completed in schools, health centres, and youth groups. There were 60 core participants in the initial workshops and an additional approximately 170 youth involved in making mini-stories. One youth said the digital storytelling project gave her the opportunity to interview her 80-year-old father, learn about his cultural stories, and share them with others. She added: "I hope I can do this kind of work for the rest of my life; sharing stories and culture through modern technology is beneficial for future generations."

On other occasions there are specific end users who need to be engaged in the evidence, not just as passive receivers, but also as participants in shaping and digesting the evidence. To this end, more complex approaches such as communities of inquiry (CoI) or communities of practice (CoP) are useful. These are groups constituted either in person or online using web-based interactive platforms to engage with a particular topic over a defined period of time. They are usually voluntary and comprise parties who are interested in the topic for use in their practice or policy development or in their community. These groups embody the co-learning aspect of evidence building along with the receiving of evidence from the facilitator, the researcher(s), and other participants. This sharing over time is a process of developing more robust "evidence" that relies not only on published scientific works, but also lived experiences of communities or individuals and cumulative experiences of practitioners and policymakers.

A group of researchers in Northern Canada used a virtual community of practice model to achieve "integrated knowledge translation" in a project involving Indigenous and non-Indigenous community service providers, civil servants, and researchers across the three territories who were studying women's homelessness (Poole & Bopp, 2015). This CoP involved researchers and research collaborators in monthly web meetings over the two-year span of the study. It allowed for a diverse multisectoral and intercultural group to read and discuss findings about complex intersections between homelessness, gender, culture, and trauma from previously published academic and grey literatures. This step formed the basis of the co-learning and was advanced by taking the time to reflect deeply on the data collected from the study interviews and focus groups with service users and service providers. Then the CoP participants considered the implications for their own individual and collective practices, setting the stage for design and implementation of a service innovation initiative to test what they learned about pathways for achieving better outcomes for homeless women (Poole et al., 2015). Throughout, new learning and practice goals were continuously set, further solidifying the CoP and commitment to uptake of the research evidence.

What Do You Transmit?

There are many and varied KT products that can be produced as a result of research projects. For example, there are traditional journal articles, books, and conference presentations. These kinds of products are expected of most academic researchers and form part of their productivity as measured by their employers in universities, colleges, hospitals, or industry. These forms of KT reach important but often limited audiences, such as other academics, government policymakers, and relevant and interested professionals. Despite limited audiences, these are extremely important outputs and are usually peer-reviewed (see Chapter 5 for a discussion of peer-reviewed literature). These kinds of outputs form the basis of "scientific evidence" and get built upon by subsequent researchers and writers. It is worth noting that, traditionally, individuals and groups who did not have access to academic libraries most often had to pay to acquire these publications. Increasingly, however, these products are in "open access" formats, meaning that anyone can read them without having to pay a fee.

In addition, there are products aimed at reaching wider audiences. These include an array of options from public service messages and announcements to infographics (pictorially based representations of evidence) to videos, speeches, websites, webinars, TED Talks, posters, FAQ (frequently asked questions) sheets, policy briefs, short lectures, or media messages. Contemporary technological innovations offer more opportunities for spreading research results to the widest audiences. Many of these avenues are available to the general public or are designed for selected audiences. Given the proliferation of accessible technology and social media, KT can often be developed to use technological channels to translate research to any audience.

Knowledge Translation Processes

It is often true that even when the evidence exists to support a change in practice or policy, the evidence is not always readily understood or accepted. One area where knowledge exists and considerable KT was done with little change is in women's use and misuse of tranquilizers. In 1978 Ruth

Cooperstock published research on sex differences in mood-modifying drugs. This research brought attention to the medicalization of women's social problems and the resultant overprescription of psychotropic drugs to women. An innovative portable kit of information that built upon this research (entitled "It's Just Your Nerves") about women's use of alcohol and tranquilizers and the connections to the experience of violence was developed by Health Canada's Ontario office. The kit was shared widely in face-to-face knowledge exchange sessions across Canada. This was followed in the 1980s by a Canada-wide theatre tour of a play entitled *Side Effects*, which told real women's stories through theatre and prompted community-based education and activism.

Since then health research groups have published reports, policy briefs (Currie, 2003), books (Rochon Ford & Saibil, 2009), and information sheets on the marketing of tranquilizers and anti-depressants to women and physicians (Saibil, 2005). These documents describe the woman-specific effects of such drugs and their patterns of use, and restate the need for sex- and gender-specific treatment and guidelines for use and cessation. Considerably more research has been done delving into this issue over the years. Yet, 40 years on, women are still prescribed these medications twice as often as men are and protocols for tapering from these drugs are still lacking. This example illustrates that the opposite can also be true: Inaccurate knowledge and practice persists even though scientific evidence has proven it wrong. This points to the importance of acknowledging the complexity of factors that affect the adoption and diffusion of information.

A famous example of KT gone wrong is the persistent belief that autism is caused by childhood vaccines. This belief began with the publication of a single journal article by Andrew Wakefield and colleagues in 1998 that was later formally rescinded as inaccurate and fraudulent by the editor of the *British Medical Journal* (Braunstein, 2011). Additional support for this position had been generated by celebrities like actress Jenny McCarthy, who promoted this information as truth based on her own personal experience when her son was diagnosed with autism in 2005. Although McCarthy rescinded this statement nine years later, damage had been done by creating an "anti-vaxxer" movement. As one British Columbia doctor pointed out: "Jenny McCarthy reaches 250,000 people on one YouTube video. Physicians can use the same medium to get to the same parents and explain the scientific evidence behind immunization. We didn't play catch up on time" (Chai, 2014). A book by Timothy Caulfield, *Is Gwyneth Paltrow Wrong about Everything?* (2015), examines the impact of fame on the diffusion of ideas and how the general public responds to these messages.

Ultimately this combination of events led to resistance by some parents in vaccinating their children, creating the need for massive public education efforts about vaccine safety in the context of resurging communicable childhood diseases such as the measles. A commentary on this situation documents the impact of this fraud and even suggests prosecution of Wakefield. The assessment of why the beliefs persist, however, is interesting in the context of understanding KT processes:

> So why do parents still believe it? The answer has a lot of moving parts. One is that immunization is a counter-intuitive notion—that the cause of a disease can create immunity from it. Another is that anecdotes are more accessible and satisfying than rigorous experimental methodology; the scientific community took so long to respond adequately—even though UK health officials immediately denounced the study's recommendations—and the media became so good at telling the bad story and so bad at telling the real story. Most understandable, though, is any parent's need to know why—why something as inexplicable as autism has happened to their child. But autism existed long before the MMR vaccine was introduced, and hundreds of millions of children have had the vaccine without any problems, much less autism. (Braunstein, 2011)

Braunstein identifies some of the more complex and hard to predict elements of knowledge construction and translation and illustrates the complexities of bringing evidence to practice. The power of anecdotes, the responsibility of the media, the need to fill vacuums, and the difficulty of explaining some evidence are examples of such complexities. In sum, the existence of good evidence is not a guarantee that change in practice, policy, or society will follow. It must be accompanied by the intent to change.

Another example of an area requiring a complex approach to KT to gain progress is the issue of alcohol use during pregnancy. Stigma, misinformation, and judgment about alcohol use, women's drinking, and fetal alcohol exposure abound. The Canadian FASD Research Network (CanFASD) is a network of researchers, policymakers, service providers, and mothers who work to translate knowledge on prevention of fetal alcohol spectrum disorder (FASD) to reach the full range of those in a position to act on FASD prevention by using multiple formats (see www.canfasd.ca). They have created booklets to educate and support women and their partners, infographics to educate service providers (see http://bccewh.bc.ca for resources) and support them in initiating empowering conversations, journal articles and commentaries (Poole & Greaves, 2013) to inform and invite action by practitioners and governments, and a popular blog (https://fasdprevention.wordpress.com) to educate people working at all levels of prevention globally. Such networks require facilitation, so researchers who facilitate extended knowledge translation efforts need to act out of a broader interest for change than simply looking for opportunities to share and promote their own work. Rather, they must act as engaged scholars.

In recent years, researchers have addressed these complex issues, or moving parts, of KT processes to try and determine how these processes actually work. For example, Greenhalgh, Robert, Macfarlane, Bate, and Kyriakidou (2004) examined and analyzed a wide range of literature to identify some concepts for understanding these issues. They proposed a conceptual model for considering the determinants of diffusion, dissemination, and implementation of innovations. The relevant elements included the attributes of the innovation (or idea), the attributes of the adopter (the person or group being influenced), a wide range of contextual factors (such as system characteristics and readiness), and a number of aspects of the KT process. They made specific suggestions as to what would move the knowledge translation field forward, such as examining the social networks of receptors and those who could influence or bridge various worlds to transmit information. The role of "boundary spanners"—individuals who actively link internal aspects of organizations to the external world—was identified as critical to bring new information and evidence forward. They also noted the importance of studying the ability of organizations or groups to absorb information and the roles of informal networking on these processes.

Ultimately the scientific evidence produced by research studies is only one part of knowledge and practice. Through authentic practices of KT, especially integrated KT, and engagement and collaboration in research processes, there are many elements that create better practices, new approaches, and improved policies. Equally important, though, are the contextual factors that shape the transmission and receipt of evidence. These factors include a range of processes and people who are sometimes supporting and sometimes subverting evidence-based decision making. In short, both knowledge construction and knowledge translation are complex, dynamic, and iterative processes.

Making Social Change

Ultimately, those of us who engage in critical social research are interested in making social change. This can be as specific as how neighbourhoods are laid out to maximize safety or promote exercise, to more general goals such as eliminating sexism or racism or homophobia, or securing human rights protections for children. Change can also be desired to reverse something. This can be as specific as lowering speed limits on city streets to reduce injuries and deaths of pedestrians, or as general as changing the Constitution to protect equality rights or reversing a law that allows discrimination that limits voting rights. Change can also be aimed at practices such as the one that required women to get their husbands or fathers to cosign a mortgage or that allowed smoking on airplanes and in hospitals. Finally, change can take aim at formal laws, such as those that did not recognize women's contribution to marital assets or those that allowed discrimination against gay and lesbian individuals.

We can also be motivated by an interest in redressing imbalances in knowledge or rectifying historical accounts. Some of these higher-order goals may not be met in a lifetime, but progress can be measured over time. Much of this progress can be seen in the context of general social movements, such as labour, anti-racism, gay rights, or feminist movements, where over time progress has been made in alleviating inequity or changing laws. Evidence and information, whether new or reframed, form a critical dimension in changing public records or public opinion. Many activists engaging in social change movements rely on the generation or regeneration of new knowledge or the recording of hidden and forgotten knowledge to promote new attitudes, revise laws, or create new practices. Sometimes films or videos serve this purpose, recalling history for new audiences. An excellent example of this is *Milk*, the movie that recounted the history of Harvey Milk, a gay activist politician in San Francisco who was shot and killed while on the job.

In 2008, the Feminist History Society was formed in Canada, comprised of five women who were central to the "second wave" feminist movement in Canada that took place from 1960 to 2010 (see http://feministhistories.ca/about/). Their mission was to generate as many books as possible detailing the history of various aspects of the feminist movement in Canada during that period. This project was inspired by the knowledge that without recording our history, it could easily be forgotten or rewritten—or worse, repeated. The project was also intended to educate future generations by creating a public record of activism in this period and to serve as a basis for generating further feminist activism. The books are published in hardcover, paperback, and ultimately in electronic formats and cover issues as diverse as how women came to feminist consciousness, the history of women and sport, biographies of various feminists, legal reform for women, immigrant women and feminism, history of Québécoise feminists, women's health, and other elements of the second wave. This exercise is a crucial piece of generating and recording versions of activists and reformers on women's rights in Canada so that evidence is preserved, achievements noted, and a basis for future feminist activism is laid down. One of the books, *Playing It Forward: 50 Years of Women and Sport in Canada* (Demers, Greaves, Kirby, & Lay, 2013) has formed the basis of the movie *Play Fair* (www.playfair.tv), bringing even wider exposure in an accessible format to the history of feminism in Canada.

How does research build support for a concept or a way of thinking? How does it converge with other events to create change? There is no one formula, as often many disparate events and people converge to generate change. Sometimes it requires a long process and an informal or formal social movement or organization to get organized. Sometimes it can be a centuries' long process or sometimes will occur over a year or two. Evidence is not the only element that shifts policy or practice, and research is not the sole ingredient of social change. But research can sometimes be key in sparking a new way of thinking, illuminating an injustice or a hazard or a problem, or feeding into social organizing. When that happens, multiple players are needed to make change.

Think tanks such as the Caledon Institute for Social Policy (see www.caledoninst.org) and the Tamarack Institute for Community Engagement (see http://tamarackcommunity.ca) in Canada are two examples of institutes devoted to making positive changes happen in the structure of Canadian society. The Tamarack Institute (2005) has studied the elements of several successful changes in Canada, ranging from the movement to lower smoking rates to introducing blue box programs for recycling, and has tried to incorporate some of these elements into future work for change. For example, it convenes community engagement via technology and measures community impact in the interests of sustaining a wide community-based movement for social change.

Sometimes it takes many parties, external events, and several methods to tackle "wicked" and persistent problems, such as poverty. Vibrant Communities was a program created to study and change the architecture of Canadian social contracts by examining employment insurance, poverty, health, and social transfers from the federal government to provinces. The Caledon Institute generated a pan-Canadian poverty reduction program within Vibrant Communities called Trail Blazers. Trail Blazers engaged 13 communities across Canada to share information and expertise, engage in a learning community, work with policymakers, and carry out innovative community-specific programming over several years. Indeed, elongating the pace of change was important because it leads to more sustainable changes.

Data collection, community mapping, and comprehensive multisector plans were the basis of the Trail Blazer program. Research and sharing evidence and information between communities was also a key piece of this initiative, linking local information with national survey data and pointing the way for change. The initiative engaged all sectors, including those experiencing poverty firsthand. The seed for the project emerged in a context of economic recession and shifts in social spending that exacerbated poverty. A group of individuals at Tamarack and Caledon, funded by a private foundation, launched the initiative. As a result, there was a focus on "living wages" to make working more rewarding than welfare; reducing barriers between federal, provincial, and municipal policies; and generating some local projects on issues like affordable housing, improving disability benefits, and enabling single mothers to finish school. This initiative lives on as Cities Reducing Poverty, with the lofty goal of improving the lives of 1 million Canadians in 100 cities across Canada.

Social change is complex and "messy" in that there is usually no one element that will ensure the desired change. Rather, a range of elements and approaches may have to be tried repeatedly and amended over time. The movement to reduce tobacco use in Canada is a case in point. It required (and still requires, despite massive reductions in smoking) a multipronged, comprehensive approach. This includes regulating products; imposing tobacco taxes; creating laws about smoking locations and access to buying and selling tobacco; restrictions on advertising, packaging, and promotion; and innovative treatment programs and prevention campaigns. None of these elements exists alone, and all of them have undergone improvements over the years. They were introduced and crafted based on experiences in other jurisdictions and on research evidence collected in Canada. While governments are key to this shift, the movement also includes a range of community groups, disease-based charities, advocacy groups, environmentalists, women's groups, and child health advocates, among others. Collectively, these groups have become known as the "tobacco control movement."

Essentially, this movement has radically altered the norms around smoking. In the 1950s in North America, medical doctors would readily help advertise cigarettes (and smoke themselves), and smoking was allowed in any location imaginable. Smoking was common in university and college classrooms in Canada as recently as the late 1970s and on planes as recently as 1989. Now, a relatively short time later, smoking is limited and marginalized, with only a few outside areas available for smoking. How did this enormous shift occur? The impetus for this movement can be traced back to the first report on the effects of smoking on health published by the US Surgeon General in 1963. What followed has been a long arduous struggle to change laws, restrict advertising, generate treatment, and launch prevention campaigns. It has been successful in reducing prevalence of smoking from over 50 per cent of the population to less than 20 per cent in Canada. However, the movement has not gone away. It has turned its attention to new products, such as vaping and e-cigarettes, hookah and nontobacco smoking, as well as to creating more sensitive approaches for groups in Canada who still exhibit high rates of smoking and need tailored approaches, such as single mothers, young pregnant women, those living on low incomes, people with mental health conditions, and Indigenous peoples.

Sometimes many disciplines are required and, over time, contribute to building a full understanding of a phenomenon. Transdisciplinarity, an approach discussed in Chapter 2, can offer a route to change by drawing from a range of areas and perspectives to shift our collective understanding of a phenomenon. Research and experiences or events can often coalesce to produce a trend, a new way of thinking, or a new language and concepts. For example, the emergent understanding of trauma over the last century has been a clear example of a mix of these elements. Contributions from various sources, disciplines, and communities, including those linked to many social movements advancing the rights of Indigenous peoples, children, women, veterans, and people with mental health issues, have coalesced to build a solid understanding of trauma, PTSD (post-traumatic stress disorder), and violence, and most recently they have worked to generate appropriate responses to these issues.

Early in the twentieth century, some 10,000 Canadian and 80,000 British soldiers returning from World War I were labelled with the condition "shell shock," a set of symptoms including crying, stress, paralysis, and shock that was thought to result from active combat. It took a whole century for the condition of PTSD to be understood, and it is now well accepted as afflicting veterans.

Now there are social programs and treatments available for returning veterans. Trauma and PTSD have become much more understood.

Another element of this building understanding emerged through the women's movement in the late twentieth century with its focus on sexual assault, rape, abuse, incest, and childhood sexual abuse. Judith Herman's landmark book *Trauma and Recovery* (1992) drew clear parallels between the effects of war on soldiers and sexual assault and abuse on women and children. This analysis forcefully expanded understandings of trauma and, ultimately, PTSD across populations and drew much-needed parallels between different populations and experiences.

An important longitudinal study in the United States called the Adverse Childhood Experiences Study (ACE) has also had a huge impact on our understanding of the impact of early life experiences. For years various disciplines and many individuals have struggled with understanding and treating difficult problems such as suicide, substance use, addiction, chronic diseases, and mental health issues. Now we have insight into the early childhood experiences that correlate with many of these issues. The ACE study followed thousands of children, documented their experiences of issues such as childhood sexual abuse, parental separation or divorce, experiencing or witnessing abuse of their mother, or having an incarcerated parent, and followed their progress in health and social outcomes. Felitti et al. (1998) concluded early on in the study that such experiences were highly correlated with suicide attempts, drug and alcohol use, and other mental health issues. Studies such as this have spawned a renewed interest in trauma and its effects.

Meanwhile, Indigenous peoples in Canada and elsewhere began reviewing their experiences of colonization, residential schools, and child welfare with a similar lens and began to popularize the notion of intergenerational trauma and cultural genocide to label the effects of these experiences. These experiences have been linked to some of the current social and health issues that are more prevalent among Indigenous peoples compared to non-Indigenous people, such as alcohol abuse and violence (Truth and Reconciliation Commission of Canada, 2015).

These multiple avenues to understanding trauma and its effects have led to a widespread acceptance and understanding of the term and have called upon both services and systems to respond in more appropriate and adequate ways. This has led to the emergence and development of both trauma-informed treatment in clinical settings (focused on treating those who disclose trauma) as well as trauma-informed practice in service and system design, which creates universally safe settings and procedures that all can benefit from (Poole & Greaves, 2012).

Working Together

Many of the issues that require social change are complicated. They require multiple players and often involve many components. Some of these issues are referred to as "wicked problems," meaning that they are big, seemingly pervasive, intertwined with other issues, and difficult to solve. Income inequality, homelessness, and climate change come to mind, as well as illiteracy, violence against women, and attitudes and practices such as misogyny, discrimination, or homophobia. Wicked problems are often attacked piecemeal, with groups or governments working on their own. But ultimately it is important to figure out strategic, comprehensive approaches. This is where research comes in and can help, but working together is essential.

The Mental Health Commission of Canada was established in 2006 and aims to reduce mental health problems and improve the mental health system in Canada (see www.mentalhealthcommission.ca). It generated a strategy and a set of ambitious initiatives for improving the lives of those affected by mental health and illness, including an anti-stigma campaign to change public opinion about mental health and illness. Another initiative was to reduce homelessness among those with chronic and significant mental health issues. But figuring out the exact way to go about this needed research.

Standard approaches to homelessness require individuals to enter treatment first for substance use or mental health issues. But five years of study in five cities across Canada clearly established that providing homes to those living on the streets with mental health conditions, known as the "housing-first" approach, was successful in improving lives, led to reduction of symptoms and less substance use, and was economically beneficial to society (Goering et al., 2014). In a randomized control trial, providing housing to over 2,000 people was compared to "treatment as usual" for 2,000 others. Results showed that housing led to entry into supports and treatment, stabilized lives, and provided security. In addition, participants in the study were engaged with the process, and some told their stories on video and in the report. This research was critical to establishing the utility and effectiveness of the housing-first approach across a range of different populations and locations. Without this research, it would be impossible to innovate in this way or to convince funders to pay for the housing-first approach.

Many social researchers intending to contribute to change-making will encounter complex issues with different stakeholders and interest groups that often have deep historical roots. Solving these issues requires creativity, innovation, collaboration, and patience. An example of the interconnectedness of problems is illustrated in the following analysis of research into ending obesity, which clearly shows that what might look like a public health or behavioural problem may be anything but.

One quickly learns that wicked problems like obesity demand both a scientific approach and a designerly approach. Because "every wicked problem is a symptom of another problem," any wicked problem is too big for a single-tiered approach. Poor people in the targeted communities don't have fresh vegetables because their neighbourhoods don't have stores that sell them; that's an economic problem. They don't drive to other areas because they can't afford cars; that's also economic. They can't take the bus because the city voted for the bus line to serve only other, less-impoverished areas; that's a policy issue. The city voted that way because more voters live in more affluent areas; now we're back to economics. And residents of more affluent areas are more likely to vote because they learned about the democratic process (education), whereas poor people might have missed those lessons because of inferior schools in their districts, which again comes down to economics (AC4D, n.d.).

Change, especially on problems that are often thought to be intractable, can be accelerated with the right evidence presented and shared in convincing and understandable ways. Effectively communicating evidence with the appropriate stakeholders—government, activists, and communities—is a key role for critical social researchers. Addressing change in a moral sense is part of being an engaged scholar or an activist researcher. This mentality takes us past a didactic presentation of information or research findings and into a territory of aiming to change life for the better. This is consistent with some of the approaches we described in Chapter 2, such as feminist, Indigenous, anti-oppressive, and engagement approaches. It is also reflective of gender transformative work, where those interested in creating interventions for women or men also design them to reduce gender inequity at the same time. These approaches not only inform how we design our research but, as we have seen, also influence our knowledge translation approaches. At the heart of social change is the desire to make things better in a meaningful way, working in conjunction with others.

Dealing with wicked problems is not just about showing up and building houses, giving things away, or delivering any direct service— even if you're in the community for the long haul. You have a moral imperative to build capacity, to enable the community to solve its own problems, lift itself up. If you're not helping the community build its ability to improve either its skills or its support network, you're not making a difference. (Hubbard, n.d.).

Summary

In this chapter we have stressed the importance of using research results to make change. This is the ultimate point of doing critical social research. In this chapter we discussed a range of ways of using research, from knowledge translation processes to influencing practice and policy development to shifting public opinion to generating large-scale social change by supporting activism and advocacy. All of these have merit, but each requires different skills in the researcher. We also described how change-making can be a complex process and how many different sectors of society, sometimes over long periods of time, must get involved to successfully make change. Think about your own project and what is possible and appropriate. Begin to plan by seeking some of these opportunities for sharing your research findings.

> Action without knowledge is wasted effort, just as knowledge without action is a wasted resource.
>
> —Lee Jong-wook, former director-general of the World Health Organization

Questions for Discussion

1. What is the difference between end-of-project knowledge translation and integrated knowledge translation? Which approach is most appropriate and feasible for your project?
2. Why is it so difficult to get evidence from research into practice?
3. Can you think of more effective ways of transmitting evidence to the general public than those currently used?
4. How do you decide what to believe?
5. Can you identify a social change that has affected you that resulted from research?
6. Why do you think the problem of overprescription of mood-altering drugs to women continues despite 40 years of research?
7. What are some "wicked problems" that concern you that could benefit from research?

Our Recommended Readings

AC4D. (n.d.). Wicked problems: Problems worth solving. Retrieved from https://www.wickedproblems.com/read.php

Canadian Institutes of Health Research. (2012). Guide to knowledge translation planning at CIHR: Integrated and end-of-grant approaches. Retrieved from http://www.cihr-irsc.gc.ca/e/documents/kt_lm_ktplan-en.pdf

Demers, G., Greaves, L., Kirby, S., & Lay, M. (2013). *Playing it forward: 50 years of women and sport in Canada.* Toronto: Feminist History Society.

Also go to www.bccewh.bc.ca, the website for the British Columbia Centre of Excellence for Women's Health, which has many examples of taking research to practice in women's health and gender and health.

CONCLUSION

In *Experience, Research, Social Change* we have discussed the importance of framing research in theoretical, ideological, and ethical contexts and conducting research in clear, logical ways. Many key issues have been raised for researchers preparing for and conducting research. Powerful social forces that affect knowledge production and use and some contemporary theories and approaches that shape the research enterprise have been identified. We have reviewed researcher roles and responsibilities, research ethics and methods, and aspects of knowledge translation and social change.

These issues are to be understood on many levels. The first level involves research practices: understanding research paradigms, making research choices, developing and applying research skills, maintaining a reflexive stance, and understanding and contextualizing research results. We have stressed the value of disciplined, rigorous research practice and the importance of an iterative research process—a process rooted most often in researchers' experiences, goals, obligations, and opportunities. The second level involves operative considerations for researchers: working in different contexts with different roles and responsibilities; developing research capacity by collaborating, mentoring, and exchanging skills with others; and translating and transferring knowledge to bring about positive social change. Finally, there is the awareness of how social forces and inequities influence both the research process as well as the utilization of knowledge, and how some individuals and groups have been excluded as producers, users, and beneficiaries of knowledge.

In the first edition of this book we understood this zone as "the margins." Almost three decades later we believe that an understanding of and research from the margins is still needed. In the past, information was often gathered and used to benefit certain individuals or groups of people to achieve or maintain personal, social, political, or economic advantage. This was accomplished by controlling the approach to research and the right to be a researcher. In this book we have presented ways to overcome these limits by creating techniques to reduce or eliminate various forms of exclusion from the process of knowledge production.

We began this book by asserting that "knowledge is power" and that understanding how knowledge is produced and used is central to understanding how power relations are defined and social relations are created or maintained. We presented some approaches to engaging different types of people and sectors in research, some of whom may not typically be involved. In addition, we maintained a critical view of methodology and research design throughout, focusing on the "so what?" questions critical social researchers need to be asking throughout the research process. This book has proposed a variety of research and knowledge translation processes that will help researchers conduct relevant and change-making critical social research.

Our goal was to write a book that presents the "how to" of doing critical social research. Along the way, we have also focused on the construction of knowledge as a political process and some of the differences in choices of research areas, research methodologies, research processes, and modes of knowledge translation. Critical social research is best characterized by a democratization of research practices and processes and equitable control over the destination and use of knowledge. But individual skills are always important to successful research, so much of this book has been oriented toward the "how to" aspects of research. We have gone into detail to help locate the research and the researcher by focusing on transparency, positionality, reflexivity, voice and representation, and ethical issues. Researchers can use similar thinking processes or pathways (but different tools) to gather, organize, and analyze data; establish themes and theory; and ultimately share research results. Fundamentally we have proposed that those influenced by the knowledge produced should, in some meaningful ways, be part of the production of that knowledge.

What Does the Future Hold for Critical Social Research?

We live in the Information Age, characterized by the proliferation of information through computerization. More than ever before, the world is faster and more transparent, and people are doing more research on more topics in a more collaborative and coordinated ways. Yet researchers must also attend to developing principles of rigorous and ethical research that fit within and keep pace with this context, thus raising new and important questions. With the daily proliferation of new information on the Internet, how can a thorough literature review ever be completed? How can we account for continuously evolving modes of communication and technologies in our research protocols? In what instances do we need to ensure direct contact with people in our research designs? What are the ethics of conducting online research, and what are the implications for current understandings of anonymity? How can we imagine new formats for knowledge translation that fit with emergent technologies and increasingly sophisticated audiences? How can we get such knowledge into channels that create social change from local to global contexts?

As critical social researchers we must always question our motivations for doing research. In all three editions of *Experience, Research, Social Change,* we have remained committed to understanding and exposing "the margins." As our social, cultural, economic, and political contexts shift, so do our conceptions of who resides in "the margins" and what issues remain marginalized. Understanding that critical social researchers inquire from and with the margins brings the researcher's values and responsibilities into clear focus. Practices for conducting research in acceptable, engaging ways and within ethical frameworks continue to evolve. Issues such as the nature of informed consent, assent, benefits, harm, rights of participants to withdraw, privacy, confidentiality, culturally sensitive research, rights to access research outcomes, covert research, and relations between researchers and the marketplace require constant and ongoing examination.

Undoubtedly we benefit from many aspects of the Information Age. We have gained access to huge amounts of information from around the world, numerous technologies to connect with individuals and groups, and a wide range of tools for collecting, managing, storing, and analyzing data. However, critical social research involves taking time to think, reflect, and evaluate our own practices and those of others. It involves actively learning research skills. While the research world gets faster and busier and hence more demanding, we hope that reflection and reflexivity do not suffer. The challenge for us all is to remain thoughtful, to transmit our collective passions for progressive social change to each other, and to share in shaping our communities' goals for knowledge. If we are able to take these approaches we will generate not only progressive social change, but also change within ourselves and our communities that will give us new direction, new questions, and the optimism that comes from creating new knowledge.

REFERENCES

AC4D. (n.d.). A designerly approach to social entrepreneurship. Wicked Problems: Problems Worth Solving. Retrieved from https://www.wickedproblems.com/1_designerly_approach_to_social_entrepreneurship.php

Adams, J., Hollenberg, D., Lui, C.W., & Broom, A. (2009). Contextualizing integration: A critical social science approach to integrative health care. *Journal of Manipulative and Physiological Therapeutics, 32*(9), 792–798. http://dx.doi.org/10.1016/j.jmpt.2009.10.006 Medline:20004808

Adler, P., & Adler, P. (1994). Observational techniques. In N. K. Denzin & Y. S. Lincoln (Eds.), *Handbook of qualitative research* (pp. 377–392). Thousand Oaks: Sage.

Afifi, A., May, S., & Clarke, V. A. (2011). Practical multivariate analysis (5th ed.). Boca Raton: CRC Press.

Alexander, B. K. (2008). *The globalisation of addiction: A study in poverty of the spirit.* Oxford: Oxford University Press.

AlleyDog.com. (n.d.). Confounding variable. Retrieved from http://www.alleydog.com/glossary/definition.php?term=Confounding%20Variable#ixzz3mEQ86Ck2

Ali, R. (2015). Rethinking representation: Negotiating positionality, power and space in the field. *Gender, Place and Culture, 22*(6), 783–800. http://dx.doi.org/10.1080/0966369X.2014.917278

Allen, D. (2004). Ethnomethodological insights into insider–outsider relationships in nursing ethnographies of healthcare settings. *Nursing Inquiry, 11*(1), 14–24. http://dx.doi.org/10.1111/j.1440-1800.2004.00201.x Medline:14962343

Aluwihare-Samaranayake, D. (2012). Ethics in qualitative research: A view of the participants' and researchers' world from a critical standpoint. *International Journal of Qualitative Methods, 11*(2), 64–81.

American Public University System. (2016). Institutional review board. Retrieved from http://www.apus.edu/community-scholars/institutional-review-board/

Arcia, A. (2014). Facebook advertisements for inexpensive participant recruitment among women in early pregnancy. *Health Education & Behavior, 41*(3), 237–241. http://dx.doi.org/10.1177/1090198113504414 Medline:24082026

Arghode, V. (2012). Qualitative and quantitative research: Paradigmatic differences. *Global Education Journal, 2012*(4), 155–163.

Babbie, E. (1998). *The practice of social research* (8th ed.). Belmont: Wadsworth.

Babbie, E., & Benaquisto, L. (2010). *Fundamentals of social research* (2nd ed.). Toronto: Nelson Education.

Bartlett, C., Marshall, M., & Marshall, A. (2012). Two-Eyed Seeing and other lessons learned within a co-learning journey of bringing together Indigenous and mainstream knowledges and ways of knowing. *Journal of Environmental Studies and Sciences, 2*(4), 331–340. http://dx.doi.org/10.1007/s13412-012-0086-8

Bauer, G. R. (2014). Incorporating intersectionality theory into population health research methodology: Challenges and the potential to advance health equity. *Social Science & Medicine, 110*, 10–17. http://dx.doi.org/10.1016/j.socscimed.2014.03.022 Medline:24704889

Baxter, P., & Jack, S. (2008). Qualitative case study methodology: Study design and implementation for novice researchers. *The Qualitative Report, 13*(4), 544–559.

Berger, R. (2015). Now I see it, now I don't: Researcher's position and reflexivity in qualitative research. *Qualitative Research, 15*(2), 219–234. http://dx.doi.org/10.1177/1468794112468475

Bernard, H. R. (2006). *Research methods in anthropology: Qualitative and quantitative approaches* (4th ed.). Lanham: Altamira Press.

Bettez, S. C. (2015). Navigating the complexity of qualitative research in postmodern contexts: Assemblage, critical reflexivity, and communion as guides. *International Journal of Qualitative Studies in Education: QSE, 28*(8), 932–954. http://dx.doi.org/10.1080/09518398.2014.948096

Bowleg, L. (2012). The problem with the phrase "women and minorities": Intersectionality—An important theoretical framework for public health. *American Journal of Public Health, 102*(7), 1267–1273. http://dx.doi.org/10.2105/AJPH.2012.300750 Medline:22594719

Braunstein, G. B. (2011, January 31). Andrew Wakefield's vaccination and autism study: Allegations of fraud with financial motivations. *Huffington Post.* Retrieved from http://www.huffingtonpost.com/glenn-d-braunstein-md/andrew-wakefields-vaccina_b_816208.html

Brackenridge, C. H. (1999). Managing myself: Investigator survival in sensitive research. *International Review for the Sociology of Sport, 34*(4), 339–410. http://dx.doi.org/10.1177/101269099034004007

Brandt, A. M. (1978). *Racism, research and the Tuskegee Syphilis Study* (Report No. 8). New York: Hastings Centre.

Bringer, J. D. (2002). *Sexual exploitation: Swimming coaches' perceptions and the development of role conflict and role ambiguity.* Unpublished doctoral dissertation, University of Gloucestershire, UK.

Briggs, C. L. (2007). *Learning how to ask: A sociolinguistic appraisal of the role of the interview in social science research.* Cambridge: Cambridge University Press.

Brown, L., & Strega, S. (2005). *Research as resistance: Critical, Indigenous and anti-oppressive approaches.* Toronto: Canadian Scholars' Press.

Canadian Institutes of Health Research. (2012). Guide to knowledge translation planning at CIHR: Integrated and end-of-grant approaches. Retrieved from http://www.cihr-irsc.gc.ca/e/documents/kt_lm_ktplan-en.pdf

Canadian Institutes of Health Research. (2013). Guidelines for health research involving Aboriginal people. Retrieved from http://www.cihr-irsc.gc.ca/e/29134.html

Canadian Institutes of Health Research. (2015a). The knowledge-to-action process. Retrieved from http://www.cihr-irsc.gc.ca/e/29418.html#6

Canadian Institutes of Health Research. (2015b). Sex, gender and health research guide: A tool for CIHR applicants. Retrieved from http://www.cihr-irsc.gc.ca/e/32019.html

Cannella, G. S. (2014). Qualitative research as living within/transforming complex power relations. *Qualitative Inquiry*, doi:10.1177/1077800414554907

Carbado, D. W., Crenshaw, K. W., Mays, V. M., & Tomlinson, B. (2013). Intersectionality: Mapping the movements of a theory. *Du Bois Review: Social Science Research on Race*, *10*(2), 303–312. http://dx.doi.org/10.1017/S1742058X13000349 Medline:25285150

Carlson, R. G. (2006). Ethnography and applied substance misuse research: Anthropological and cross-cultural factors. In W. R. Miller & K. M. Carroll (Eds.), *Rethinking substance abuse: What science shows and what we should do about it* (pp. 201–219). New York: Guilford Press.

Carney, T. F. (1983). *Qualitative methods in communication studies: A new paradigm research manual.* Windsor: University of Windsor, Department of Communication Studies.

Carpiano, R. M., & Daley, D. M. (2006). A guide and glossary on post-positivist theory building for population health. *Journal of Epidemiology and Community Health*, *60*(7), 564–570. http://dx.doi.org/10.1136/jech.2004.031534 Medline:16790824

Carter, S. M., & Little, M. (2007). Justifying knowledge, justifying method, taking action: Epistemologies, methodologies, and methods in qualitative research. *Qualitative Health Research*, *17*(10), 1316–1328. http://dx.doi.org/10.1177/1049732307306927 Medline:18000071

Castellano, M. B. (2000). Updating Aboriginal traditions of knowledge. In G. J. Sefa Dei, B. L. Hall, & D. G. Rosenberg (Eds.), *Indigenous knowledges in global contexts: Multiple readings of our world.* Toronto: University of Toronto Press.

Caulfield, T. (2015). *Is Gwyneth Paltrow wrong about everything? When celebrity culture and science clash.* Toronto: Penguin Canada.

Chai, C. (2014, April 16). Jenny McCarthy backtracking on anti-vaccination, but is it too late? *Global News.* http://globalnews.ca/news/1274553/jenny-mccarthy-backtracking-on-anti-vaccination-but-is-it-too-late

Clow, B., Pederson, A., Haworth-Brockman, M., & Bernier, J. (2009). *Rising to the challenge: Sex- and gender-based analysis for health planning, policy and research in Canada.* Halifax: Atlantic Centre of Excellence for Women's Health Halifax.

Code, L. (1991). *Knowledge and subjectivity: What can she know? Feminist theory and the construction of knowledge*. Ithaca: Cornell University Press.

Cole, A .L., & Knowles, J. G. (2001). *Lives in context: The art of life history research*. Lanham: Altamira Press.

Community Research Ethics Office. (2012). Ethics and community research. Retrieved from http://www.communityresearchethics.com/background/

Cooperstock, R. (1978). Sex differences in psychotropic drug use. *Social Science & Medicine, 12*(3B), 179–186. Medline:725615

Crenshaw, K.W. (1989). Demarginalizing the intersection of race and sex: A black feminist critique of antidiscrimination doctrine, feminist theory and antiracist politics. *University of Chicago Legal Forum, 1989*, 138–167.

Creswell, J.W. (1998). *Qualitative inquiry and research design: Choosing among five traditions*. London: Sage.

Creswell, J.W. (2014). *Research design: Qualitative, quantitative, and mixed methods approaches* (4th ed.). Los Angeles: Sage.

Crowe, S., Cresswell, K., Robertson, A., Huby, G., Avery, A., & Sheikh, A. (2011). The case study approach. *BMC Medical Research Methodology*. doi:10.1186/1471-2288-11-100

Currie, J. (2003). Manufacturing addiction: The over-prescription of benzodiazepines and sleeping pills to women in Canada. Retrieved from http://bccewh.bc.ca/wp-content/uploads/2012/05/2003_Manufacturing-Addiction.pdf

Curry, R. M., & Cunningham, P. (2000). Co-learning in the community. *New Directions for Adult and Continuing Education, 2000*(87), 73–82. http://dx.doi.org/10.1002/ace.8708

Day, S. (2012). A reflexive lens: Exploring dilemmas of qualitative methodology through the concept of reflexivity. *Qualitative Sociology Review, 7*(1), 60–85.

D'Cruz, H., Gillingham, P., & Melendez, S. (2007). Reflexivity, its meanings and relevance for social work: A critical review of the literature. *British Journal of Social Work, 37*(1), 73–90. http://dx.doi.org/10.1093/bjsw/bcl001

Del Basto, M., & Lewis, A. (1997). *A guide to social research*. Scarborough, ON: International Thomson Publishing.

Del Favero, M. (2016). Academic disciplines. StateUniversity.com. Retrieved from http://education.stateuniversity.com/pages/1723/Academic-Disciplines.html

deMarrais, K. (2004). Qualitative interview studies: Learning through experience. In K. DeMarrais & S. D. Lapan (Eds.), *Foundations for research: Methods of inquiry in education and the social sciences* (pp. 51–68). Mahwah: Lawrence Erlbaum Associates.

Demers, G., Greaves, L., Kirby, S., & Lay, M. (2013). *Playing it forward: 50 years of women and sport in Canada*. Toronto: Feminist History Society.

Denzin, N. K. (1970). *The research act: A theoretical introduction to sociological methods*. Chicago: Aldine Publishing.

Denzin, N. K. (1988). *The research act: A theoretical introduction to sociological methods*. New York: McGraw-Hill.

Denzin, N. K., & Lincoln, Y. S. (2000). Introduction: The discipline and practice of qualitative research. In N. K. Denzin & Y. S. Lincoln (Eds.), *Handbook of qualitative research* (2nd ed., pp. 1–29). Thousand Oaks: Sage.

Denzin, N. K., & Lincoln, Y. S. (2003). (Eds.) *The landscape of qualitative research: Theories and issues*. London: Sage.

DePoy, E., & Gitlin, L. N. (2011). *Introduction to research* (4th ed.). St. Louis: Mosby.

Dhamoon, R. K. (2011). Considerations on mainstreaming intersectionality. *Political Research Quarterly, 64*(1), 230–243. http://dx.doi.org/10.1177/1065912910379227

Discipline. (2005). *Merriam-Webster's collegiate dictionary* (11th ed.). Springfield, MA: Merriam-Webster.

Duneier, M. (1999). *Sidewalk*. New York: Douglas & McIntyre Ltd.

Edwards, R., & Ribbens, J. (1998). Living on the edges: Public knowledge, private lives, personal experience. In J. Ribbens & R. Edwards (Eds.), *Feminist dilemmas in qualitative research: Public knowledge and private lives*. London: Sage.

Esterberg, K. G. (2002). *Qualitative methods in social research*. Boston: McGraw-Hill.

Etherington, K. (2007). Ethical research in reflexive relationships. *Qualitative Inquiry, 13*(5), 599–616. http://dx.doi.org/10.1177/1077800407301175

Fantz, A., & Brumfield, B. (2015, November 19). More than half the nation's governors say Syrian refugees not welcome. CNN. Retrieved from http://www.cnn.com/2015/11/16/world/paris-attacks-syrian-refugees-backlash/

Federal, Provincial, and Territorial Advisory Committee on Population Health. (1999). *Toward a healthy future: Second report on the health of Canadians*. Retrieved from http://publications.gc.ca/collections/Collection/H39-468-1999E.pdf

Ferlatte, O., Dulai, J., Hottes, T. S., Trussler, T., & Marchand, R. (2015). Suicide related ideation and behavior among Canadian gay and bisexual men: A syndemic analysis. *BMC Public Health, 15*(1), 597. http://dx.doi.org/10.1186/s12889-015-1961-5 Medline:26136235

Felitti, V. J., Anda, R. F., Nordenberg, D., Williamson, D. F., Spitz, A. M., Edwards, V., . . . & Marks, J. S. (1998). Relationship of childhood abuse and household dysfunction to many of the leading causes of death in adults: The Adverse Childhood Experiences (ACE) Study. *American Journal of Preventive Medicine, 14*(4), 245–258. http://dx.doi.org/10.1016/S0749-3797(98)00017-8 Medline:9635069

Fine, M., & Weis, L. (2003). *Silenced voices and extraordinary conversations: Re-imagining schools*. New York: Teachers College Press.

Fine, M. (1994). Working the hyphens: Reinventing self and others in qualitative research. In N. K. Denzin & Y. S. Lincoln (Eds.), *Handbook of qualitative research* (pp. 70–82). Thousand Oaks: Sage.

Finson, S. D. (1985). *On the other side of silence: Patriarchy, consciousness and silence— Women's experiences of theological education*. Unpublished thesis, Boston University, Boston.

Fletcher, C. (2003). Community-based participatory research relationships with Aboriginal communities in Canada: An overview of context and process. *Pimatisiwin: A Journal of Aboriginal and Indigenous Community Health* 1(1): 27–62.

Flicker, S., Savan, B., McGrath, M., Kolenda, B., & Mildenberger, M. (2008). "If you could change one thing …" What community-based researchers wished they could have done differently. *Community Development Journal: An International Forum, 43*(2), 239–253. http://dx.doi.org/10.1093/cdj/bsm009

Flinders, D. J. (1992). In search of ethical guidance: Constructing a basis for dialogue. *Qualitative Studies in Education, 5*(2), 101–115.

FluidSurveys Team. (2014, October 8). Response rate statistics for online surveys: What numbers should you be aiming for? Retrieved from http://fluidsurveys.com/university/response-rate-statistics-online-surveys-aiming/

Flyvbjerg, B. (2011). Case study. In N. K. Denzin & Y. S. Lincoln (Eds.). *The SAGE handbook of qualitative research* (3rd ed., pp. 301–316). Thousand Oaks: Sage.

Fook, J. (1999). Critical reflectivity in education and practice. In B. Pease & J. Fook (Eds.), *Transforming social work practice: Postmodern critical perspectives.* Sydney: Allen & Unwin.

Fornssler, B., McKenzie, H. A., Dell, C. A., Laliberte, L., & Hopkins, C. (2013). "I got to know them in a new way": Rela(y/t)ing rhizomes and community-based knowledge (brokers') transformation of Western and Indigenous knowledge. *Cultural Studies, Critical Methodologies.* doi:10.1177/1532708613516428

Freire, P. (1985). *The politics of education.* South Hadley, MA: Bergin and Garvey Publishers.

Freire, P. (2000). *Pedagogy of the oppressed* (30th anniversary ed.). New York: Bloomsbury. (Original work published 1970)

Fry, P. (n.d.) Literature review template. Thompson Rivers University Writing Centre. Retrieved from https://www.tru.ca/__shared/assets/Literature_Review_Template30564.pdf

Glaser, B. G., & Strauss, A. L. (1967). *The discovery of grounded theory: Strategies for qualitative research.* New York: Aldine de Gruyter.

Glassner, B., & Corzine, J. (1982). Library research as fieldwork: A strategy for qualitative analysis. *Sociology and Social Research, 66*(3), 305–319.

Goering, P., Veldhuizen, S., Watson, A., Adair, C., Kopp, B., Latimer, E., . . . & Aubry, T. (2014). *National at home/Chez soi Final Report.* Calgary: Mental Health Commission of Canada.

Goffman, E. (1974). *Frame analysis.* New York: Harper Colophon Books.

Gostin, L. O., & Powers, M. (2006). What does social justice require for the public's health? Public health ethics and policy imperatives. *Health Affairs, 25*(4), 1053–1060. http://dx.doi.org/10.1377/hlthaff.25.4.1053 Medline:16835186

Graham, I. D., Logan, J., Harrison, M. B., Straus, S. E., Tetroe, J., Caswell, W., & Robinson, N. (2006). Lost in knowledge translation: Time for a map? *Journal of*

Continuing Education in the Health Professions, 26(1), 13–24. http://dx.doi.org/ 10.1002/chp.47 Medline:16557505

Gratton, C., & Jones, I. (2004). *Research methods for sport studies.* London: Routledge.

Greaves, L. (1996). *Smoke screen: Women's smoking and social control.* Halifax: Fernwood.

Greaves, L., & Ballem, P. (2001). *Fusion: A model for integrated health research.* Vancouver: BC Centre of Excellence for Women's Health.

Greaves, L. J., & Bialystok, L. R. (2011). Health in all policies—All talk and little action? *Canadian Journal of Public Health, 102*(6), 407–409.

Greaves, L., Pederson, A., & Poole, N. (2014). *Making it better: Gender-transformative health promotion.* Toronto: Women's Press.

Greaves, L., Poole, N., & Boyle, E. (Eds.). (2015). *Transforming addiction: Gender, trauma, transdisciplinarity.* New York: Routledge.

Greaves, L., Poole, N., Okoli, C. T. C., Hemsing, N., Qu, A., Bialystok, L., & O'Leary, R. (2011). *Expecting to quit: A best practices review of smoking cessation interventions for pregnant and postpartum women* (2nd ed.). Vancouver: British Columbia Centre of Excellence for Women's Health.

Greenhalgh, T., Robert, G., Macfarlane, F., Bate, P., & Kyriakidou, O. (2004). Diffusion of innovations in service organizations: Systematic review and recommendations. *Milbank Quarterly, 82*(4), 581–629. http://dx.doi.org/10.1111/j.0887-378X.2004.00325.x Medline:15595944

Guilianotti, R. (1995). Participant observation and research into football hooliganism: Reflections on the problems of entree and everyday risks. *Sociology of Sport, 12,* 1–20.

Hankivsky, O. (2012). Women's health, men's health, and gender and health: Implications of intersectionality. *Social Science & Medicine, 74*(11), 1712–1720. http://dx.doi.org/10.1016/j.socscimed.2011.11.029 Medline:22361090

Hankivsky, O., Grace, D., Hunting, G., Ferlatte, O., Clark, N., & Fridkin, A., … Laviolette, T. (2012). Intersectionality-based policy analysis. In O. Hankivsky (Ed.), *An intersectionality-based policy framework* (pp. 33–45). Vancouver: Institute for Intersectionality Research and Policy.

Harding, S. (1987). Introduction: Is there a feminist method? In S. Harding (Ed.), *Feminism and methodology: Social sciences issues* (pp. 1–14). Bloomington: Indiana University Press.

Hayes, M., Ross, I. E., Gasher, M., Gutstein, D., Dunn, J. R., & Hackett, R. A. (2007). Telling stories: News media, health literacy and public policy in Canada. *Social Science & Medicine, 64*(9), 1842–1852. http://dx.doi.org/10.1016/j.socscimed.2007.01.015 Medline:17337317

Henwood, K. (2008). Qualitative research, reflexivity and living with risk: Valuing and practicing epistemic reflexivity and centering marginality. *Qualitative Research in Psychology, 5*(1), 45–55. http://dx.doi.org/10.1080/14780880701863575

Herman, J. (1992). *Trauma and recovery: The aftermath of violence from domestic abuse to political terror.* New York: Basic Books.

Hesse-Biber, S. (2010). Qualitative approaches to mixed methods practice. *Qualitative Inquiry, 16*(6), 455–468. http://dx.doi.org/10.1177/1077800410364611

Holloway, I., & Biley, F. C. (2011). Being a qualitative researcher. *Qualitative Health Research, 21*(7), 968–975. http://dx.doi.org/10.1177/1049732310395607 Medline:21266705

hooks, b. (1992). *Black looks: Race and representation.* Boston: South End.

Hopkins, C., & Fornssler, B. (2014). Honouring our strengths: Indigenous culture as intervention in addictions treatment. Retrieved from http://www.addictionresearchchair.ca/creating-knowledge/national/honouring-our-strengths-culture-as-intervention/

Hochschild, A. R., & Machung, A. (1989). *The second shift: Working parents and the revolution at home.* New York: Viking.

Horowitz, C. R., Robinson, M., & Seifer, S. (2009). Community-based participatory research from the margin to the mainstream: Are researchers prepared? *Circulation, 119*(19), 2633–2642. http://dx.doi.org/10.1161/CIRCULATIONAHA.107.729863 Medline:19451365

Hsiung, P. C. (2008). Teaching reflexivity in qualitative interviewing. *Teaching Sociology, 36*(3), 211–226. http://dx.doi.org/10.1177/0092055X0803600302

Hubbard, R. (n.d.). Ryan Hubbard, on wicked problems. Wicked Problems: Problems Worth Solving. Retrieved from https://www.wickedproblems.com/1_ryan_hubbard.php

International Development Research Community. (2015). Cities and climate change: Call for proposals. Retrieved from http://www.idrc.ca/EN/Funding/Grants/Pages/GrantsDetails.aspx?CallID=21

Janesick, V. J. (2004). *Stretching exercises for qualitative researchers* (2nd ed.). London: Sage.

Jellinek, E. M. 1960. The disease concept of alcoholism. New Haven: Hillhouse Press. http://dx.doi.org/10.1037/14090-000

Johnson, A., & Sackett, R. (1998). Direct systematic observation of behavior. In H. R. Bernard (Ed.), *Handbook of methods in cultural anthropology* (pp. 301–332). Walnut Creek: AltaMira Press.

Johnson, J. L., Greaves, L., & Repta, R. (2007). *Better science with sex and gender: A primer for health research.* Vancouver: Women's Health Research Network.

Johnson, T. C. (2013, October 9). The value of partially completed surveys. ServiceTick. Retrieved from https://www.servicetick.com/blog/the-value-of-partially-completed-surveys/

Josselson, R. (2007). The ethical attitude in narrative research: Principles and practicalities. In D. J. Clandinin (Ed.), *Handbook of narrative inquiry: Mapping a methodology* (pp. 537–566). Thousand Oaks, CA: Sage. http://dx.doi.org/10.4135/9781452226552.n21.

Kaiser, K. (2009). Protecting respondent confidentiality in qualitative research. *Qualitative Health Research, 19*(11), 1632–1641. http://dx.doi.org/10.1177/1049732309350879 Medline:19843971

Keller, S. (2015). Clinical decision making in mental health. Unpublished master's thesis (RHSC 589B), University of British Columbia, Vancouver.

Kelly, D. M. (2000). *Pregnant with meaning: Teen mothers and the politics of inclusive schooling*. New York: Peter Lang.

Kenny, C., Faries, E., Fiske, J., & Voyageur, C. (2004). A holistic framework for Aboriginal policy research. Retrieved from http://www.publications.gc.ca/collections/Collection/SW21-114-2004E.pdf

Kessel, F., & Rosenfield, P. L. (2008). Toward transdisciplinary research: Historical and contemporary perspectives. *American Journal of Preventive Medicine, 35*(2 Suppl), S225–S234. http://dx.doi.org/10.1016/j.amepre.2008.05.005 Medline:18619403

Kincheloe, J. L., & McLaren, P. (2005). Rethinking critical theory and qualitative research. In N. K. Denzin & Y. S. Lincoln (Eds.), *The SAGE handbook of qualitative research* (3rd ed., pp. 303–342). California: Sage.

Kirby, S. L. (2005, November 1). Role models and muddles. Keynote address at the Point of View: Voices Inspiring Equity for Women in Sport and Physical Activity conference, Canadian Association for the Advancement of Women and Sport, Winnipeg.

Kirby S. L. (2009). Racialized communities and police services (RCAPS) community consultation phase II, personal fieldnotes.

Kirby, S. L., Greaves, L., & Hankivsky, O. (2000). *The dome of silence: Sexual harassment and abuse in sport*. Halifax: Fernwood.

Kirby, S. L., Greaves, L., & Reid, C. (2006). *Experience, research, social change: Methods beyond the mainstream*. Toronto: University of Toronto Press.

Kirby, S. L., & McKenna, K. (1989). *Experience, research, social change: Methods from the margins*. Toronto: Garamond Press.

Kirby, S. L., & SQS (Sum Quod Sum). (2000). Sexual orientation and images of deviance: Report on a needs assessment survey of senior gays and lesbians. In L. Beamon (Ed.), *New perspectives on deviance: The construction of deviance in everyday life* (pp. 109–118). Toronto: Prentice-Hall.

Klein, R. D. (1983). How to do what we want to do: Thoughts about feminist methodology. In G. Bowles & R. D. Klein (Eds.), *Theories on women's studies*. London: Routledge.

Krause, S. (2013). Beyond non-domination: Agency, inequality and the meaning of freedom. *Philosophy and Social Criticism, 39*(2), 187–208. http://dx.doi.org/10.1177/0191453712470360

Krieger, S. (1983). *The mirror dance: Identity in a women's community*. Philadelphia: Temple University Press.

Kristin Does Theory. (n.d.). Understanding W. E. B. Du Bois' concept of double consciousness. [Weblog post]. Retrieved from http://kristindoestheory.umwblogs.org/understanding-w-e-b-du-bois-concept-of-double-consciousness/

Kuhn, A., & McAllister, K. E. (Eds.). (2006). *Locating memory: Photographic acts*. New York: Berghahn Books.

Laerd Statistics. (2013). One-sample t-test using SPSS Statistics. Retrieved from https://statistics.laerd.com/spss-tutorials/one-sample-t-test-using-spss-statistics.php#procedure

Landy, A. (2015). *Community engagement through the lens of intersectionality*. Unpublished Master of Science research proposal, Simon Fraser University, Burnaby, British Columbia.

Lewis, D. (1991). Data extraction as text categorization: An experiment with the MUC-3 corpus. In Proceedings, Third Message Understanding Conference (MUC-3), San Mateo, California.

Lincoln, Y. S., & Guba, E. G. (2005). Paradigmatic controversies, contradictions, and emerging confluences. In N. K. Denzin & Y. S. Lincoln (Eds.), *Handbook of qualitative research* (3rd ed., pp. 191–215). Thousand Oaks, CA: Sage.

Locke, K. (2015). Intersectionality and reflexivity in gender research: Disruptions, tracing lines and shooting arrows. *International Studies in Sociology of Education*, 25(3), 169–182. http://dx.doi.org/10.1080/09620214.2015.1058722

Lofland, J., & Lofland, L. (1995). *Analyzing social settings: A guide to qualitative observation and analysis* (3rd ed.). Belmont, CA: Wadsworth.

Lohse, B. (2013). Facebook is an effective strategy to recruit low-income women to online nutrition education. *Journal of Nutrition Education and Behavior*, 45(1), 69–76. http://dx.doi.org/10.1016/j.jneb.2012.06.006 Medline:23305805

Luger, C. (2015, December 1). CBC blocks all comments on Indigenous-related articles. Indian Country Today Media Network.com. Retrieved from http://indiancountrytodaymedianetwork.com/2015/12/01/cbc-blocks-all-comments-indigenous-related-articles-162618

Lupton, D. (2012, November 28). 30 tips for successful academic research and writing. [Weblog post]. Retrieved from http://blogs.lse.ac.uk/impactofsocialsciences/2012/11/28/lupton-30-tips-writing/

Maiter, S., Joseph, A. J., Shan, N., & Saeid, A. (2013). Doing participatory qualitative research: Development of a shared critical consciousness with racial minority research advisory group members. *Qualitative Research*, 13(2), 198–213. http://dx.doi.org/10.1177/1468794112455037

Malterud, K. (2001). Qualitative research: Standards, challenges, and guidelines. *Lancet*, 358(9280), 483–488. http://dx.doi.org/10.1016/S0140-6736(01)05627-6 Medline:11513933

Marelli, F. B. (2016). Qualitative research methods and methodology: Analysis is more than coding. ATLAS.ti. Retrieved from http://atlasti.com/qualitative-research-methods/

Marshall, C., & Rossman, G. B. (2016). *Designing qualitative research* (6th ed.). Los Angeles: Sage.

Maté, G. (2010). *In the realm of hungry ghosts: Close encounters with addiction.* Toronto: Vintage Canada.

Mays, N., & Pope, C. (2000). Qualitative reesearch in health care: Assessing quality in qualitative research. *British Medical Journal, 320*(7226), 50–52.

McCabe, J. L., & Holmes, D. (2009). Reflexivity, critical qualitative research and emancipation: A Foucauldian perspective. *Journal of Advanced Nursing, 65*(7), 1518–1526. http://dx.doi.org/10.1111/j.1365-2648.2009.04978.x Medline:19457011

McCauley, C. (1989). The nature of social influence in groupthink: Compliance and internalization. *Journal of Personality and Social Psychology, 57*(2), 250–260. http://dx.doi.org/10.1037/0022-3514.57.2.250

McCoy, K. (2012). Toward a methodology of encounters: Opening to complexity in qualitative research. *Qualitative Inquiry, 18*(9), 762–772. http://dx.doi.org/10.1177/1077800412453018

McIntosh, P. (1989, July/August). White privilege: Unpacking the invisible backpack. *Peace and Freedom Magazine,* 10–12.

Mead, M. (2001). *Coming of age in Samoa: A psychological study of primitive youth for western civilisation.* New York: Perennial Classics. (Original work published 1930)

Mesel, T. (2013). The necessary distinction between methodology and philosophical assumptions in healthcare research. *Scandinavian Journal of Caring Sciences, 27*(3), 750–756. http://dx.doi.org/10.1111/j.1471-6712.2012.01070.x Medline:22935081

Miller, J., & Glassner, B. (2004). The "inside" and the "outside": Finding realities in interviews. In D. Silverman (Ed.), *Qualitative research: Theory, method and practice.* London: Sage.

Minkler, M. (2005). Community-based research partnerships: Challenges and opportunities. *Journal of Urban Health 82*(Suppl 2), ii3–ii12. doi:10.1093/jurban/jti034

Morgan, D. (1988). *Focus groups as qualitative research.* Vol. 16. London: Sage.

Morgan, D. (2004). Focus groups. In S. N. Hesse-Biber & P. Levy (Eds.), *Approaches to qualitative research: A reader on theory and practice* (pp. 263–285). New York: Oxford University Press.

Moritz, M. (2013). Teaching ethnographic research through a collaborative project. *Anthropology News,* 11–12.

Morse, J. (1994). Designing funded qualitative research. In N. Denzin & Y. Lincoln (Eds.), *Handbook of qualitative research* (pp. 220–235). Thousand Oaks: Sage.

Morse, J. (2010). Simultaneous and sequential qualitative mixed methods designs. *Qualitative Inquiry, 16*(6), 483–491.

Mosselson, J. (2010). Subjectivity and reflexivity: Locating the self in research on dislocation. *International Journal of Qualitative Studies in Education: QSE, 23*(4), 479–494. http://dx.doi.org/10.1080/09518398.2010.492771

Mountjoy, M., Brackenridge, C., Arrington, M., Blauwet, C., Carska-Shappard, A., Fasting, K., . . . & Budgett, R. (2016). The IOC consensus statement: Harassment and abuse (non-accidental violence) in sport. *British Journal of Sports*

Medicine. Retrieved from http://bjsm.bmj.com/content/early/2016/04/26/ bjsports-2016-096121.short?rss=1

Nencel, L. (2014). Situating reflexivity: Voices, positionalities and representations in feminist ethnographic texts. *Women's Studies International Forum, 43*, 75–83.

Neuman, W. L. (2004). *Basics of social research*. Boston: Pearson.

Nicholls, R. (2009). Research and Indigenous participation: Critical reflexive methods. *International Journal of Social Research Methodology, 12*(2), 117–126. http://dx.doi. org/10.1080/13645570902727698

Njelesani, J., Gibson, B. E., Nixon, S., Cameron, D., & Polatajko, H. J. (2013). Towards a critical occupational approach to research. *International Journal of Qualitative Methods, 12*(1), 207–220.

NOVA. (1993). *Deception: The Tuskegee Syphilis Study* [Television broadcast]. New York and Washington, DC: Public Broadcasting System.

Oakley, A. (1981). *Subject women*. New York: Pantheon Books.

Ochocka, J., & Janzen, R. (2014). Breathing life into theory: Illustrations of community-based research—Hallmarks, functions and phases. *Gateways: International Journal of Community Research & Engagement, 7*(1), 18–33. http://dx.doi.org/10.5130/ijcre. v7i1.3486

Ochocka, J., Moorlag, E., & Janzen, R. (2010). A framework for entry: PAR values and engagement strategies in community research. *Gateways: International Journal of Community Research & Engagement, 3*, 1–19. http://dx.doi.org/10.5130/ijcre.v3i0.1328

Office for Human Research Protections. (1993). Introduction. In *Institutional review board guidebook*. Retrieved from http://www.hhs.gov/ohrp/archive/irb/irb_ introduction.htm

Office of Research Ethics. (2004). Human research ethics. Retrieved from https:// ethics.research.ubc.ca/

Panel on Research Ethics. (2014). Tri-council policy statement: Ethical conduct for research involving humans. Retrieved from http://www.pre.ethics.gc.ca/eng/ policy-politique/initiatives/tcps2-eptc2/Default/

Patton, M. Q. (1999). Enhancing the quality and credibility of qualitative analysis. *Health Services Research, 34*(5), 1189–1208.

Patton, M. Q. (2001). *Qualitative research & evaluation methods* (3rd ed.). St. Paul: Sage.

Patton, M. Q. (2014). *Qualitative research and evaluation methods* (4th ed.). Thousand Oaks: Sage.

Paul, R., & Elder, L. (2005). *Ethical reasoning*. Dillon Beach, CA: The Foundation for Critical Thinking.

Pawlychka, C. (2010). *Redefining justice: The framing of contemporary restorative justice in film*. Unpublished master's thesis, University of Manitoba, Winnipeg.

Pay Equity Commission. (2016). What is the gender wage gap? Retrieved from http://www.payequity.gov.on.ca/en/GWG/Pages/what_is_GWG.aspx

Payton, M. (2005). *The Prentice Hall guide to evaluating online resources with Research Navigator*. Upper Saddle River: Prentice Hall.

Peele, S. (1987). A moral vision of addiction. *Journal of Drug Issues, 17*(2), 187–215. http://dx.doi.org/10.1177/002204268701700205

Picard, A. (2013, October 13). Exposing Canada's ugly mental-health secret. *Globe and Mail*. Retrieved from http://www.theglobeandmail.com/life/health-and-fitness/health/exposing-canadas-ugly-mental-health-secret/article14828590/

Poland, B. (1998, November). *Social inequalities, social exclusion and health: A critical social science perspective on health promotion theory, research and practice*. Paper presented at the Symposium on Health Promotion Research: Status and Progress, Bergen, Norway.

Pomerantz, S. (2008). *Girls, style, and school identities: Dressing the part*. New York: Palgrave McMillan. http://dx.doi.org/10.1057/9780230612501

Ponic, P., & Jategaonkar, N. (2011). Balancing safety and action: Ethical protocols for photovoice research with women who have experienced violence. *Arts & Health*, 1–14. doi:10.1080/17533015.2011.584884

Poole, N. & Greaves, L. (Eds.). (2012). *Becoming trauma informed*. Toronto: Centre for Addiction and Mental Health.

Poole, N., & Greaves, L. (2013). Alcohol use during pregnancy in Canada: How policy moments can create opportunities for promoting women's health. *Canadian Journal of Public Health, 104*(2), e170–e172. Retrieved from journal.cpha.ca/index.php/cjph/article/viewFile/3700/2768 Medline:23618212

Poole, N., & Bopp, J. (2015). Using a community of practice model to create change for Northern homeless women. *First Peoples Child & Family Review, 10*(2), 122–130.

Poole, N., Bopp, J., Schmidt, R., Fuller, L., Hache, A., Hrenchuk, C., . . . & Youngblut, R. (2015). Repairing the holes in the net: Improving systems of care for Northern homeless women with mental health challenges. Retrieved from http://bccewh.bc.ca/wp-content/uploads/2015/09/RTN-Summary_August-9-2015.pdf

Prus, R., & Irini, S. (1982). *Hookers, rounders and desk clerks: The social organization of the hotel community*. Toronto: Gage Publishing Limited.

Punch, M. (1994). Politics and ethics in qualitative research. In N. K. Denzin & Y. S. Lincoln (Eds.), *Handbook of qualitative research* (pp. 83–97). London: Sage.

Ramo, D. E., & Prochaska, J. J. (2012). Broad reach and targeted recruitment using Facebook for an online survey of young adult substance use. *Journal of Medical Internet Research, 14*(1), e28. http://dx.doi.org/10.2196/jmir.1878 Medline:22360969

Rank, M. (2004). The blending of qualitative and quantitative methods in understanding childbearing among welfare recipients. In S. N. Hesse-Biber & P. Levy (Eds.), *Approaches to qualitative research: A reader on theory and practice* (pp. 81–97). New York: Oxford University Press.

Reason, P., & Bradbury, H. (2001). Introduction: Inquiry and participation in search of a world worthy of human aspiration. In P. Reason & H. Bradbury (Eds.), *Handbook of action research: Participative inquiry and practice* (pp. 1–10). London: Sage.

Reid, C., Tom, A., & Frisby, W. (2006). Finding the "action" in feminist participatory action research. *Action Research, 4*(3), 315–330. http://dx.doi.org/10.1177/1476750306066804

Reid, C., Brief, E., & LeDrew, R. (2009). *Our common ground: Cultivating women's health through community-based research.* Vancouver: Women's Health Research Network.

Reid, C., & LeDrew, R. (2013). The burden of being "employable": Under- and unpaid work and women's health. *AFFILIA: Journal of Women and Social Work, 28*(1), 79–93. http://dx.doi.org/10.1177/0886109913476944

Reid, C., Landy, A., & Leon, P. (2013). Using community-based research to explore common language and shared identity in the therapeutic recreation profession in British Columbia, Canada. *Therapeutic Recreation Journal, 47*(2), 69–88.

Reimer-Kirkham, S., Varcoe, C., Browne, A. J., Lynam, M. J., Khan, K. B., & McDonald, H. (2009). Critical inquiry and knowledge translation: Exploring compatibilities and tensions. *Nursing Philosophy, 10*(3), 152–166. http://dx.doi.org/10.1111/j.1466-769X.2009.00405.x Medline:19527437

Reinharz, S. (1983). Experiential analysis: A contribution to feminist research. In G. Bowles & R. D. Klein (Eds.), *Theories of women's studies* (pp. 162–191). Boston: Routledge & Kegan Paul.

Researcher Information Services. (n.d.). Guidance notes for the application of behavioural ethical research. Retrieved from http://dev.rise.ubc.ca/Common/_rise/Help/BREB_Guidance_Notes.html#topic2-36

Richards, T. J., & Richards, L. (1994). Using computers in qualitative research. In N. Denzin & Y. Lincoln (Eds.), *Handbook of qualitative research* (pp. 445–462). London: Sage.

Rochon Ford, A., & Saibil, D. (Eds.). (2009). *The push to prescribe.* Toronto: Women's Press.

Roer-Strier, D., & Sands, R. G. (2015). Moving beyond the "official story": When "others" meet in a qualitative interview. *Qualitative Research, 15*(2), 251–268. http://dx.doi.org/10.1177/1468794114548944

Rosenfield, P. L. (1992). The potential of transdisciplinary research for sustaining and extending linkages between the health and social sciences. *Social Science & Medicine, 35*(11), 1343–1357. http://dx.doi.org/10.1016/0277-9536(92)90038-R Medline:1462174

Saibil, D. (2005). SSRI antidepressants: Their place in women's lives. Women and Health Protection. Retrieved from http://www.whp-apsf.ca/en/documents/ssri.html

Salminen, A.-L., Harra, T., & Lautamo, T. (2006). Conducting case study research in occupational therapy. *Australian Occupational Therapy Journal, 53*(1), 3–8.

Sandelowski, M. (1995). Sample size in qualitative research. *Research in Nursing & Health, 18*(2), 179–183. http://dx.doi.org/10.1002/nur.4770180211 Medline:7899572

Sandelowski, M. (2000). Combining qualitative and quantitative sampling, data collection, and analysis techniques in mixed-method studies. *Research in Nursing & Health, 23*(3), 246–255. http://dx.doi.org/10.1002/1098-240X(200006)23:3<246::AID-NUR9>3.0.CO;2-H Medline:10871540

Schiebinger, L., Klinge, I., Sánchez de Madariagao, I., Paik, H.Y., Schraudner, M., & Stefanick, M. (Eds.). (2011–2015). Pregnant crash test dummies: Rethinking standards and reference models. Gendered Innovations in Science, Health & Medicine, Engineering and Environment. Retrieved from http://genderedinnovations. stanford.edu/case-studies/crash.html

Scotland, J. (2012). Exploring the philosophical underpinnings of research: Relating ontology and epistemology to the methodology and methods of the scientific, interpretive, and critical research paradigms. *English Language Teaching, 5*(9), 9–16. http://dx.doi.org/10.5539/elt.v5n9p9

Sedlack, R., & Stanley, J. (1992). *Social research: Theory and methods.* London: Allyn and Bacon.

Sheppard, M., Newstead, S., Di Caccavo, A., & Ryan, K. (2000). Reflexivity and the development of process knowledge in social work: A classification and empirical study. *British Journal of Social Work, 30*(4), 465–488. http://dx.doi.org/10.1093/bjsw/30.4.465

Shields, S.A. (2008). Gender: An intersectionality perspective. *Sex Roles, 59*(5–6), 301–311. http://dx.doi.org/10.1007/s11199-008-9501-8

Shuttleworth, M. (n.d.). Hawthorne effect. Explorable. Retrieved from https://explorable.com/hawthorne-effect

Silverman, D. (2005). *Doing qualitative research* (2nd ed.). London: Sage.

Smith, L.T. (1999). *Decolonizing methodologies: Research and indigenous peoples.* Dunedin, NZ: University of Otago Press.

Smith, L.T. (2012). *Decolonizing methodologies: Research and Indigenous peoples* (2nd ed.). London: Zed Books.

Smith, S. (2014). *Seeking wellness: Living with depression and chronic pain: A multiple case study.* Unpublished master's thesis, University of British Columbia, Vancouver.

Snow, D.A., Rochford, E. B., Worden, S. K., & Benford, R. D. (1986). Frame alignment processes, micromobilization and movement participation. *American Sociological Review, 51*(4), 464–481. http://dx.doi.org/10.2307/2095581

Snow, D.A., & Benford, R. D. (1988). Ideology, frame resonance and participant mobilization. *International Social Movement Research, 1,* 197–217.

Social Sciences and Humanities Research Council. (2015). Guidelines for the merit review of Aboriginal research. Retrieved from http://www.sshrc-crsh.gc.ca/ funding-financement/merit_review-evaluation_du_merite/guidelines_research-lignes_directrices_recherche-eng.aspx

Social Sciences and Humanities Research Council. (2016). Connection Program. Retrieved from http://www.sshrc-crsh.gc.ca/funding-financement/umbrella_ programs-programme_cadre/connection-connexion-eng.aspx

Stake, R. E. (2005). Qualitative case studies. In N. K. Denzin & Y. S. Lincoln (Eds.). *The SAGE handbook of qualitative research* (3rd ed., pp. 443–466). Thousand Oaks: Sage.

St. Denis, V. (2004). Community-based participatory research: Aspects of the concept relevant for practice. In W. Carroll (Ed.), *Critical strategies for social research* (pp. 292–319). Toronto: Canadian Scholars' Press.

Strauss, A. L., & Corbin, J. (1988). *Basics of qualitative research: Techniques and procedures for developing grounded theory* (2nd ed.). London: Sage.

Stutchbury, K. K., & Fox, A. (2009). Ethics in educational research: Introducing a methodological tool for effective ethical analysis. *Cambridge Journal of Education, 39*(4), 489–504. http://dx.doi.org/10.1080/03057640903354396

Surgeon General of the United States. (1963). Smoking and health: Report of the advisory committee of the surgeon general of the public health service.

Symon, G., & Cassell, C. (Eds.). (2012). *Qualitative organizational research: Core methods and current challenges.* Los Angeles: Sage.

Szyjka, S. (2012). Understanding research paradigms: Trends in science education research. *Problems of Education in the 21st Century, 43,* 110–118.

Tamarack Institute. (2005). Creating Canadian movements for social change. Retrieved from http://tamarackcommunity.ca/downloads/M4C/m4c_report.pdf

Taylor, C., & White, S. (2000). *Practising reflexivity in health and welfare: Making knowledge.* Buckingham: Open University Press.

Taylor, D. (n.d.). The literature review: A few tips on conducting it. University of Toronto Health Sciences Writing Centre. Retrieved from http://www.writing.utoronto.ca/advice/specific-types-of-writing/literature-review

Tom, A. R. (2005). *The stages of writing.* Unpublished manuscript, University of British Columbia.

Tom, A. R., Fingeret, H.A., Niks, M., Dawson, J., Dyer, P., Harper, L., McCue, M., & Morley, A. (1994). *Suspended in a web of relationships: Collaborative ethnographic evaluation.* Durham: Literacy South.

Truth and Reconciliation Commission of Canada. (2015). *Honouring the truth, reconciling for the future: Summary of the final report of the Truth and Reconciliation Commission of Canada.* Retrieved from http://www.trc.ca/websites/trcinstitution/File/2015/Exec_Summary_2015_06_25_web_0.pdf.

Tubey, R., Rotich, J. K., & Bengat, J. K. (2015). Research paradigms: Theory and practice. *Research on Humanities and Social Sciences, 5*(5), 224–228.

Tuli, F. (2010). The basis of distinction between qualitative and quantitative research in social science: Reflection on ontological, epistemological and methodological perspectives. *Ethiopian Journal of Education and Science, 6*(1), 102–103.

UBC Office of Research Ethics. (n.d.). UBC clinical research ethics general guidance notes. Retrieved from https://ethics.research.ubc.ca/ore/ubc-clinical-research-ethics-general-guidance-notes#art16pt2

Wakefield, A. Murch, S. H., Anthony, A., Linnell, J., Casson, D. M., Makil, M., . . . & Walker-Smith, J. A. (1998). Ileal-lymphoid-nodular hyperplasia, non-specific colitis, and pervasive developmental disorder in children. *The Lancet,* 637–641.

Wang, C., & Burris, M. A. (1997). Photovoice: Concept, methodology, and use for participatory needs assessment. *Health Education & Behavior*, *24*(3), 369–387. http://dx.doi.org/10.1177/109019819702400309 Medline:9158980

Warner, R., Zahraei, S., Farah, D., Nandlal, J., Jaskulka, I., Peters, V., Cheung, G., Sarang, A., Wynter, P. (2008). Best practices in developing anti-oppressive, culturally competent supporting housing: Project background document. Supportive Housing and Diversity Group. Retrieved from http://www.fredvictor.org/uploads/File/SHAD-background-web.pdf

Watts, J. (2006). The outsider within: Dilemmas of qualitative feminist research within a culture of resistance. *Qualitative Research*, *6*(3), 385–402. http://dx.doi.org/10.1177/1468794106065009

Writing Centre at the University of Wisconsin—Madison. (2014). *The writer's handbook: How to proofread.* Retrieved from https://writing.wisc.edu/Handbook/Proofreading.html

Yellow Bird, M. (2013). Neurodecolonization: Applying mindfulness research to decolonizing social work. In M. Gray, J. Coates, M. Yellow Bird, & T. Heatherington (Eds.), *Decolonizing social work.* Burlington, VT: Ashgate.

Yin, R. K. (2009). *Case study research: Design and methods* (4th ed.). Thousand Oaks: Sage.

Young, M. I. (2005). *Pimatisiwin: Walking in a good way—A narrative inquiry into language as identity.* Winnipeg: Ptarmagon Press.

Zimmer, M. (2012, October 19). Thoughts on privacy and the use of Facebook to recruit research subjects. Retrieved from http://www.michaelzimmer.org/2012/10/19/thoughts-on-privacy-and-the-use-of-facebook-to-recruit-research-subjects/

INDEX

Figures and tables are indicated by page numbers in italics